# A COUNTRY CALLED

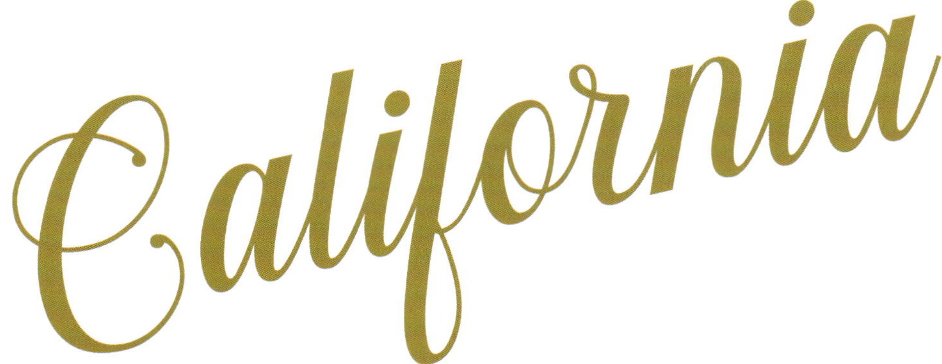


## PHOTOGRAPHS 1850s TO 1960s

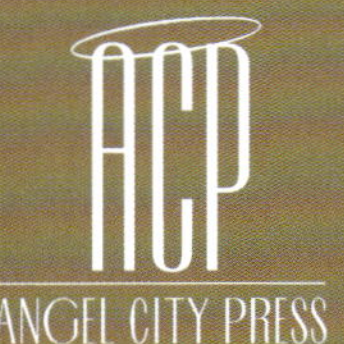
ACP
ANGEL CITY PRESS

# A COUNTRY CALLED

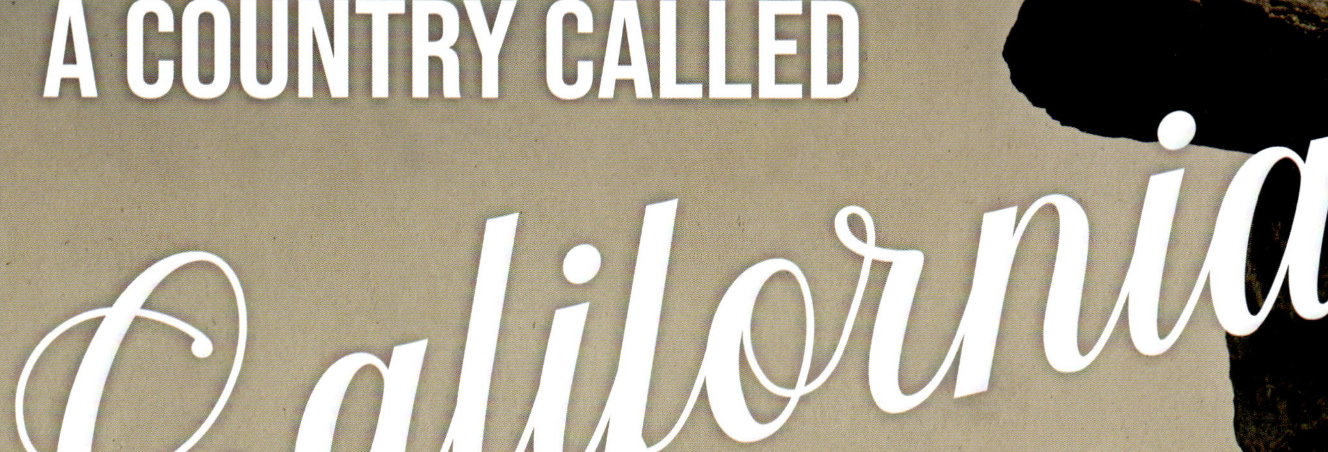


## PHOTOGRAPHS 1850s TO 1960s

STEPHEN WHITE

Foreword by LYNELL GEORGE

*Dedicated to the photographers,
both men and women, whose daring and courage
sent them out across the state of California.*

# CONTENTS

# CALIFORNIA'S STILL THINKING OF WATER

**by Suzanne Lummis**

Or—we all are. Or, maybe it's just me.
I was raised up in frozen water blanketing
the ascending and descending land—water wind-
whipped through air. In the photo that does
not exist, I'm a kid standing on the edge of lonely
Highway 40 above Donner Pass, and not
the pretty, fluffy stuff this time but hard, fast
pellets of ice redden my face, the school bus

running late. I'll just bet (in this photo that doesn't exist)
I'm thinking of the "party" that followed
Mister Donner, *how cold they must have been*, starved,
ragged, falling dead in the snow, poor babies,
poor mothers of babies.
I still think of them sometimes when stuck
on the 110, in L.A.—first freeway in the U.S.!
(in the East they were toll roads, not free)—

or worse, the exasperating 101. Now I'm hot—
what's wrong with my air conditioning? *At least*
*I'm not struggling on foot over the snowbound Sierras*
*in the brutal, notorious Winter of 1846,*
I think.     Water. In the dry West, the Southwest driest
of all, which is Southern California, both south
and far west, we can never get enough, sell enough, own
enough water, though Water has had enough of us.

Men construct dams, feats of engineering, sublime,
glorious, how cathedrals must have seemed
to peasants of the 16th century. They swallow vast, rich
hollows of land.     *Moving water.* Our rivers are different.
Here, rivers not only move but are *moved*, not so much
"stolen," as some claim, not *quite* illegal, just acquired
by trickery and sneaked out of town in the dark,
or wide desert daylight.
In a photo that doesn't exist, this time I'm on a bus, Greyhound,
and it's hot but different heat, the flat, plain-speaking
sunlight of the San Joaquin, the Great Central Valley,
and beyond the window, row after row of food—soon
to be food, or else wasted. Miles of crops. Californians are thirsty
and hungry. The whole country is hungry. Ravenous.
It cries to be fed. Look. Lettuce, sugar beets, grapes, oh
strawberries! Oh orchards of oranges, that other Gold.

California gold. I am packed and heading for Fresno State—
Fresno! Yes, a desolate place, back then, and therefore
ideal for poets. But the bounty of the Valley needs
water (not poets)—how ever, from anywhere, borrowed,
transported, reclaimed, from deep ground or surface. It needs
people to harvest, and they come--from Oaxaca, Sinaloa,
Nogales, speaking their language, working with swift hands.
They've never seen an American, they say, who can work fast.

It's true. My brother has a friend, Frank—university guy—
who wanted to join them and worked alongside them
for a year—then two years. . . . He was young, in his prime,
in the best shape of his life, but he was born into softness.
Try as he might, and try harder, he could never keep up,
not even with the women or boys, not even
with aging men, weathered but muscled, their hands
in flight.          We began here with *Thinking*.

You who eat these fruits, tomatoes, bread from these grains,
and mock California . . . And, you who call farm workers "unskilled,"

. . . something to think about.

<:>

Elsewhere, some believe California is L.A. and L.A. is Hollywood,
but these days
not even Hollywood is Hollywood.
And Hollywood is everywhere.

I have heard some call Hollywood "phony."

In a photo that does not exist---or might—Esther Williams steps onto
the diving board, slips from the violet-blue satin cloak
that had concealed her all the way down, and now she's
no, not naked, of course—it's 1952, no one was naked—all
in black, a black leotard shining like planetarium sky. And she lifts
her arms over her head for that exquisite swan dive into
the jewel blue pool.

It's all real. She really made that dive—there were no strings—
that air she passed through, true air,
that blueness,
genuine water.

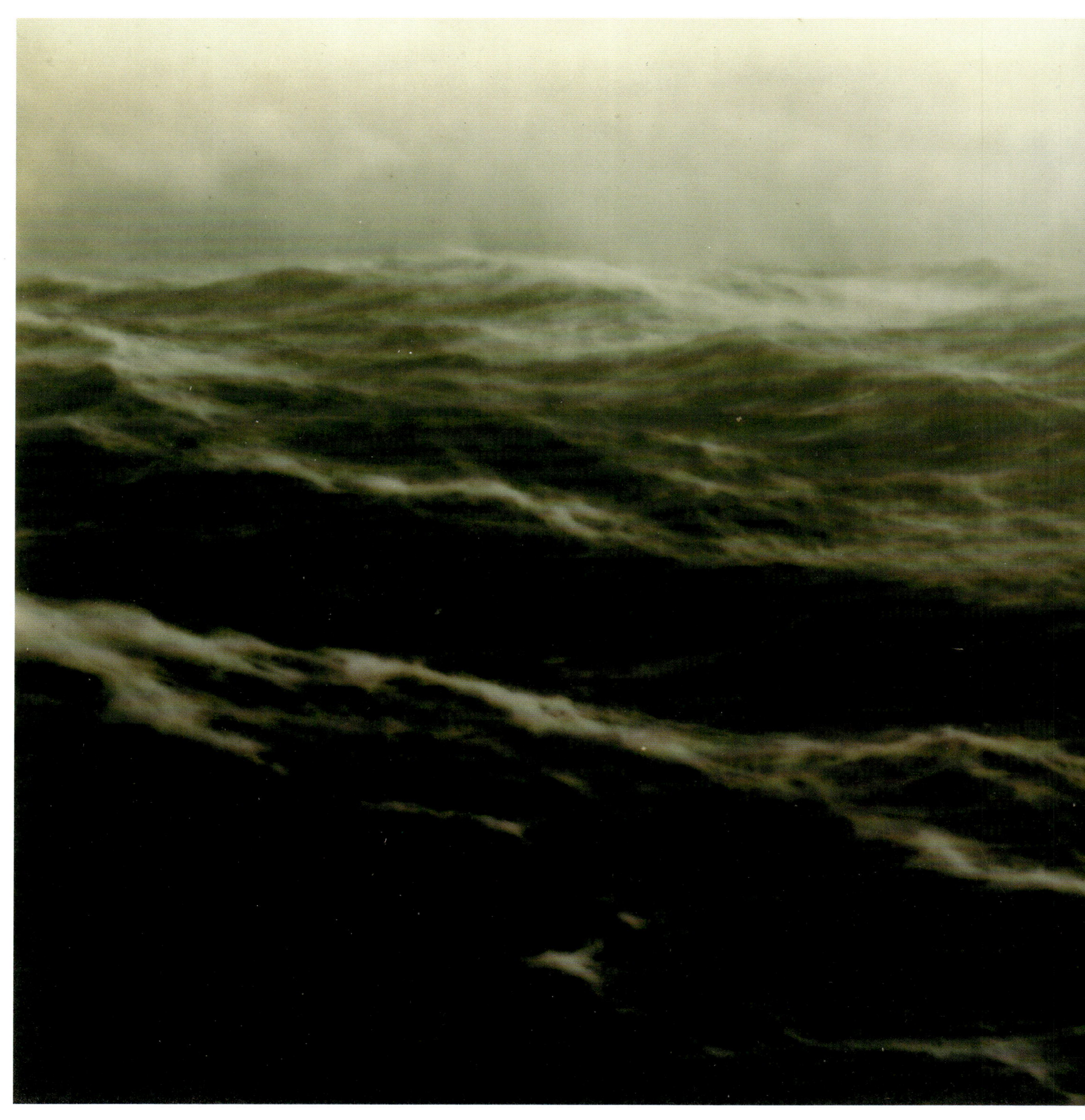

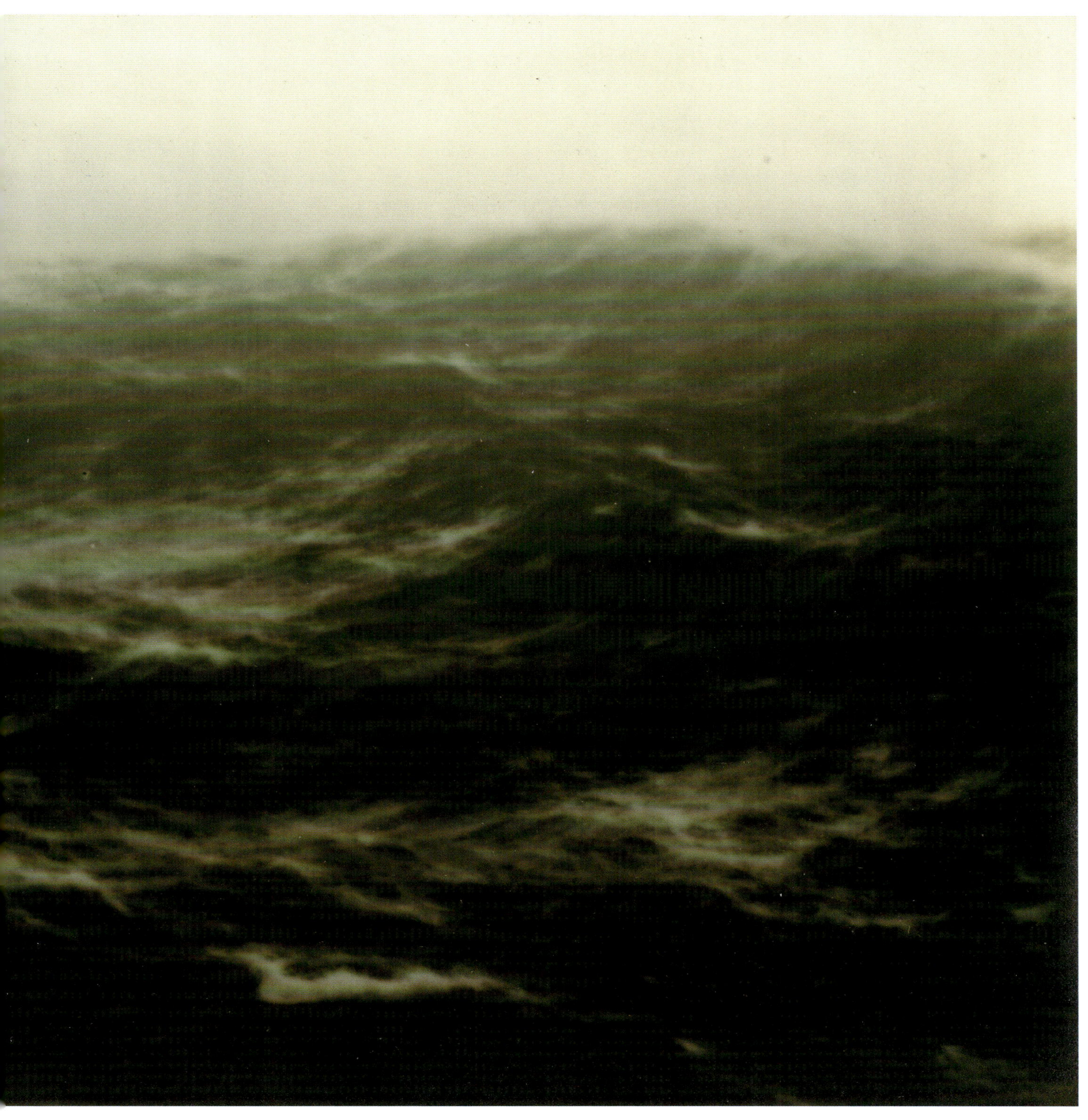

Leopold Hugo; Untitled (The Pacific); toned gelatin silver print; ca. 1930; 6⅝ × 13⅛ in.
*The Pacific Ocean runs the length of California's 840-mile coastline; Hugo's poetic interpretation gives a feel of the infinite space that makes the coast of California so unique.*

FOREWORD

# "ONLY MORE SO"

**by Lynell George**

Even still, this late in its complicated story, California prevails—not simply as a location, but an intention. Seekers still refer to the Golden State and its attendant dream, but for my family, the destination functioned more as a promise. It was a goal, a site of activation. Intersecting with California was a necessary component to unlock a very particular promise: a different you, a better chance, a new way of seeing. That promise, of course, varied, but once declared, was assured.

My forebears hail from the East Coast and from the Deep South, on my paternal and maternal sides respectively. Their migration to California began in the 1940s, and their reasons for re-situating their lives and perspectives were not dissimilar to those of other Black Americans who felt restless, hindered, or fed up and more than ready to break free of old ways or limits. They needed more space simply to be.

I've often wondered who in my family saw California first. What region—Northern or Southern? What description of its physicality—urban or rural—imprinted? What aspect took root and grew wild in their imaginations? What, if they could name it, called them from afar? Did "California"—the notion of it—emerge through someone's stories—letters home or back-porch talk? Did it come into focus as an elaborate description of Eden nestled against a coastline? What were the lures and promised benefits? Its potential-building qualities? What did they envision?

Ever since I can remember, I know that those citrus-crate images of orchards and farms painted a particular Arcadia that seldom matched reality, but if you squinted and held your head at just the right angle you might be able to see it—and thus see yourself in it.

Not too long ago, I was tasked with sorting through generations of my relatives' mementoes, organizing relics to send off to far-flung cousins. I found all manner of souvenirs of my relatives' journey to, and life within, California. Many of the memories were photographs. They'd put themselves into the landscapes they had dreamed of for so long. There were beachside snapshots, backyard meals under shaggy palm trees, sunsets over mountains and beaches. Christmas under the palm trees. In the process of sorting, I hit on a poignant keepsake. A single, fragile white teacup adorned with delicate hand-painted oranges under which the word "California" was inscribed, in a thin but fanciful green flourish. While I didn't happen upon those popular novelty postcards of railroad flatcars [Page 187] dwarfed by exaggeratedly enormous citrus fruit, that sold the region to the curious, this delicate tourist keepsake held the same sort of power. A promise of abundance. Maybe it was first purchased as a souvenir and then made its way back across the country, then back again? Or maybe it was purchased much later as a reminder of what the promise was and a nudge to continue working to make certain it was kept.

No one in my family spoke of any other place as they did of California—not even their beloved ancestral hometowns or their most wished-for destination across oceans. California figured in a very particular way in their stories: it was a launching pad. It was the elusive element that would make everything right. Acquiring a California address wasn't about starting again—it was getting started. Finally.

As the novelist and essayist Wallace Stegner famously asserted in a 1967 contemplation of the state of the state for *Saturday Review*: "Like the rest of America, California is unformed, innovative, ahistorical, hedonistic, acquisitive, and energetic—only more so." Many of us live within the cacophony of this observation in the everyday rhythm of our lives: California is its own extraordinary territory moving at its own time signature. We didn't need to see the world, when the world was California.

I recall the photographs that populated the social studies and history textbooks I grew up with in my Southern California classrooms, that taught us of the wonders of the Golden State—the California we both looked back on and looked forward to. These photos of jagged coasts [Page 31] and waves crashing against rocks [Page 35], stands of ages-old redwoods in their towering magnificence [Page 36], of mountain ranges, a grid of newly laid foundations that only hinted at cities being born, were backdrops for us, like our parents and grandparents, to place ourselves within. Set against text that highlighted movement, growth, expansion, we were encouraged to think big and outside the limits of convention. California, we came to believe, not just through words but through imagery, was the only location on the planet where impossibility could be made real, where cities grew out of deserts, where water could be routed anywhere, where roads connected distances carrying you from shoreline to snow in just under a couple of hours. In other words, California was the place where you could not just have it all, but be of it all.

Yet, as a first-generation native of this place, the California I came to know and navigate was one of incongruity. In a very specific way, I walked into those idealized frames, and pushed into their very edges to have a look around. Juxtaposed against the startling beauty was the menace of disaster—at any moment that pastoral earth beneath you could pitch and yaw, that stunning stretch of shoreline could be toxic [Page 37], that row of freshly painted bungalows fronted by neatly edged lawns could sometimes hide desperate, end-of-the road stories. As I came to learn, there was nothing quite like the sharp blade of California noir.

How do we come to balance the image with reality? How did my family? These images of plenty—citrus, coastline, mountains, vast stretches of land—told only one layer of a story. The East Coast family drove across the country with *The Negro Motorist Green Book* in their glove box to help them navigate safely through the county's racially exclusionary and thus deadly expanses; the Deep South side arrived on the Jim Crow cars of trains leaving the known limits of their birth-homes for what they saw and intuited in the imagery of California as something limitless. Of course California was dotted with a network of racist sundown towns and restrictive housing covenants. Those beautiful bungalows were something they had to risk their lives for—the first deep nicks in the dream as they came to know. But they saw something greater in a possibility they thought they could write for themselves. The vastness of the imagery suggested that. It was for many of them a blank slate to picture themselves a different way, living among other similar-minded lodestars who were willing to gamble on the unknown and consider what it might be to be a person you'd never been before.

Many of the images contained on these pages feel like both dreams and promises, worlds to find yourself in. All the same, as the region shape-shifts and its numbers grow—the state, projected to hit forty-four million residents by 2040—I wonder if I would have chosen California for myself. It seems I have inherited not just my relatives' keepsakes but their restlessness; a drive to do things my own way. Every day, I walk in their footsteps, inside the contours of their dream, parsing the un-kept promises. I see fewer of the features that pulled them here. I know that that became true for my elders too. But there are still aspects of California that stirs something inside me too, especially when it catches me unawares: a quality of light, the sharp scent of wilderness in an urban space. It forces me to imagine not so much what they saw, but what they were inspired to build against those imperfect backdrops—a landscape that could be as breathtaking as it could be merciless. They took broken pieces of a promise and cut a path deep into their own California, into their own future, and built something sturdy enough to pass on. I live in their after image.

# A COUNTRY CALLED CALIFORNIA

INTRODUCTION

The precise moment I began to think about California as a separate country eludes me. I have traveled all over the world and found each country to have certain characteristics. In recent years, much of what made these countries distinctive from each other has changed into a kind of generic global conglomeration, but California in many ways still feels like an exception to me.

I grew up in California, living first in San Francisco, then San Mateo, San Jose, and finally Los Angeles. The San Fernando Valley was my home from fourth grade through high school. That valley of my youth was a segregated, tough place with gangs, car clubs, and a strong Midwestern and Southern influence. Racism against Hispanics and African Americans was common, and anti-Semitism was pervasive.

Today, the Valley is an aggregate of Asians, Hispanics, and Europeans, all together making a population of about two million, larger than that of many states. Like my valley, my state has changed and evolved from its violent, racist past to a more accepting and open-minded present. California has become a proponent of reform and protections of minorities and women. According to the State of California's Department of Justice, our civil rights laws enforce non-discrimination by "business establishments, including discrimination on the basis of race, color, religion, sex, ancestry, national origin, disability, medical condition, genetic information, sexual orientation, citizenship, primary language, immigration status, and other protected classifications." Yet, as recent protests and demonstrations have shown, California still has a way to go to achieve equal and fair opportunity for all.

What does it mean, then, to be a Californian? To live in California is to be a special kind of American; a free and innovative individual who can create opportunity and "surf" the Pacific Rim in search of the good life. To imagine California as a country is to fabricate a dream state of mind. The reality, however, remains that California is one of fifty states: we are subject to federal rules and regulations, we pay income tax to the federal government, we travel on American passports, and, like all states big and small, we have only two senators representing our forty million residents who generate a powerful economy, providing a wealth that is the envy of the world.

In an article titled "Best States for Business 2019: California" *Forbes* states, "If it were a country, California's $3.1 trillion economy would be the fifth biggest in the world, ranked between Germany and the United Kingdom. The state represents 15 percent of the U.S. economy. Home prices in the state are the highest in the nation at a median of $592,000, having doubled from the lows of 2011 and surpassing their pre-recession highs in 2017." According to a May 2021 report by the California Association of Realtors, as of April 2021 the median single-family home set a record of $813,980 statewide.

When I started reflecting on the ideas at the heart of this book, I began to decipher the many elements of California and in its history that define the place. The state has a long coastline with large ports facing the Pacific Rim, making it a prime center for shipping to

Asia. Despite its frequent droughts and wildfires, California has arguably the best climate in the country, affording opportunities in agriculture, tourism, and a lifestyle that has spawned innovations in food, health and fitness, sports and recreation, and tourism. From an international economic point of view, California has been at the forefront of industries specializing in oil exploration and production, entertainment, aerospace and automotive design and manufacturing, shipping, fashion, education, medical and pharmaceutical research, and, of course, technology.

While continuing to explore the idea of California being its own country, I proceeded to mine my collection of photographs to support the concept of "A Country Called California"—if only in my imagination. During the past thirty years, my collection of California photography has swelled to almost a thousand images, including everything from artwork by famous photographers such as Ansel Adams and Edward Weston to quirky images by unknown photographers, all reinforcing the state's exceptional status.

Many of these photographs bring to light fascinating anecdotes whereby I have come to see California as a land built on unique origin stories and compelling myths, which are part of—yet surprisingly independent from—the union that surrounds it. Before California became a state in 1850, it was a part of Mexico at a time when the American government was interested in expanding its holdings. To pry the state away from Mexico, John Fremont, an early explorer of California, received covert orders from the American government as early as 1846 to take control of the state through a series of complicated steps and clever maneuvers. When Fremont finally secured California from the Mexican government, a final generous surrender to the opposition in the Cahuenga Pass in Los Angeles was initiated. Around 1890, Isaac Taber photographed a building in Monterey [Page 120] that housed Fremont's troops in 1846 as he went about his mission to seize the state.

The gold rush started before California joined the United States in 1850, but the Mexican-American War did not slow the influx of gold-hungry characters who flowed in from all across the country and foreign places for a chance at fame and fortune. One of those risk-takers and hopefuls was a miner, William Pitt, who appears to have arrived in the mid-1850s. In a letter to a friend, Pitt revealed his cold-country origins when he urged his friend to "take sleigh rides enough for you and [name crossed out] and a white one for me and I will dig some gold for you."

Even though he said in the letter that he made between two and six dollars a day—"We live first rate," he wrote—Pitt did not want his friend to come out to California. "There is a great many folks here that would be glad to go home if they could," he explained, "and they could after a while if they would save their money but there is a gambling house close by here. I have been in there and seen men loose [*sic*] the last cent they had and I have seen some win forty or fifty dollars in a few minutes and then off and get drunk and come back loose it all again and some will work all day and spend it at night. That is the way with one half of the folks in California." In many ways, the dream of this open country has always outdone the reality.

The importance of photography to California's history cannot be overlooked. In addition to photographing the inhabitants and their many historic adventures, photographers achieved international fame for their artistic interpretations of the California landscape. In the early 1870s, Eadweard Muybridge, an English photographer, gained immortality by developing a method that allowed Leland Stanford to prove that a horse ran with all four feet off the ground at the same time. Decades before the Lumière brothers and others captured the "moving picture," Muybridge set up a series of cameras side by side, each with a string stretched across the racetrack to trigger the shutters and record the progressive movement of the galloping horse.

Most frequently known for the series of motion studies done at the University of Pennsylvania, Muybridge is also known for his striking Yosemite landscapes, photographs of the Modoc War, and a mammoth plate panorama of San Francisco. But there is another story told in great detail by Rebecca Solnit in her captivating biography of Muybridge, titled *River of Shadows*. After the photographer learned of his wife's affair with a well-traveled scoundrel, Harry Larkyns, he followed Larkyns to near the town of Calistoga, shot him dead, and stood trial for first-degree murder—only to be acquitted.

From the gold rush forward, violence and crime ruled in California: claim jumping, robberies, fraud, murders, and many other crimes hampered the development of California even before it became a state. Even then, erratic lawlessness continued after the state was taken over by the American government. California's isolating geography kept it somewhat beyond the grasp of the federal government back East, which was nominally in charge.

When the Depression hit, many cities suffered revenue shortages, and San Diego was no exception. Nevertheless, the 1935 California Pacific International Expo in Balboa Park attracted over seven million visitors. As a consequence, the city fathers decided to continue the popular attraction again the following year. In 1936, new buildings and concepts were installed at the Expo. One of these was the building that housed "Front Page," a collection of tantalizing stories and photographs supposedly snatched from the front pages of newspapers between the years 1910 to 1935—stories seemingly ripped from the headlines [Page 190]. Included in the exhibition were photographs of gangsters, murderers, shipwrecks, fires, and other disasters. Many of these had occurred in our own "Golden State" and were then seized upon by the kind of sensationalized journalism popular in the Hearst papers.

A number of the panels displayed inside the building showed scenes from catastrophic events with anywhere from eight to twenty original photographs to a panel. To draw people inside, several photographs were blown up and the oversized prints were mounted in front of the building, including the famous image of Ruth Snyder in the electric chair as well as Dillinger, dead, the crime boss, Al Capone, and the ramming of the Santa Clara County jail by vigilantes intent on hanging two kidnappers [Page 191]. Though not exactly intended for educational purposes, this was very possibly the first exhibition of photojournalism.

From the gold rush forward, California evolved on an uneven path. Our treatment of minorities reflected the ambivalence that pervaded the population. The Chinese Exclusion Act of 1882 was meant to curb Chinese immigration to California by banning the Chinese for ten years and denying them naturalization. Encouraged by California businesses, this became a federal law signed by President Chester Arthur.

Sixty years later, the Japanese American community was subjected to a federal law signed in 1942 by Franklin D. Roosevelt that forced legal residents from their homes and jobs into concentration camps set up throughout California and the West. To make matters worse, the detainees were expected to sign a loyalty oath and agree to fight in a war in Europe while their loved ones languished behind barbed wire in the camps. Those who refused to fight or declare total allegiance to the United States were termed "No-Nos" and transferred to Tule Lake [Page 129], the harshest of the camps. Yet many incarcerated Americans of Japanese descent joined the 442nd infantry regiment, which became the most decorated regiment during the war.

This has always been the California paradox: a land of sunshine and laughter mixed with hardship and struggles. The famous photograph of Dorothea Lange's migrant mother contrasts with visitors at a dude ranch having a cowboy breakfast, while a city leveled by an earthquake and fire contrasts with an urban sprawl, as seen in the panorama from Mount Lowe [Page 52].

The stories are endless. Often the most interesting can be found around a rather innocuous photograph, such as that of a memorial service conducted in front of the Jewish Worker's Hall for Isadore Berkowitz. Berkowitz, a handyman who worked at a summer camp for the children of various workers' groups, was arrested with six other people including the camp cook, the piano player and her visiting mother, the camp manager, a cleaning lady, and a nineteen-year-old counselor and college student named Yetta Stromberg. Their crime? Nobody knew exactly. But once the six were placed in the San Bernardino jail, the district attorney decided to charge them with a violation of the anti-red flag law enacted in 1919 "as a symbol or emblem of opposition to organized government." Most likely unaware of the 1919 law, each morning Stromberg flew a homemade red flag with a hammer and sickle painted on it, while the children stood beside their beds and recited a pledge to the working classes.

On August 3, 1929, several cars filled with American Legionnaires rode into the camp along with the San Bernardino DA, also a Legionnaire. They searched the grounds, found the flag and a small box of Communist literature, and arrested the five women and Berkowitz. A short time later, they were all released on bail of $1,000 each, raised by the International Labor Defense that also arranged for an attorney to defend them.

At the trial, five of the six defendants were found guilty, and only the visiting mother was acquitted. Before sentencing, Berkowitz hanged himself in the Worker's Cooperative Center, leading to the photograph that showed the attendees at the memorial service. Four of the defendants received sentences of six months to five years in San Quentin. Stromberg was sentenced to one to ten years in San Quentin, where women were housed until 1933. The American Civil Liberties Union, founded in 1920, joined in the appeal, and the case was petitioned all the way to the Supreme Court of the United States. In Stromberg versus California in 1931, the court ruled by a 7–2 margin that the California law was illegal, as it violated both the first and fourteenth amendments. At the time of the ruling, over thirty states had enacted red flag restrictions. Though the Supreme Court ruling came too late to rescue Berkowitz, it confirmed the independent spirit of Californians when faced with injustice.

Attracted by this same independent spirit were the pioneers who came out to California through the years on a temporary basis or to settle here permanently. They presented a cross-section of artists, innovators, intellectuals, and fast talkers. Pictured here are individuals as diverse as Teddy Roosevelt, Charlie Chaplin, Albert Einstein, John Muir, Allen Ginsberg, Charles Lindbergh, President McKinley, and Evelyn Nesbit. Einstein spent three winters in Pasadena teaching at Caltech. Roosevelt toured Yosemite with John Muir.

Among these individuals, Evelyn Nesbit holds a particular interest for me. In her day, she was as famous as Marilyn Monroe. Starting in her mid-teens, she hit it big in New York, becoming a highly successful model to famous artists. A young woman whose face appeared on many magazine covers, Nesbit became an actress who attracted a following that included Stanford White, John Barrymore, and Harry Thaw. She was the famous "Girl on the Red Velvet Swing" (the swing was located in the apartment of architect Stanford White). Eventually, Nesbit became White's teenaged mistress; but through manipulation and courtship, Thaw managed to marry her. However, his mental illness took hold in the form of a double fixation, smothering Nesbit and obsessing about the man who had deflowered her, namely White. This culminated in Thaw shooting White after a show at Madison Square Garden in 1906 and subsequently serving years in a mental hospital, during which time Nesbit divorced him.

With her only son, Russell Thaw, and daughter-in-law living in Los Angeles, Nesbit ventured west to Brentwood during her waning years. Much to my surprise, I later learned from one of the four grandchildren that they remained uninformed of their grandmother's notoriety and fame while growing up, until as young adults they read her obituary. To them, she was their grandma who made pottery and cookies, babysat, and told them bedtime stories.

A plethora of stories hides behind the photographs selected here, each one telling fascinating and intriguing tales. These visual narratives are the foundation upon which my California dreamscape is built.

**Stephen White**
June 2021

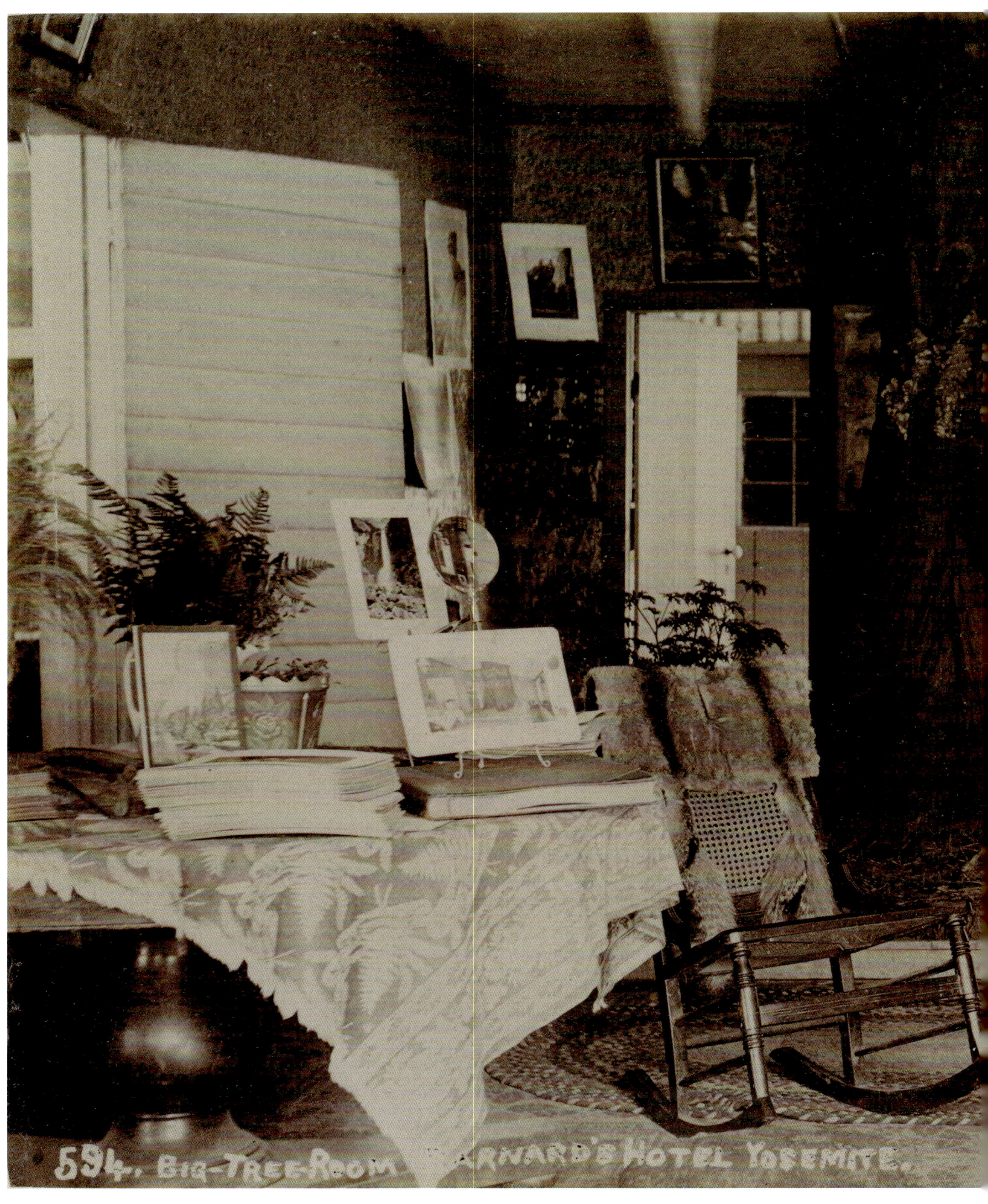
594. BIG-TREE-ROOM BARNARD'S HOTEL YOSEMITE.

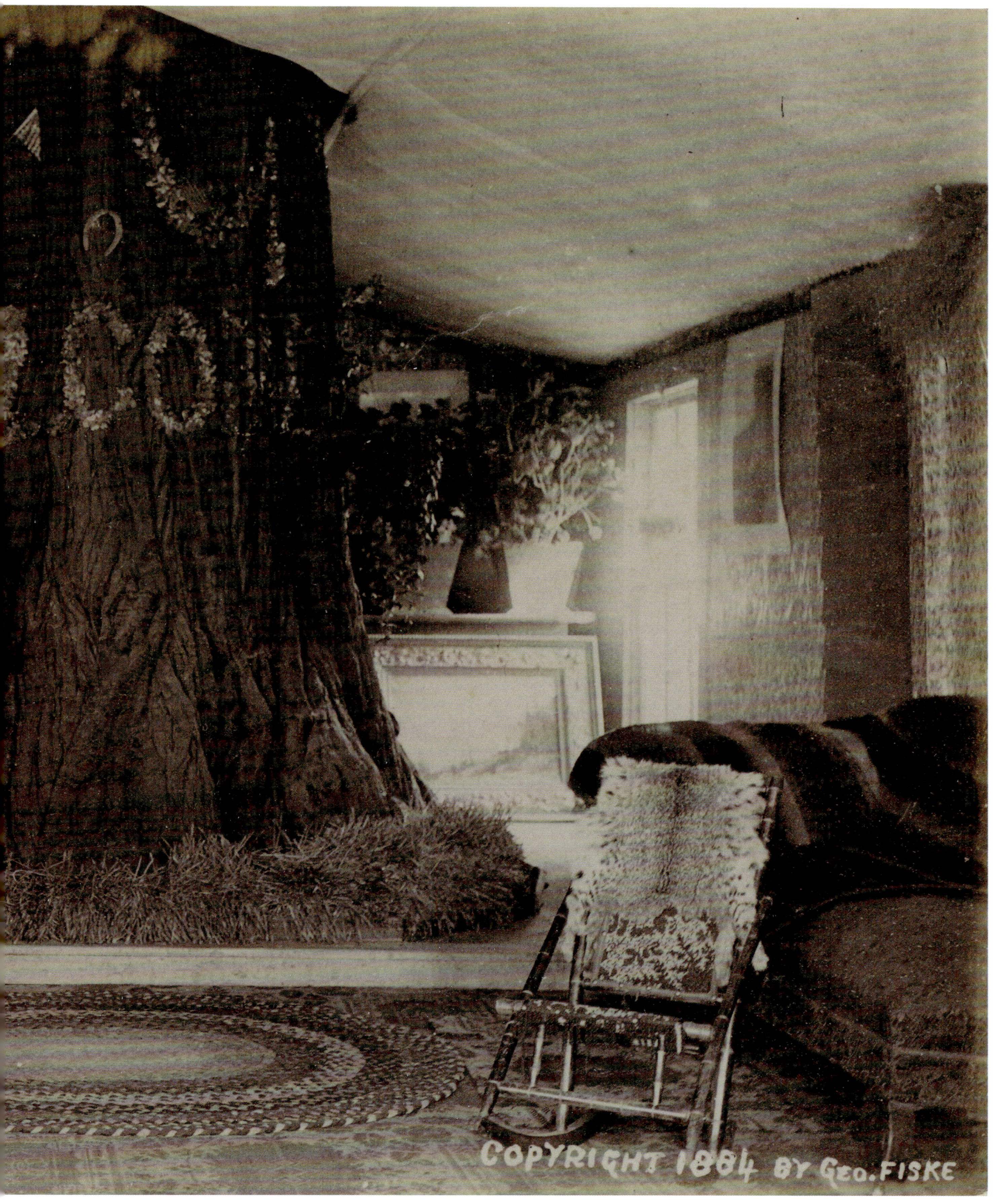


George Fiske; *Big Tree Room, Barnard's Hotel, Yosemite*; albumen print; 1884; 4¼ × 7⅛ in.
*Part of an expansion of Hutchings House, the room encompassed a 175-foot-tall incense cedar tree.*

## SONG OF THE REDWOOD TREE

**by Jonathan Spaulding**

In the middle of the nineteenth century, empirical science and imperial conquest reshaped the world. In those expansive and covetous times, photographs recorded a planet overrun by white men convinced that their manifest destiny led them inevitably toward world domination.

In the 1840s, shortly after photography was developed in Europe and crossed the Atlantic, the discovery of gold in the foothills of the Sierra Nevada sent news of California around the world. Cameras came ashore from the ships that crowded into San Francisco Bay, along with the rats and the prospectors. Back in Brooklyn, the poet Walt Whitman had read the news. He saw the photographs, too. He never actually set foot in California, but its conquest and transformation represented something profoundly American, he thought, something global in its import. It marked a crucial step in a grand saga: the European-American empire now spanned the globe.

However much he hailed the conquest of California, Whitman sensed the devastation that would come in its wake. He felt the power in the land, now threatened and under siege. Two poems, published four years apart, capture the optimistic rush of transcontinental conquest and the nagging awareness that a beautiful bit of earth was being desecrated in the process. These twin emotions of triumph and regret would shape depictions of California for more than a century.

Whitman's "Passage to India," published in 1870, celebrated the completion of the transcontinental railroad across the American West and the opening of the Suez Canal, linking the ancient Mediterranean with Asia. These triumphs of engineering and capital completed a global circuit of commerce and culture, completing the "passage to India" long envisioned by those who sought the wealth of the world for their own. The course of empire was now clear. The world was the white man's oyster. But Whitman found hope in something most white men feared: the racial mixing that would inevitably follow.

> Lo, soul! seest thou not God's purpose from the first?
> The earth to be spann'd, connected by network,
> The races, neighbors, to marry and be given in marriage,
> The oceans to be cross'd, the distant brought near,
> The lands to be welded together.

While he hailed the march of empire, the poet sensed the power of the Far West, the forces of nature the ax attacked. "Song of the Redwood Tree," published in 1874, recalls the chants, not democratic but deathly, he imagined among the forests of California as the loggers did their work. Whitman channeled the spirit of an ancient tree, soon to die. However unlikely, he imagined that the tree was fine with it.

(For know I bear the soul befitting me, I too have consciousness,
identity,
And all the rocks and mountains have, and all the earth,)
Joys of the life befitting me and brothers mine,
Our time, our term has come.

The mighty redwood sang its dying song accompanied by a chorus of forest spirits, "dryads" and "hamadryads" in Whitman's classical turn. The spirits, like the trees, bow to the new lords of the land and head for the exits. Arcadian nymphs peopled the mystic forests, greeting the onward-marching axmen. Indigenous people, caretakers of the land for thousands of years, make no appearance. It was not only Whitman who left indigenous people out. The photographers did the same. It was as if photographers and poets found indigenous Californians inconvenient, a truth to be ignored. The unpeopled landscape in these photographs was standard practice in the day, a "representational genocide" in writer Rebecca Solnit's piquant phrase.

The photographs collected here depict the triumphs of modern California: great cities, vast productive fields, homes for millions. They offer reassuring glimpses of islands of beauty, preserved bits of the California that once was. Occasionally, they show the devastation that accompanied the state's rise.

Ansel Adams, the most renowned of California's photographers, knew indigenous people personally from his residence in Yosemite. But he rarely photographed them. His landscapes exist in a mythic space, out of time, out of touch with the destruction that surrounded him while he worked. The Sierra peaks look plucked from the moment of creation, the hand of God swirling among the clouds.

If the natural beauty of California has been an inspiration to the world, its history has been a cautionary tale. It took the students of Adams and later generations of photographers to turn their lenses on the sorry consequences of empire. The destruction of California over the last two centuries is by now well known and well documented. What is less well documented are the beginnings of a restoration, the slow healing of the land that can happen if we put our best effort into it.

Along the redwood coast, dams are coming down. Salmon are beginning to reclaim their spawning grounds. Clear cuts and raging infernos need not be our reality. Indigenous people, despite the odds, are still here and they are beginning to educate the broader public on how to manage the land sustainably, with respect for all its life. Here is a potential new chapter in the great saga of California and the world. Here is a subject worthy of a new generation of photographers.

That "murmuring, fateful, giant voice, out of the earth and sky" that Whitman heard can still speak to us, if we walk quietly enough to listen. Maybe that redwood tree is telling us it really would rather live.

Edward Weston; Untitled (Rocks); gelatin silver print; ca. 1930; 9⅝ × 7⅝ in.
*Rocks are everywhere, but a great photographer can draw out the natural beauty and order within.*

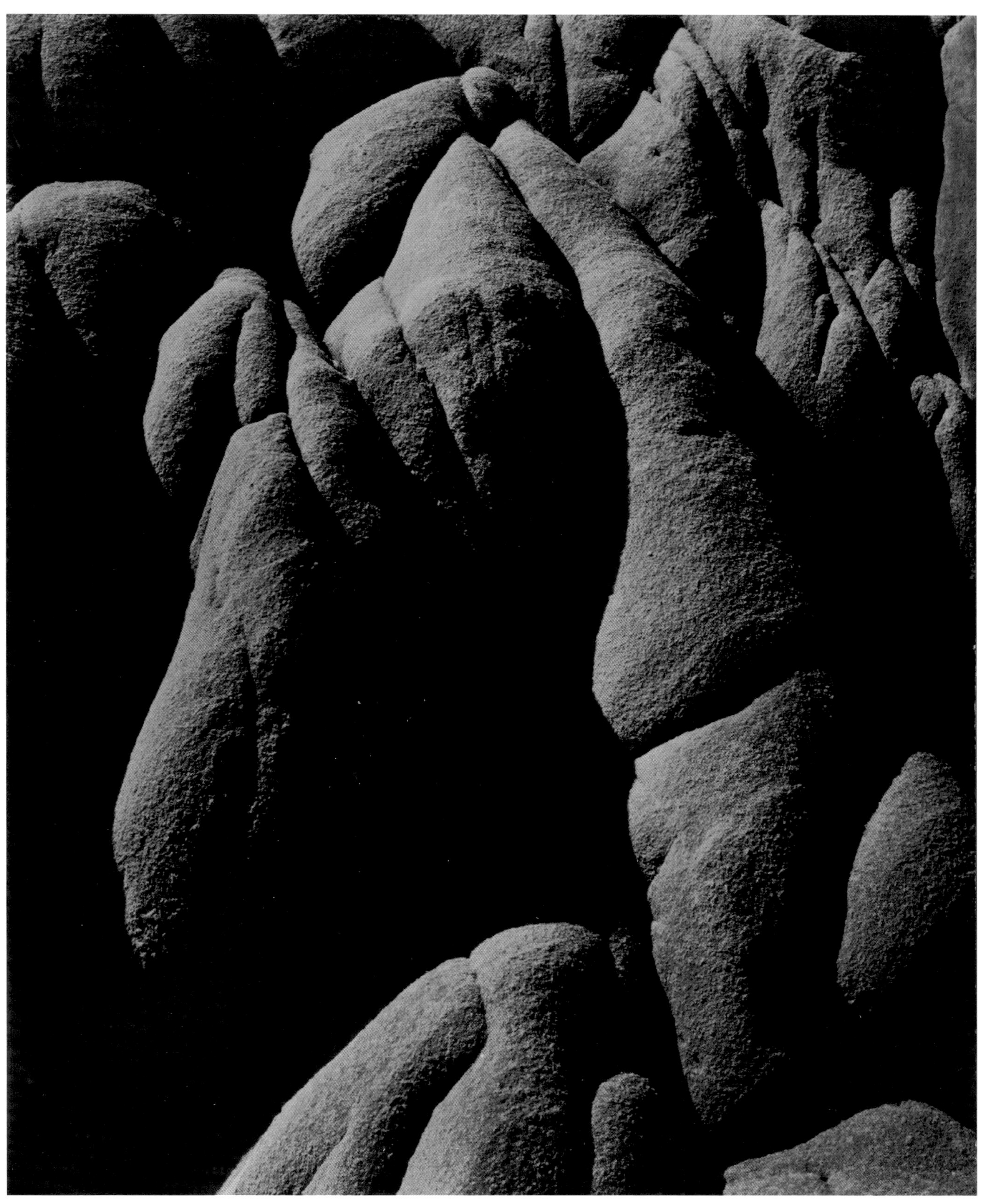

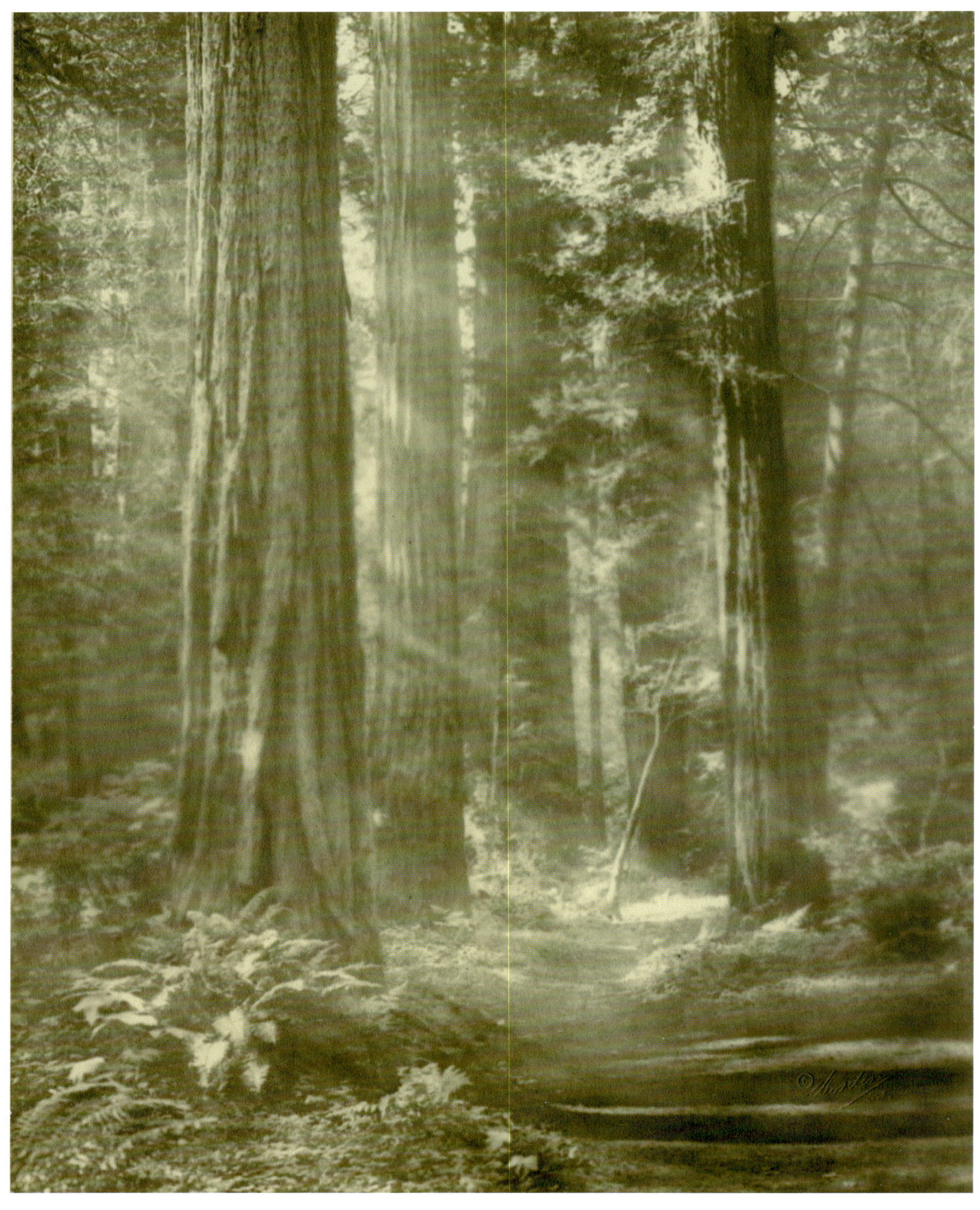

Willard E. Worden; Redwoods California; gelatin silver print; ca. 1910; 9¼ × 7¼ in.
*Worden, a Bay Area photographer at the turn of the century, captures the unique beauty and strength of light playing out among the redwood trees. Redwoods are primarily located in Northern California and considered one of the great wonders of the state.*

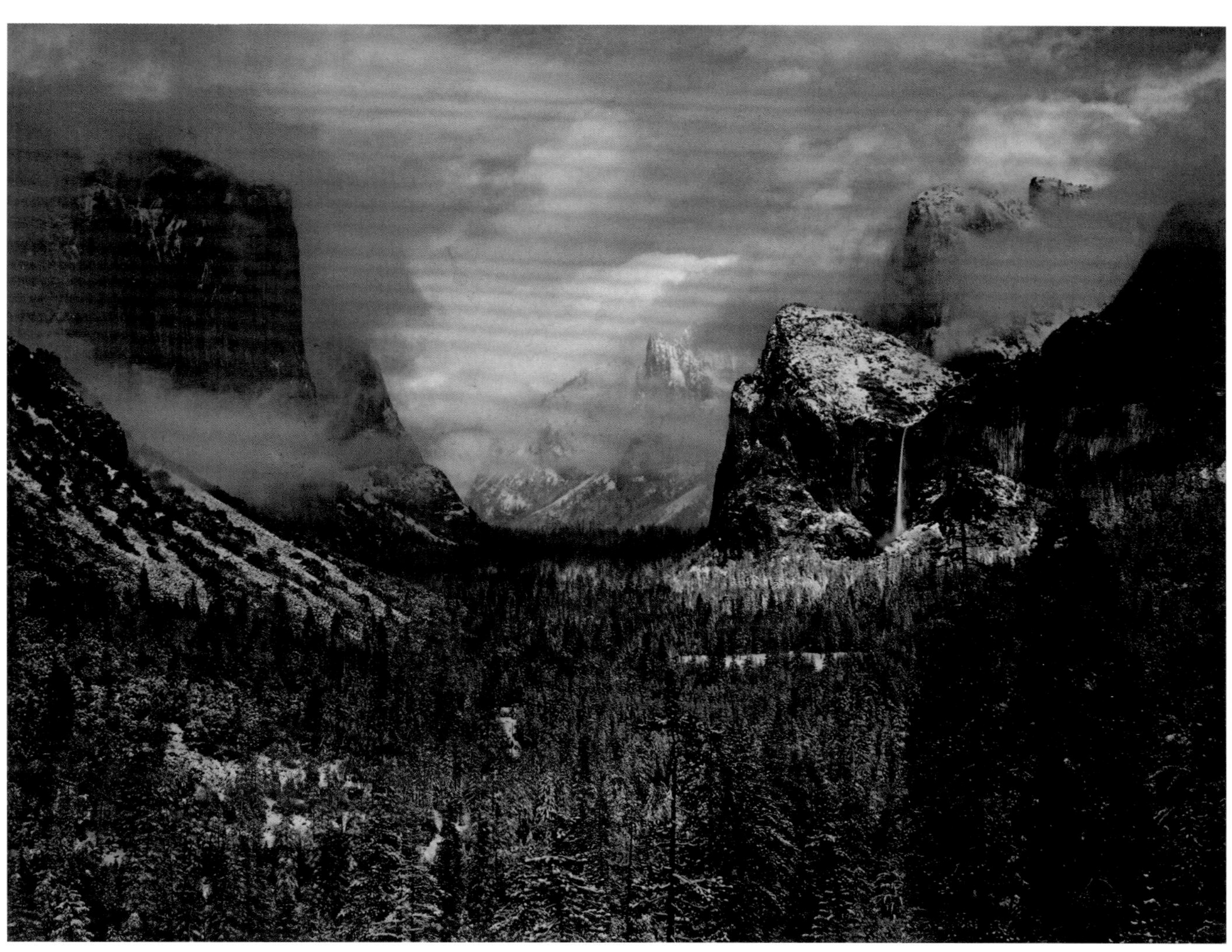

Ansel Adams; Clearing *Winter Storm*; gelatin silver print; ca. 1955; 15⅛ × 19⅜ in.
*This iconic Adams print of the basin of Yosemite has the surface patina of an old master painting, with scratches and cracks throughout. This particular print has historic as well as aesthetic interest. Originally attached to a Masonite board, it was shown in Yosemite and San Francisco as part of an exhibition titled,* This is the American Earth. *The exhibition, sponsored by the Sierra Club, is credited with initiating the environmental movement. Reproduced in the catalogue* This Is the American Earth, *published 1960.*

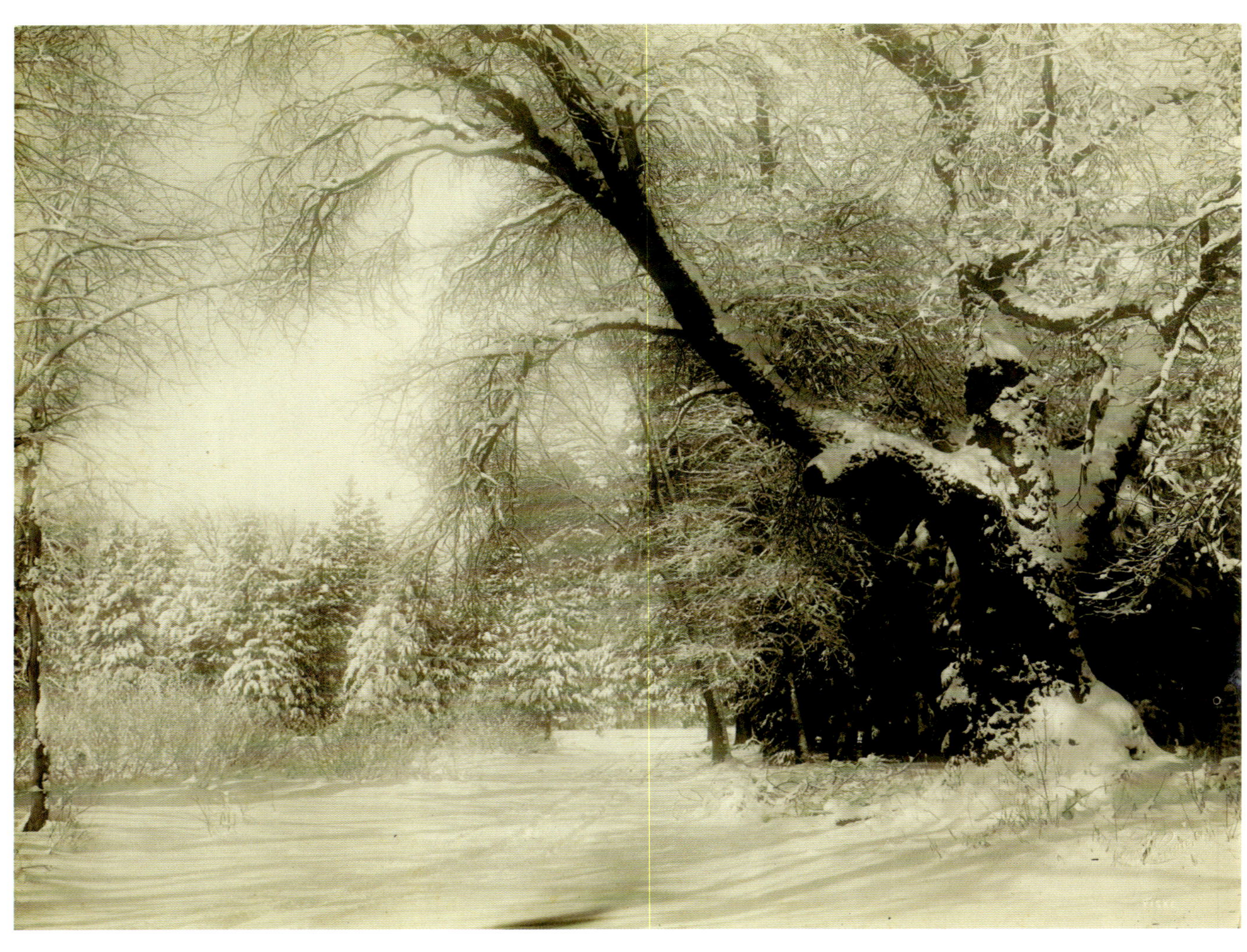

George Fiske; *Fairyland*; gelatin silver print; ca. 1910; 10 × 13⅛ in.
*Fiske lived and worked in Yosemite for more than fifty years. While most of his photographs were albumen, toward the end of his life, he produced a series of larger silver prints of his beloved Yosemite Valley.*

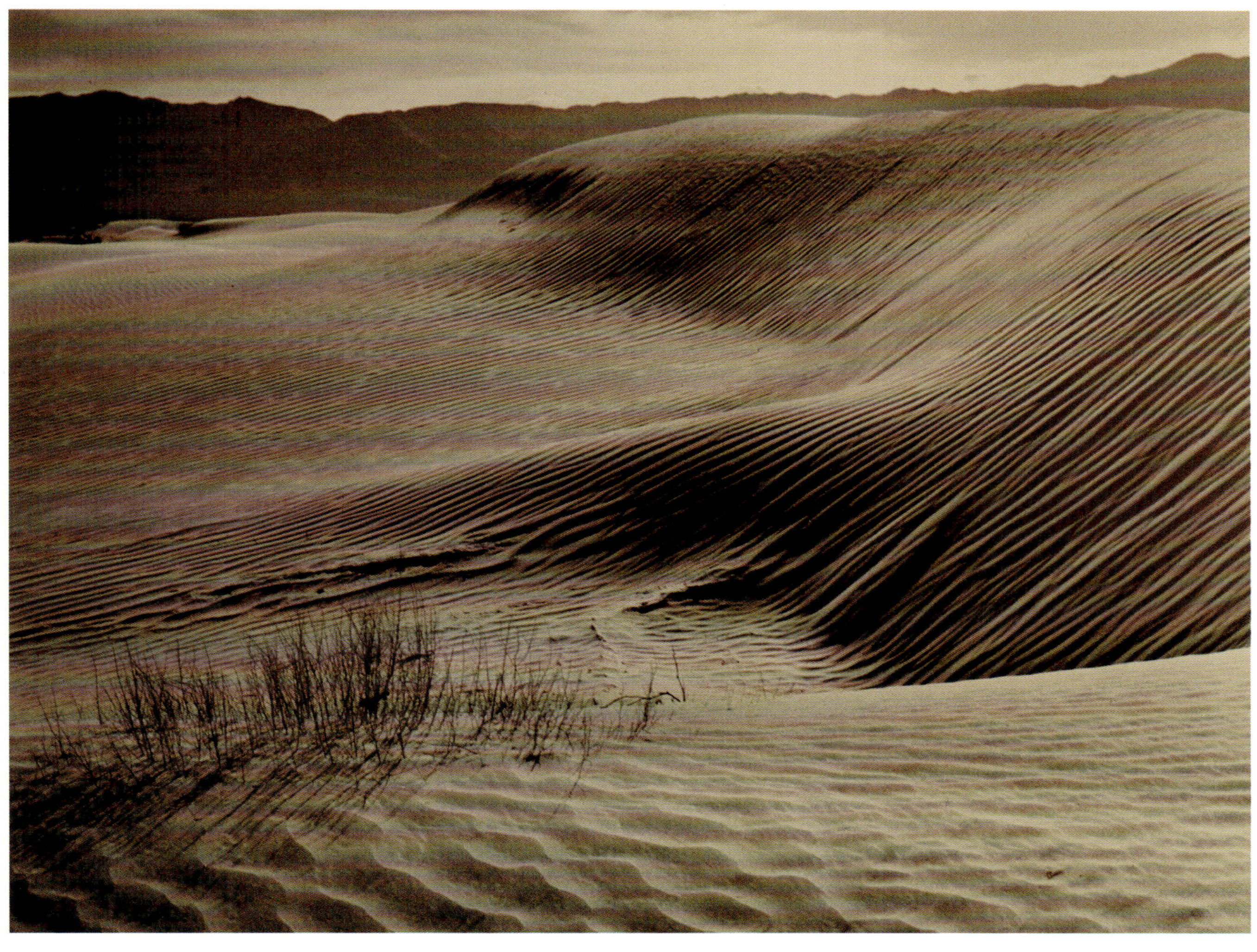

Floyd Evans; *Sand Falls*; chlorobromide print; ca. 1930; 13⅜ × 17⅜ in.
*Evans lived in Pasadena and was a member of the Los Angeles Camera Club.*

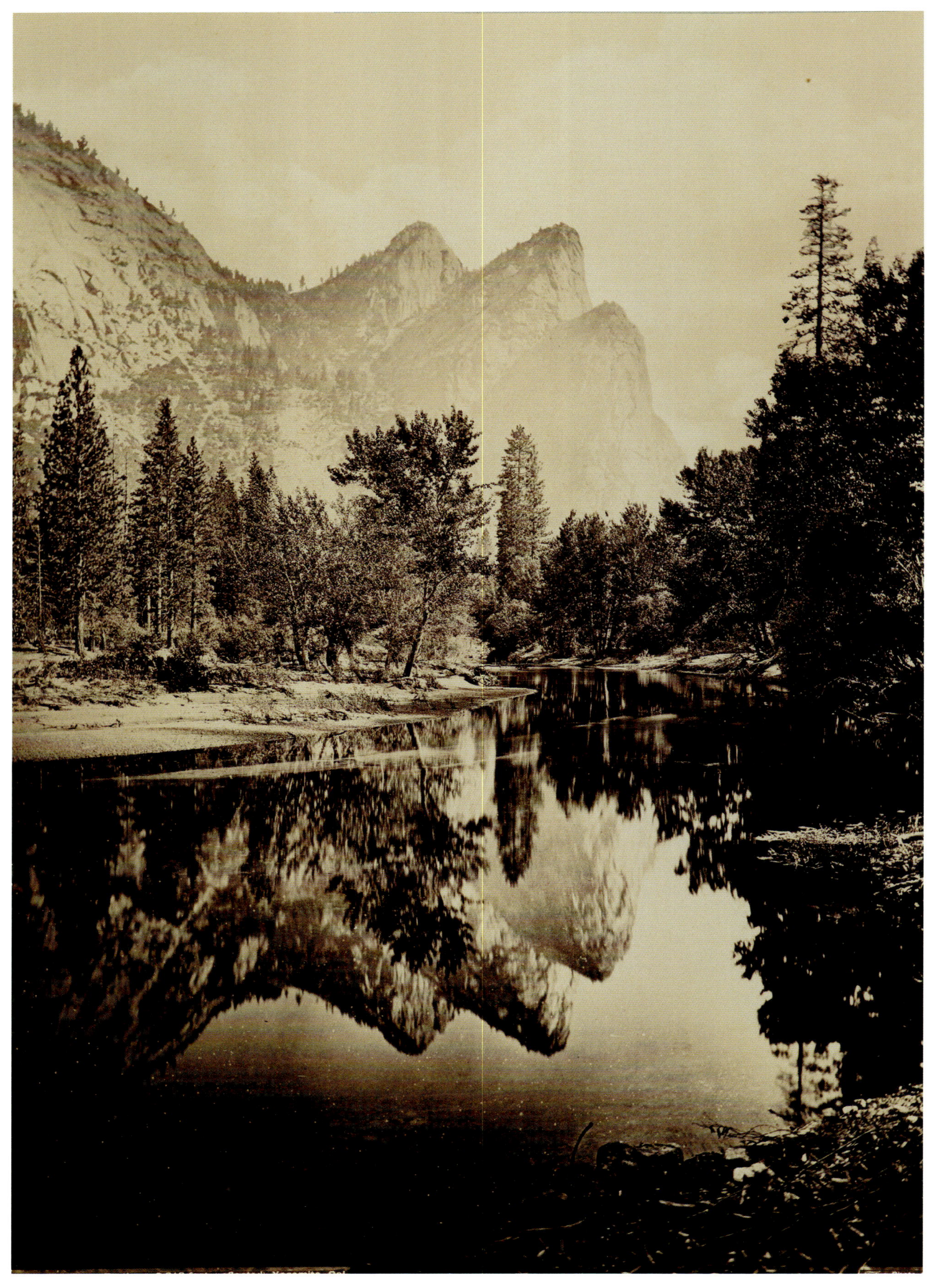

Carleton E. Watkins; Untitled (Three Brothers, Yosemite); albumen print; ca. 1872; 21 × 14½ in.
*Watkins is considered to be one of the greatest American photographers of the nineteenth century for his large-scale landscapes of the American West.*

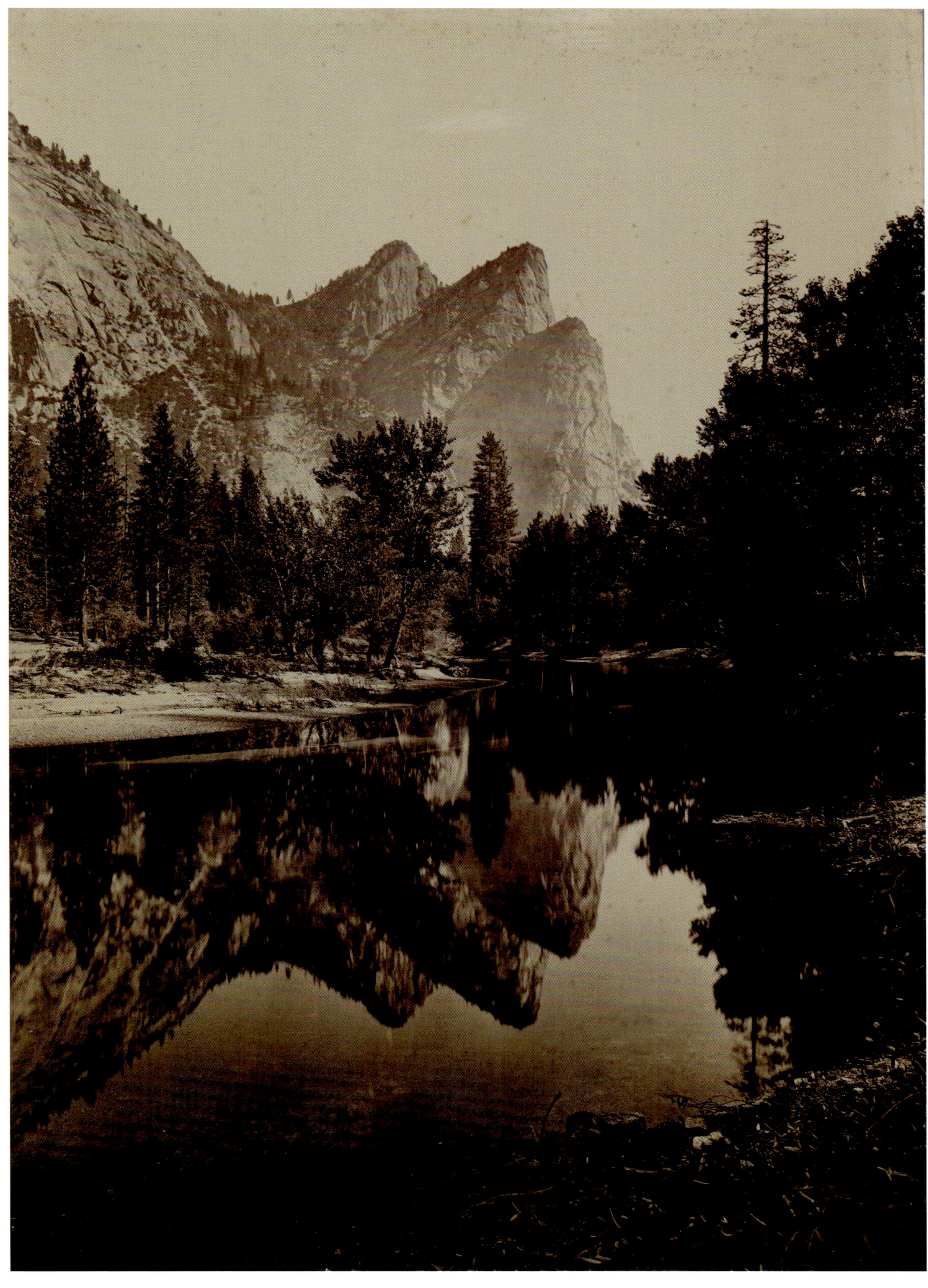

Carleton E. Watkins/Isaiah W. Taber; Untitled (Three Brothers); albumen print; ca. 1872; 20½ × 16 in.
*Taber took over many of Watkins's photographs after the latter declared bankruptcy in 1872. Taber operated a photographic studio in San Francisco.*

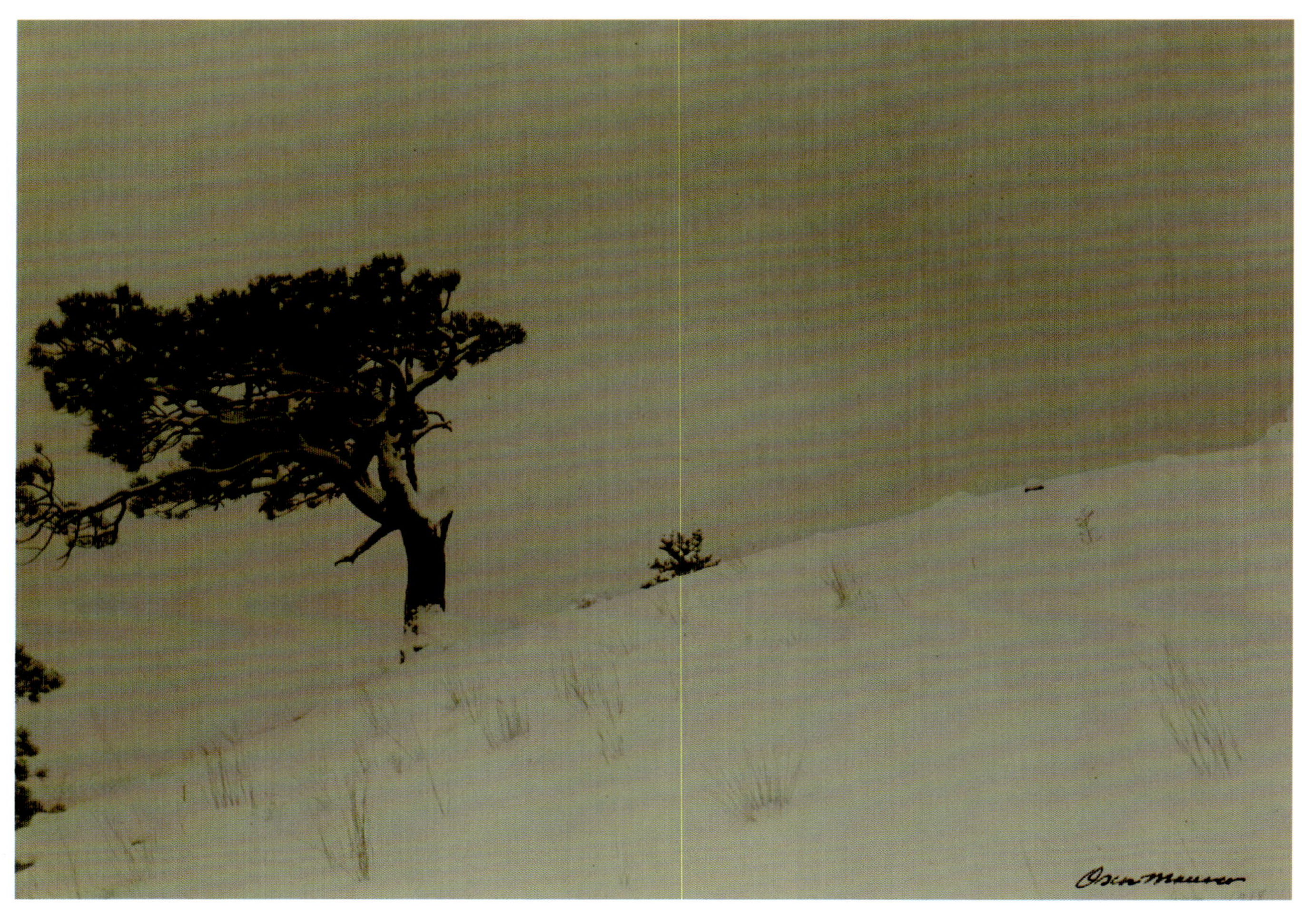

Oscar Maurer; Untitled (Windswept Tree); gelatin silver print; ca. 1910; 7⅛ × 10 in.
*Maurer, from San Francisco, was an associate of the Photo-Secession, a group of art photographers selected by Alfred Stieglitz. He published Maurer's work in his magazine,* Camera Work.

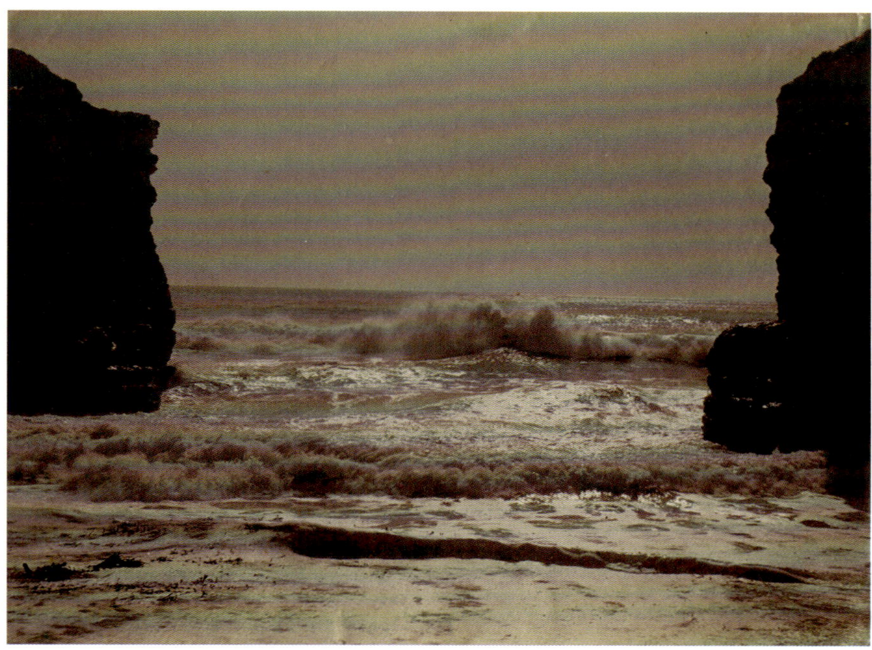

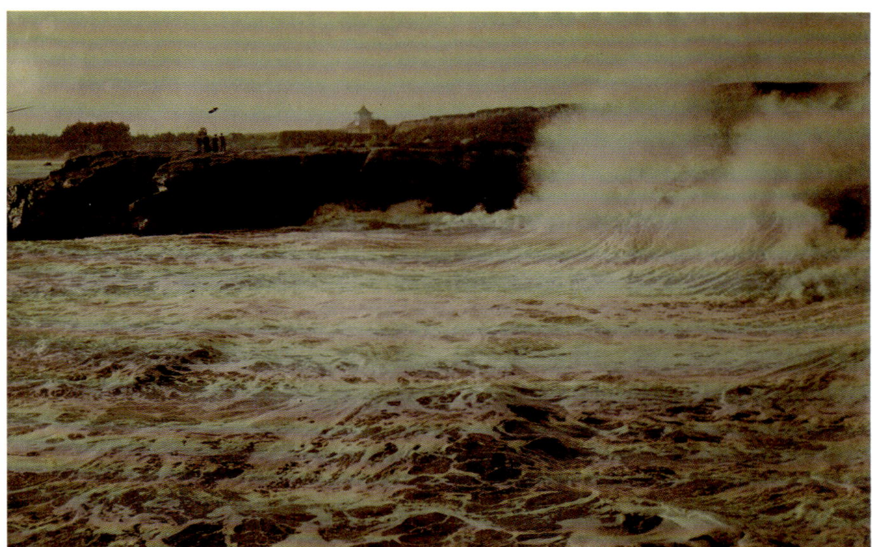

TOP: Unknown Artist; Untitled (Santa Cruz surf sequence); toned gelatin silver print; 1900; 5 × 8 in. (each)

MIDDLE: Unknown Artist; Untitled (Santa Cruz surf sequence); toned gelatin silver print; 1900; 5 × 8 in. (each)

BOTTOM: Unknown Artist; Untitled (Santa Cruz surf sequence); toned gelatin silver print; 1900; 5 × 8 in. (each)

*Middle print shows a group of people gathered near the lighthouse.*

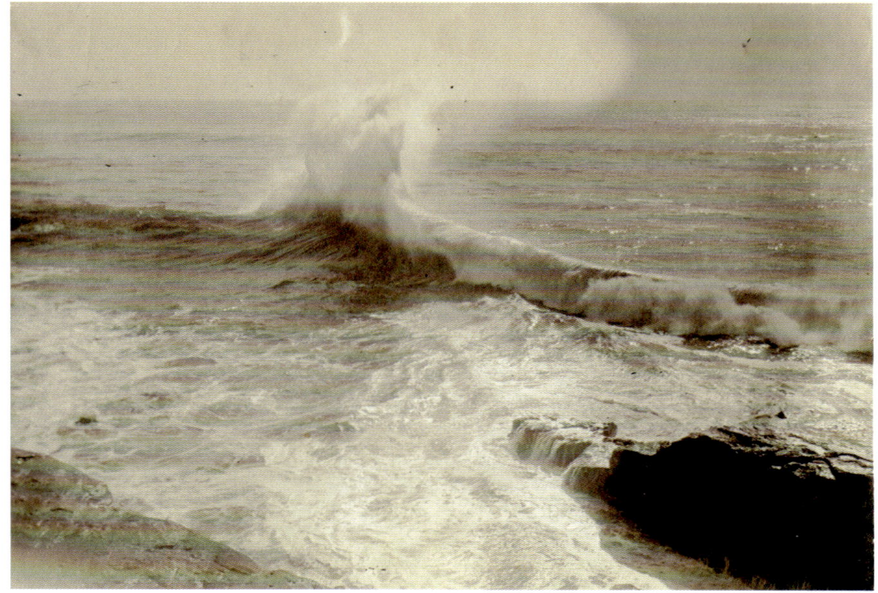

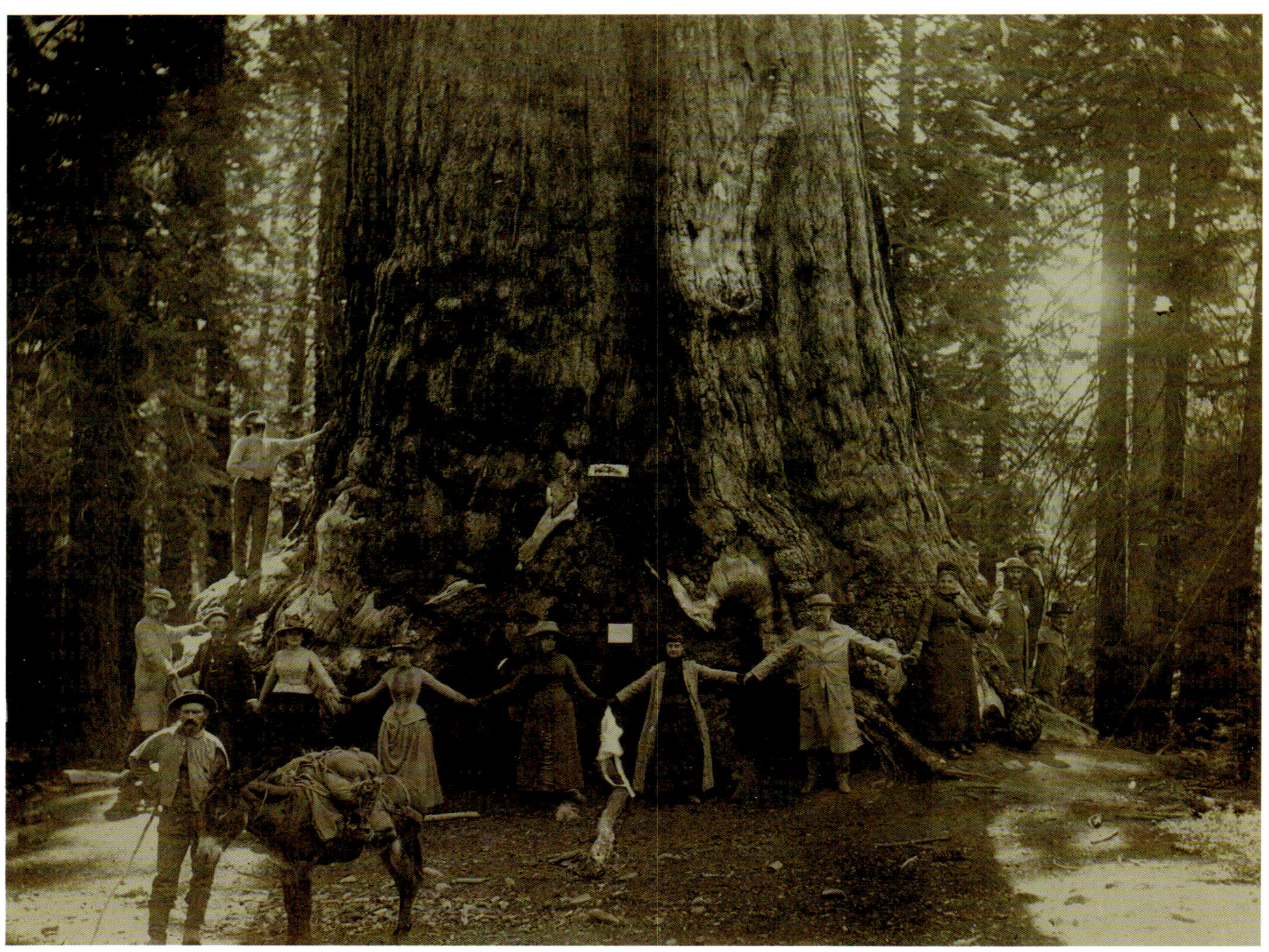

Unknown Artist; Untitled (The Henry Cowell Redwoods State Park); albumen print; ca. 1885; 7 × 9 in.
*A popular tree for tourists visiting the Santa Cruz Big Trees. This tree, about 1,500 years old, has a circumference of fifty-two feet and a height of 285 feet.*

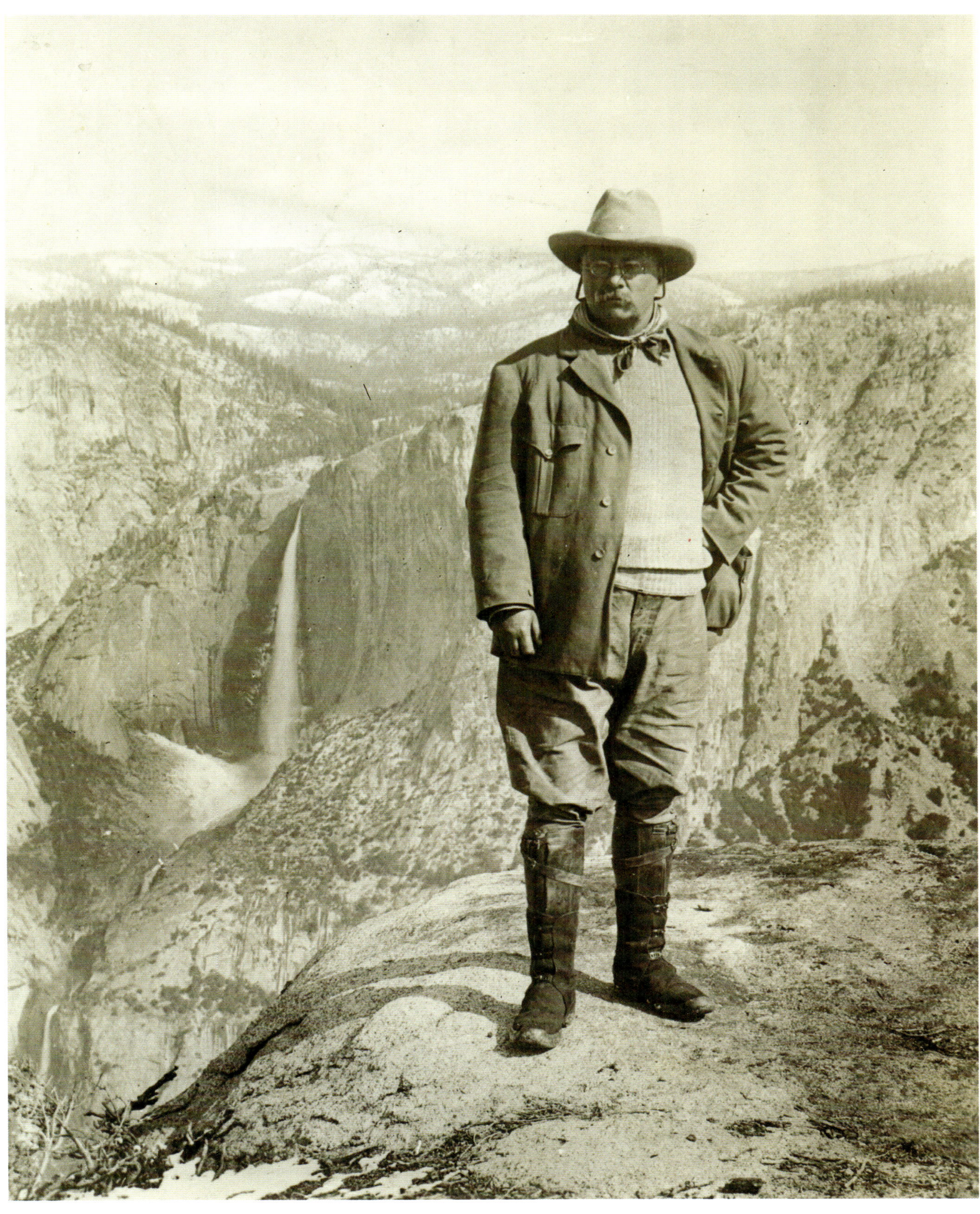

Underwood and Underwood (attributed); Untitled (Teddy Roosevelt in Yosemite); gelatin silver print; 1903, printed ca. 1930; 9¼ × 7¼ in.
*Teddy Roosevelt took a three-day trek through Yosemite with John Muir in 1903. Three years later, he designated Yosemite Valley and the Mariposa Grove to be under the protection of the federal government through the American Antiquities Act of 1906.*

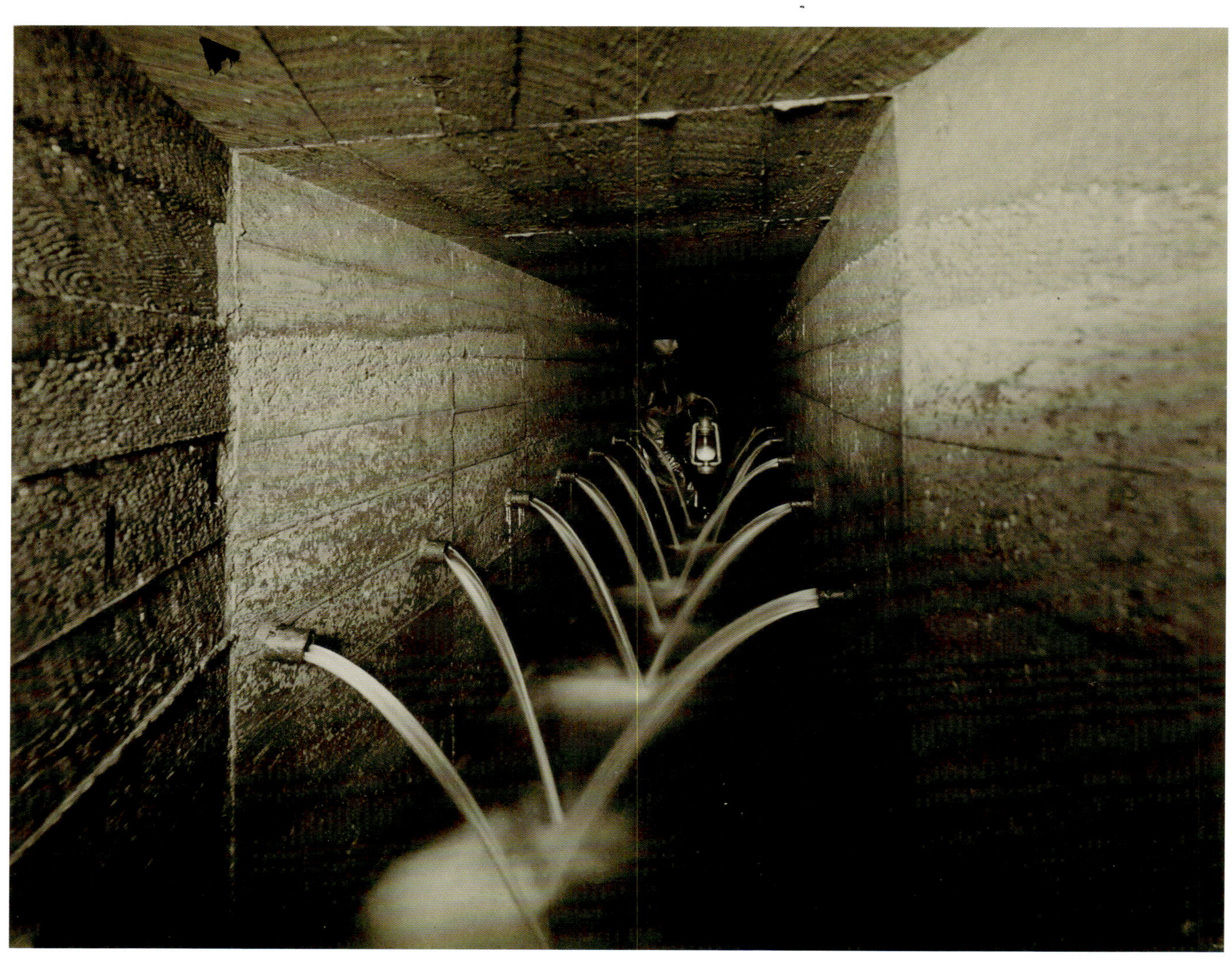

Unknown Artist; Untitled (The Sunol filter gallery); gelatin silver print; ca. 1930; Mounted: 8⅞ × 10⅞ in. / Image Size: 7⅝ × 9½ in.
*Part of the process of bringing water to San Francisco through the Hetch-Hetchy dam project.*

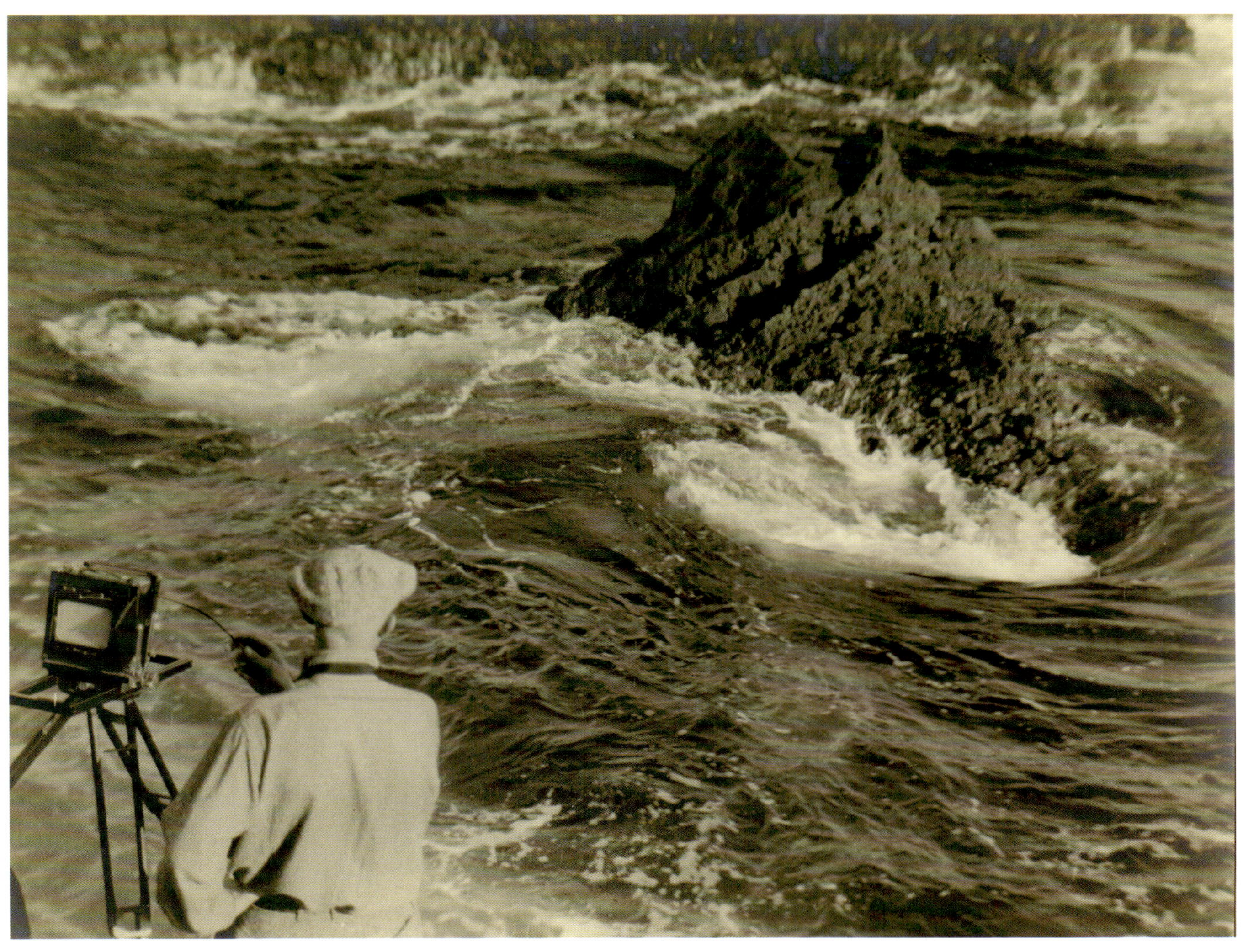

Dain Tasker; Untitled (Photographing the waves); gelatin silver print; ca. 1920; 10⅛ × 13⅛ in.
*Tasker, a radiologist who lived in Los Angeles, is best known for the series of x-rays of flowers he took in the 1930s.*

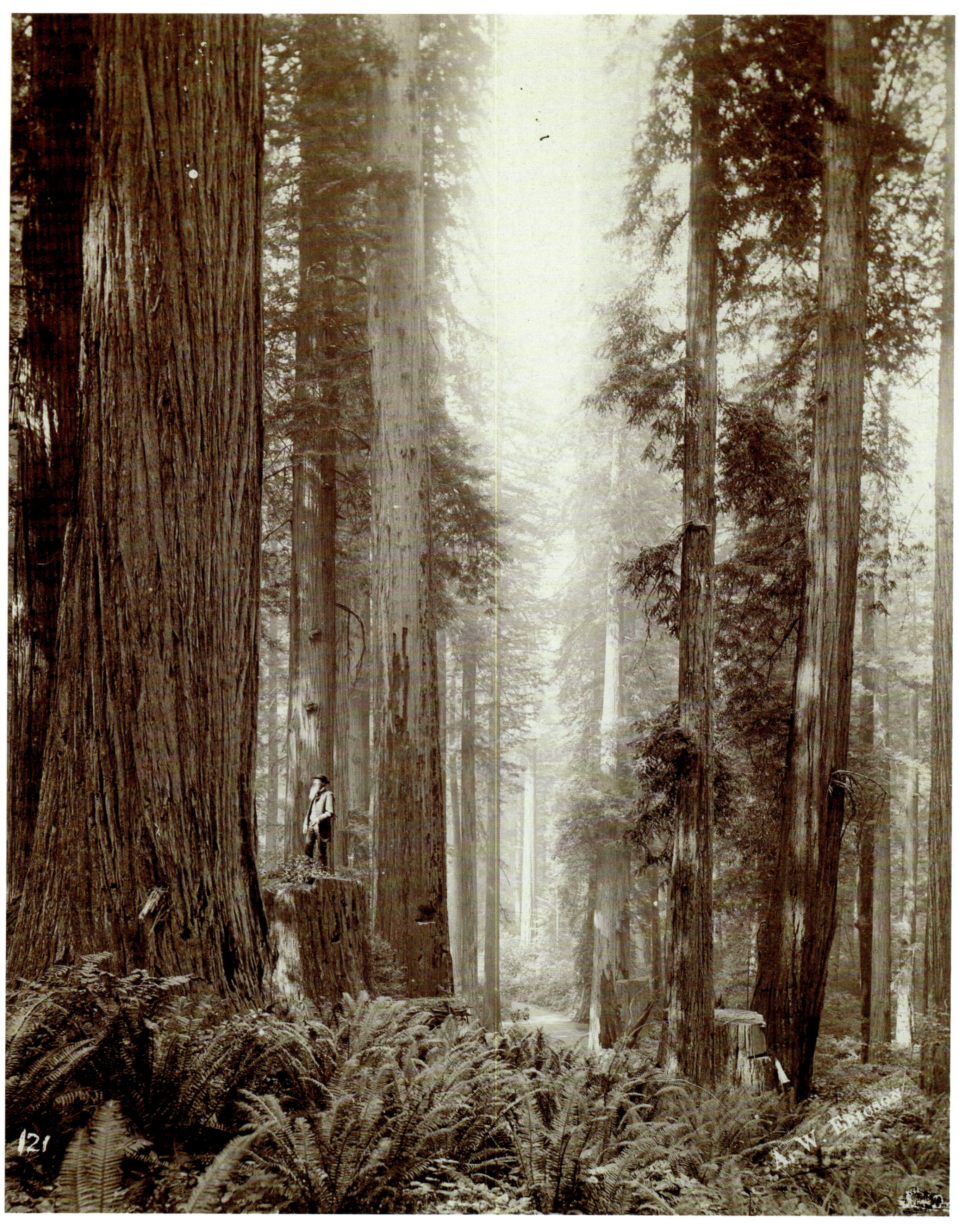


Augustus William Ericson; *Scene of the California Redwoods*; aristotype print; ca. 1900; 9 × 7 in.
*Possibly depicts John Muir standing on a stump.*

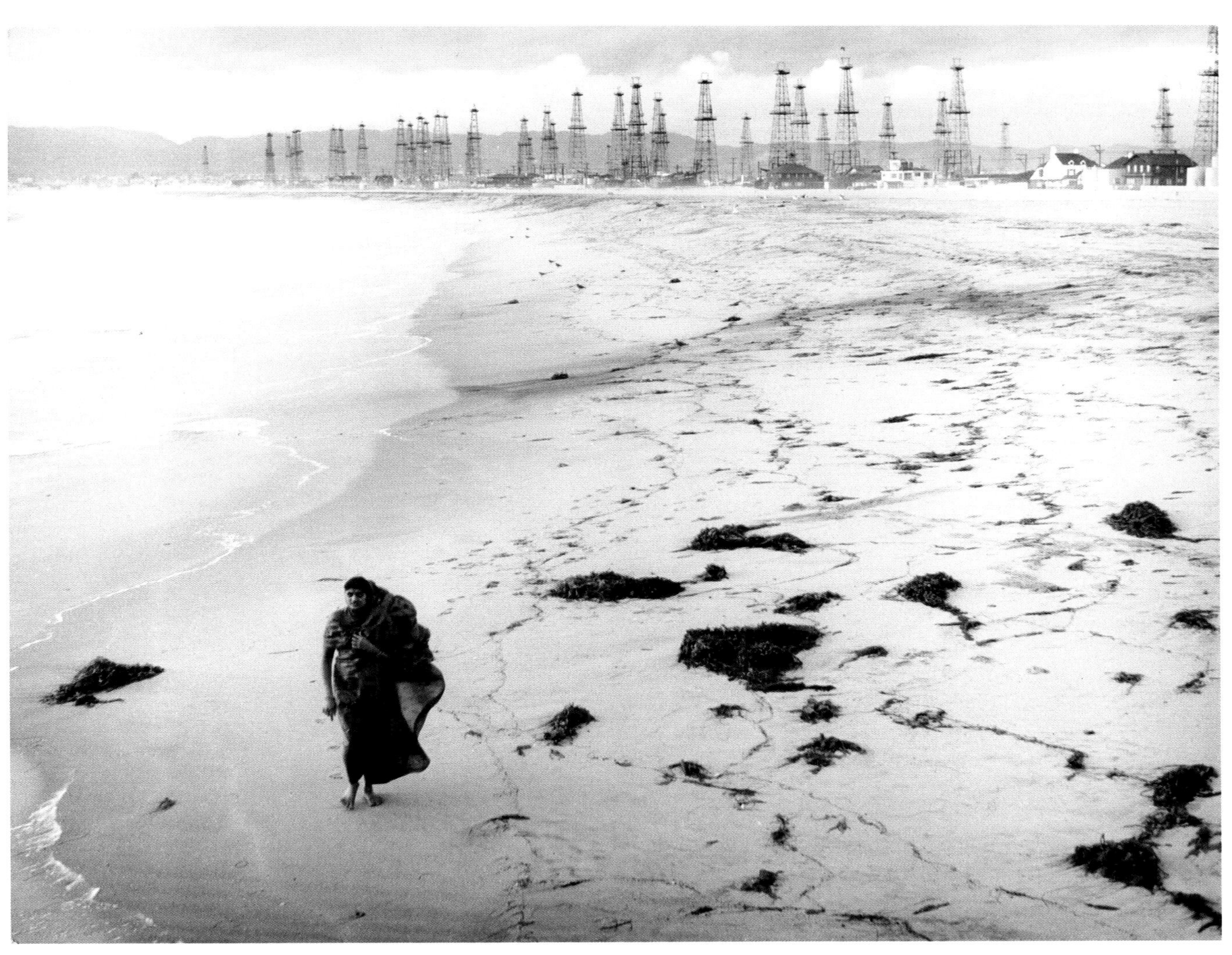

S.H. Linden; Untitled (Woman walking along Venice Beach); gelatin silver print; 1959; 11 × 14 in.
*With the discovery of oil in Los Angeles in the 1890s, the number of oil wells exploded, and the city's population followed, reaching more than one million by 1930.*

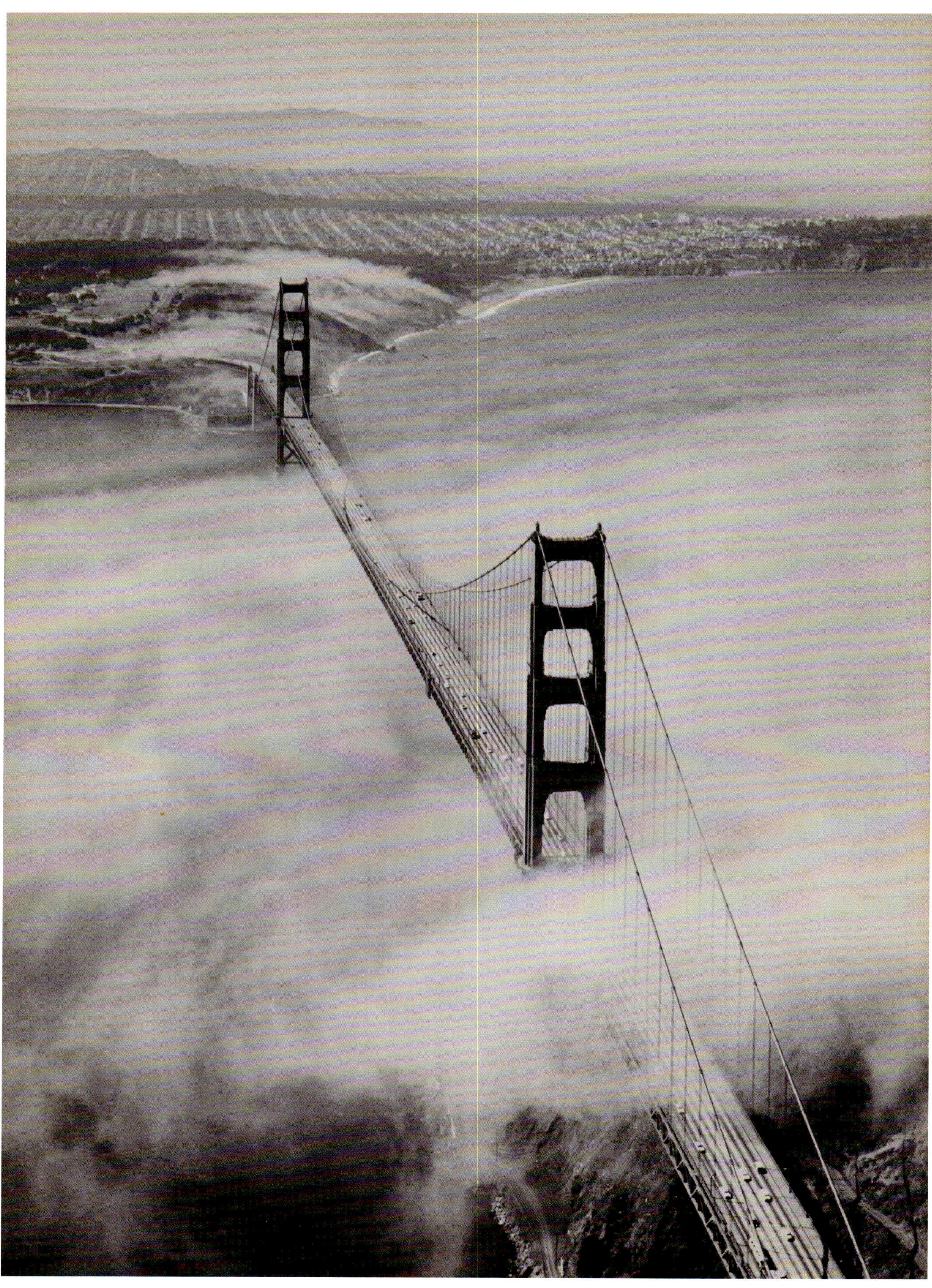

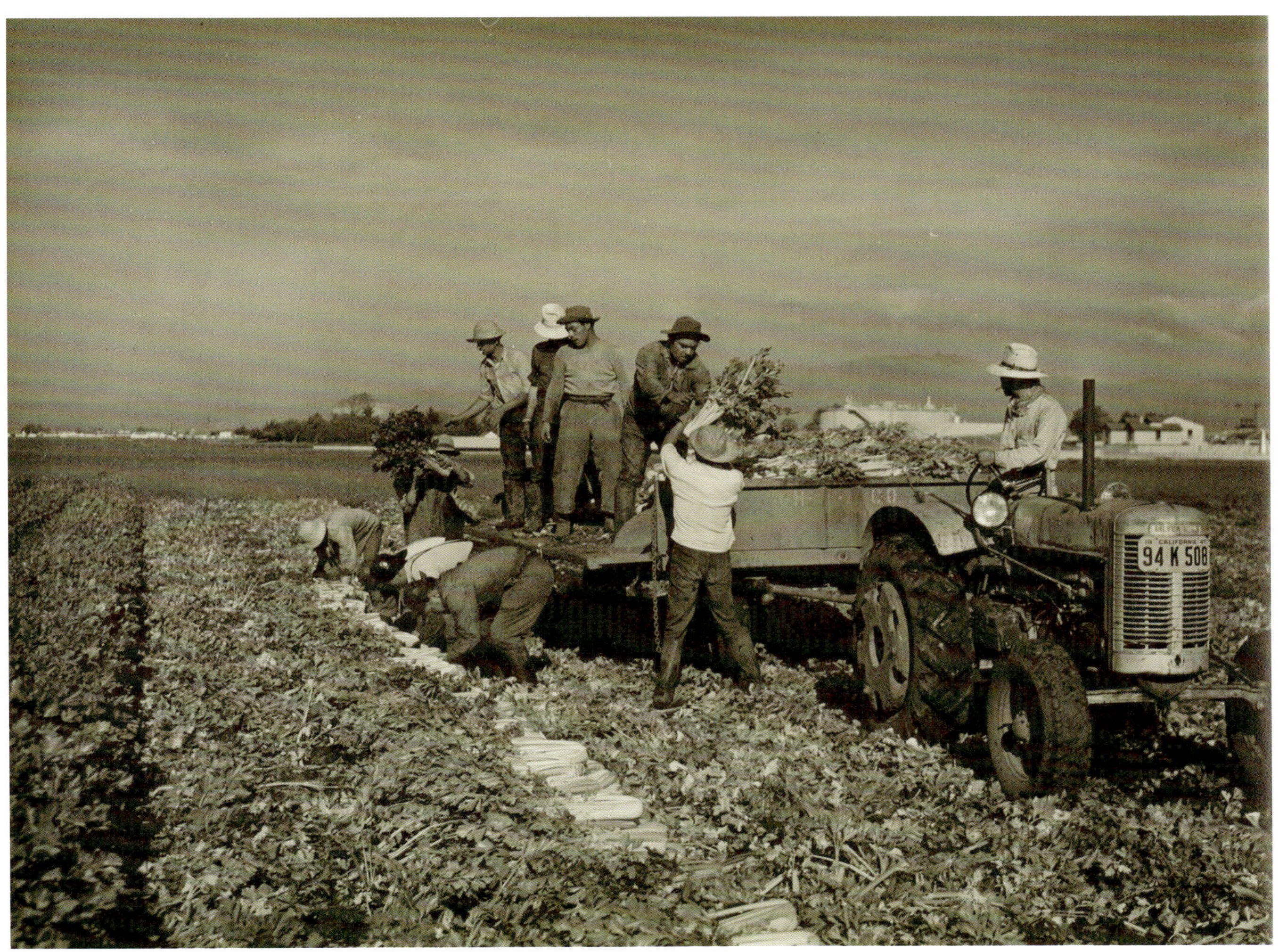


Hi Worth; Untitled (Harvesting celery); gelatin silver print; 1947; 10⅞ × 14 in.
*Worth photographed for the Pasadena City Schools in the 1940s.*

OPPOSITE: Ted Castle; *The Golden Gate Bridge*; gelatin silver print; ca. 1960; 16¼ × 11⅛ in.
*Castle worked for Time-Life and had work included in The Family of Man at New York's Museum of Modern Art, the iconic exhibition curated by Edward Steichen.*

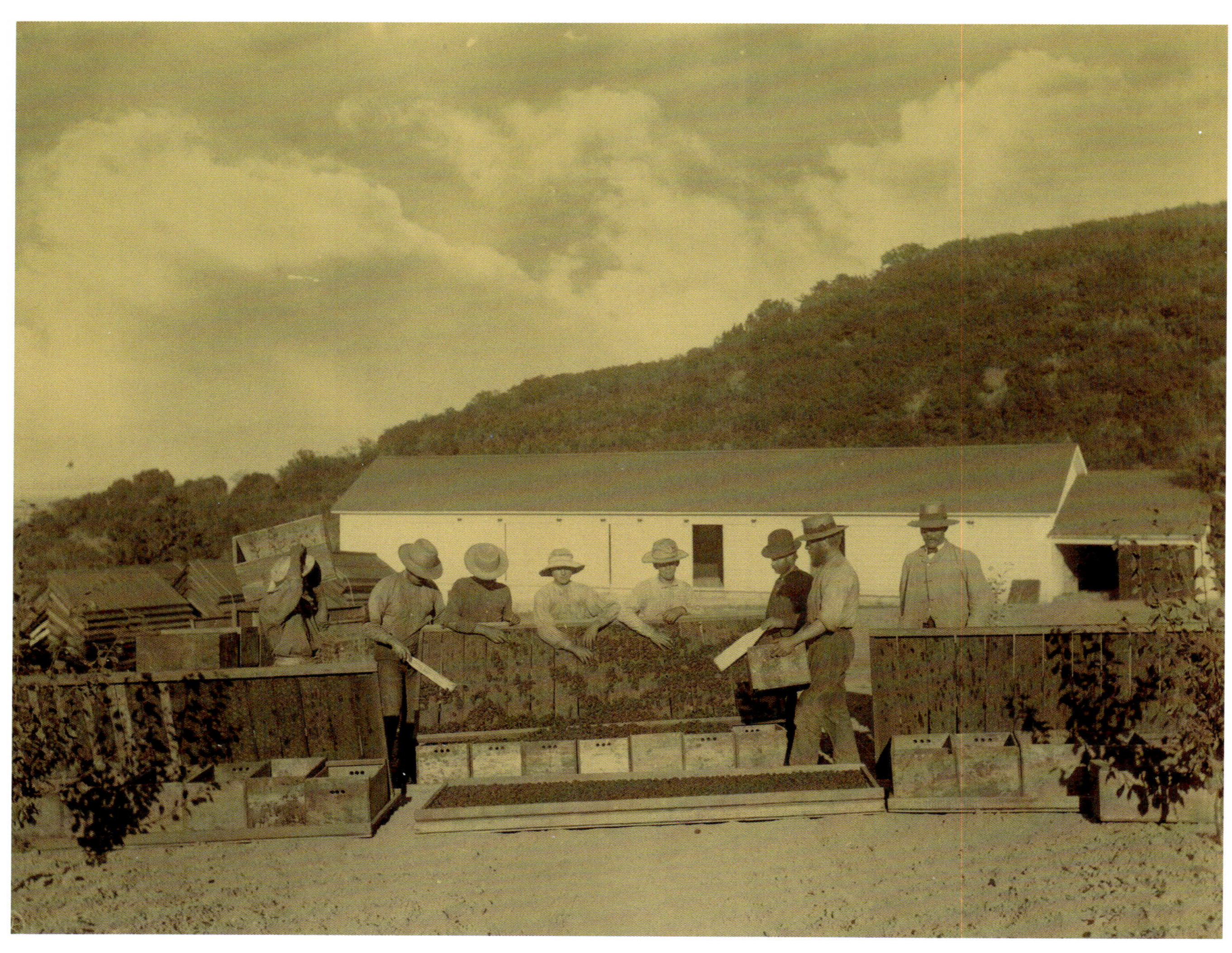

Isaiah W. Taber; *Assorting Prunes by Hand, Santa Clara County, California*; albumen print; ca. 1880; 7½ × 9½ in.
*Today, workers are used to sort out bad fruit and vegetables and assist in the various mechanized processes.*

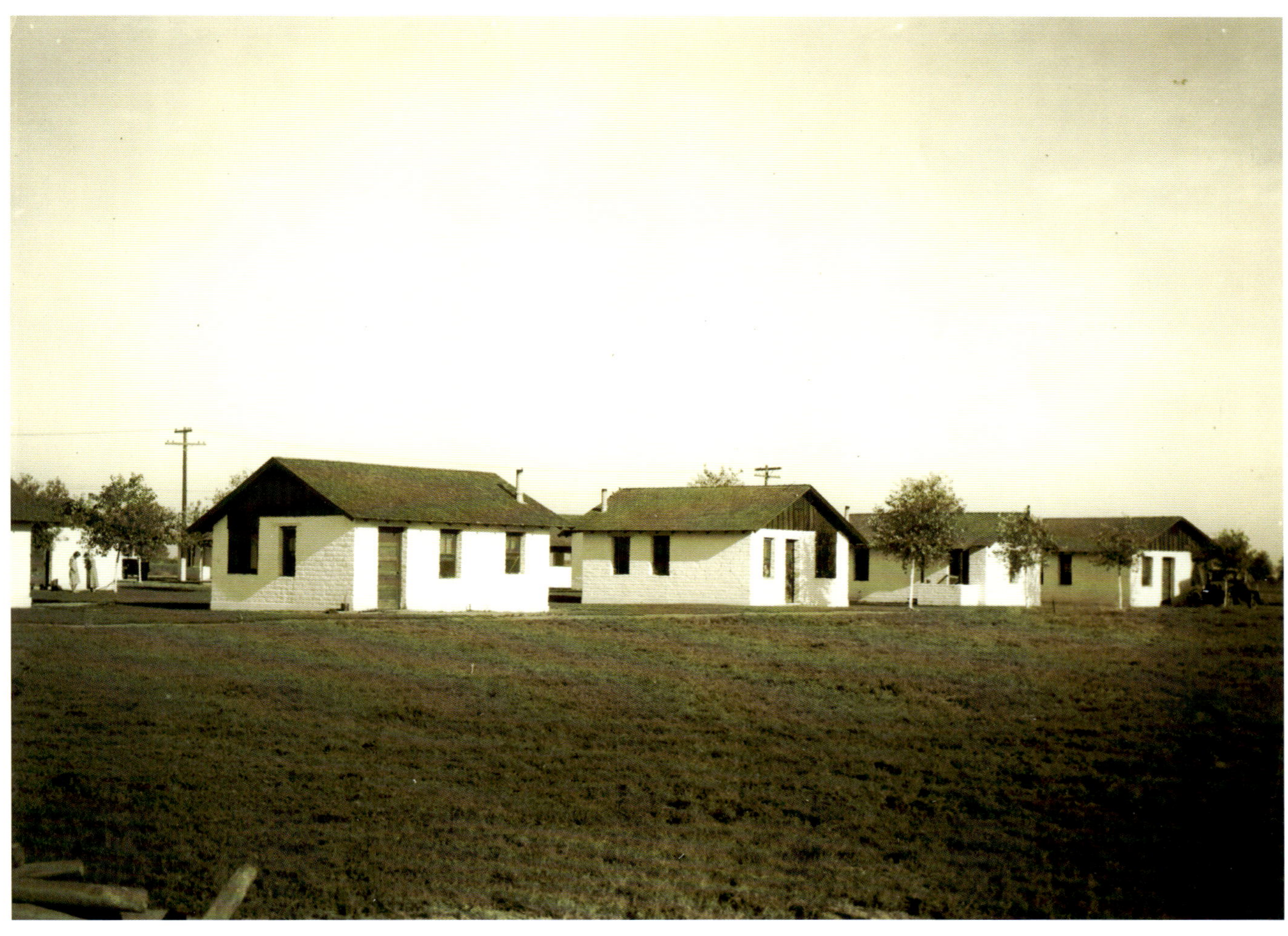

F. Hal Higgins; *Village of New Adobe Cottages Built on the Hoover Greenfield Ranch*; gelatin silver print; ca. 1935; 7¼ × 9½ in.
*After losing the election to Franklin D. Roosevelt in 1932, Herbert Hoover returned to farming, including this 22,000-acre ranch near Bakersfield, California. Higgins photographed agriculture extensively throughout California and other states. His Library of Agricultural Technology has 225,000 photographs and other items and was purchased by the University of California, Davis Library in 1959.*

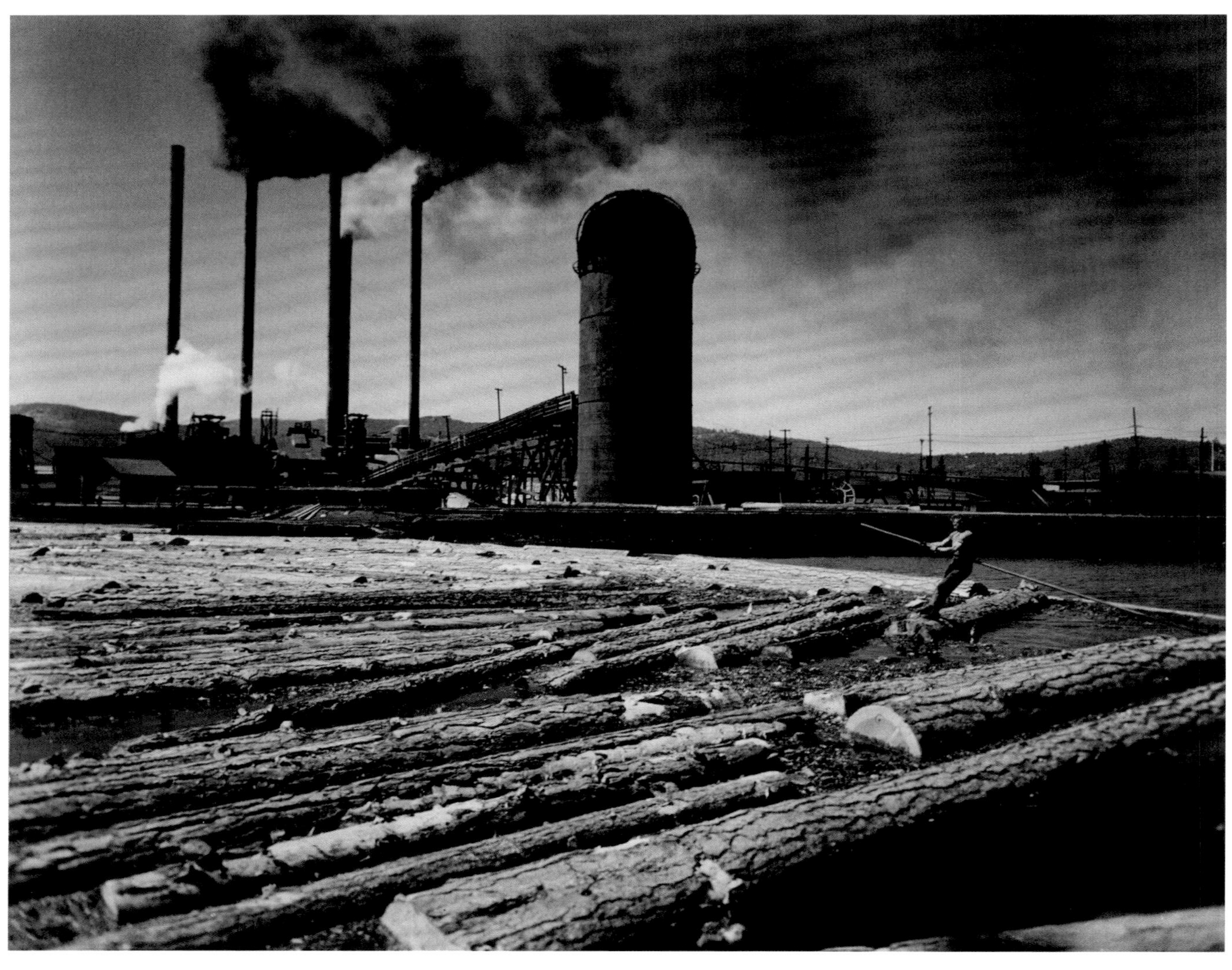

Berenice Abbott; *Number 23 Mill Pond, The Red River Lumber Company*; gelatin silver print; 1943; 14¾ × 18½ in.
*One of a series made for the Red River Lumber Company in Westwood, California. Abbott, most famous for her New York photographs in the 1930s, also discovered, printed, and helped preserve the work of the French photographer Eugene Atget.*

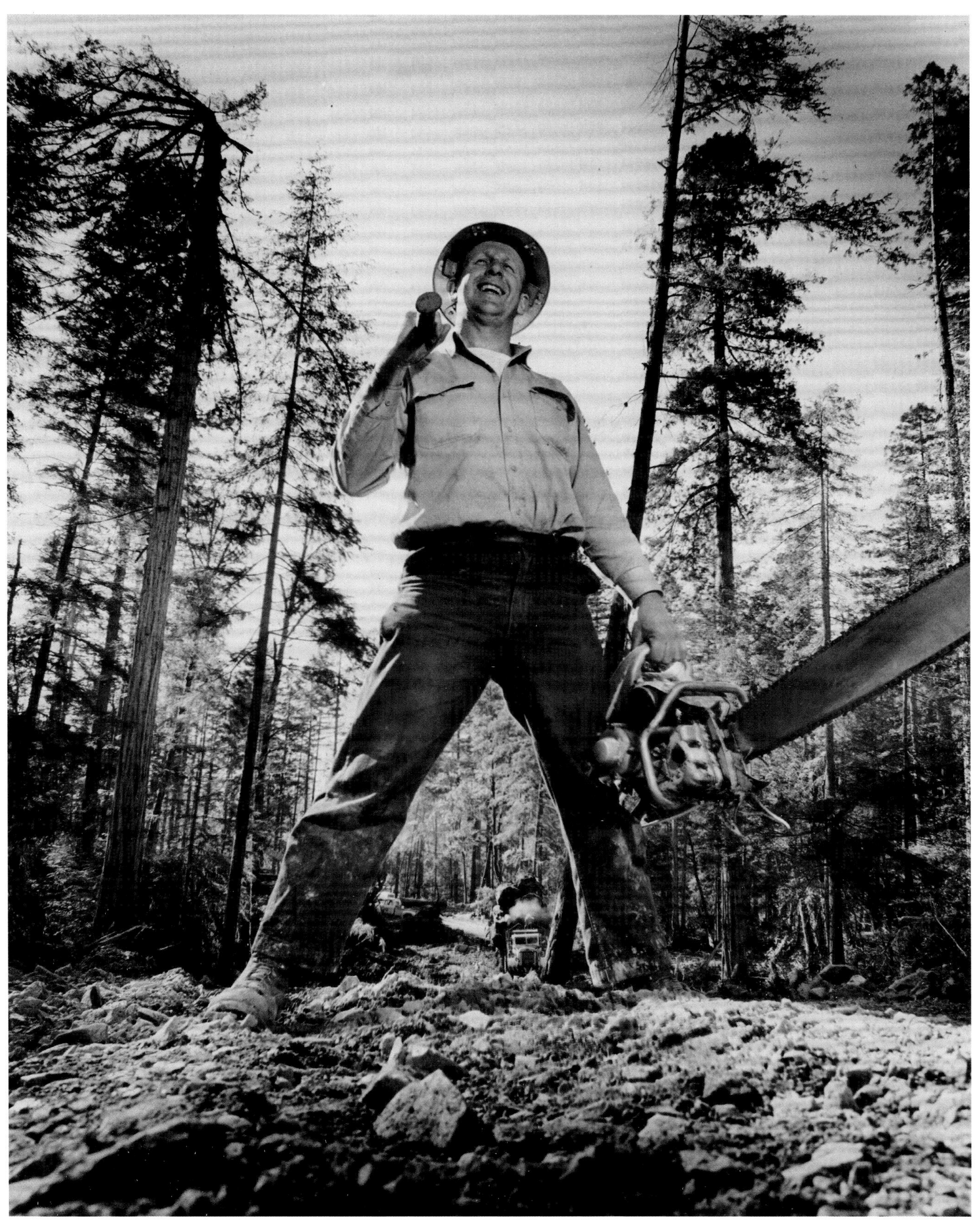

Otto Hagel; *Lumberjack, California*; gelatin silver print; ca. 1960; 19¾ × 15½ in.
*Paul Bunyan-sized character with saw in hand, ready to fell more trees. Hagel and his wife Hansel Mieth worked for* Fortune *and* Life *magazines, respectively, and homesteaded 640 acres near Santa Rosa around 1940.*

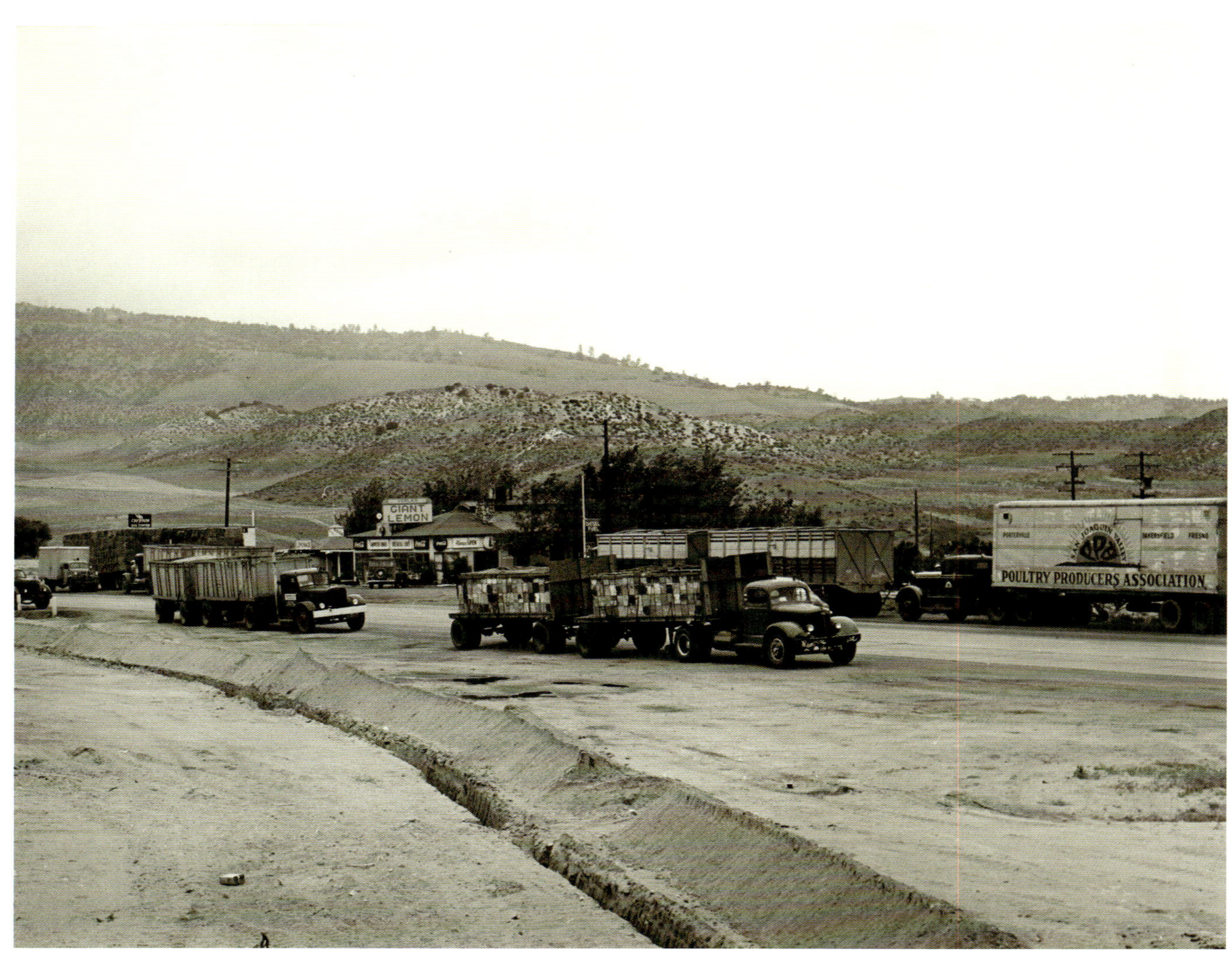


Hi Worth; Untitled (Trucks hauling produce past the Giant Lemon); gelatin silver print; ca. 1950; 11 × 13⅞ in.
*Trucking was the key to quickly moving freshly picked farm products to wholesale warehouses in California cities.*

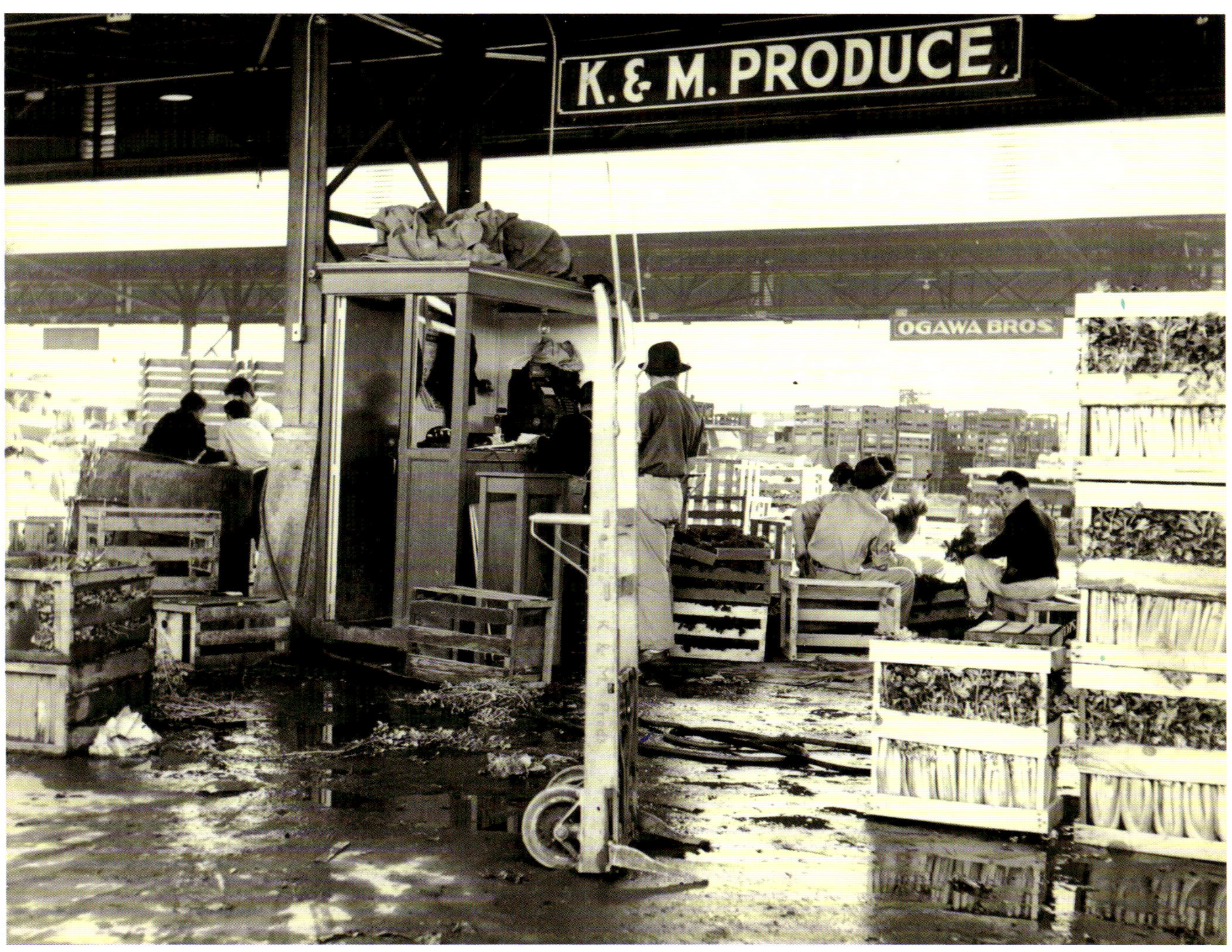


Unknown Artist; Untitled (Ogawa Brothers, K & M Produce, Los Angeles); gelatin silver print; ca. 1935; 7½ × 9½ in.
*Prior to their internment in 1942, Japanese American farmers produced one-third of all crops grown in California, which were transported throughout the state.*

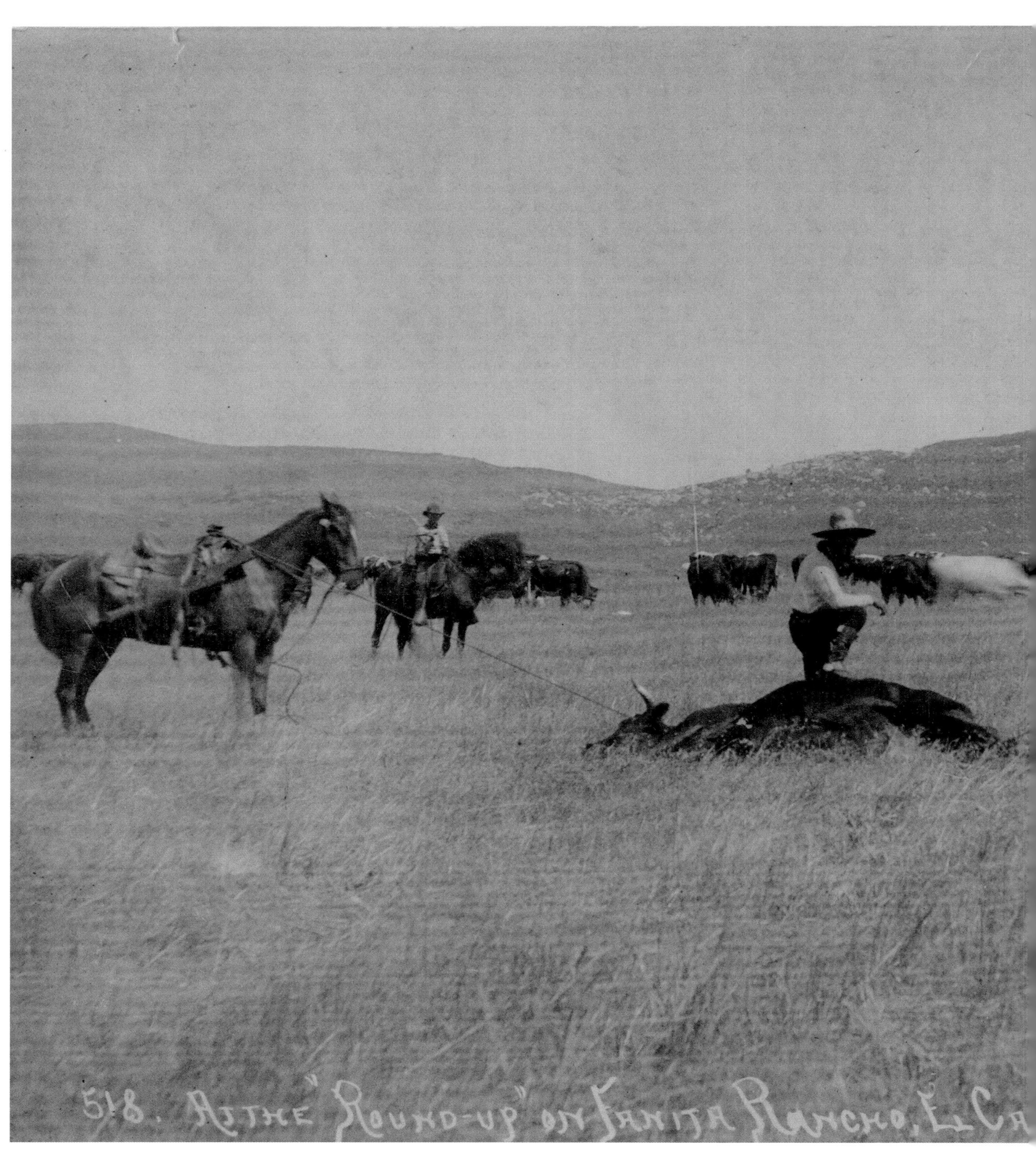
518. At the "Round-up" on Janita Rancho, El Ca

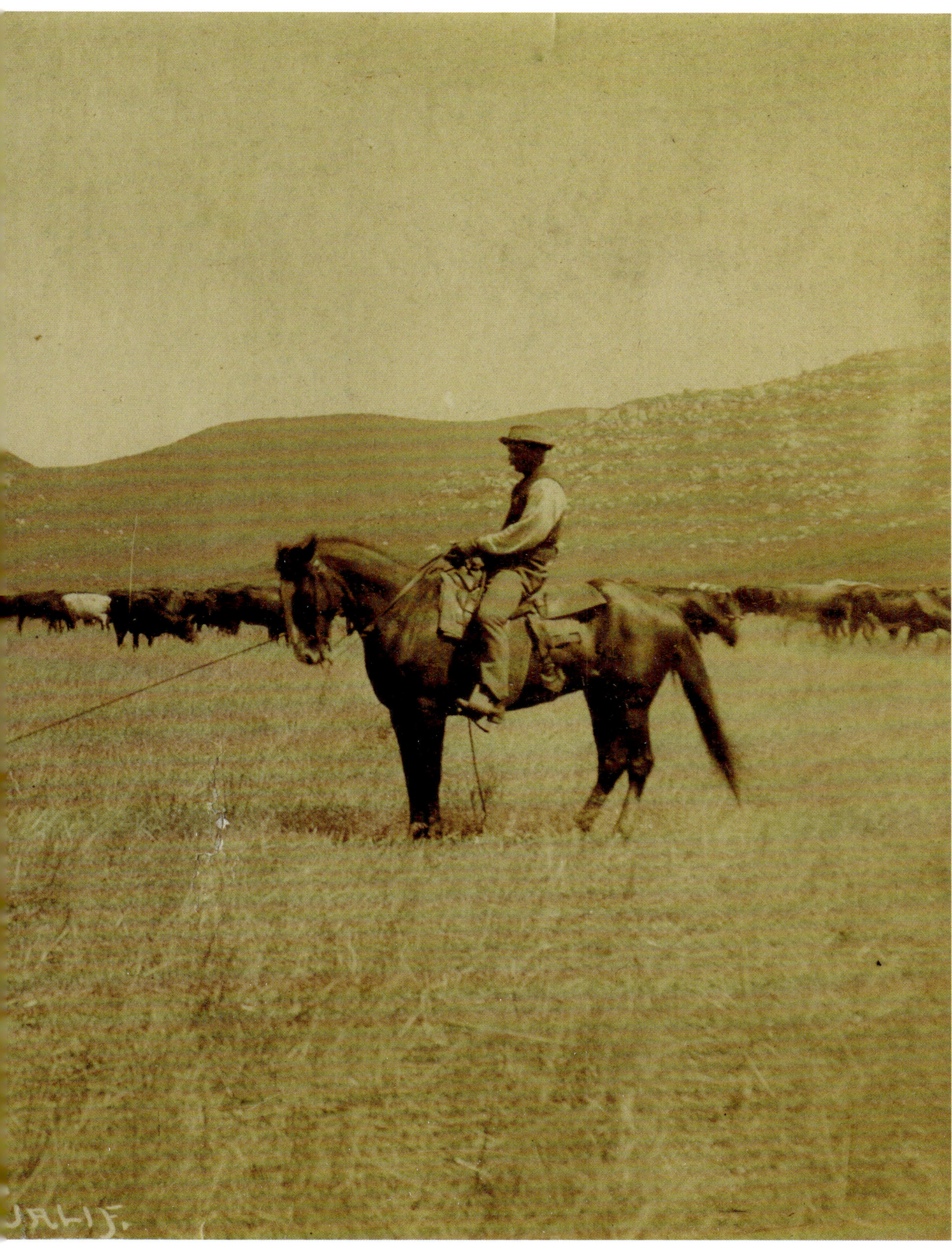

Francis Parker; *At the Round-Up, Fanita Rancho, El Cajon*; toned gelatin silver print; ca. 1900; 4 ¼ × 7 ¼ in.
*The Fanita Rancho was located in the El Cajon Valley near the town of Santee and consisted of several thousand acres.*

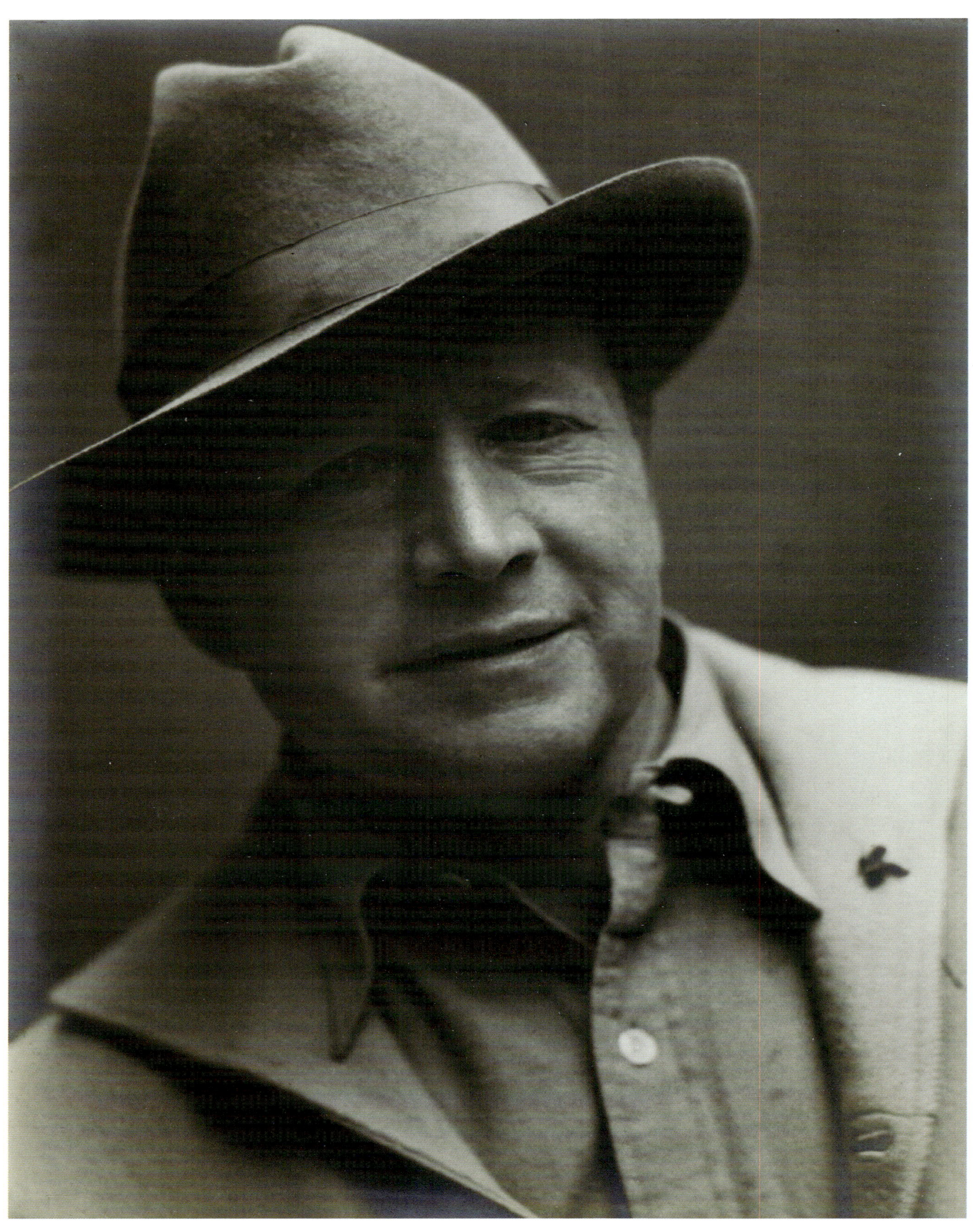

Edward Weston; Untitled; gelatin silver print; ca. 1935; 9¾ × 7½ in.
*The subject is not identified, but might be a labor contractor working in the Salinas Valley. There is no other known print of this image.*

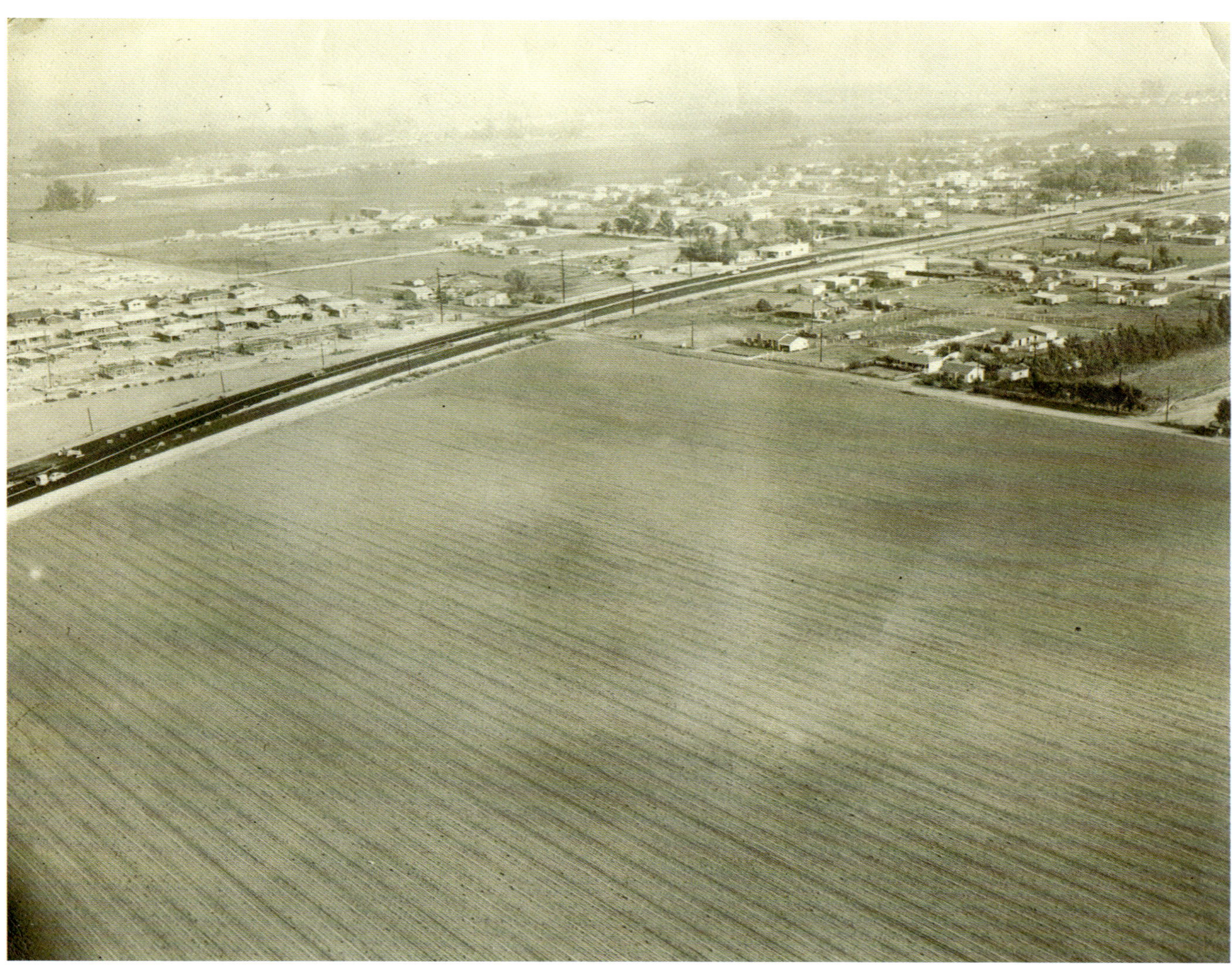

Mell Kilpatrick; Untitled (Suburbia, Orange County); gelatin silver print; ca. 1950; 10⅜ × 13 in.
*Kilpatrick worked as a photographer for the* Santa Ana Register *newspaper and specialized in photographing car crashes. He has been dubbed the "Weegee of the West," after the famous New York photographer noted for his photographs of murders and other disasters. Kilpatrick is best known for his early photographs of Disneyland, and is the subject of a book titled* Car Crashes and Other Sad Stories.

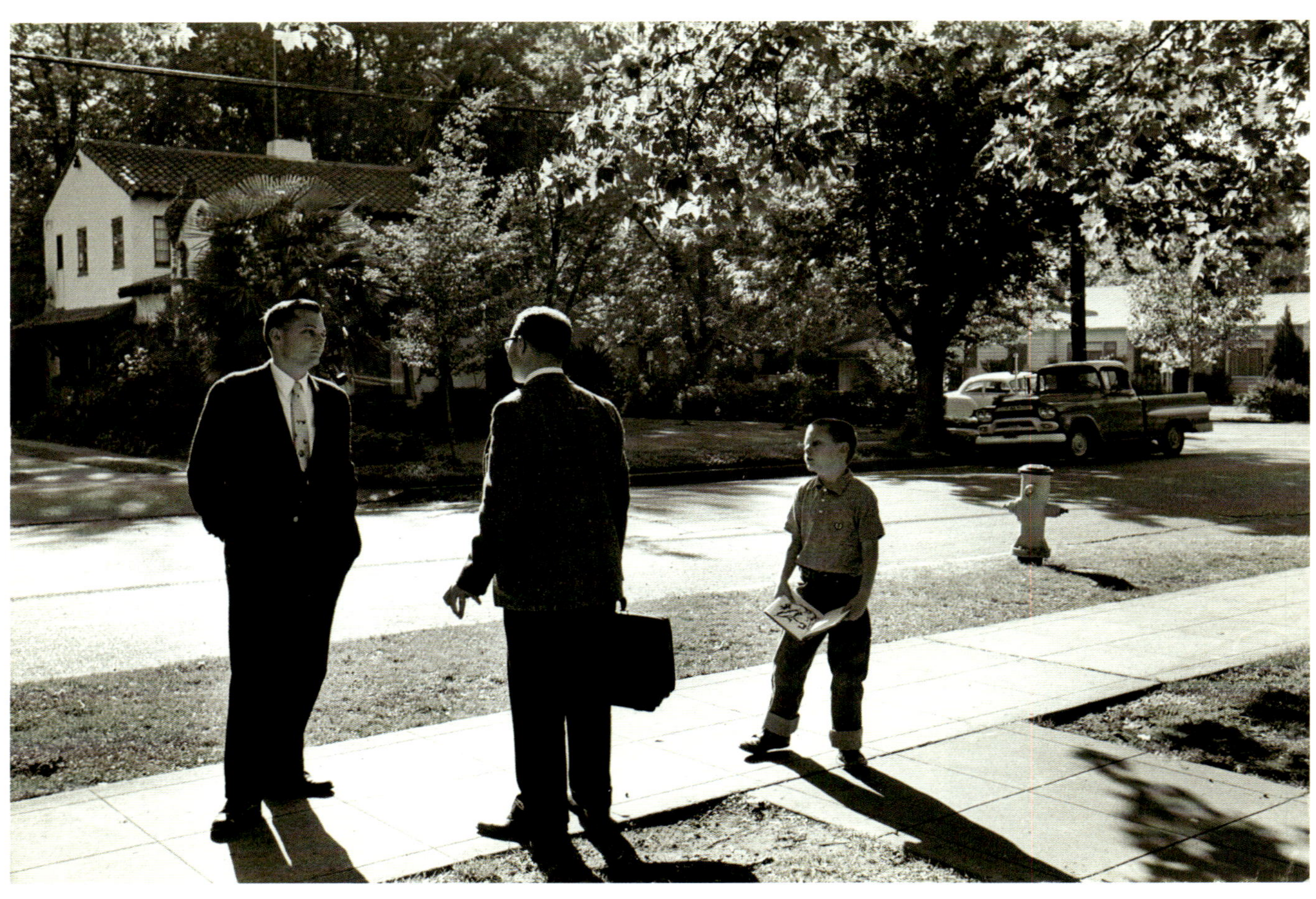

Joe Munroe; Untitled (A suburban street); gelatin silver print; ca. 1965; 7½ × 10¾ in.
*This bucolic suburban scene represented the American Dream for many hard-working Americans.*

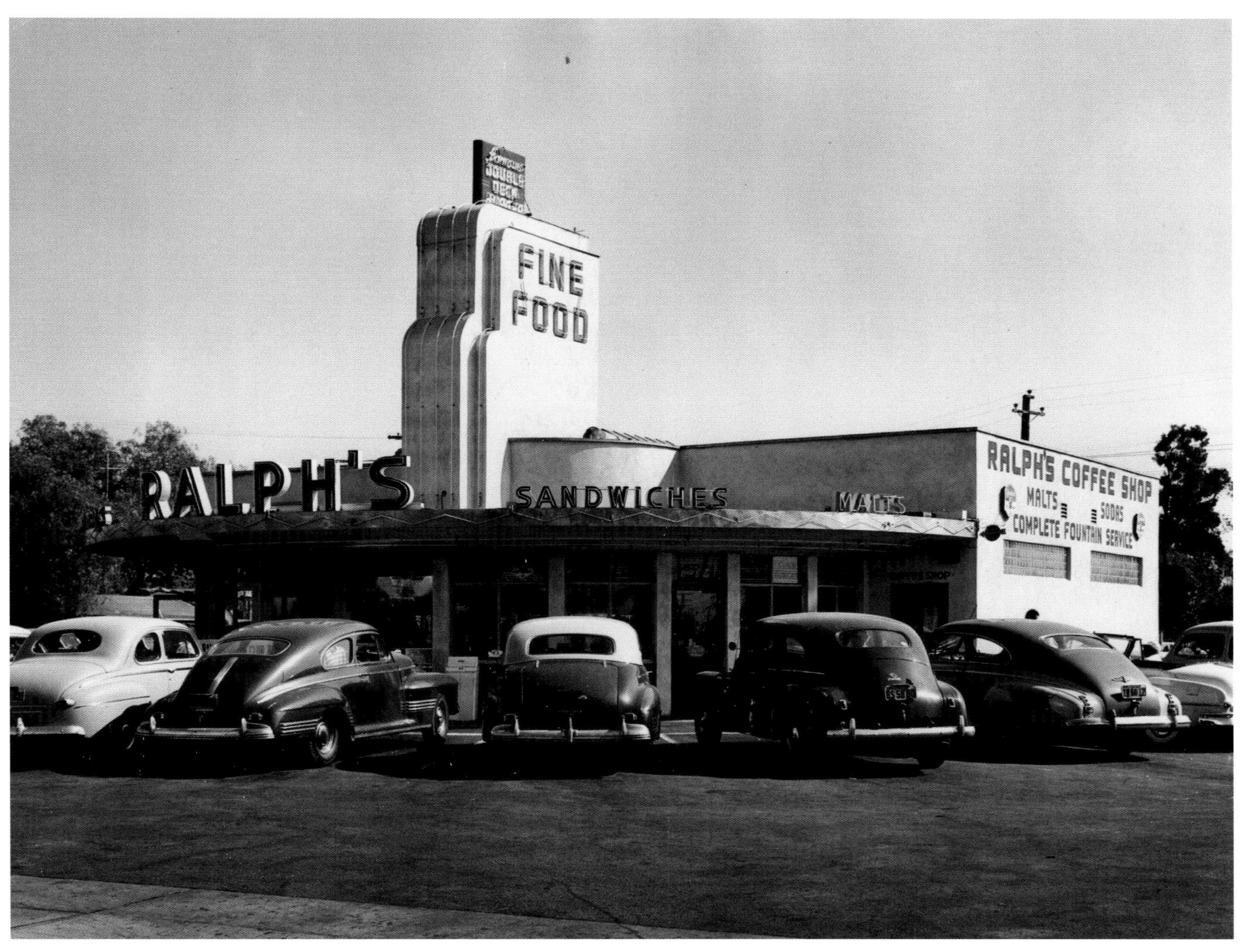


Stuart Weber; Untitled (Ralph's Drive In, Pasadena); gelatin silver print; 1949; 7½ × 9¾ in.
*Weber worked for many years as a commercial photographer in Los Angeles. He specialized in photographing supermarket displays that appeared as advertisements in* Life *magazine.*

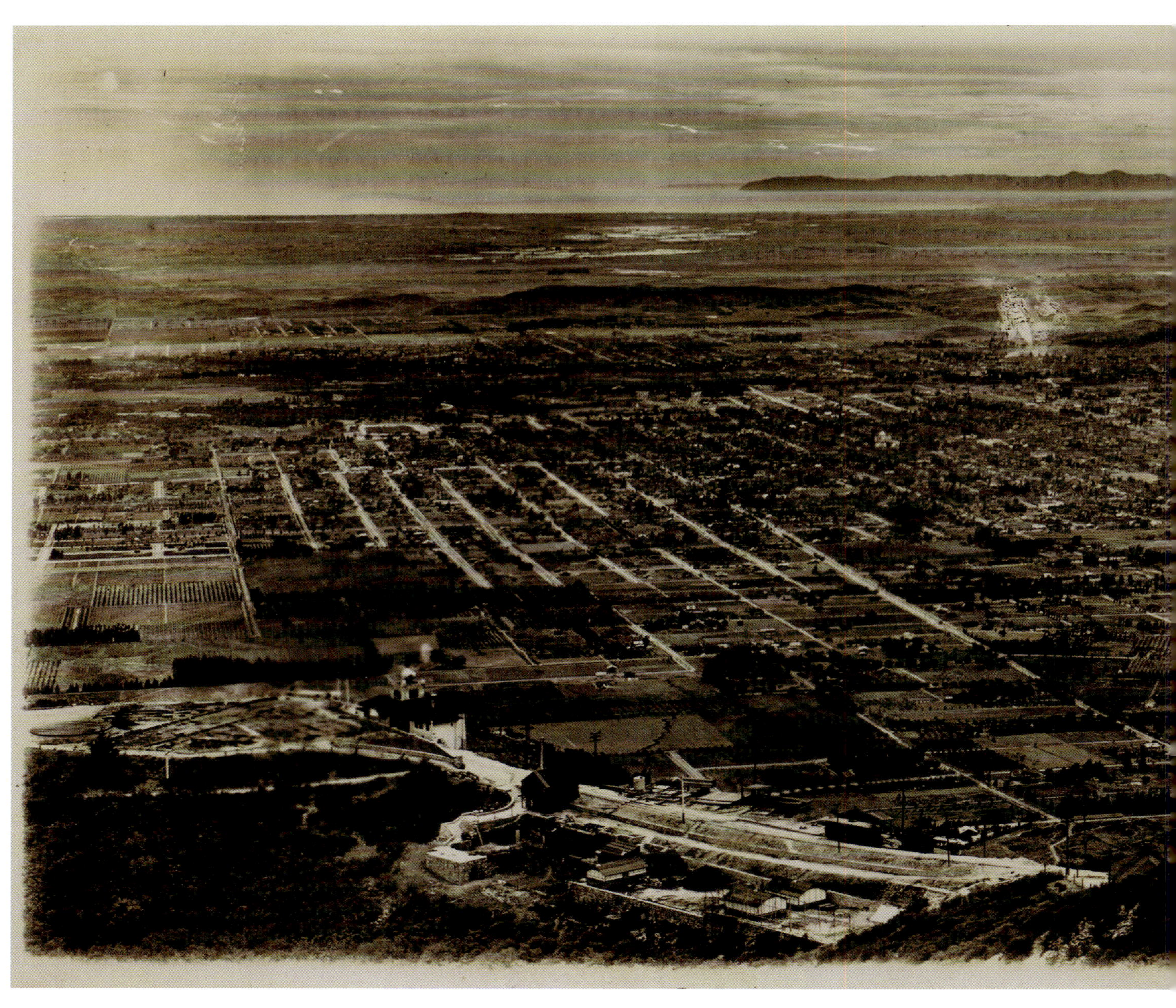

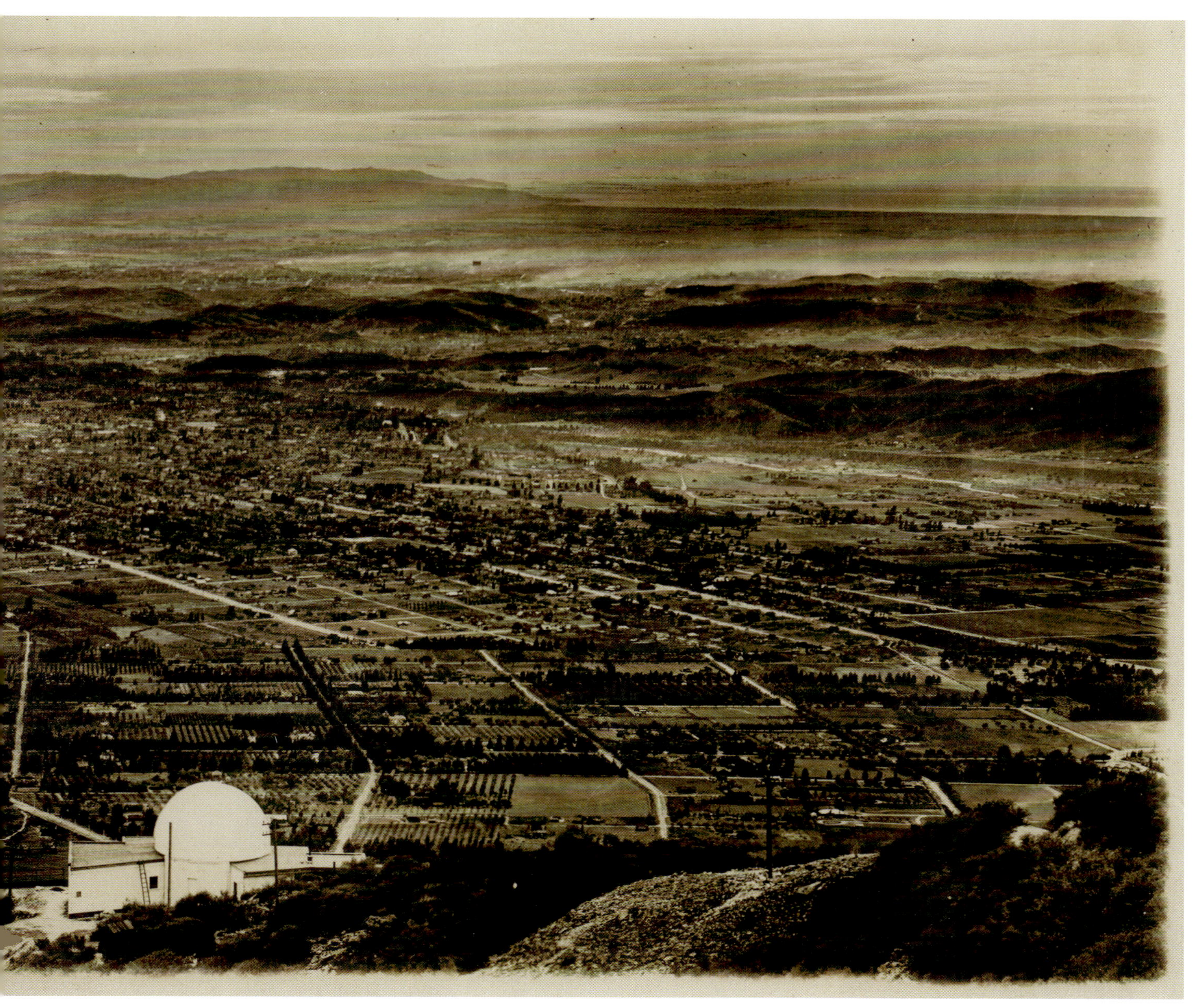

Unknown Artist; Untitled (L.A. from Mount Lowe); gelatin silver print; ca. 1900; 4 × 9¼ in.
*The Los Angeles sprawl was clearly visible a hundred years ago.*

PART 2: THE CITY RISES

## THE SPECULATIVE CITY

**by Catherine Gudis**

It might seem strange to describe the rise of California's cities as unsettling. Prospecting and speculation, migrations and mobility, new starts, possibilities, and inventions: these emblems of the California city rising were actually about unsettling the people here before, unsettling the land itself, and unsettling expectations and value systems based on rootedness and assimilation.

Unsettlement is especially useful for speculation. Something is speculative when its sure value can't be supported, as with real estate, when the market value grows based on belief in future changes. To speculate is to wonder and to conjecture without firm evidence. That's why it goes so well with "prospecting"—to look out for and search. Both are about trying to see the future while still in the here and now. Both seek to extract value based on uncertainty and unsettlement.

The camera in the nineteenth and twentieth centuries was among the tools of speculation and prospecting. It was used to see and sell places and people. This fits what photo historians also describe as the speculative gaze, objectifying its subject and colonizing the view, even as it pretends to serve as an empirical form of knowledge.

Photography instantiated the city itself, fixing its image in memory and fact onto glass, paper, metal, and then film, domesticating even an outlaw state built on violent removals of indigenous peoples and immigrants and the extractions of natural resources, from oil and water to gold and other minerals. By the time California had entered the union in 1850, San Francisco was home to over 25,000 people, half of whom were foreign born; soon thereafter, Southern Californians struck citrus and then black gold.

The photos here narrating the "rise of the city" ought to unsettle us as we wonder about the gaps, silences, and shadows. Whose land are we speculating on? Who is missing? On whose backs does the city rise? How can we understand the visual genealogies of those who are represented, and why might they be depicted in this way?

Nineteenth-century photographers like Robert Vance, William Shew, and Arnold Genthe used daguerreotypes, ambrotypes, cabinet cards, and landscape views to help clients stake their claims by circulating images of themselves near and far. Gold rush families [Page 61] as well as other migrants used the photographic medium as a virtual means of "proving up," to use the homesteading term. These photos recorded improvements and cultivation necessary in order to legally settle "unused" land according to federal acts of 1872 and thereafter. Portraits, once the exclusive domain of the wealthy, became an accessible and expressive photographic tool to assert one's social status and standing, or to fashion oneself as a merchant of the emerging middle class. Portraits also became integral to surveillance culture, particularly after the passage of the Chinese Exclusion Act in 1882, which banned new immigration from China except among the merchant class. Photographs became a part of extensive immigration files used to determine legal status, and were later required for identity cards and passports.

Shew and Genthe had studios not far from one another and proximate to San Francisco's Chinatown. Genthe regularly captured scenes of people in Chinese dress [Page 131], reproducing a sense of "otherness" while also containing this exoticism within the racialized boundaries of Chinatown, as if documenting a surely "vanishing race." Shew turned his viewfinder toward himself surrounded primarily by Chinese men in Western garb [Page 135], verifying their entrepreneurial standing. The young girl and boy in the image offer further assertions of social status, suggesting familial bonds and domesticity—hallmarks of middle-class urban society.

Middle-class urbanity is also evident in John Hodson's Sacramento studio photograph of two seated young women and two young men—all Black, all well-dressed and well-coiffed—who play out a scene of leisure and privilege [Page 60]. They too offer a visual taxonomy of upward mobility (what W.E.B. DuBois might have deemed the talented tenth) and ensure that the historical archive doesn't leave behind only racializing visual records of violence, criminalization, or otherness.

Other photographers of the city's rise in the late nineteenth and twentieth centuries, Carleton Watkins among them, joined government and geological survey teams, or, like the Huddleston Brothers, were miners with knowledge of the soil and mastery of the panorama. In the 1920s, the youngest brother, Freeman Huddleston, devised a pilot-less dirigible to hold his camera high in the sky (a predecessor to drones today) as the Aerograph Co. He gained a bird's-eye view of the land and landscape as he also participated in its transformation from dirt to real estate. In 1924, his aerograph captured the gush of oil spewing high from Union Oil Company's derricks and pumps in Long Beach [Page 77], joining discoveries by gold prospector Edward Doheny at the Los Angeles City Oil Field around downtown, which made L.A. home to the largest number of urban oil fields in the U.S. The view of First Street in Echo Park lined with houses and derricks [Page 76] exposes L.A.'s engines of development as powered by oil deposits far beneath the surface. The photos show what we can no longer see with the naked eye, but whose remnants still reside just below street level, where the wells lie idle, but their environmental and health impacts remain active.

Sometimes we can read this past quite literally in the signs captured in photographs, like the traveling wagon carrying a billboard promotional for "Jack London Socialist Candidate for Mayor" of Oakland in 1901 [Page 64], as well as commercial signage, such as that for the Pekin Curio Shop in Old Chinatown, on Los Angeles Street near Alameda Avenue in downtown L.A. [Page 78]. Constructed in the 1840s for the Lugo family, the adobe building in the photo was the only two-story structure in El Pueblo at L.A.'s founding. By the 1880s—only a decade after the same streets had witnessed eighteen Chinese boys and men murdered in the violent race riot and Chinatown Massacre of 1871—the Lugo Adobe housed Japanese and Chinese art, as part of what was promoted as an "exotic shopping district." Its appeal was magnified through such Chamber of Commerce events as La Fiesta de Los Angeles, whose pageant-parade offered sequential tableaux featuring different racial groups, including in 1895 an 800-foot Chinese dragon operated by 150 men [Page 132]. Spectacles like this one simultaneously commemorated the city's multicultural past, and, as historian William Deverell describes, ensured a nostalgic "whitewashing" of it, to secure a sense of homogeneity in the present.

The site of the Lugo Adobe became State Historic Landmark No. 301, having retained Chinese merchants of the Pekin Curio shop as well as the Hop Sing Benevolent Society, United Christian Church Chinese Mission, and Hai Hong Grocery and Merchandise over the decades, flourishing even after the rest of Old Chinatown was bulldozed and Union Station rose in its place in 1939—just a year before the opening of the Arroyo Seco Parkway, the first freeway in the U.S. (Will Connell's photo commemoration of this engineering marvel is overlaid with a cautionary thirty-five-miles-per-hour sign at a treacherous curve on the route [Page 81].) Later freeway expansions ultimately took out these last storefronts of Old Chinatown (including the Lugo Adobe), paved over, despite community opposition, to make way for the ramps to the Hollywood Freeway from 1949 to 1951.

New Chinatown became marked instead—both in L.A. and in San Francisco—by spectacular signs, often in neon (see, for instance Walter Fong's *Chinatown at Night* [Page 67]) and with "chop suey" typeface. These aimed to fabricate an Orientalized identity dramatizing the ethnic enclave as a shadowy place, much like the noir films of the 1940s and 1950s that also helped construct the city's multiracial neighborhoods as a place of potential danger and criminal activity. The two suited Chinese men in Max Yavno's c. 1947 photograph [Page 134], who might be detectives, mobsters, or innocent bystanders, also seem straight out of a noir film. A similarly portentous feeling is conveyed in Mell Kilpatrick's 1950s photo [Page 74], which is dominated by a close-up of the sharply ironed creases in a man's suit pants, seen from behind and helping frame the poster advertisement pasted on the distant building for *A Cry in the Night*, a thriller featuring a police captain's daughter (Natalie Wood) who is abducted by an unhinged sociopath (Raymond Burr).

The noir city was ultimately an expression of the racial xenophobia that also fueled white flight and urban renewal. That might be why Taizo Kato's 1920s photograph of The Korin feels ghostly [Page 94]. The stylized writing of the Kodak sign on the awning suggests how small immigrant business and corporate industry intertwined to shape the city. Kato and his partner Kamejiro Sawa operated three Korin shops, all near Little Tokyo, with the main shop and gallery at 408 W. Sixth Street. Kato's image of 408 offers a literal and figurative window into photography as both a commercial and artistic undertaking, with Japanese and Japanese American artists here at its center. Among the items on display are pictorial photographs, paintings, and portraits, including one featuring the Hollywood silent movie star and leading lady Tsuru Aoki, known for both stylized depictions of Japanese femininity and American assimilation [Page 94]. The photos allow us to imagine a palimpsest of the city, as we know what will follow from the ascendancy of Japanese Americans in Little Tokyo and Japanese enclaves across California and the Pacific Coast. This is captured in a press photo of Harie Shiwo [Page 128], taken as she awaits her forced removal in 1942 from Los Angeles to the concentration camp at Manzanar.

It is challenging to gaze upon the pre-World War II photographs in "The Rise of the City" knowing what is to come, especially when one can see the formal similarities between such images as the Adohr milk bottles (they bore the name of the owner's wife Rhoda, spelled backwards [Page 95]) and the LAPD arrests of youth during the 1965 Watts uprising [Page 107]. Both use shadows to formally structure the scene. They are jarring when looked at in tandem—in one case to sell a commodity and in the other to convey a mortal threat, not just at the hands of police but due to structural forces proscribing Black economic sustenance in the city. In this sense, as with other commercial images commissioned by insurance, power, or construction companies, the photograph plays a different, actuarial role in speculating life span or documenting its demise.

In all of these cases, the city and the photographs that capture its rise and fall unsettle our presumptions of certainty and stability even as they offer evidence of the historical layers constructing the very ground on which we all stand in California today.

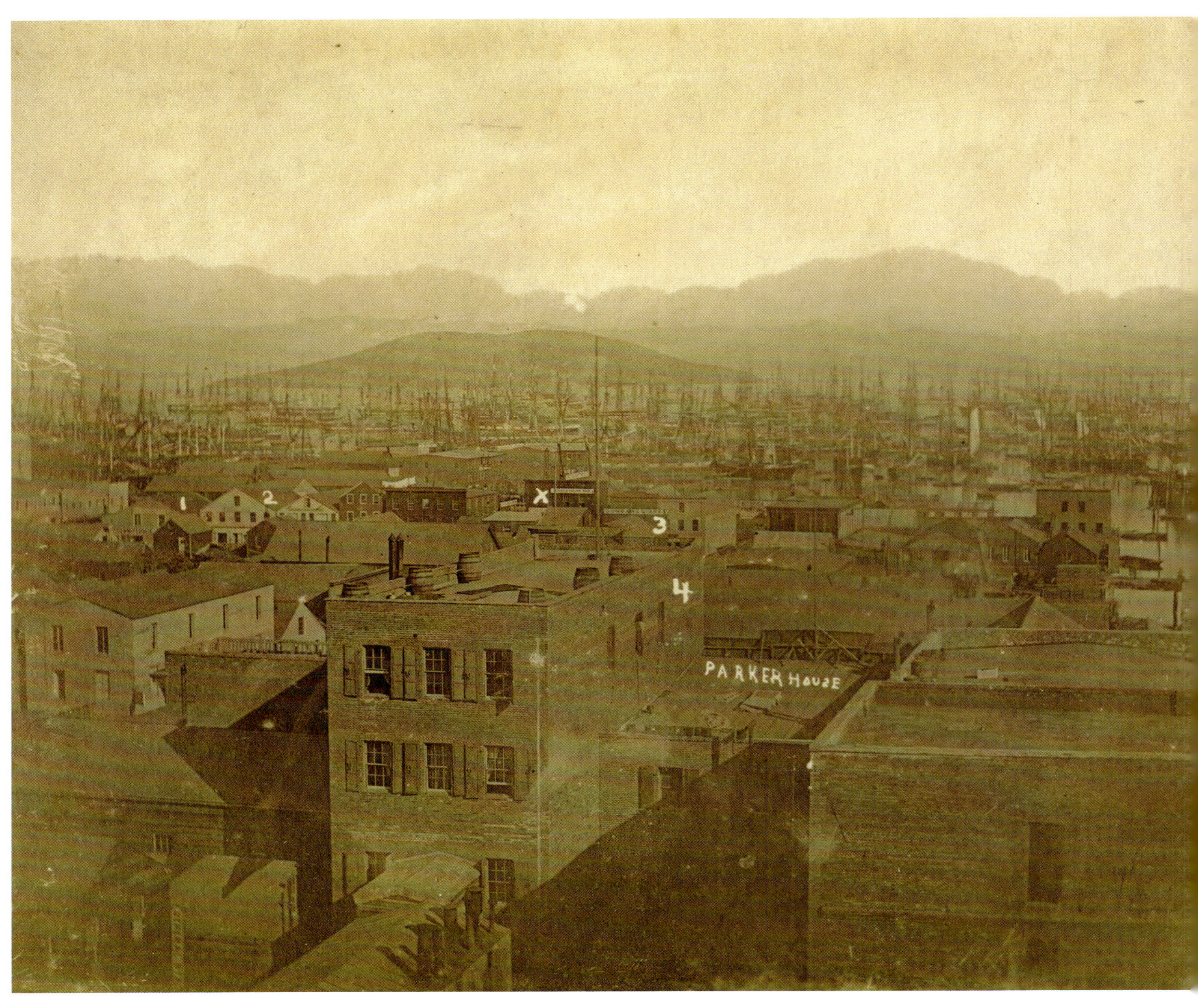
1
2
X
3
4
PARKER HOUSE

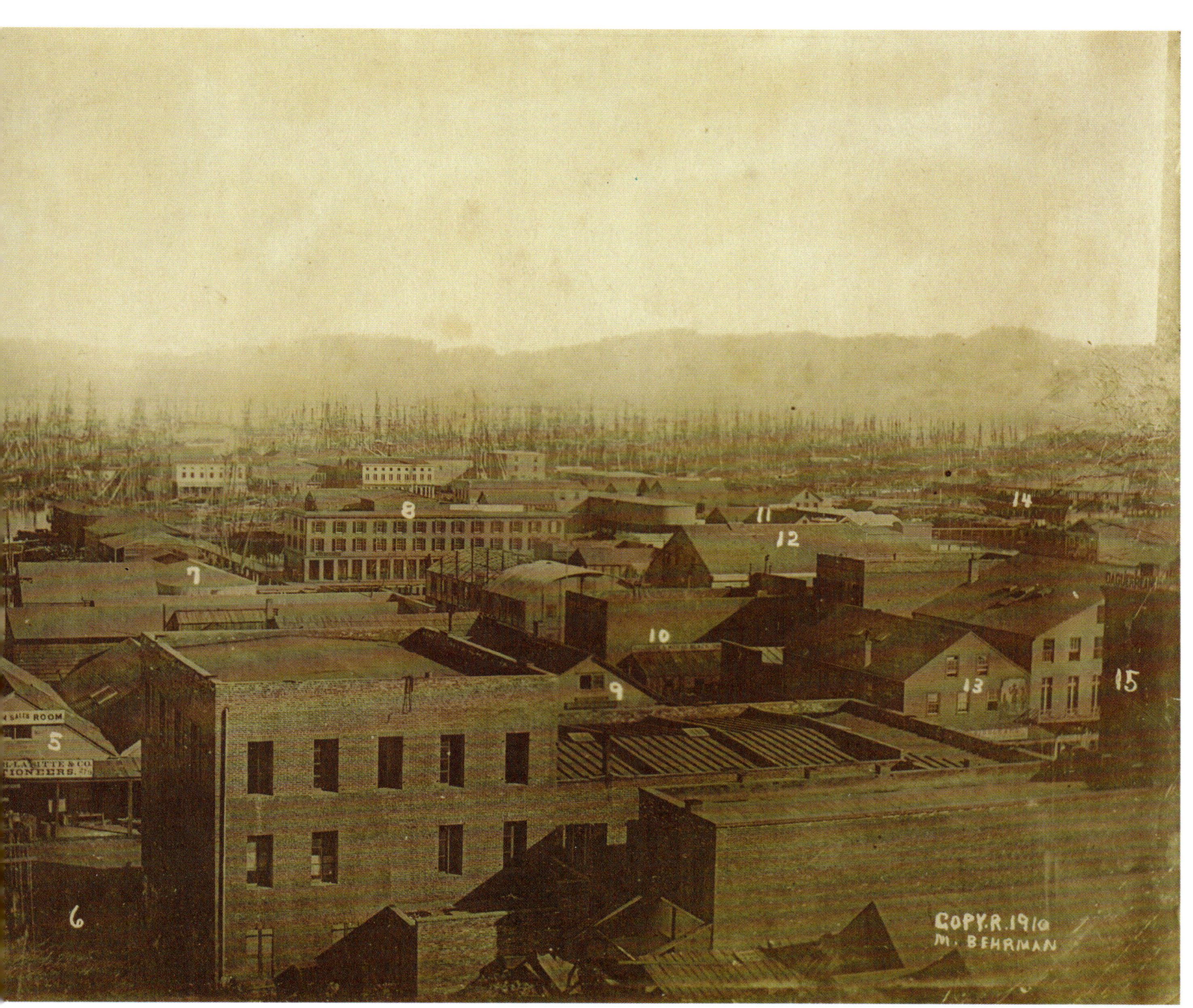


William Shew (attributed), reprinted ca. 1910 by Martin Behrman; *Panorama of the San Francisco Waterfront*; gelatin silver print; ca. 1851, copied 1910; 6¼ × 15⅛ in.
*One part of the original panorama daguerreotype is located in the Bancroft Library, University of California, Berkeley.*

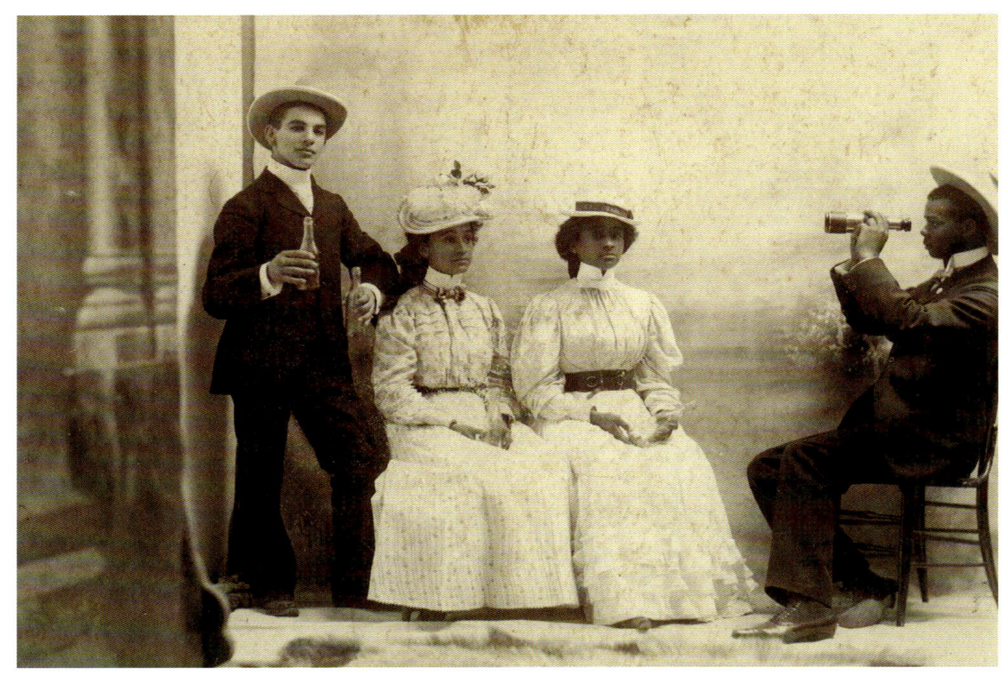

Burton M. Hodson; Untitled (Four young people in a photo studio); gelatin silver print; ca. 1900; cabinet card, 3⅞ × 5⅛ in.
*Hodson's father, John, operated a photo gallery in Sacramento from the early 1880s and later added a gallery in San Francisco.*

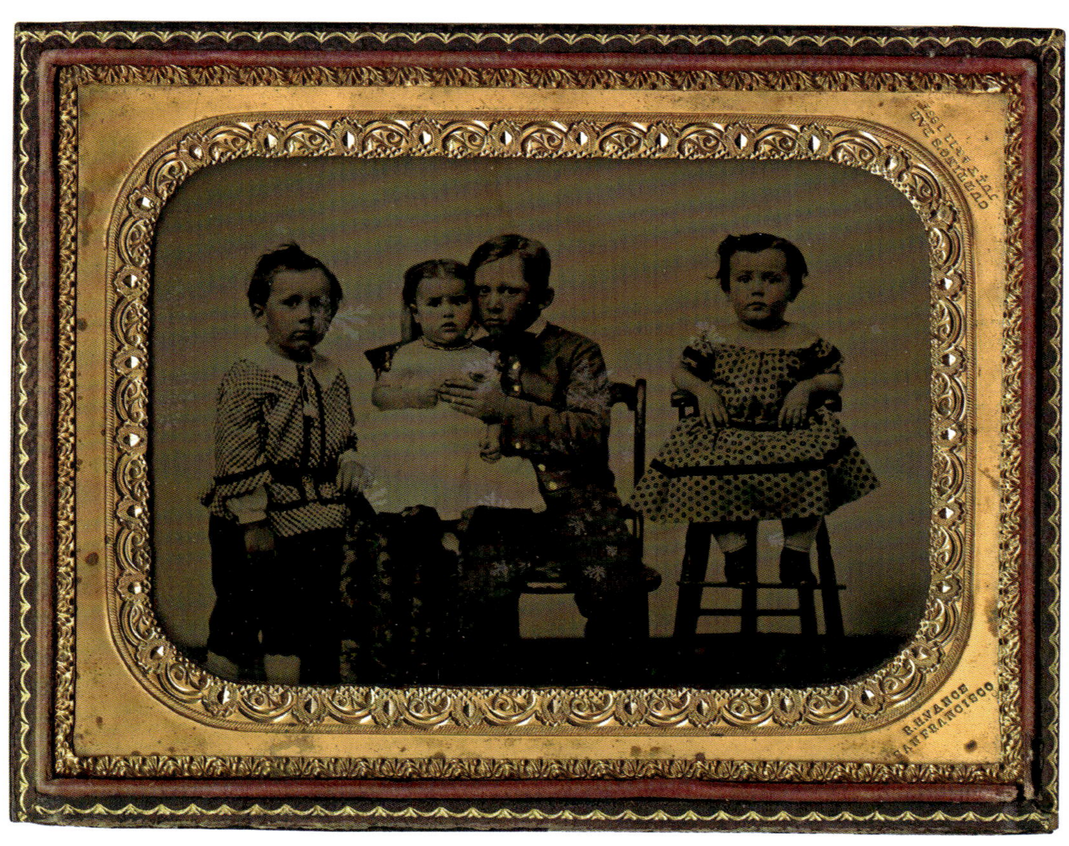

R.H. Vance; Untitled (Gold Rush children in San Francisco); ambrotype; ca. 1855; 4¼ × 5½ in.
*Vance opened his studio in San Francisco in 1851. Prior to that he had studios in Boston, Dover, New Hampshire, and Valparaíso, Chile.*

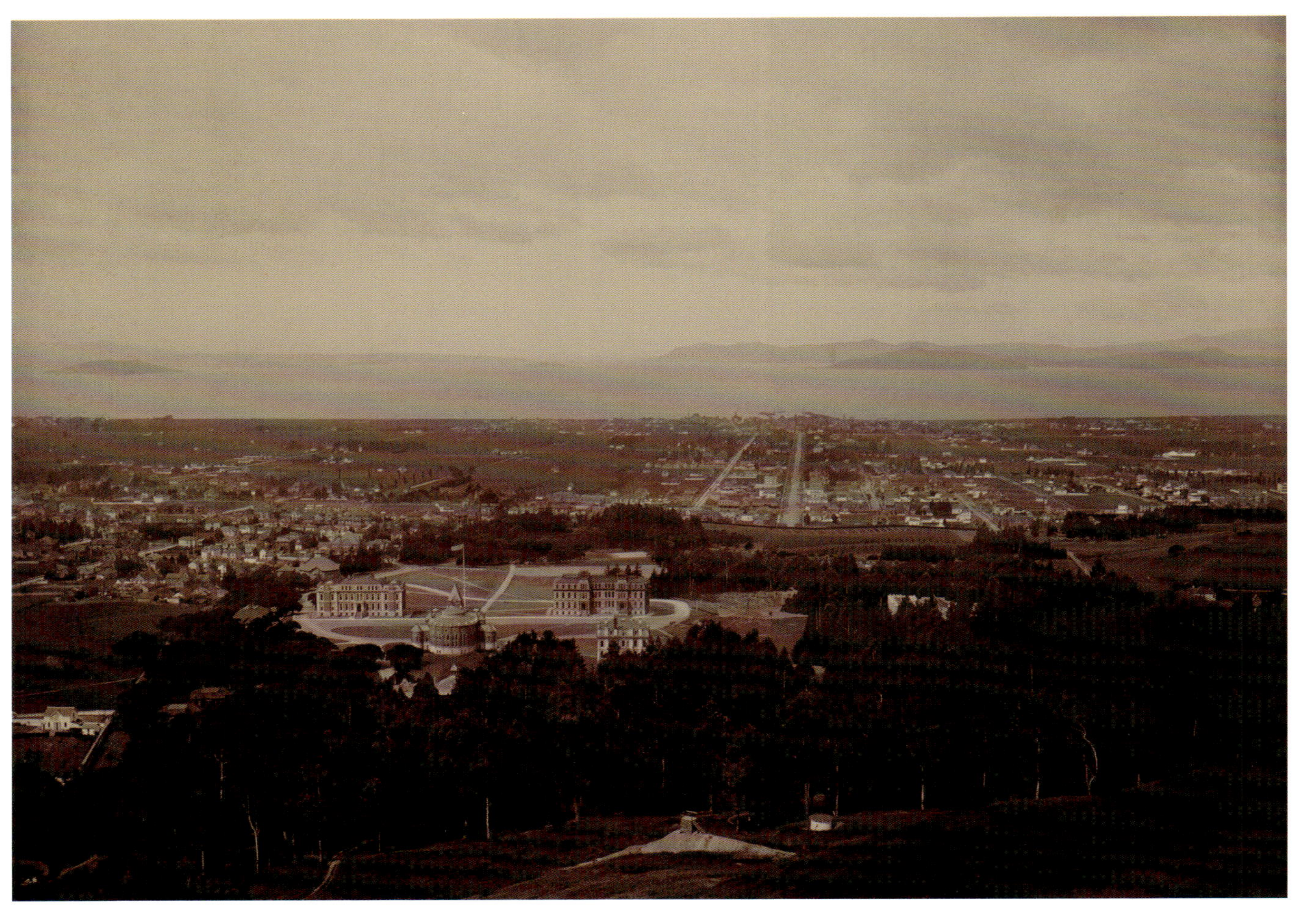

Carleton E. Watkins; Untitled (Berkeley from the hills above the University of California); albumen print; ca. 1874; 15⅜ × 21⅜ in.
*The University of California opened its doors in 1869. The following year its regents agreed to accept women on an equal footing with men, a decision made a hundred years ahead of Ivy League schools.*

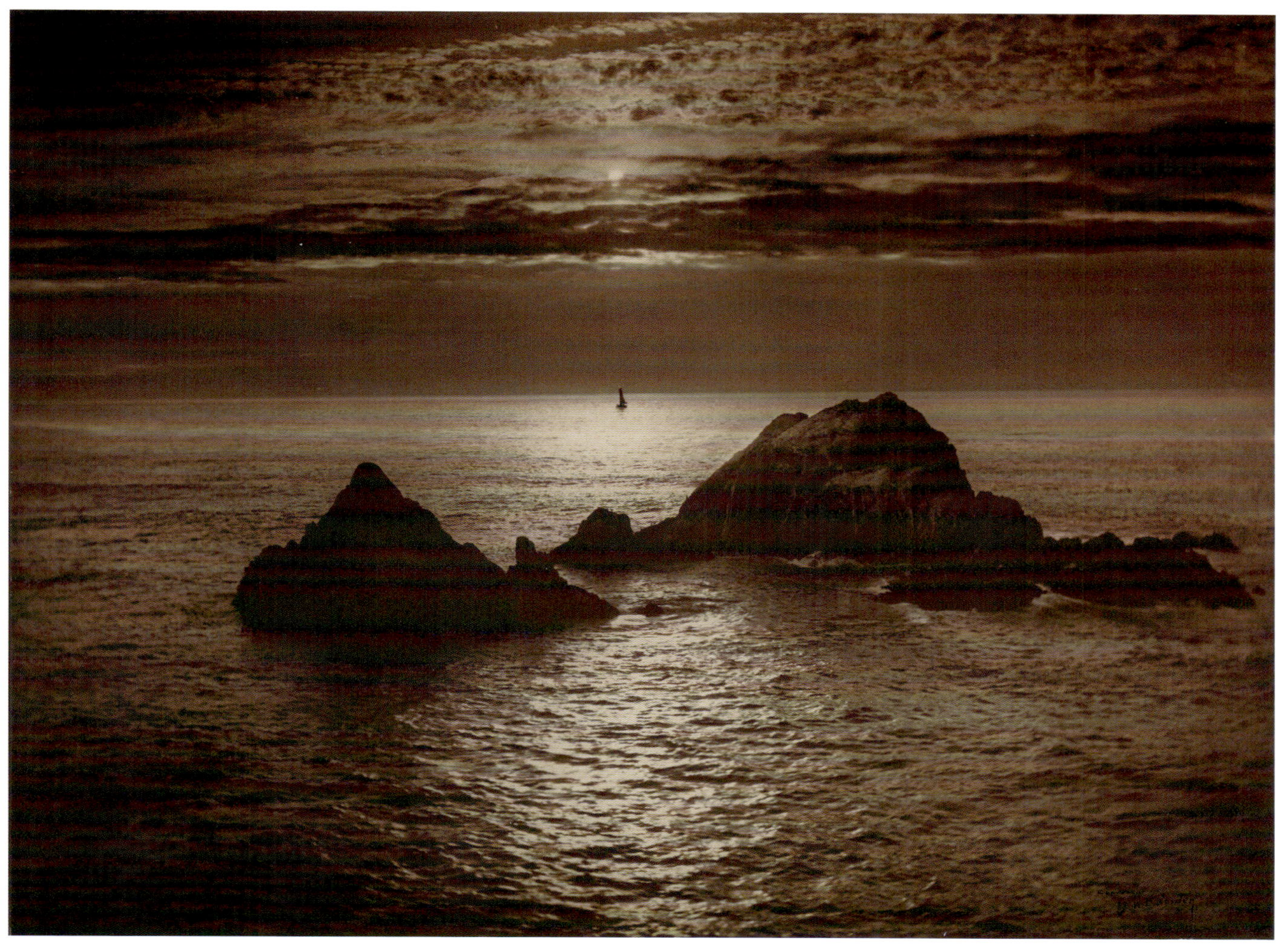

Willard E. Worden; Untitled (Ship arriving in San Francisco Bay); toned gelatin silver print; ca. 1900; 18 × 23¾ in.
*Worden was the subject of a 2015 one-man exhibition at the W.H. de Young Museum in San Francisco. The Golden Gate Bridge spanning the bay opened in 1937.*

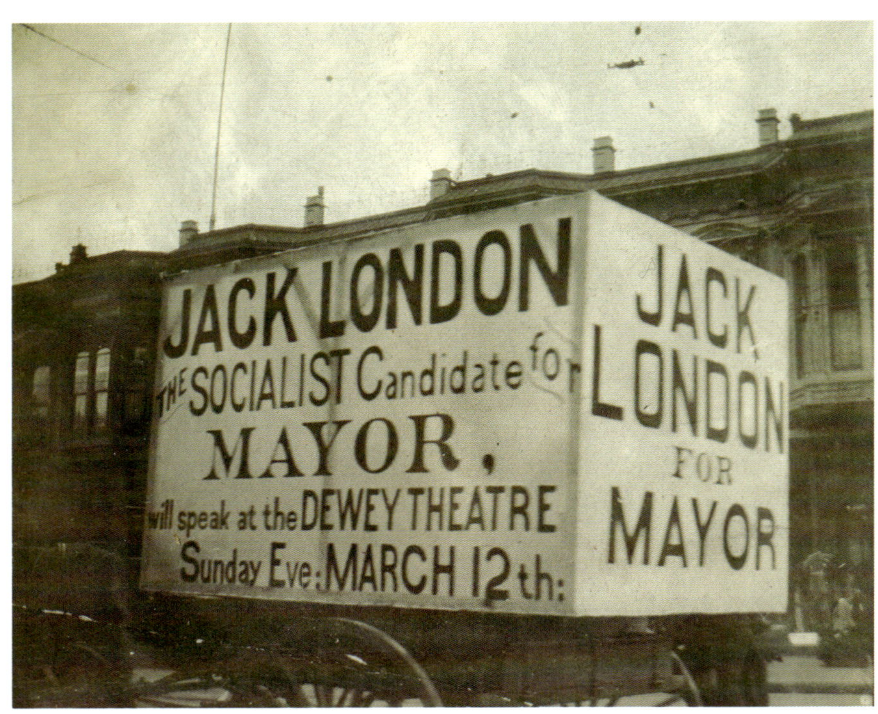


John Dicks Howe; *Jack London Socialist Candidate for Mayor, Oakland*; gelatin silver print; 1901; 3½ × 4½ in.
*As the Socialist candidate for mayor, London received 245 votes and lost the election.*

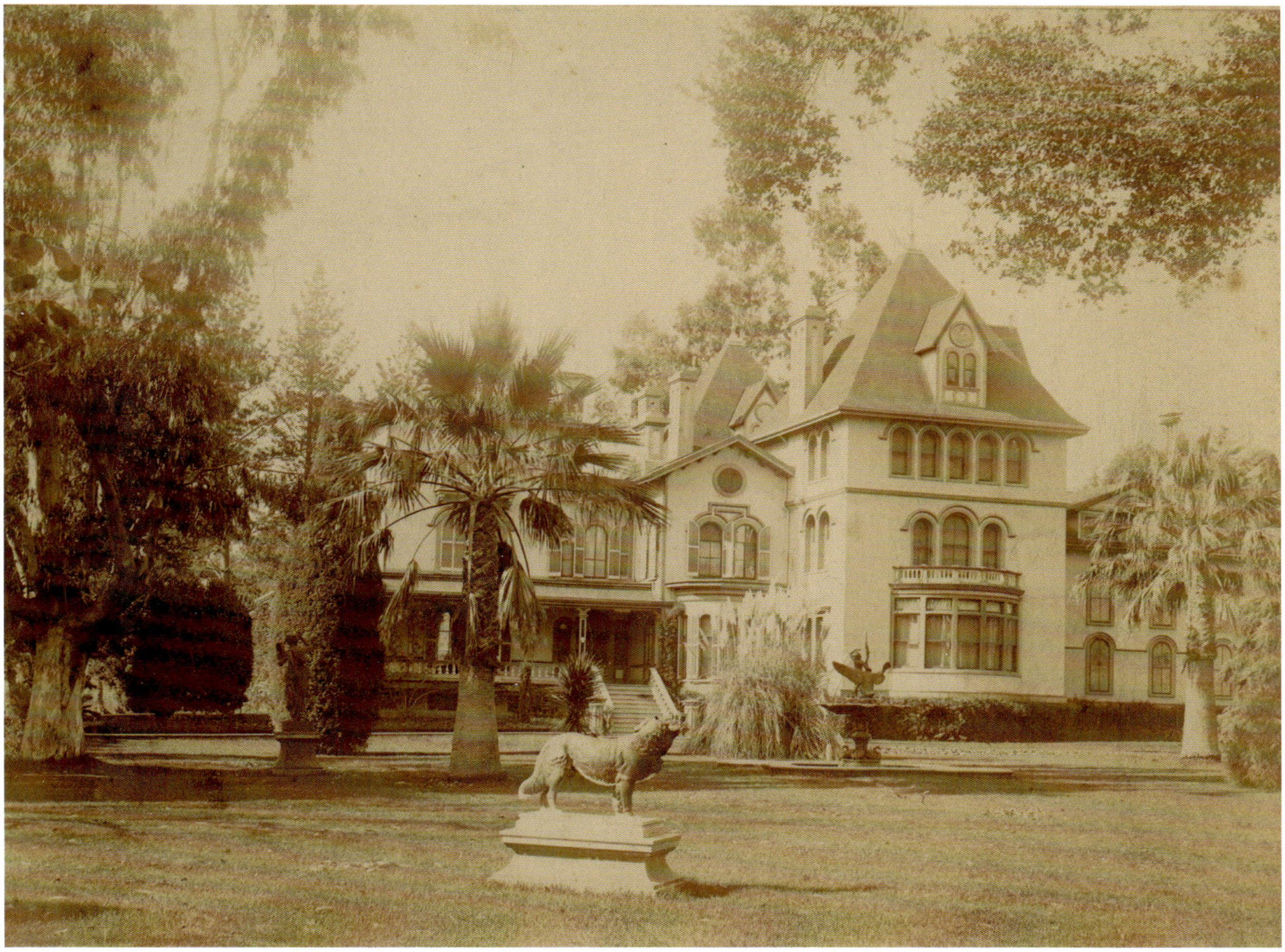

TOP: Unknown Artist; *Leland Stanford Residence, Palo Alto*; gelatin silver print; ca. 1890; 6 × 8 in.

RIGHT: Unknown Artist; *Leland Stanford*; albumen print; ca. 1890; 6 ¼ × 4⅛ in. *After their only son died from typhoid fever in 1884, Stanford and his wife decided to build a university on their 8,000-acre Palo Alto farm.*

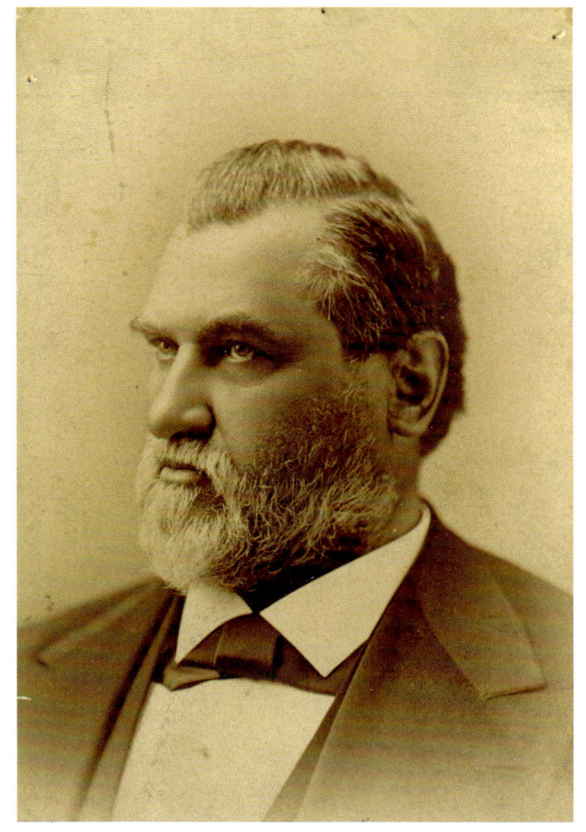

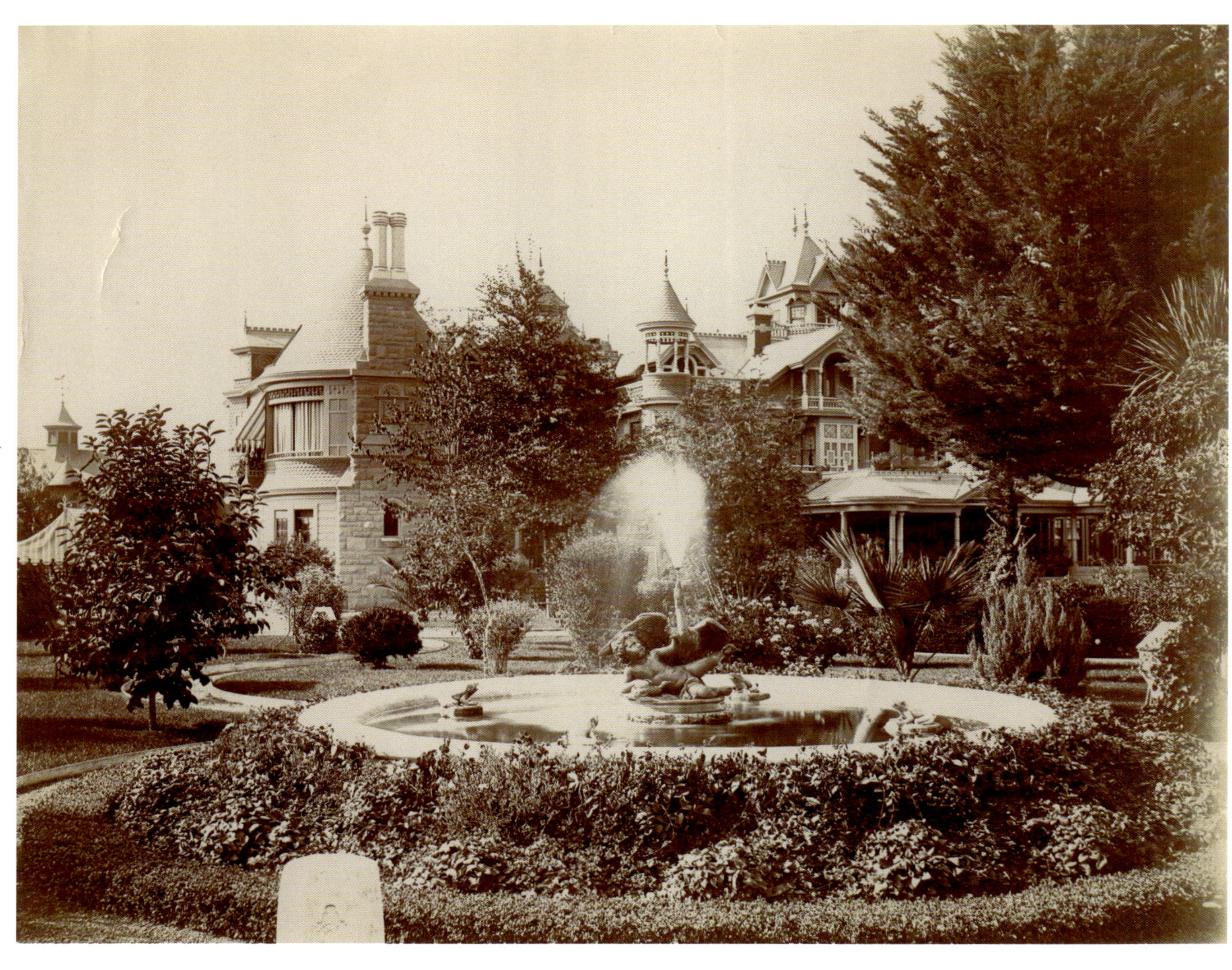

Andrew P. Hill; *The Winchester Mystery House, San Jose*; aristotype print; ca. 1890; 7½ × 9½ in.
*Hill was a photographer and painter who lived in San Jose. Sarah Winchester, widow of the gun manufacturer, kept adding on to her home in order to keep local workers employed, according to an 1895 article in the* San Francisco Chronicle. *At the time of her death, in 1922, the house contained 160 rooms and 10,000 windows, but only thirteen bathrooms. The Winchester Mystery House remains a popular attraction in San Jose.*

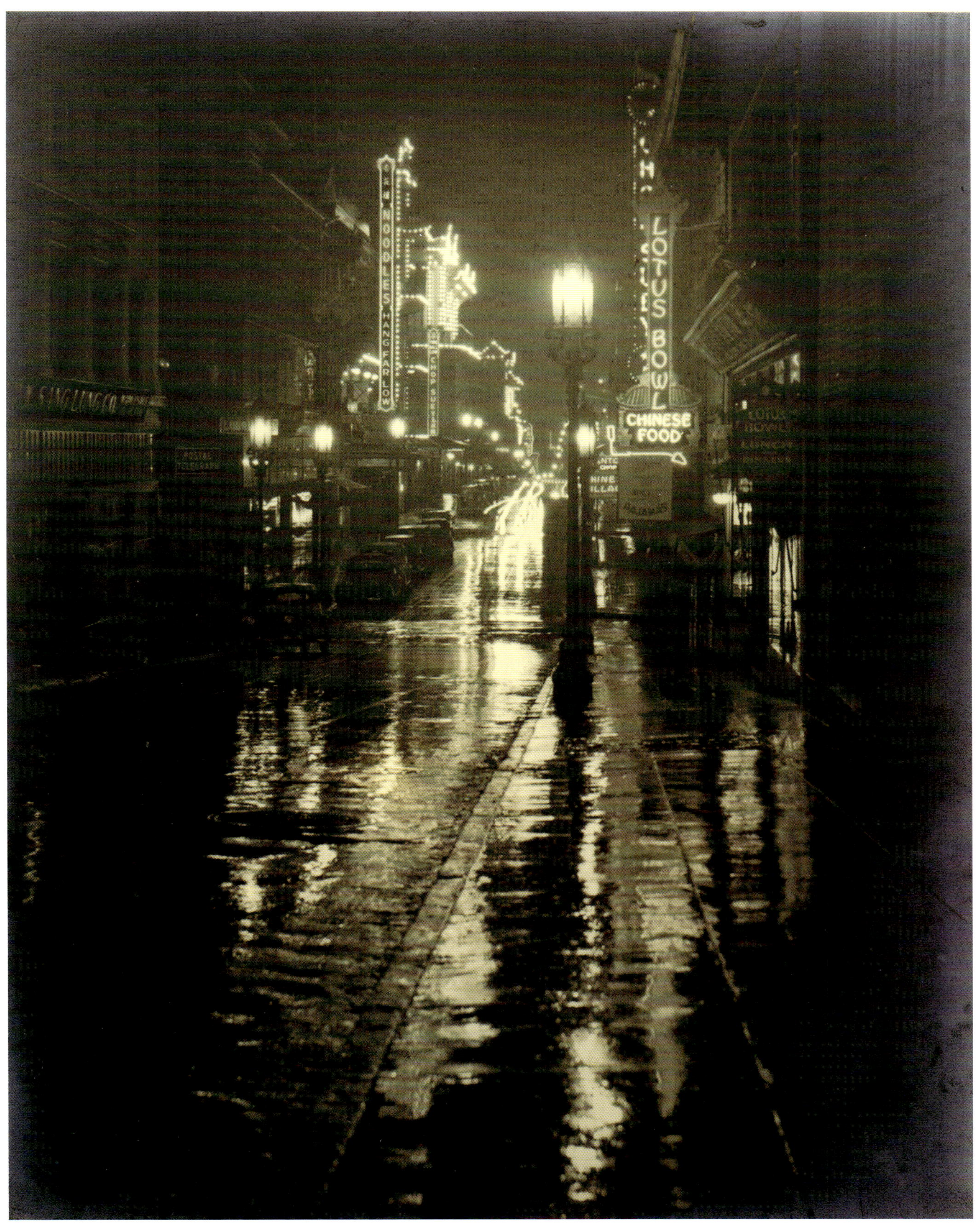


Wallace Fong; Untitled (Chinatown, San Francisco); gelatin silver print; 1937; 13½ × 10¾ in.
*Fong worked as a photographer for the* Chinese Digest *in San Francisco, a publication that began in 1935.*

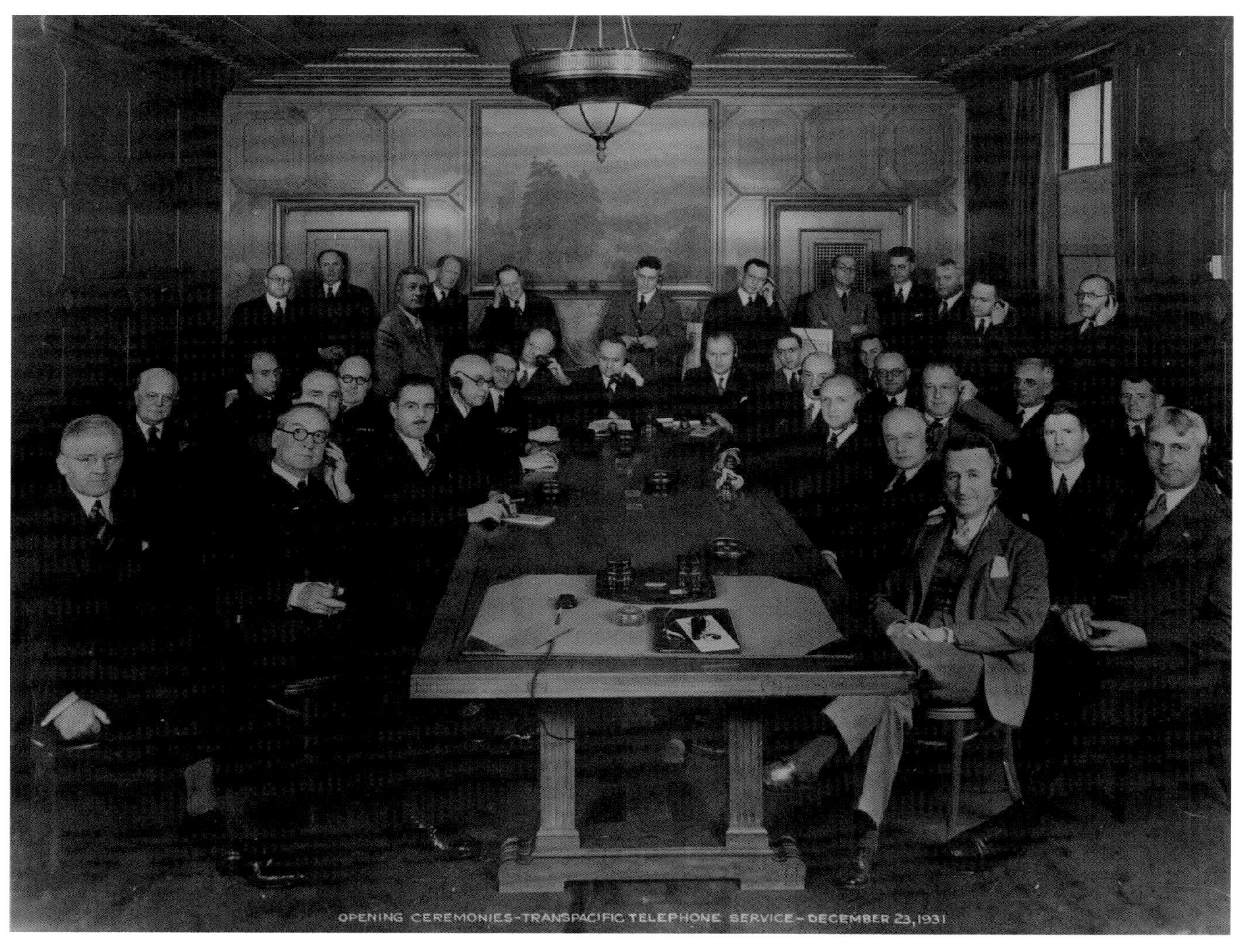


Unknown Artist; *Opening Ceremonies, Transpacific Telephone Service*; gelatin silver print; December 23, 1931; 10½ × 13¼ in.
*Twenty-nine years after completion of the first telegraph cable between California and Hawaii, an AT&T affiliate in California and the Mutual Telephone Company of Hawaii made voice calls between San Francisco and Honolulu possible.*

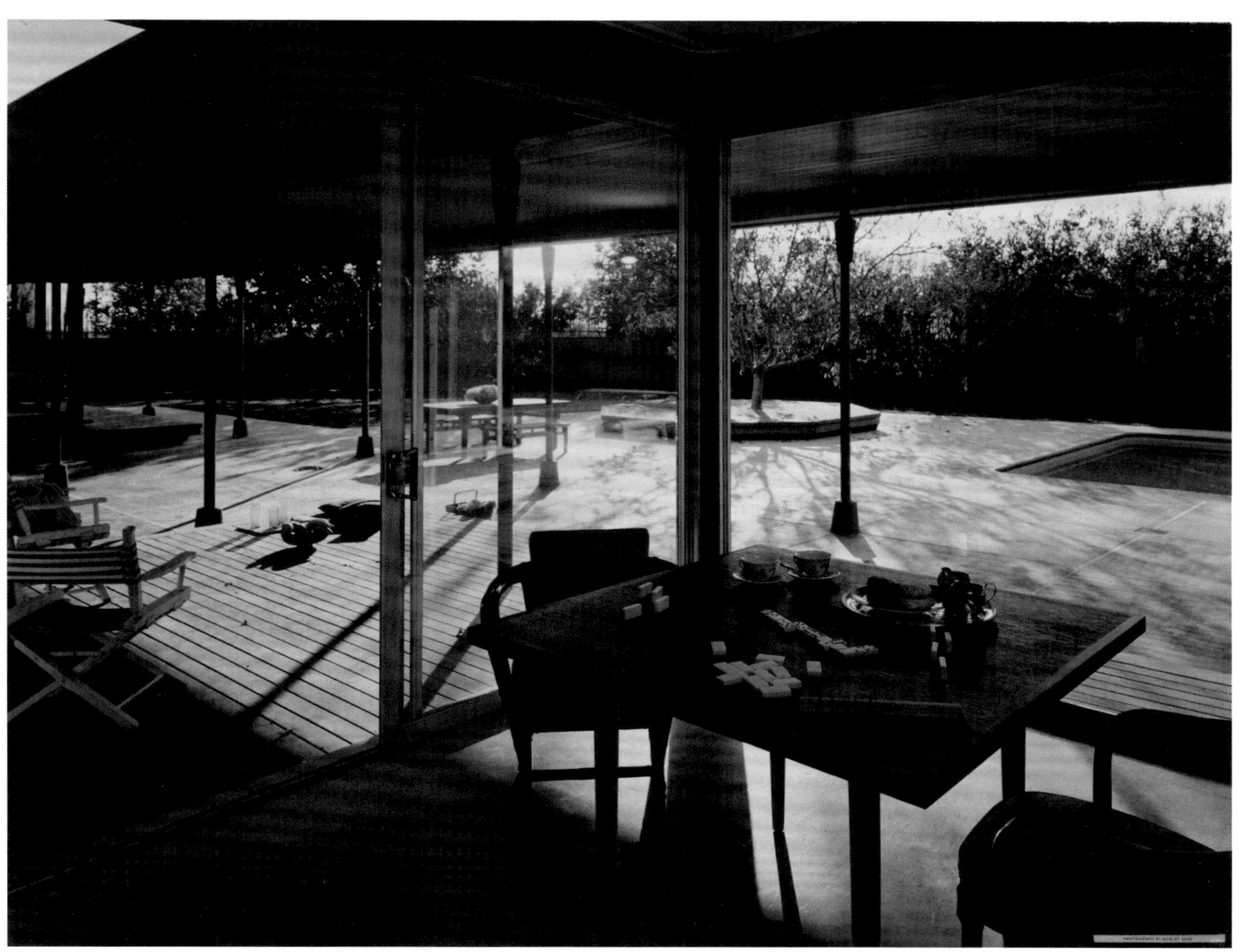

Morley Baer; Untitled (Modernist Berkeley residence); gelatin silver print; ca. 1950; 15 ¼ × 19¾ in.
*Baer was recruited by Ansel Adams to teach at the San Francisco Art Institute.*

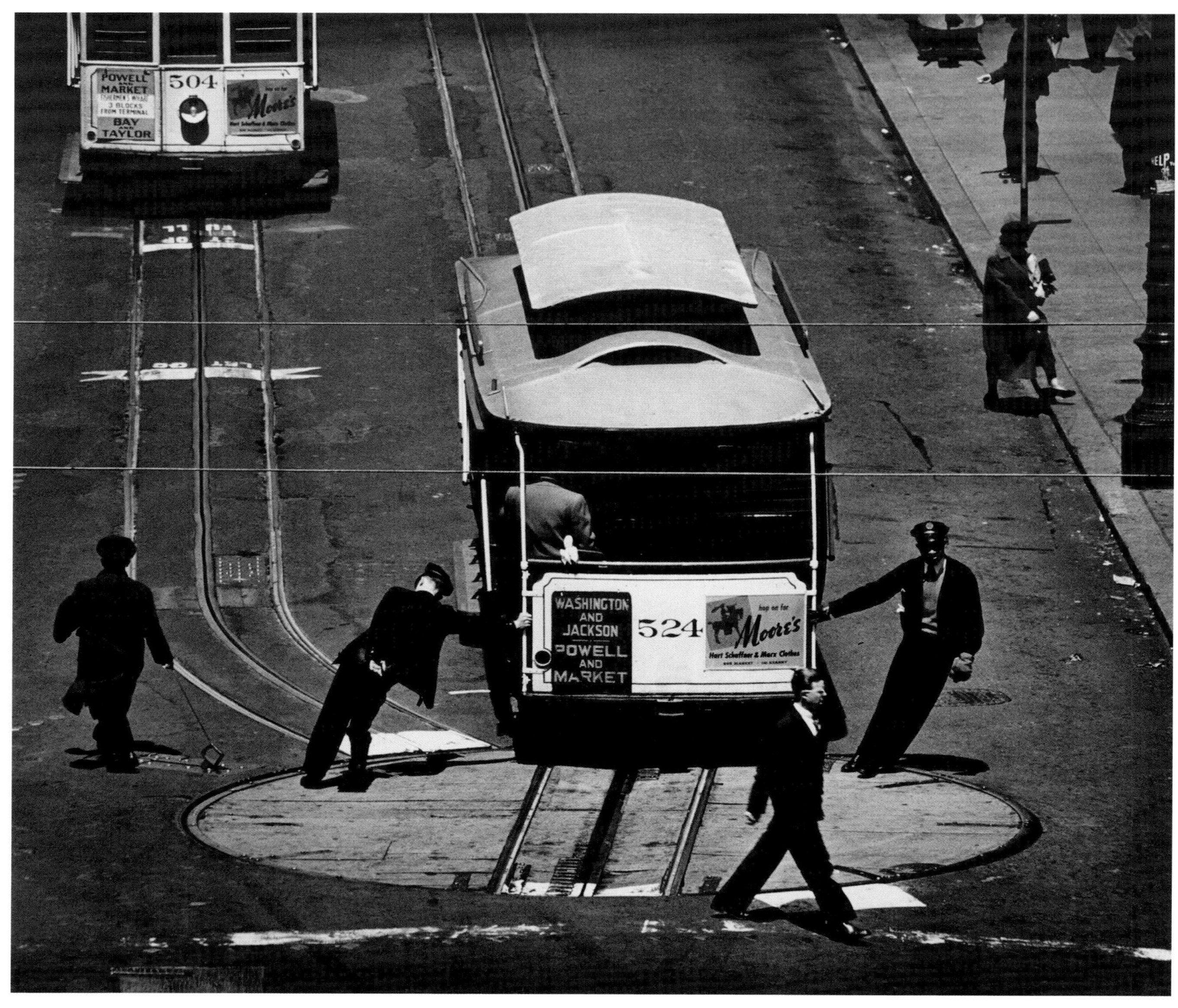


Max Yavno; *Turning the Cable Car, San Francisco*; gelatin silver print; 1948, printed later; $15\frac{3}{8} \times 17\frac{1}{8}$ in.
*Yavno illustrated* The San Francisco Book *with writer Herb Caen. This image was on the cover of* The Photography of Max Yavno *by Ben Maddow.*

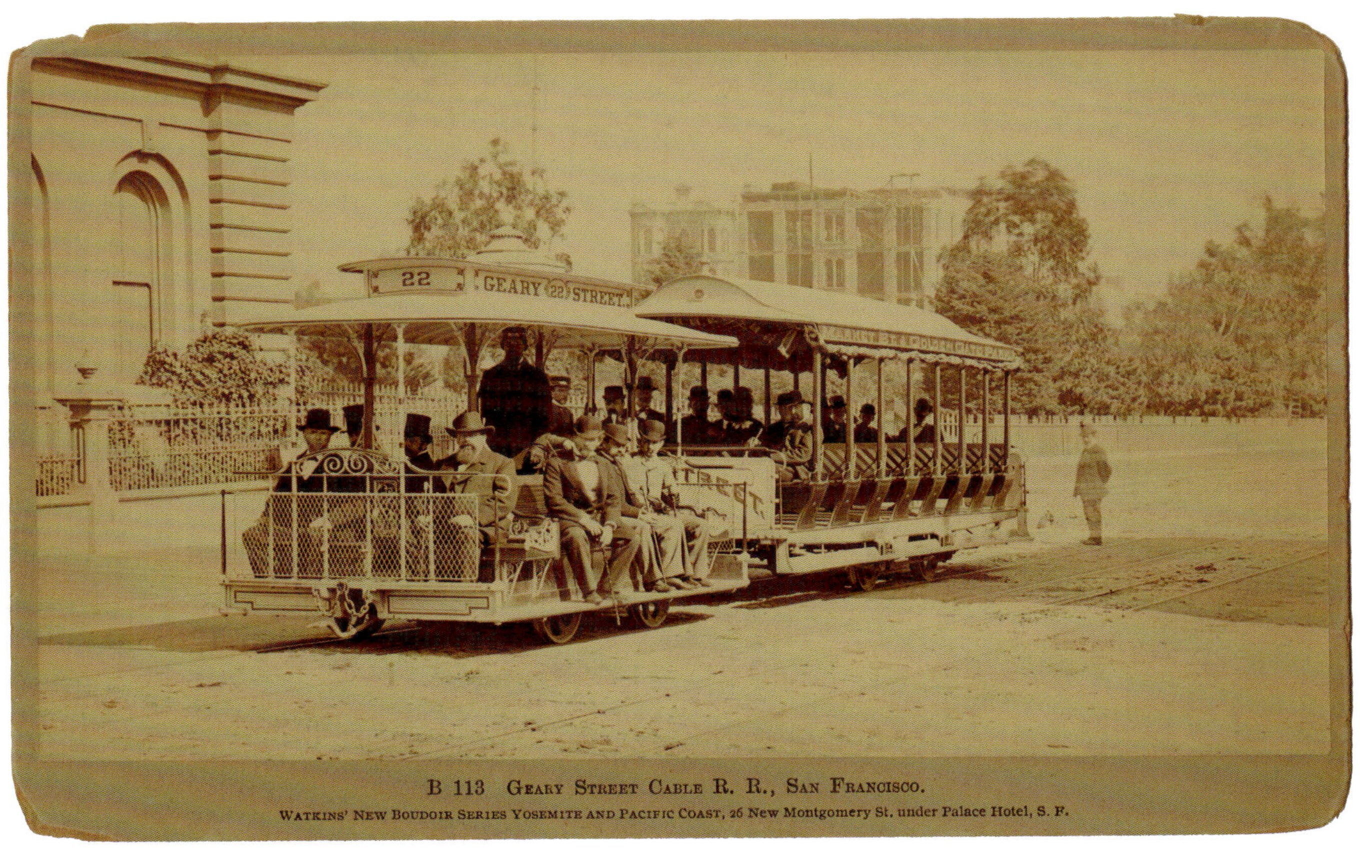


Carleton E. Watkins; *Geary Street, Cable Railroad, San Francisco*; albumen print; ca. 1880; 4½ × 8 in.
*The cable car was first utilized in San Francisco in 1873.*

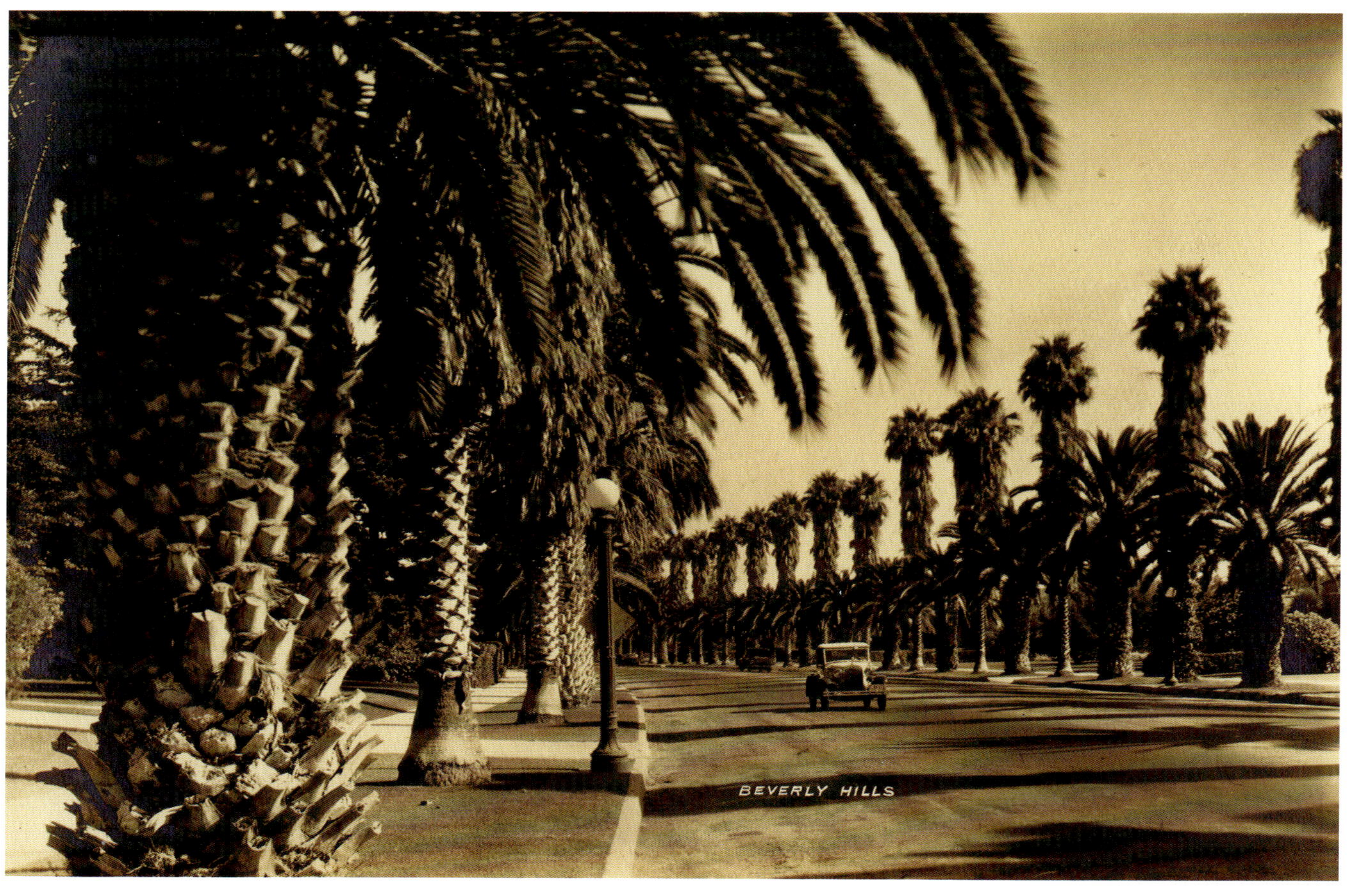


Unknown Artist; Untitled (Beverly Hills, street of palms); gelatin silver print; ca. 1920; 6½ × 9½ in.
*Many of the streets in Beverly Hills are wider than those in the surrounding areas, and palm trees are a common sight.*

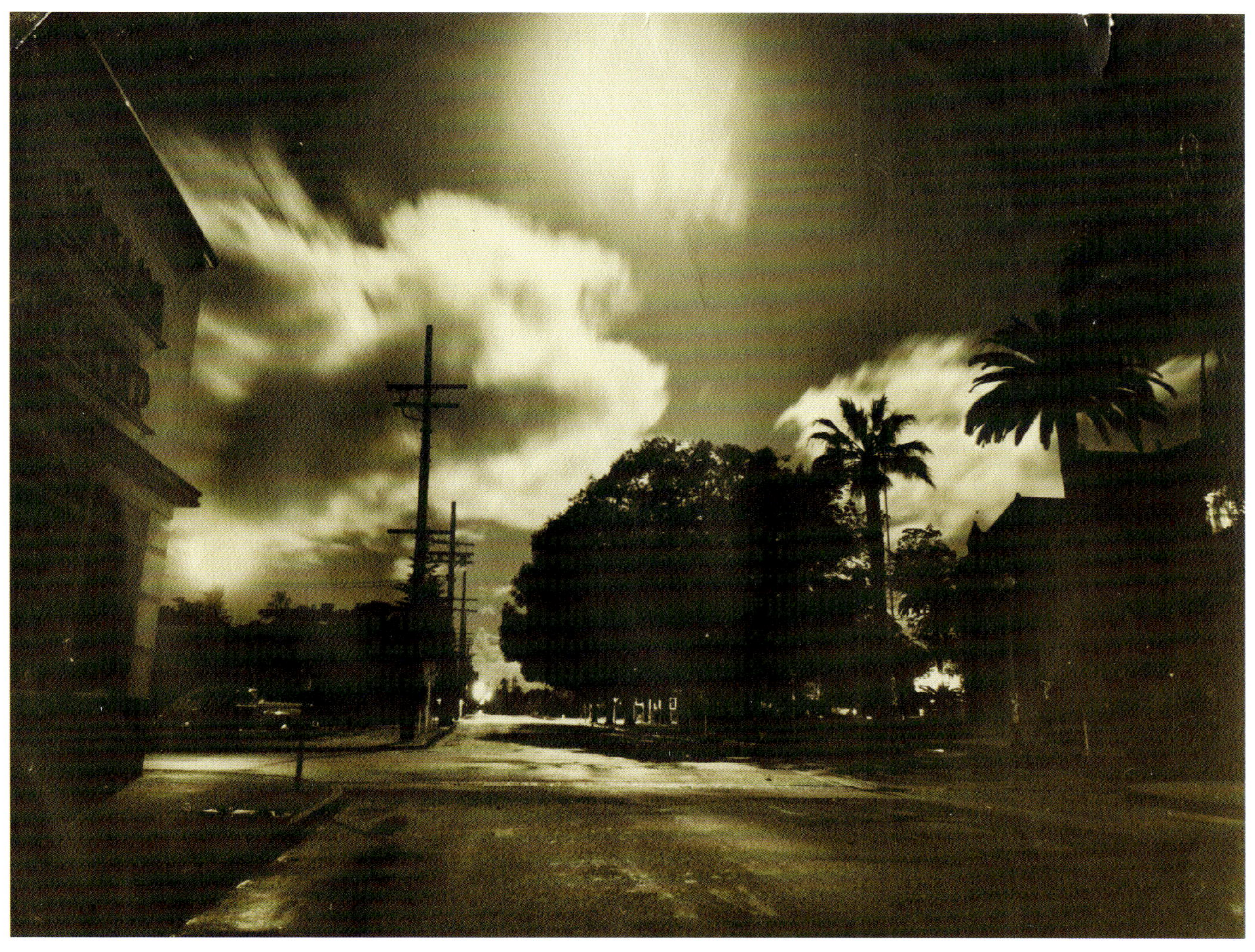

Mell Kilpatrick; Untitled (The noir city); gelatin silver print; ca. 1950; 10⅛ × 13¼ in.
*A scene reminiscent of a detective film.*

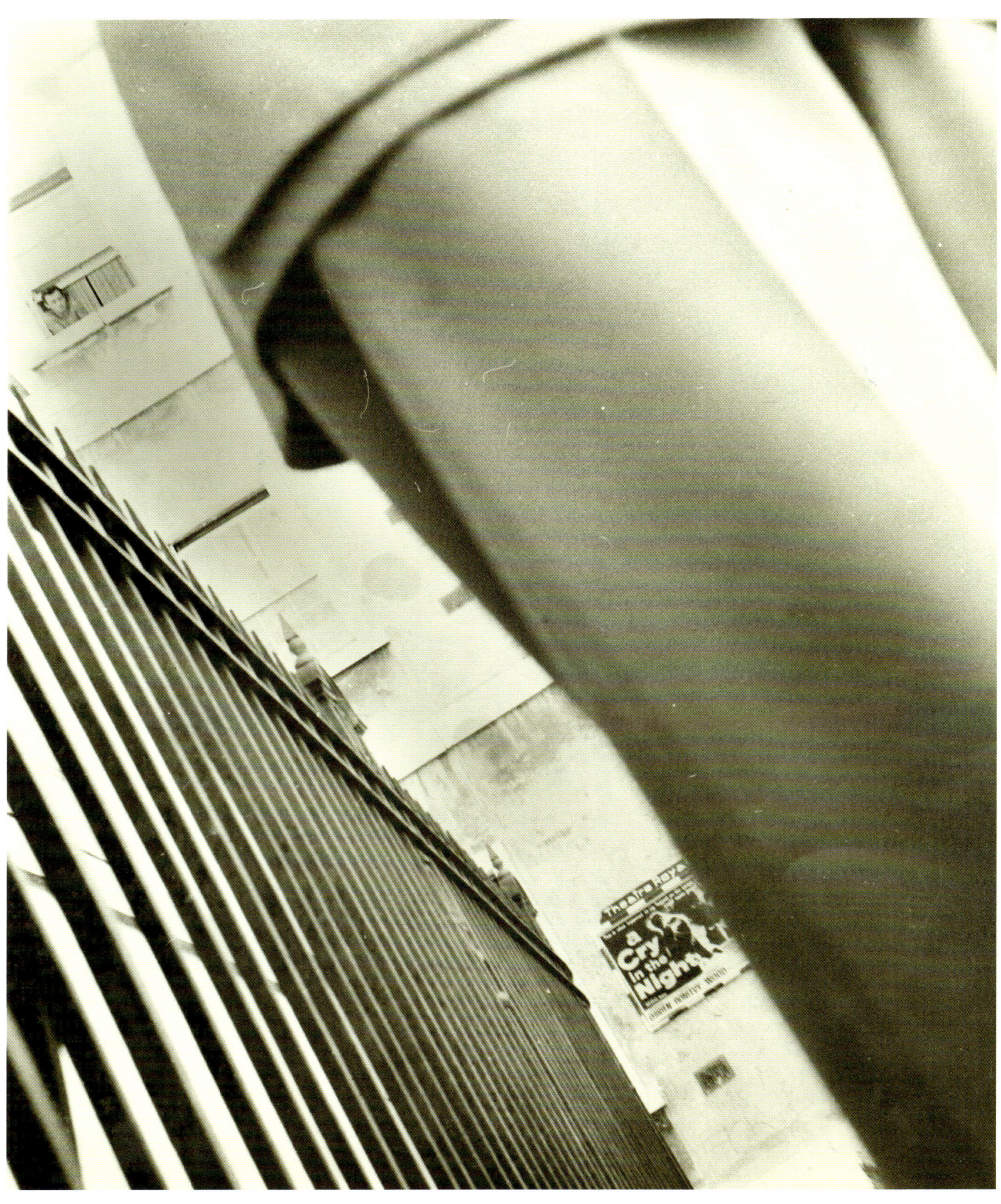


Mell Kilpatrick; Untitled (A poster advertises *The Cry in the Night*); gelatin silver print; ca. 1950; 12¾ × 10½ in.
*This piece brings to mind John Fante's Los Angeles noir novels.*

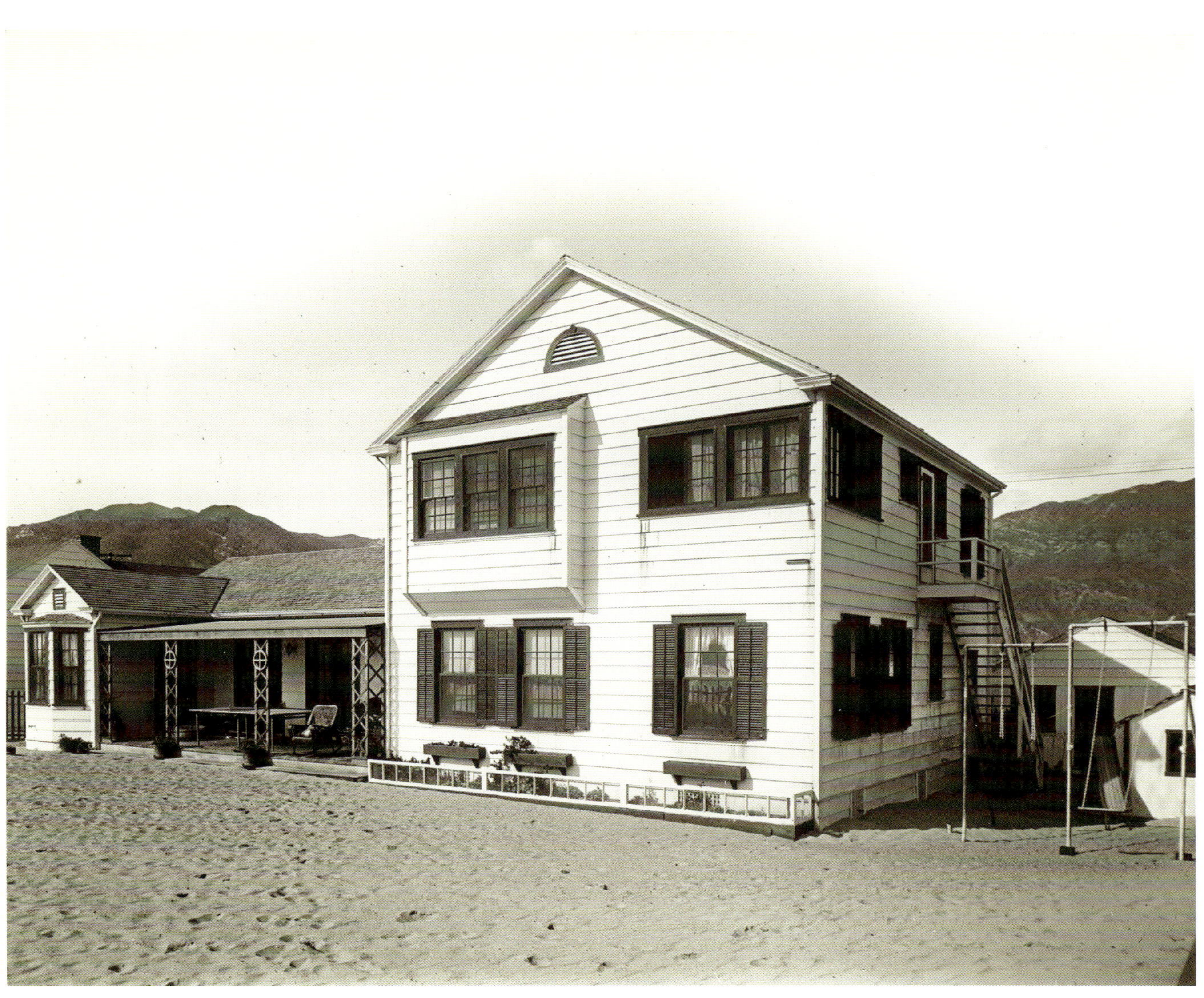

Stagg Photo Service; *Schulberg's Facing Ocean*; gelatin silver print; ca. 1940; 7⅞ × 9½ in.
*A novelist and screenwriter, Schulberg wrote the screenplay for the 1954 film* On the Waterfront, *and won an Academy Award for it, then followed up with a book released a year later that became a bestseller.*

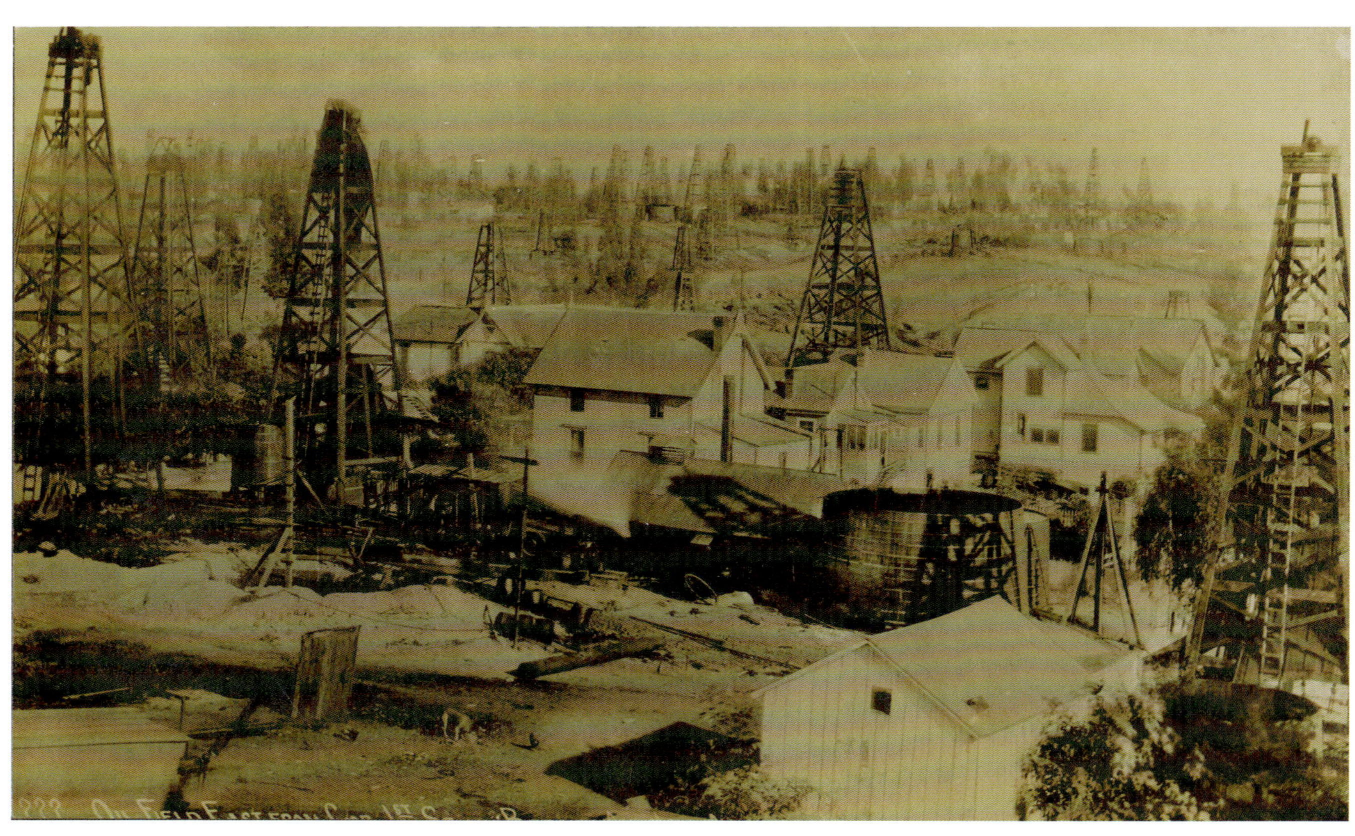

Unknown Artist; *Oil Wells and Houses, Looking East from First Street*; gelatin silver print; ca. 1910; 5⅝ × 9 ¼ in.
*Los Angeles was a city of oil wells developed during the twentieth century.*

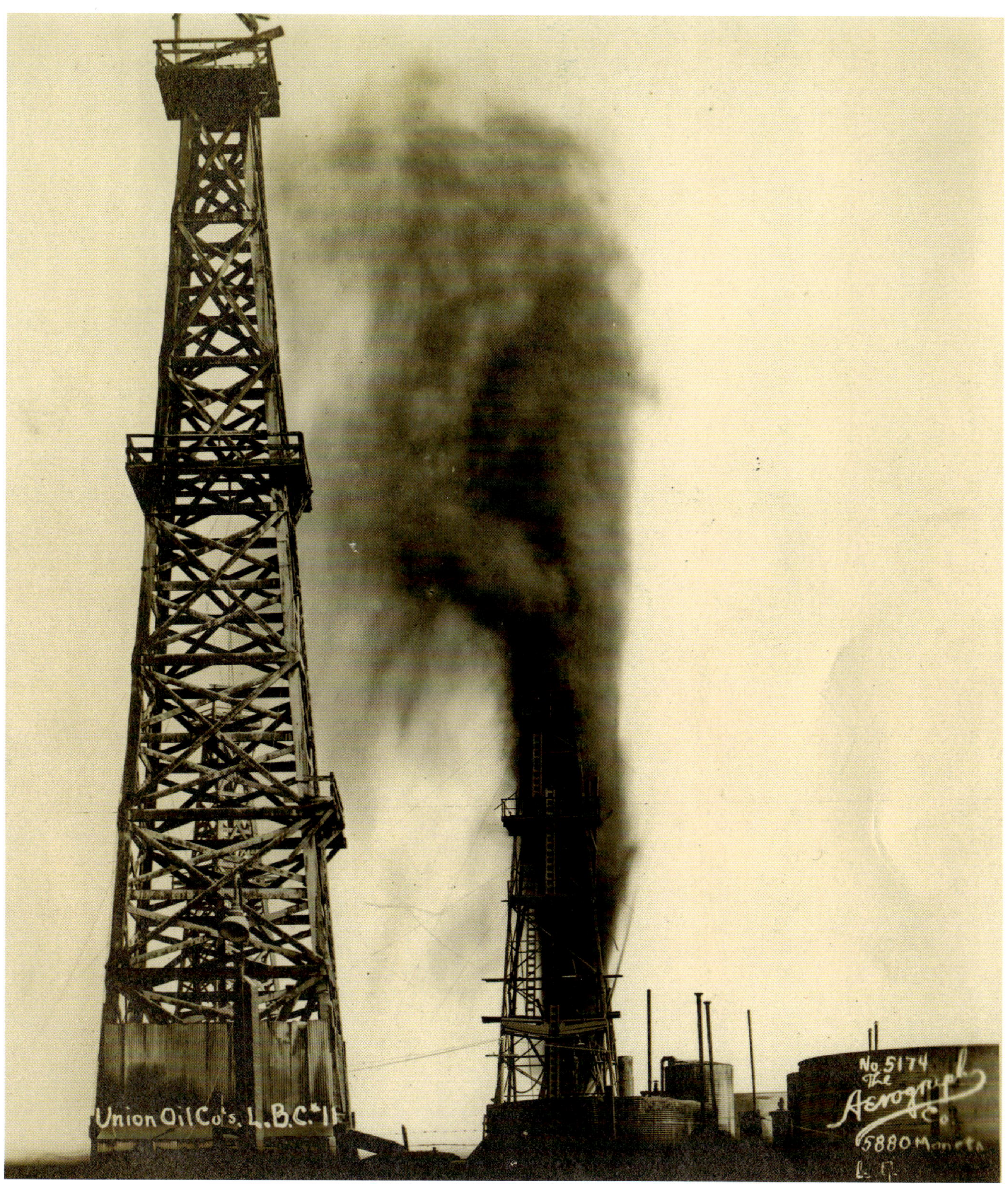


Aerograph Company Los Angeles; *Union Oil Companies L.B.C. #11*; gelatin silver print; ca. 1930; 9 ¼ × 8 in.
*From the turn of the twentieth century, oil wells began appearing across Los Angeles, even in the downtown area.*

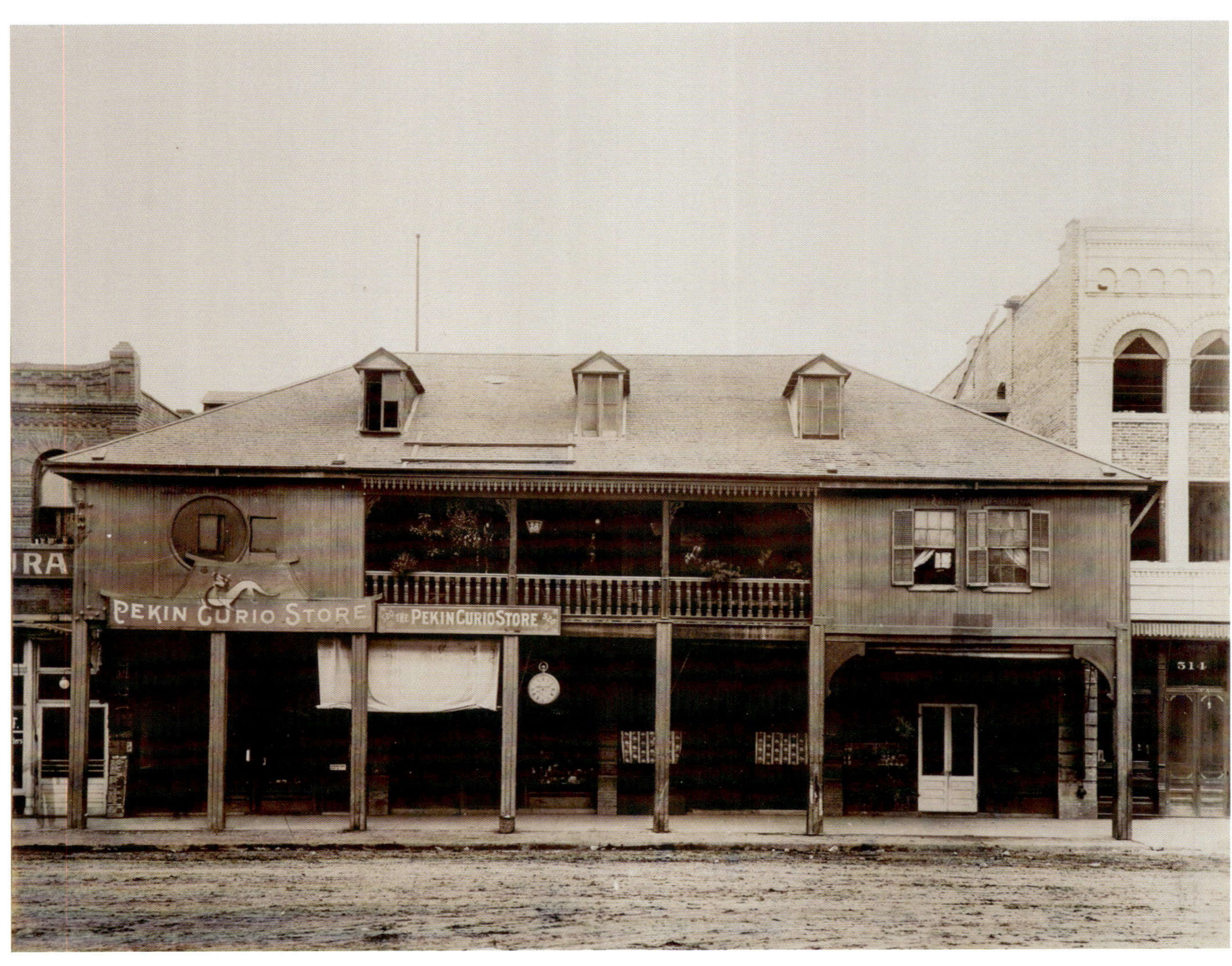


Unknown Artist; Untitled (Pekin Curio Shop, Chinatown, Los Angeles); gelatin silver print; ca. 1900, printed later; 16 × 20 in.
*Originally the location of the Lugo House, this site later became the Washington Hotel and then the Pekin Curio Shop in an area now called Old Chinatown. The adobe building was located on Los Angeles Street as part of the Plaza, but fell victim to redevelopment and was demolished in 1951.*

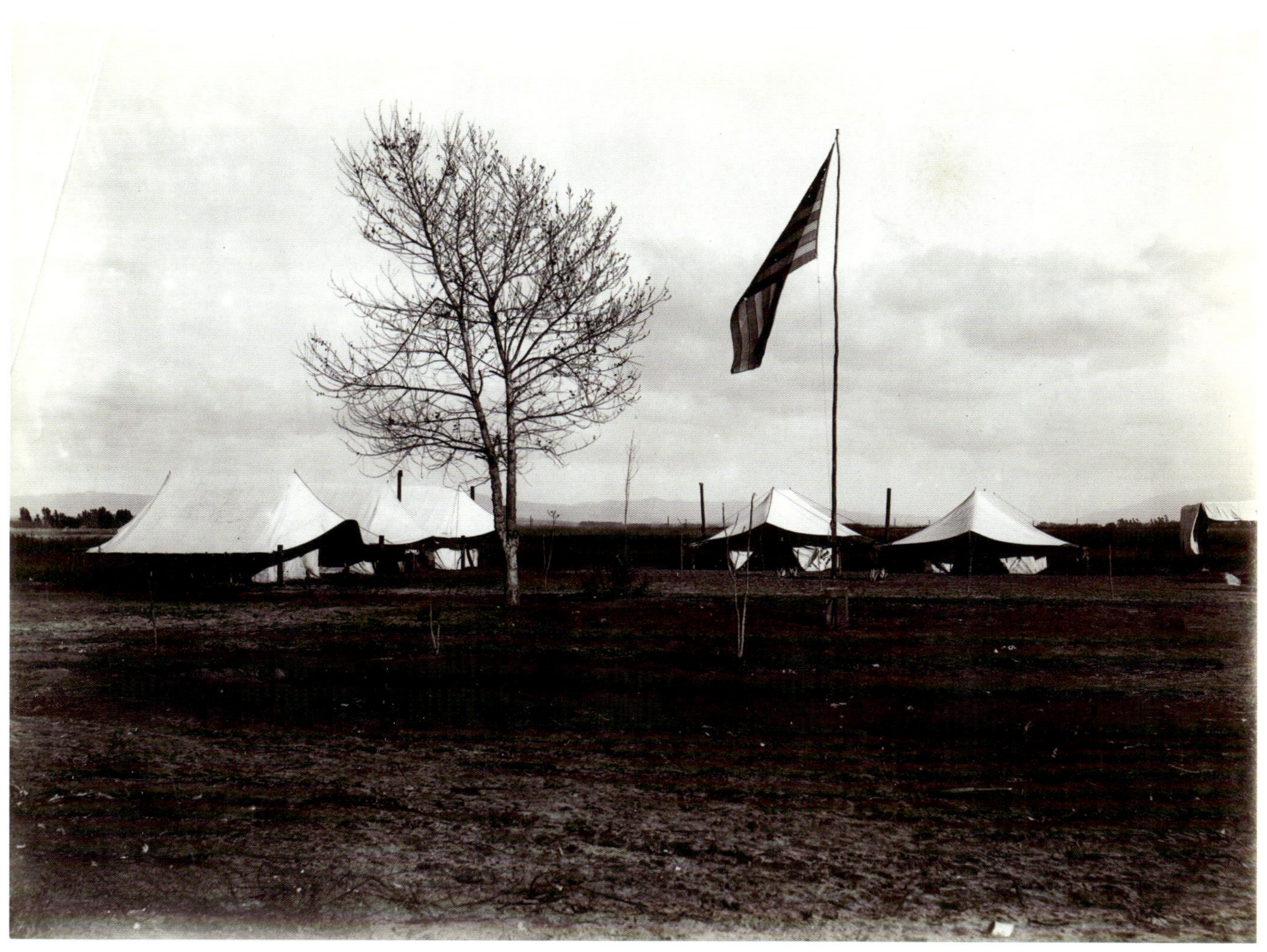

Carleton E. Watkins; *L.A. Plains Coast Survey Camp*; gelatin silver print; 1889; 7⅛ × 9½ in.
*Watkins accompanied George Davidson on an earth-measuring expedition through Central and Southern California.*

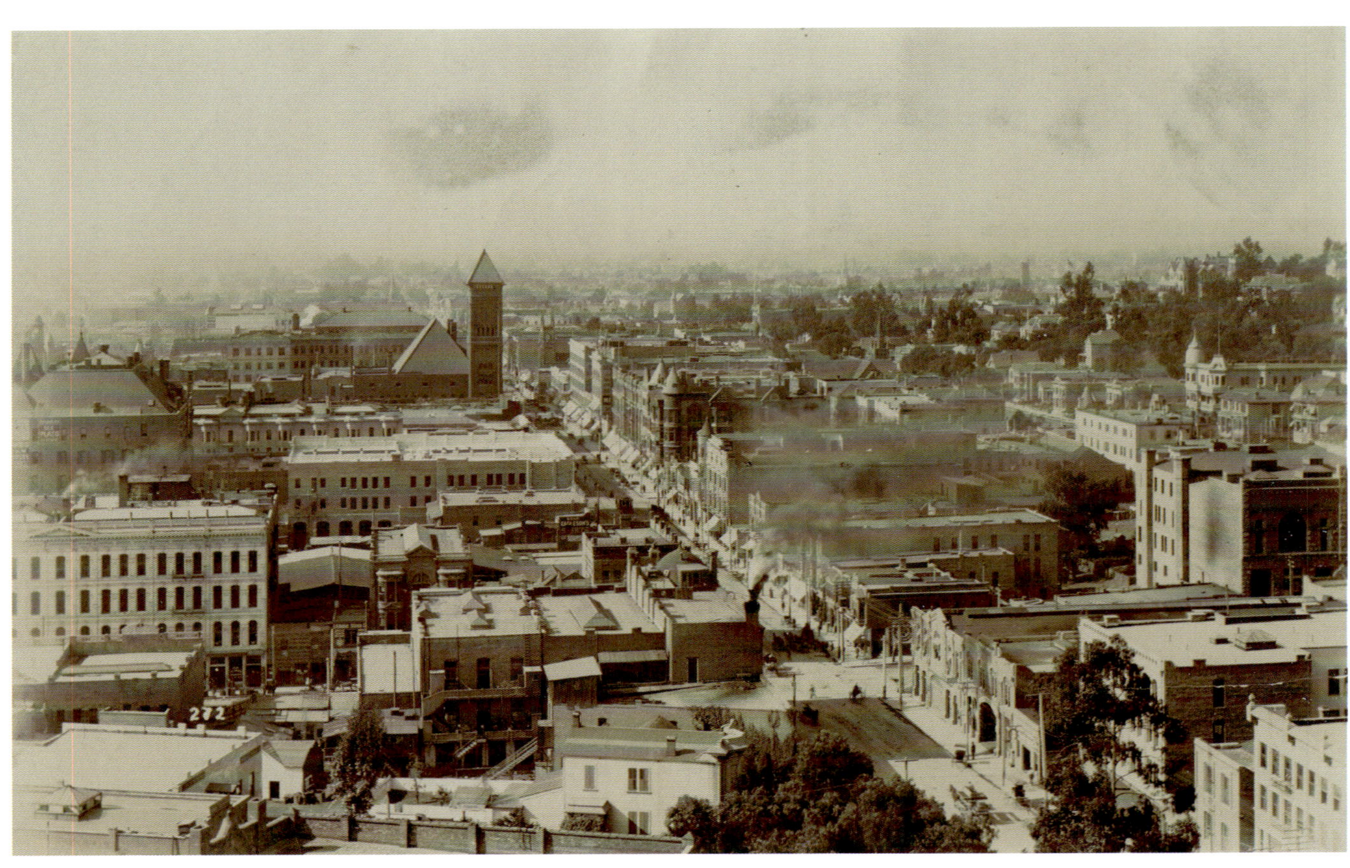


Unknown Artist; *Los Angeles*; gelatin silver print; ca. 1890; 5 × 7⅞ in.
*The population of Los Angeles had reached 50,000 by the 1890s.*

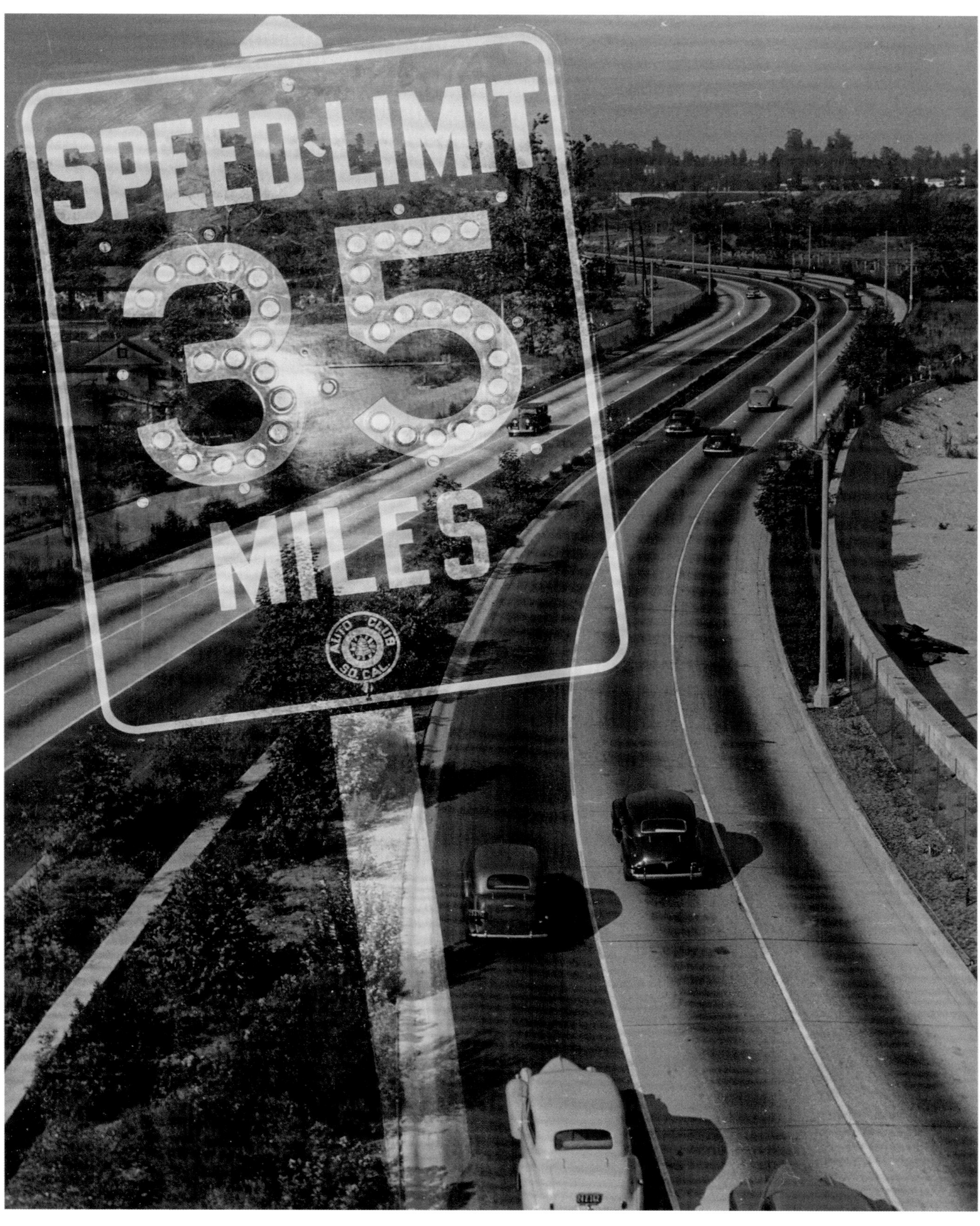


Will Connell; Untitled (Pasadena Freeway); gelatin silver print; ca. 1950; 19½ × 15⅜ in.
*The first segment of what was originally called the Arroyo Seco Parkway opened in 1938, the first freeway in the Western United States. Connell, a major force in photography in Los Angeles in the 1920s and 1930s, taught in the photography program at Art Center School, where Ansel Adams also taught classes.*

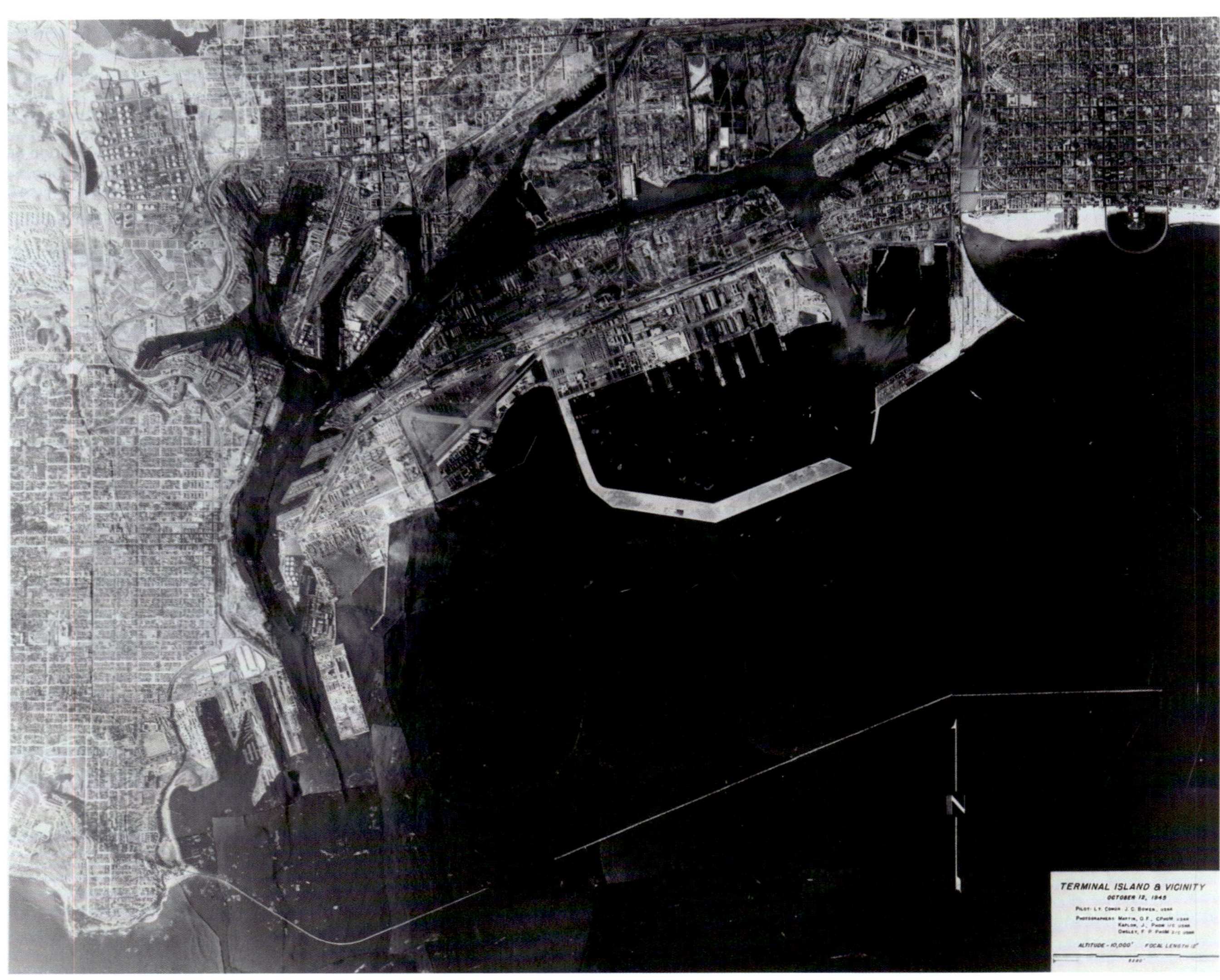


O.F. Martin; *Aerial view of Terminal Island*; gelatin silver print; October 1945; 15½ × 19 in.
*Until World War II, Fish Harbor was a thriving Japanese American community of fishermen and cannery workers and their families. During the war, Terminal Island became a center of shipbuilding, after the Japanese residents were taken to internment camps.*

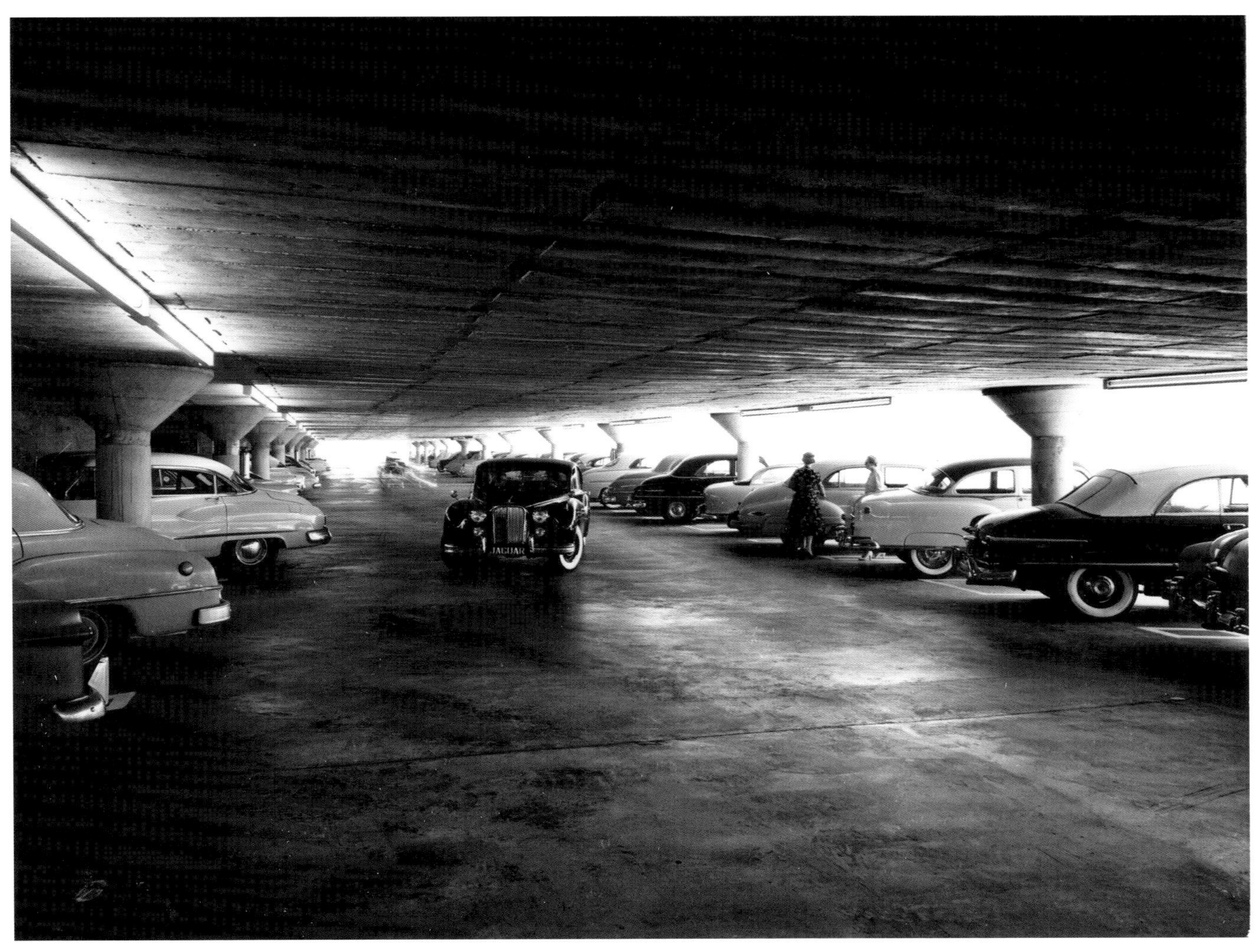


Julius Shulman; *Parking Lot for the May Company at Wilshire and Fairfax*; gelatin silver print; ca. 1954; 8½ × 10⅞ in.
*The May Co. department store corner is now the site of the Academy Museum of Motion Pictures.*

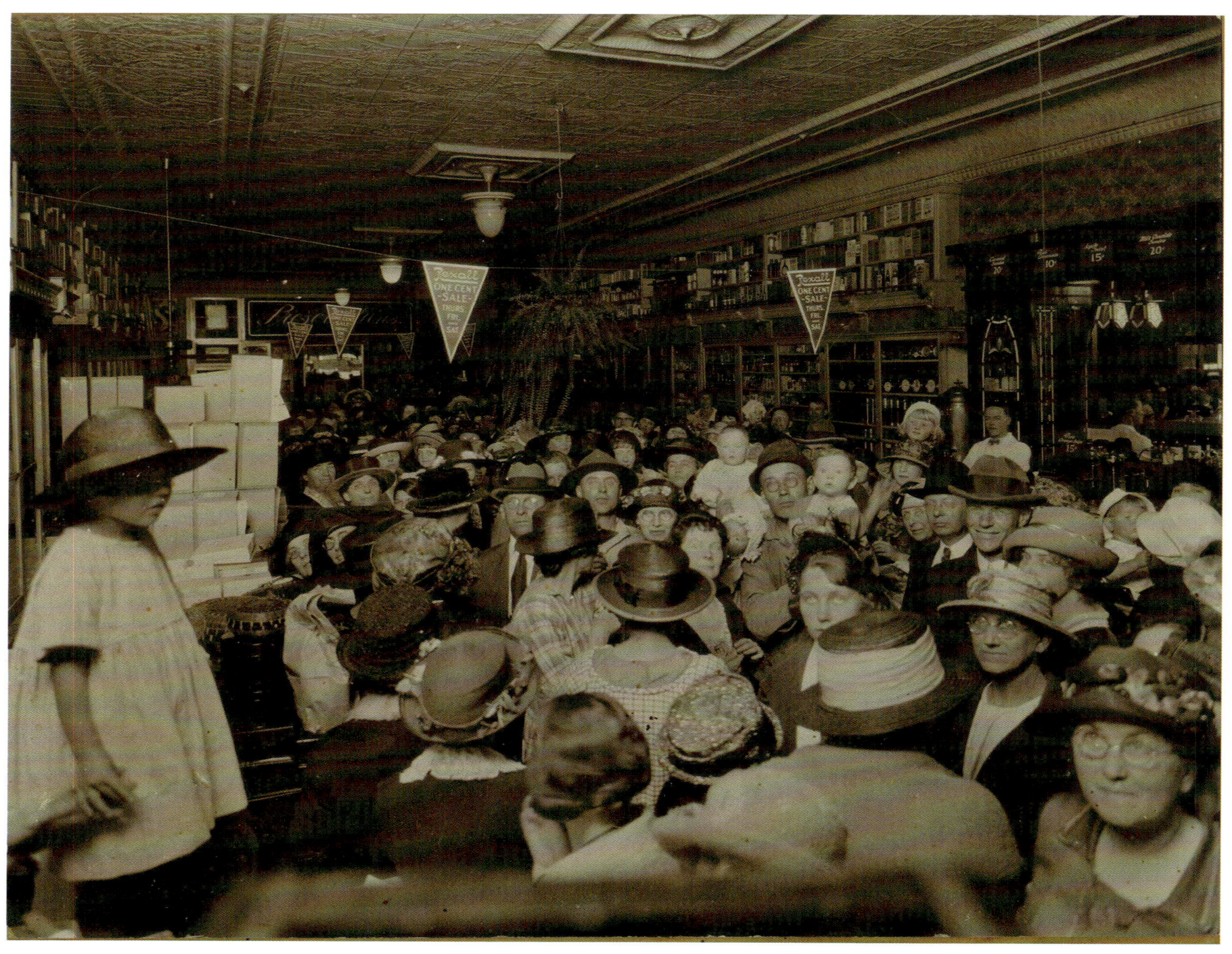


Unknown Artist; *Keystone "One-Cent" Sale, Rexall Drug Store, Riverside*; gelatin silver print; April 12, 1921; 7½ × 9½ in.
*Rexall's "One-Cent Sale" was introduced nationally in 1915 as a successful promotion in which the customers bought an item and received a second one for an additional penny. Included in* The Photograph and the American Dream 1840–1940, *the catalog for the show of the same name at the Van Gogh Museum in Amsterdam, 2001 to 2002.*

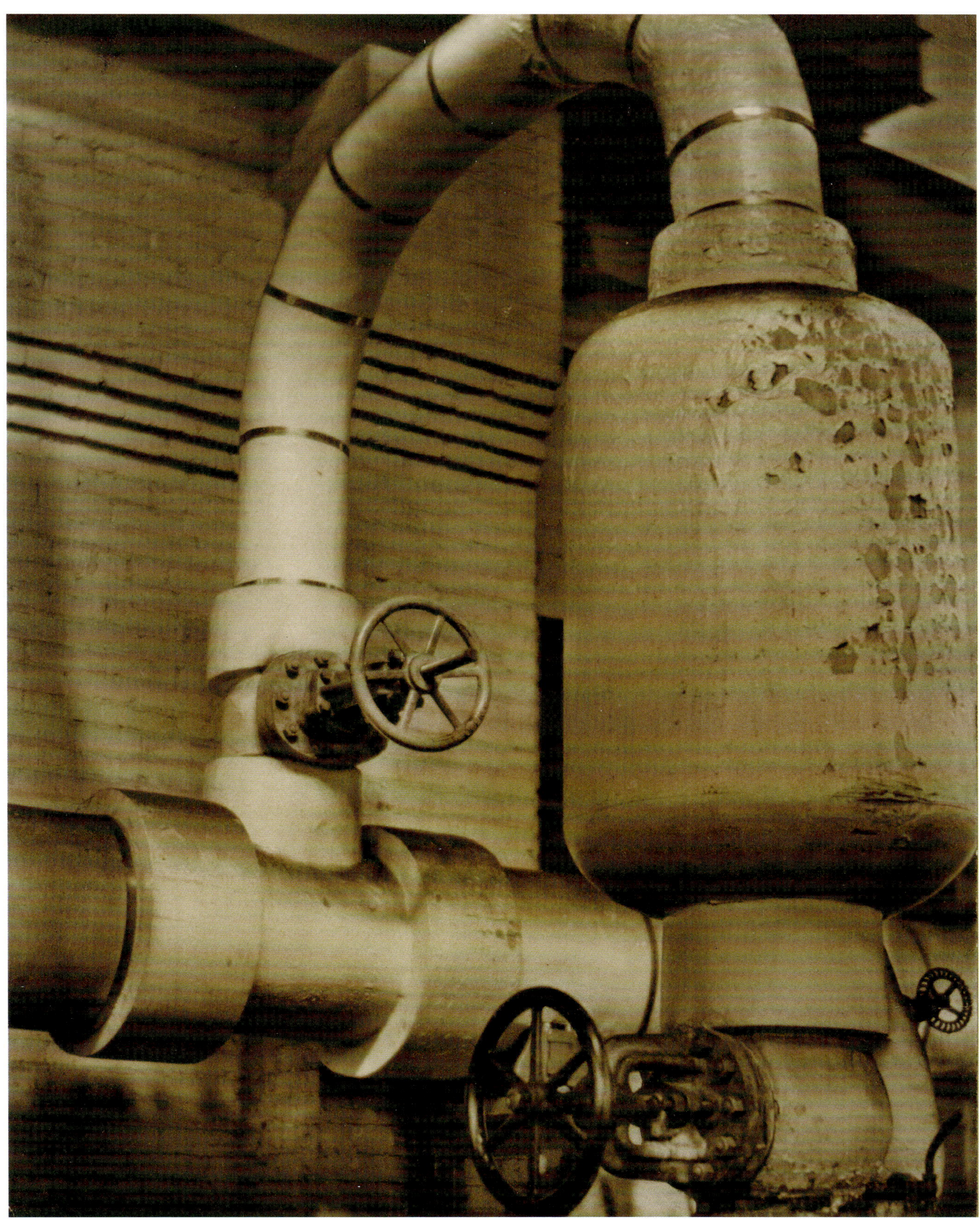

Edward Weston; Untitled (Valves); palladium print; ca. 1923; 9⅜ × 7¼ in.
*An early unknown Weston reveals his fascination with shapes, years before he developed his series on forms. From the collection of photographer Toyo Miyatake. Although born in Chicago, Weston spent the majority of his life in California and is considered one of the state's greatest photographic artists.*

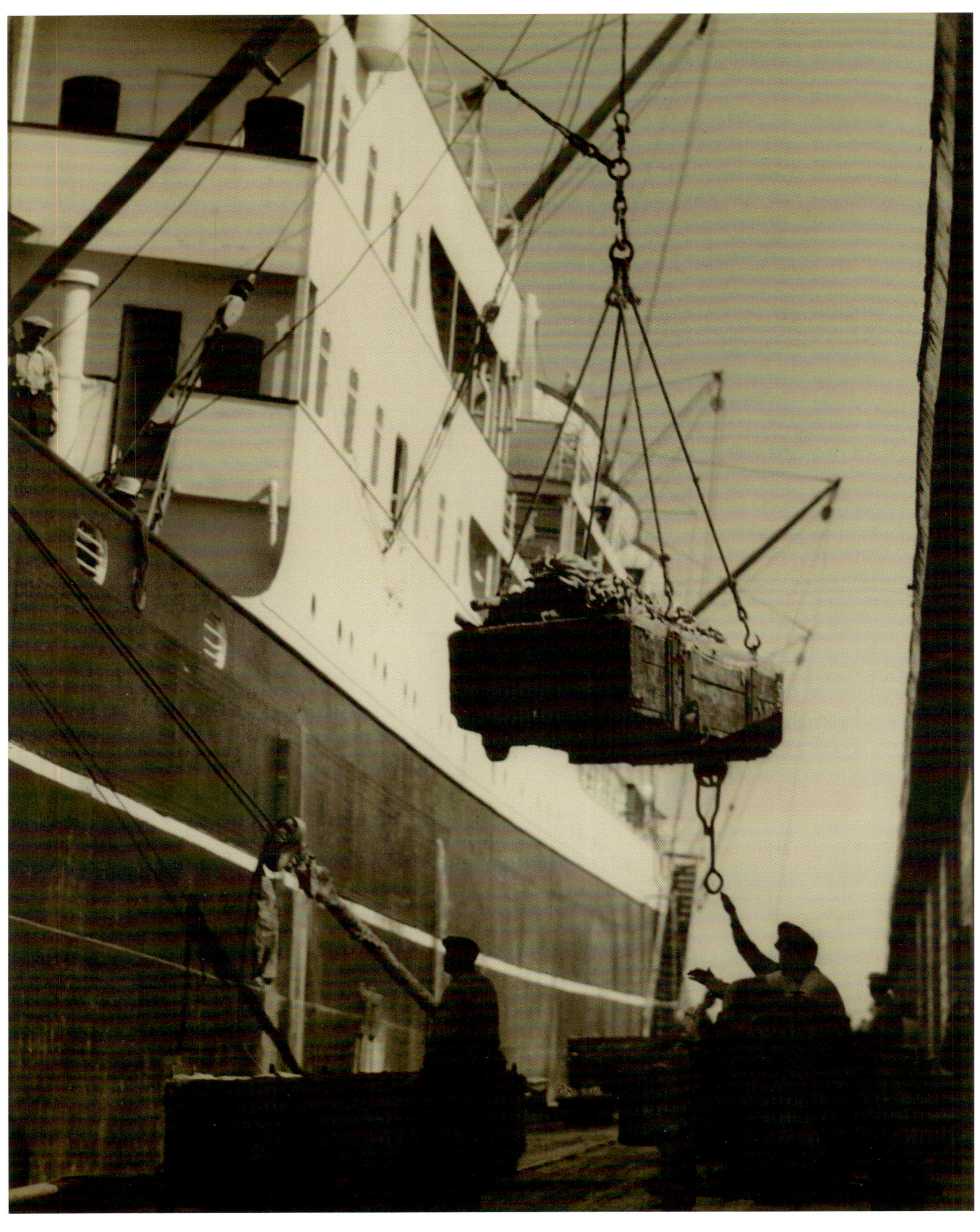

Kirby Kean; Untitled (Bananas unloading from cargo ship); gelatin silver print; ca. 1940; 14 × 11 in.
*Kean studied at Art Center School with Will Connell and James N. Doolittle, and worked as Doolittle's assistant for many years.*

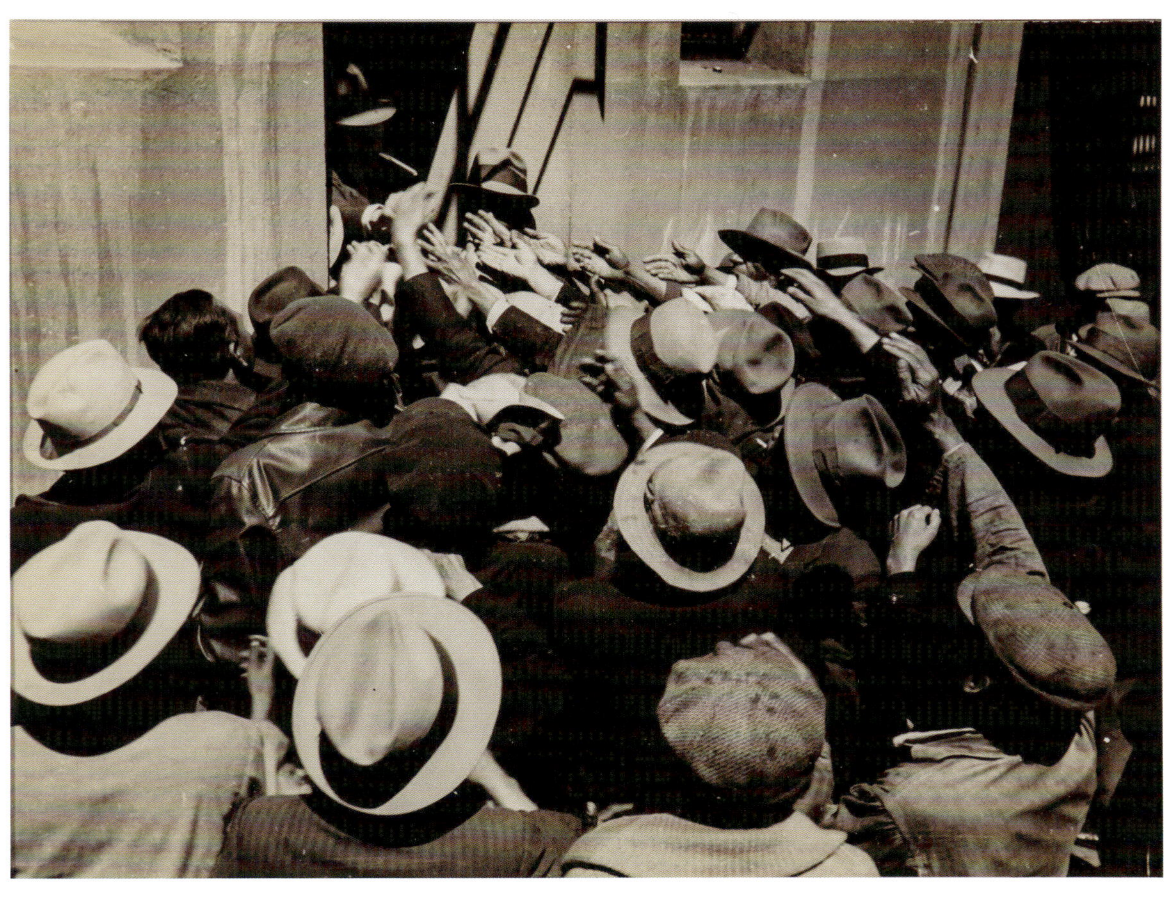

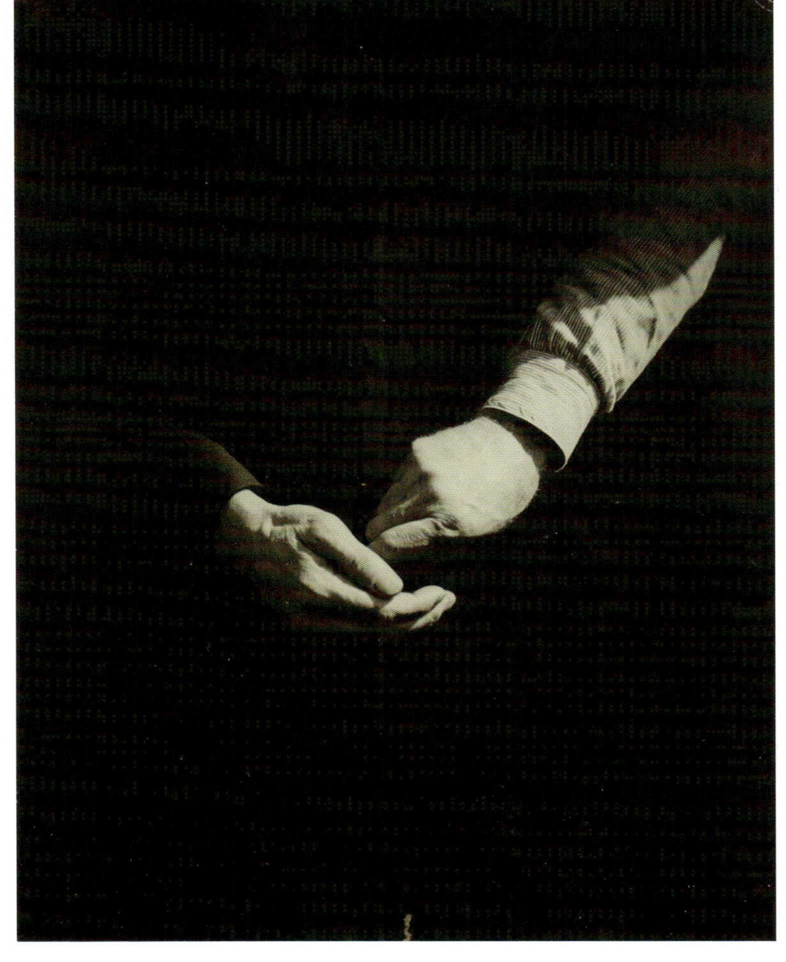

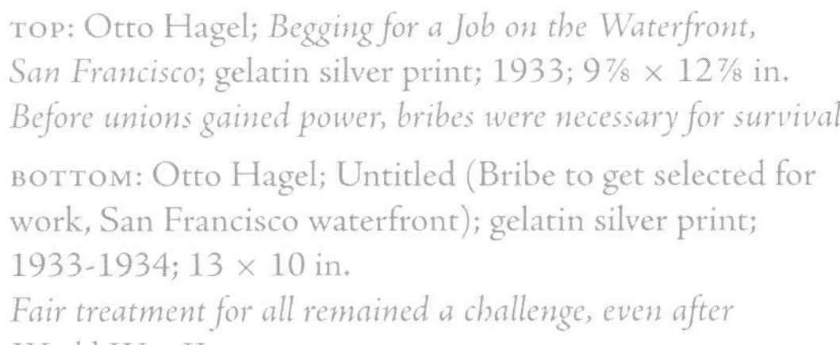

TOP: Otto Hagel; *Begging for a Job on the Waterfront, San Francisco*; gelatin silver print; 1933; 9⅞ × 12⅞ in.
*Before unions gained power, bribes were necessary for survival.*

BOTTOM: Otto Hagel; Untitled (Bribe to get selected for work, San Francisco waterfront); gelatin silver print; 1933-1934; 13 × 10 in.
*Fair treatment for all remained a challenge, even after World War II.*

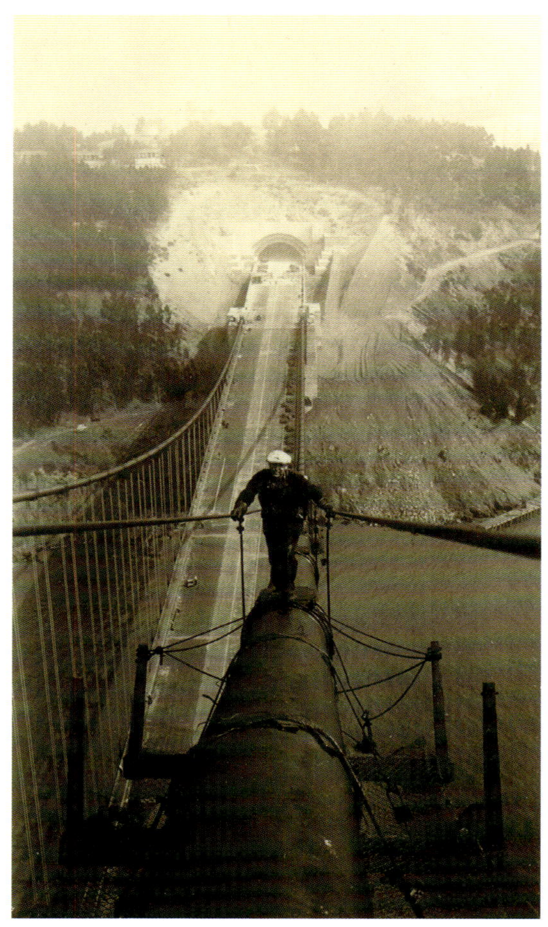

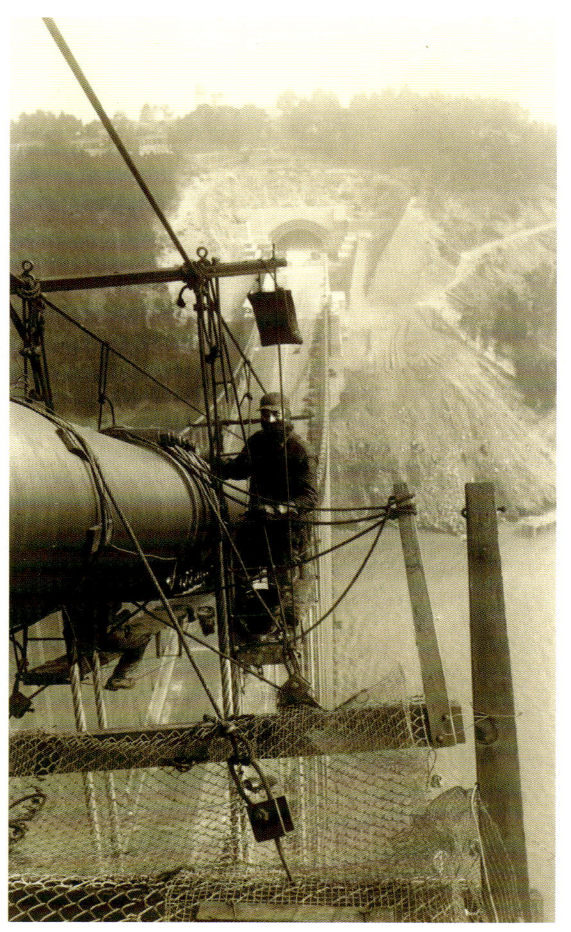

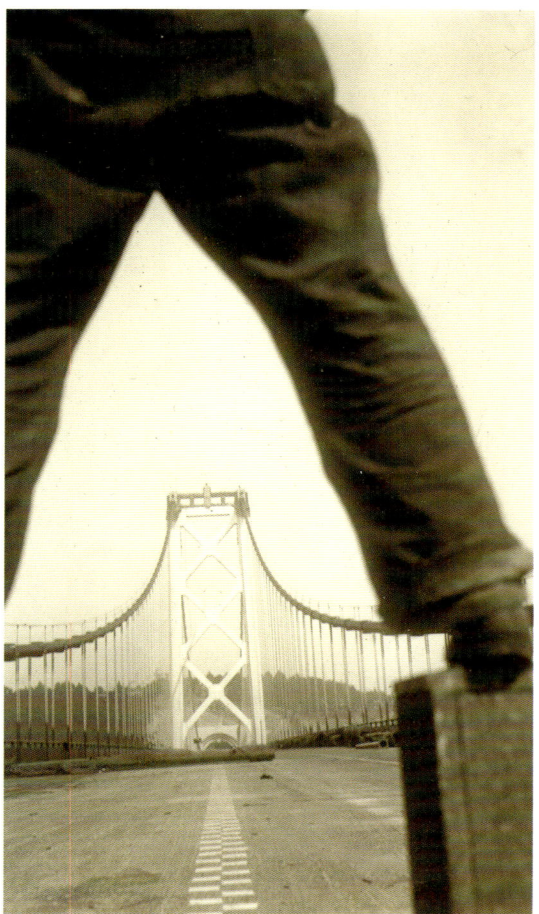

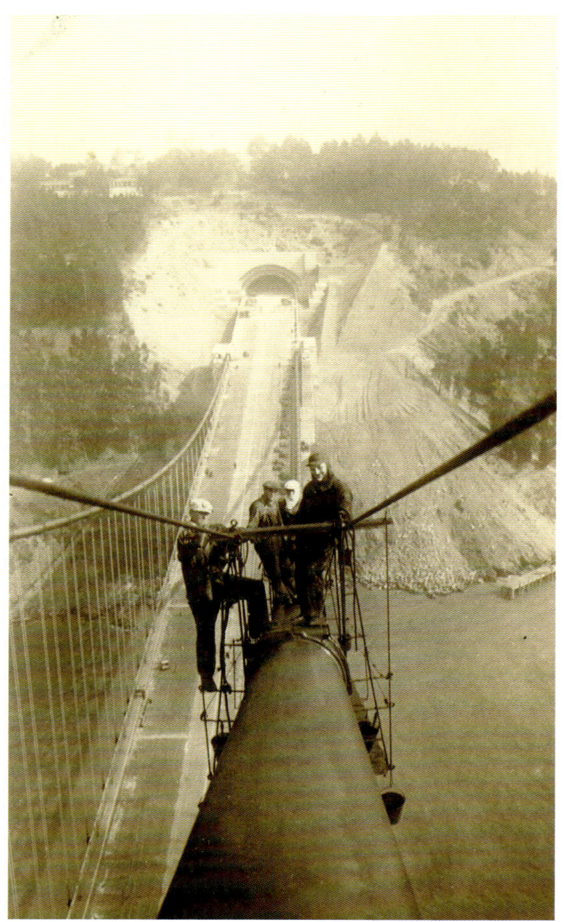

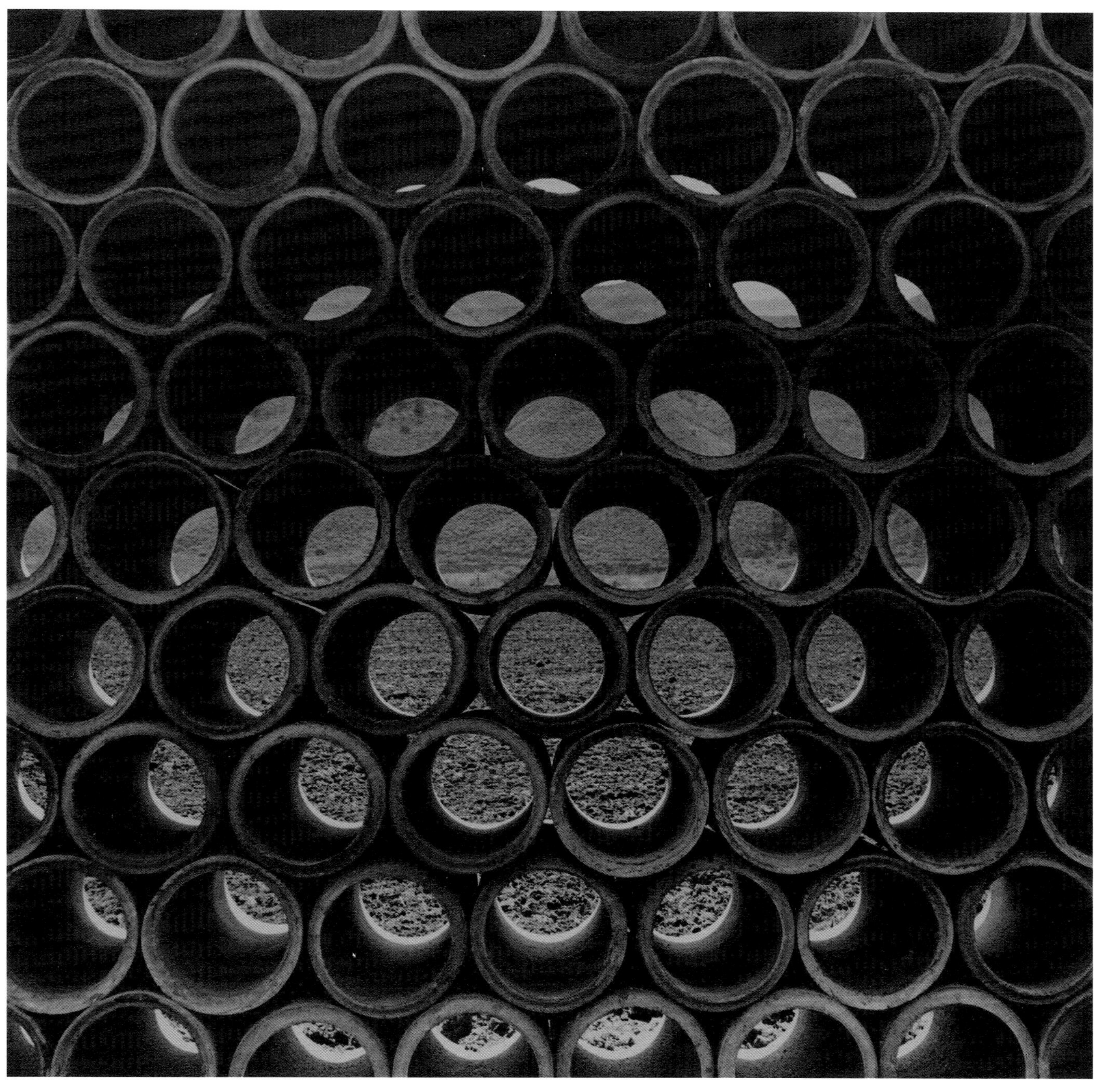

Fred Archer; Untitled (Landscape, through pipes, Piru, California); gelatin silver print; ca. 1930; 10 × 10 in.
*Archer produced some of the first abstract photographs in the United States, perhaps as early as 1919. He was a member of the Camera Pictorialists in Los Angeles, and he taught at Art Center School before founding the Fred Archer School of Photography.*

OPPOSITE, CLOCKWISE FROM TOP LEFT:
Unknown Artist; Untitled (Bay Bridge under construction); gelatin silver print; October 1935; 4¼ × 3¾ in.
Unknown Artist; Untitled (Bay Bridge under construction); gelatin silver print; October 1935; 4¼ × 3¾ in.
Unknown Artist; Untitled (Bay Bridge under construction); gelatin silver print; October 1935; 4¼ × 3¾ in.
Unknown Artist; Untitled (Bay Bridge under construction); gelatin silver print; ca. 1935; 4⅜ × 2⅝ in.
*These four photographs were taken by an amateur photographer who playfully, skillfully, and daringly recorded the dangers and camaraderie of the construction crew, of which he was a member.*

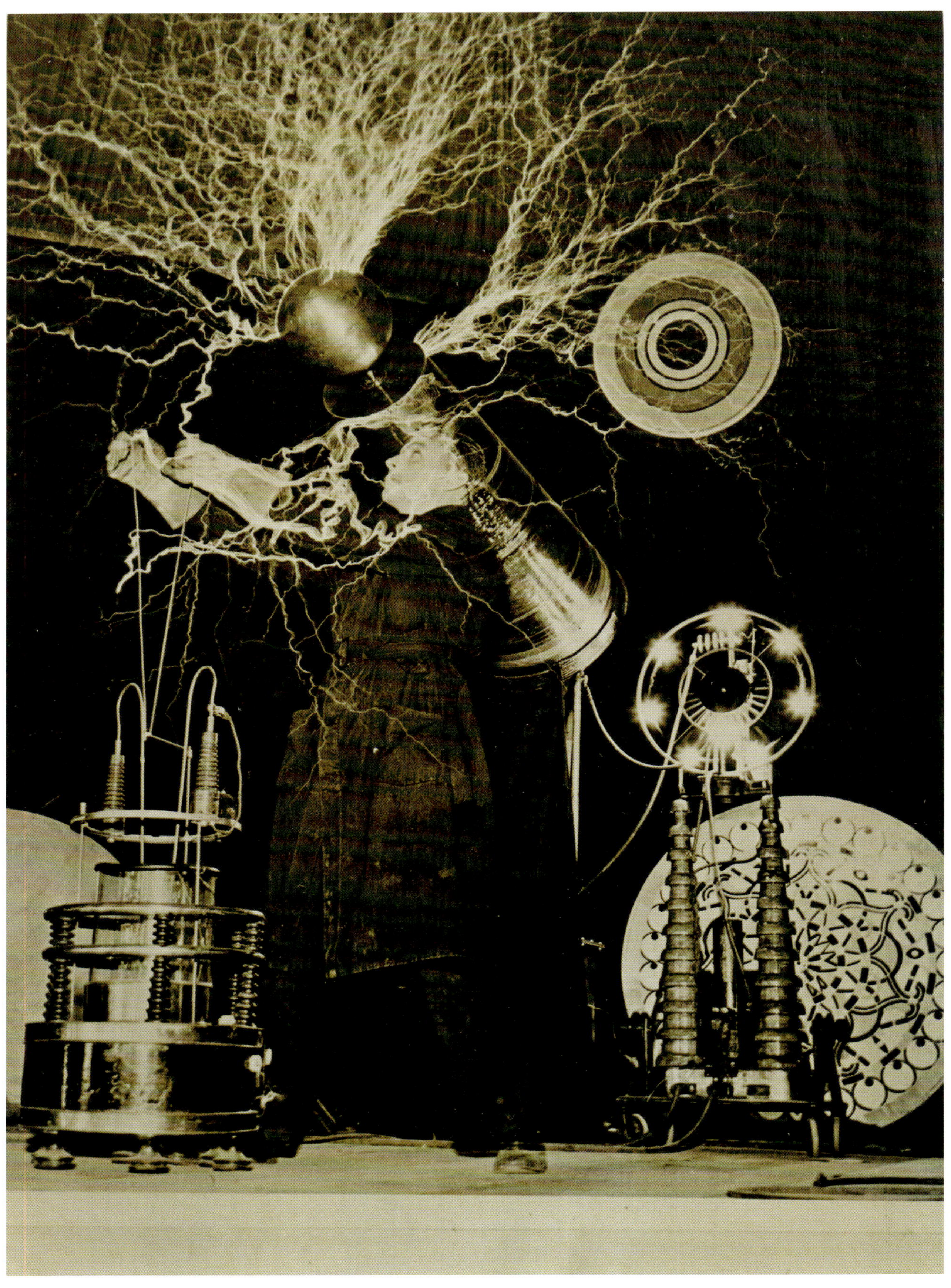

The New York Times; *A Display of Electricity in Los Angeles to Celebrate the Completion of Boulder Dam in 1936*; toned gelatin silver print; 1936; 6 × 4¾ in.
*This extraordinary display of California nuttiness celebrated the completion of digging for the massive dam in the Nevada desert that brought water to California.*

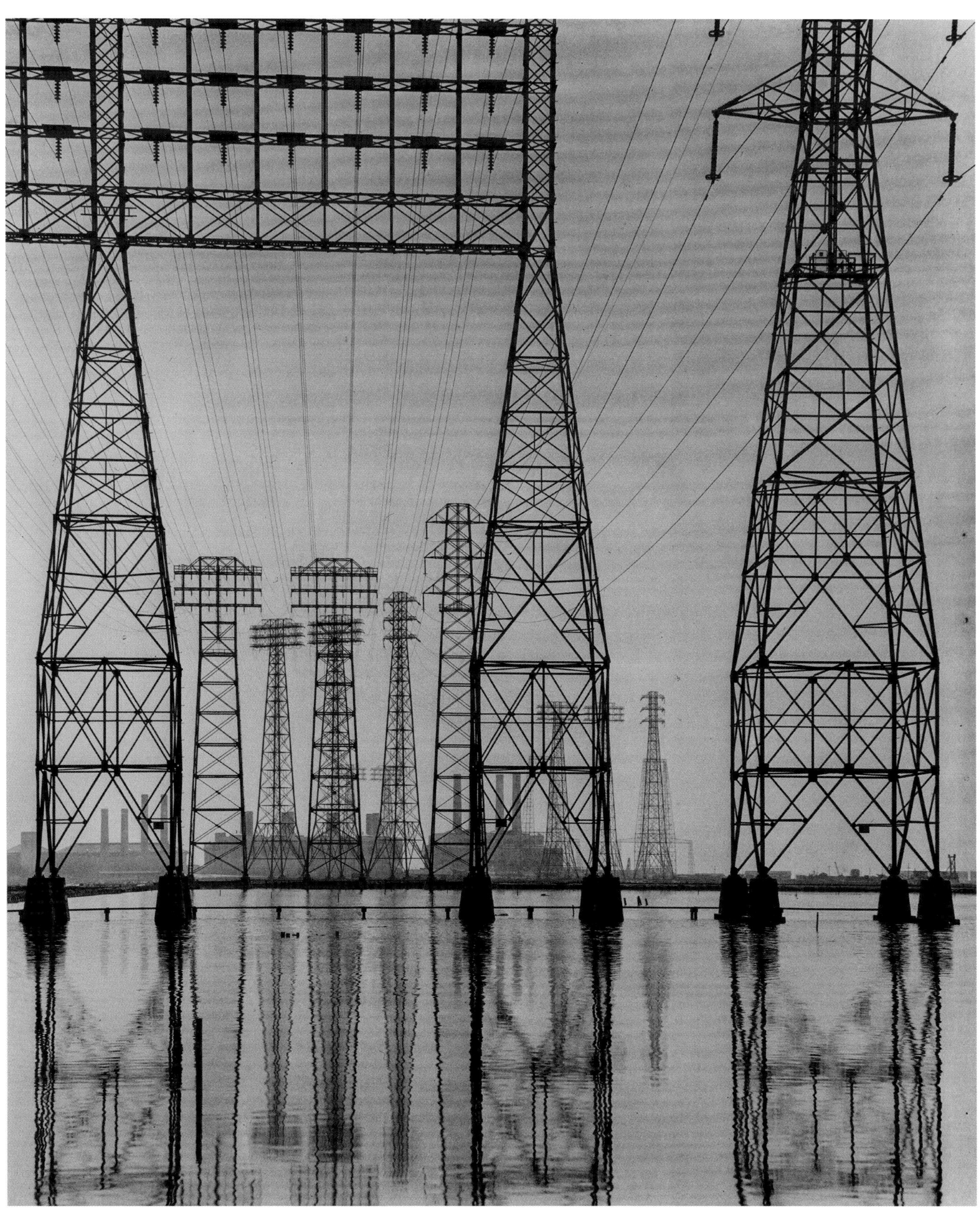

Will Connell; Untitled (Electrical transmission); gelatin silver print; ca. 1950; 19½ × 15¼ in.
*This image of the Southern California Edison transmission towers in Long Beach was Connell's most celebrated photograph. It was featured in* US Camera *magazine in 1963, two years after his death, along with a tribute article.*

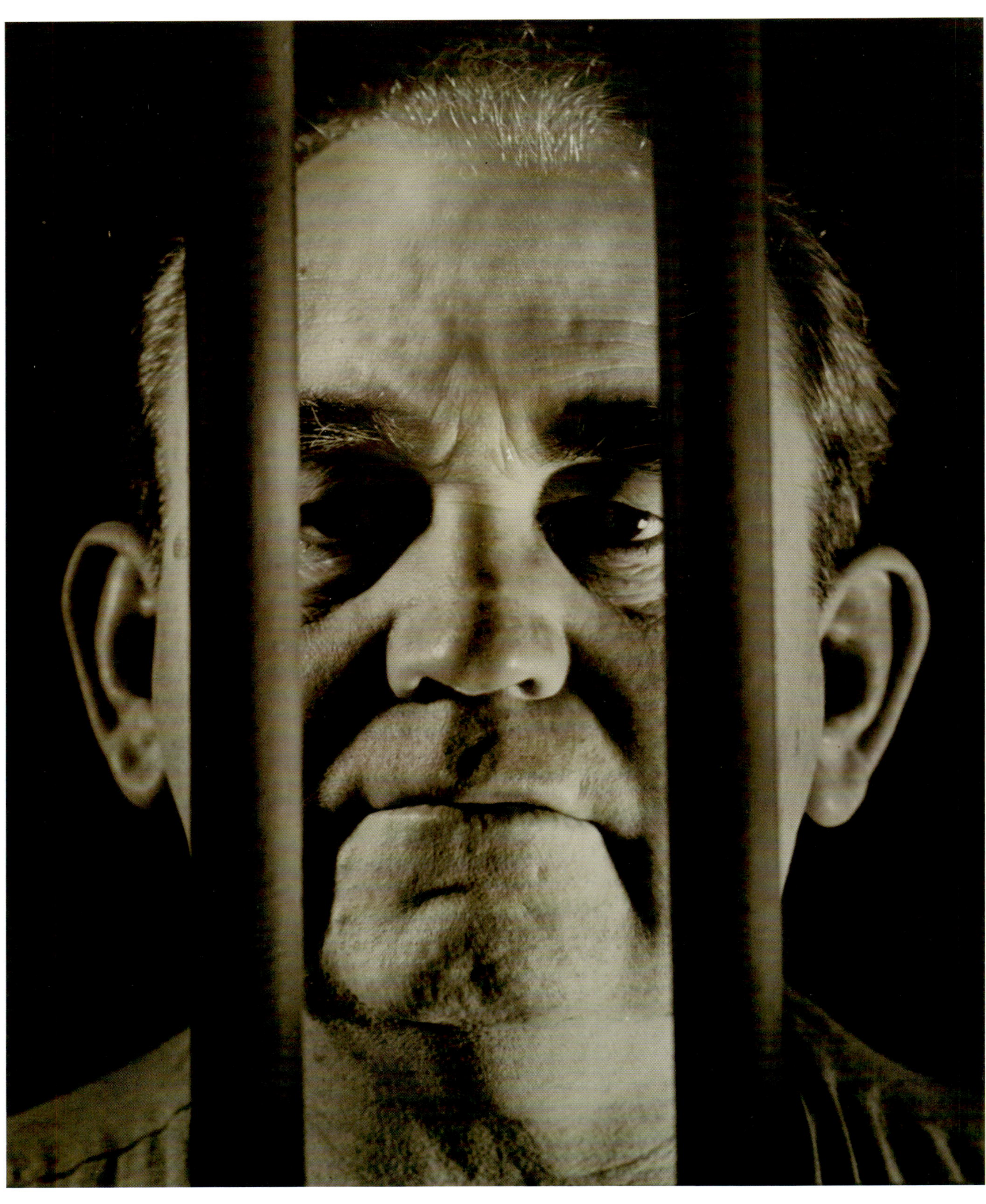

Otto Hagel; *Tom Mooney* (Labor leader in San Quentin); gelatin silver print; 1933; 12⅞ × 10¼ in.
*Mooney, a radical labor leader and a thorn in the side of local business, was apparently framed and accused of the "Preparedness Day" bombing in 1916, and sentenced to death. A request from President Woodrow Wilson to California's Governor William Stephens led to Mooney's sentence being commuted to life, but he was pardoned after serving twenty-two years in San Quentin.*

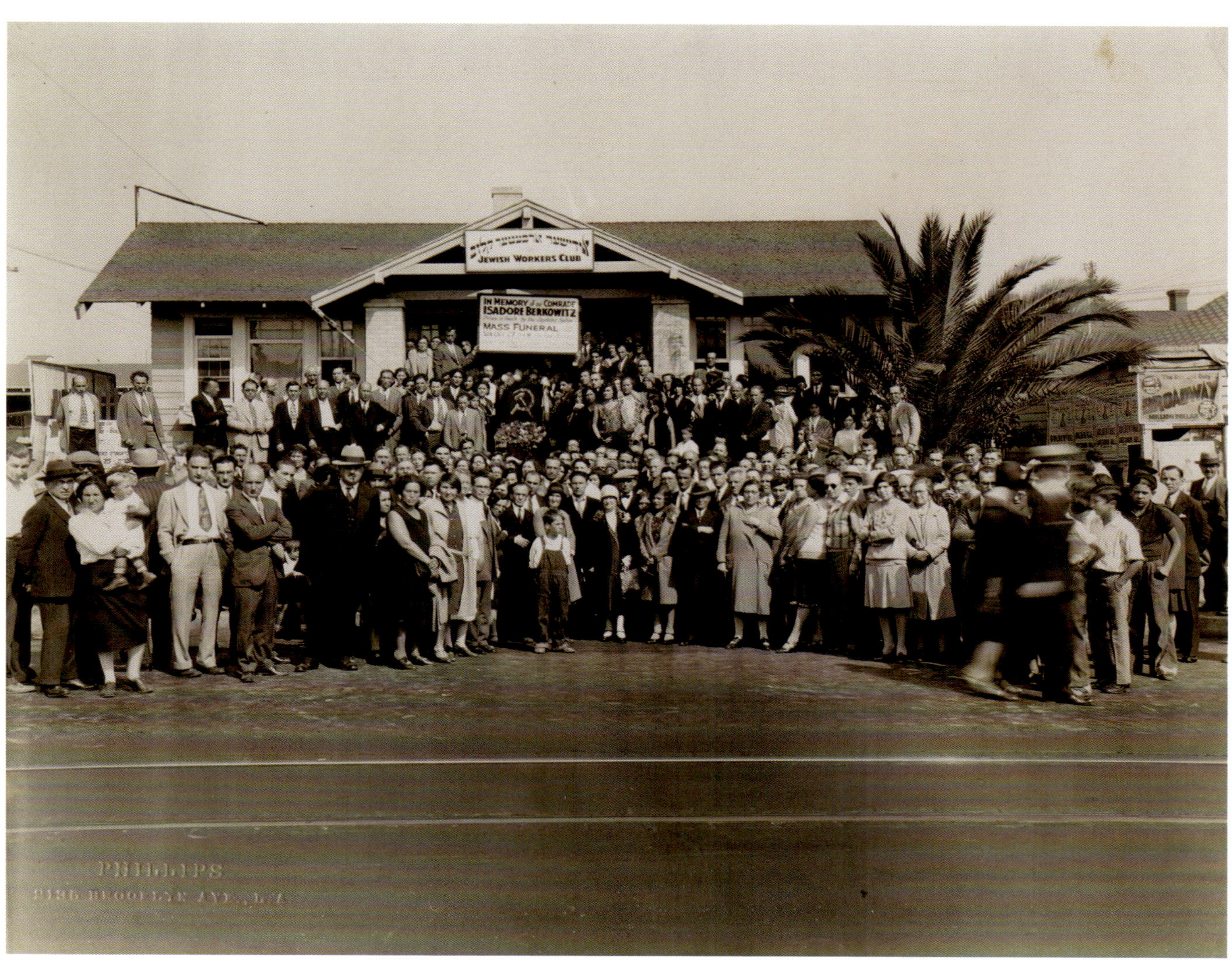



Phillips; *Memorial for Isadore Berkowitz*; gelatin silver print; 1929; 7½ × 9¼ in.
*Berkowitz was one of a group arrested for violating the 1919 California Red Flag Law. He was working as a custodian in a summer camp run by the Jewish Workers Union. Convicted, he hanged himself in the Worker's Cooperative Center in Los Angeles. The Supreme Court ruled the Red Flag Law unconstitutional in 1931. Phillips had a studio at 2135 Brooklyn Ave. in Boyle Heights.*

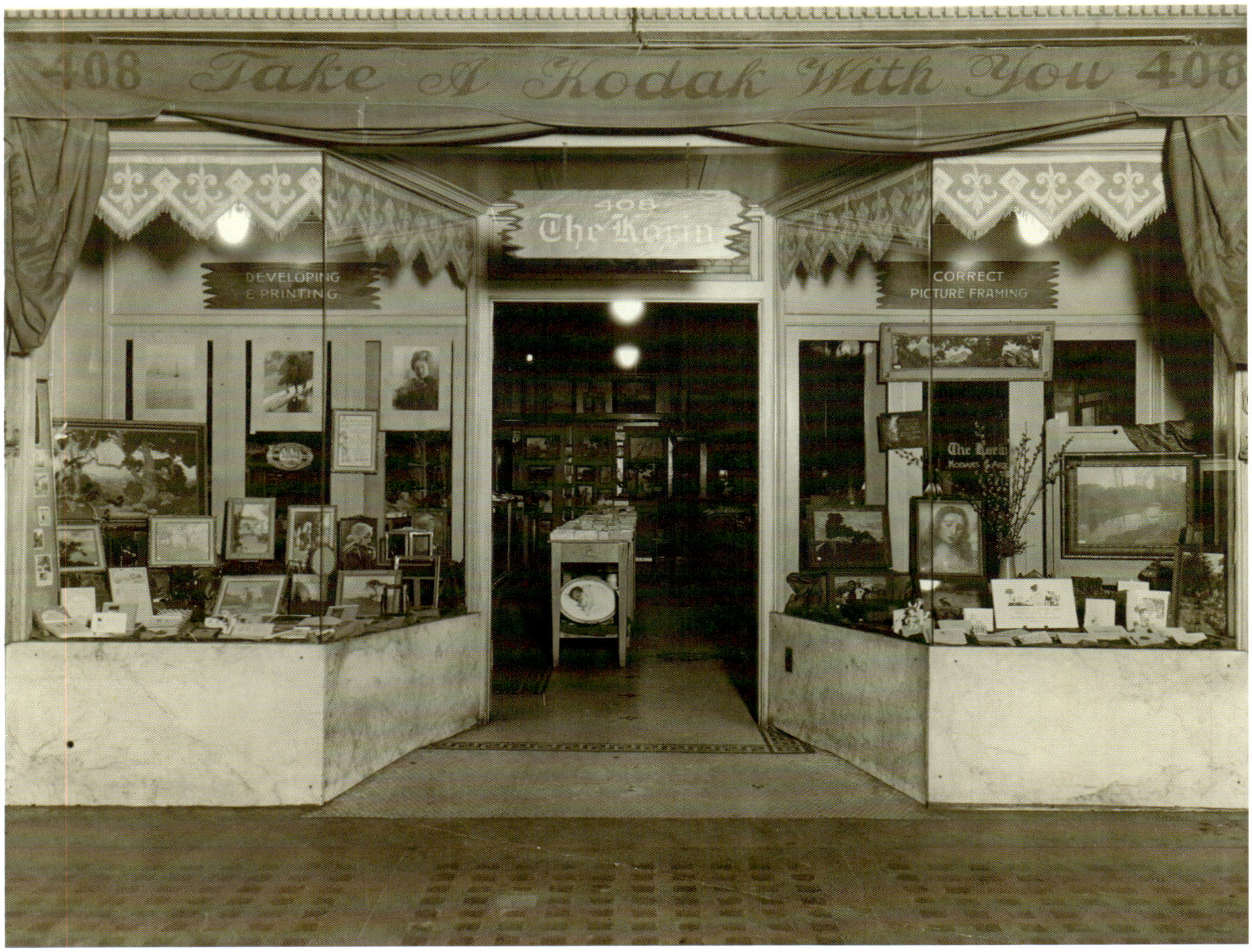

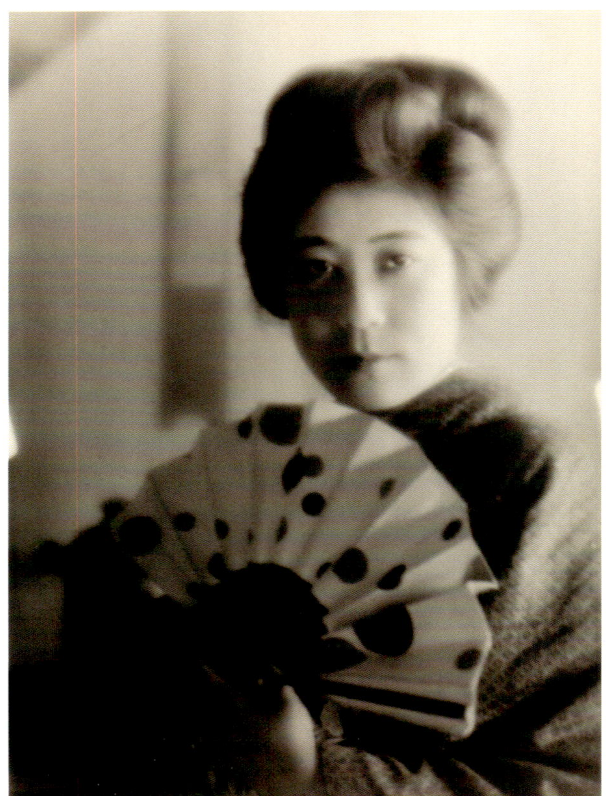

TOP: Taizo Kato; Untitled (Korin Camera Supply, Sixth Street Los Angeles); gelatin silver print; ca. 1923; 8 × 10 in.

LEFT: Taizo Kato; Untitled (Portrait of Tsuru Aoki, actress); gelatin silver print; ca. 1923; 14 × 11¼ in.

*Portrait of Tsuru Aoki in Japanese dress is displayed in the window of the camera store. Left: The portrait of Aoki. Aoki was the first Japanese actress to receive top billing in a Hollywood film. She was married to Sessue Hayakawa, and they starred together in a number of films between 1914 and 1920. Star power sold, even then.*

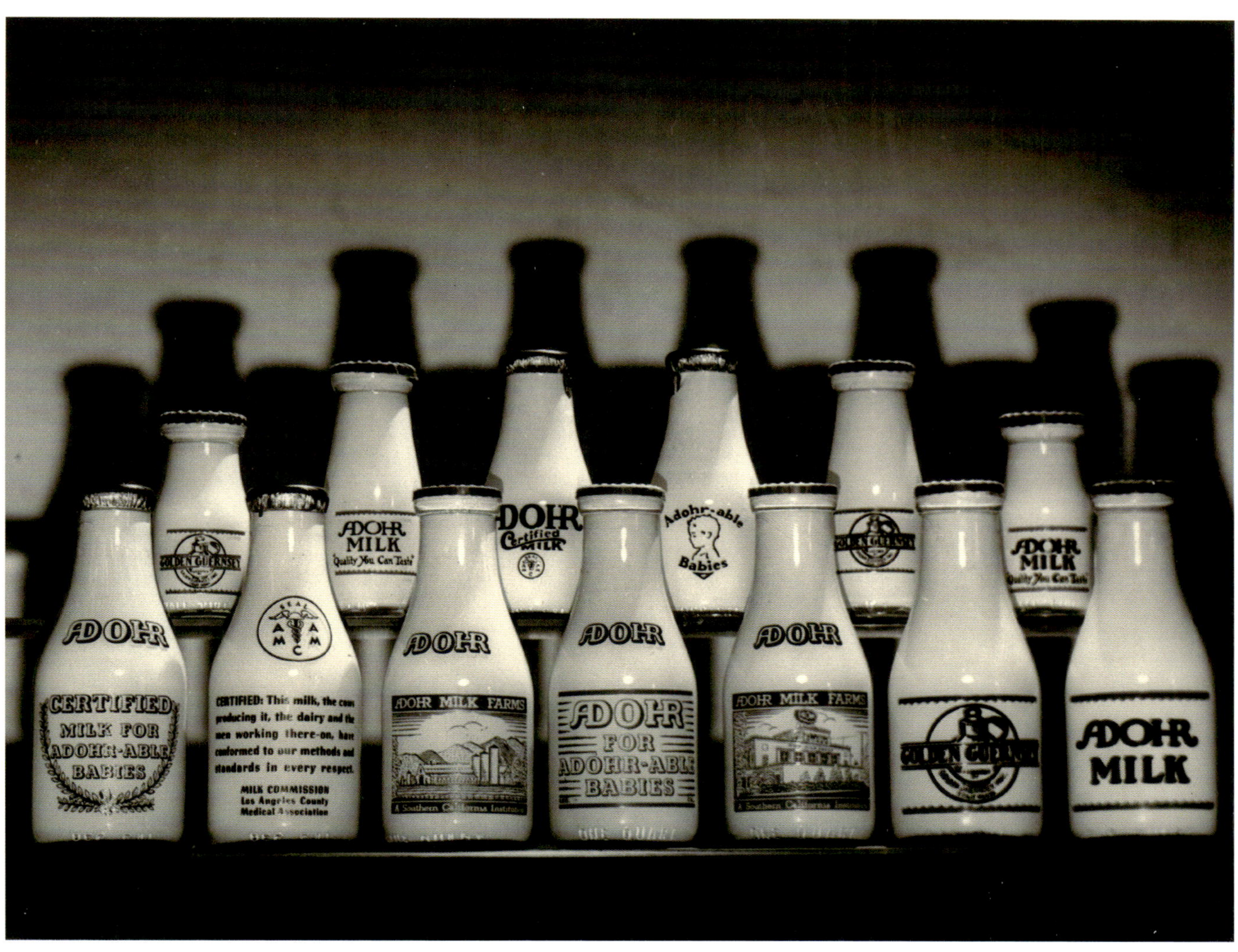


Frank Judson; Untitled (Milk display for Adohr Farms); gelatin silver print; ca. 1936; 7¼ × 9¼ in.
*Judson taught photography at Art Center School for many years in the 1930s and early 1940s.*

Dorothea Lange; *Migrant Mother*; gelatin silver print; 1936, printed ca. 1960; 13¼ × 10 in.
*The most iconic of all Depression-era photographs, Lange's image of Florence Thompson and her children was shot in a migrant farm worker's camp near Nipomo, in Central California.*

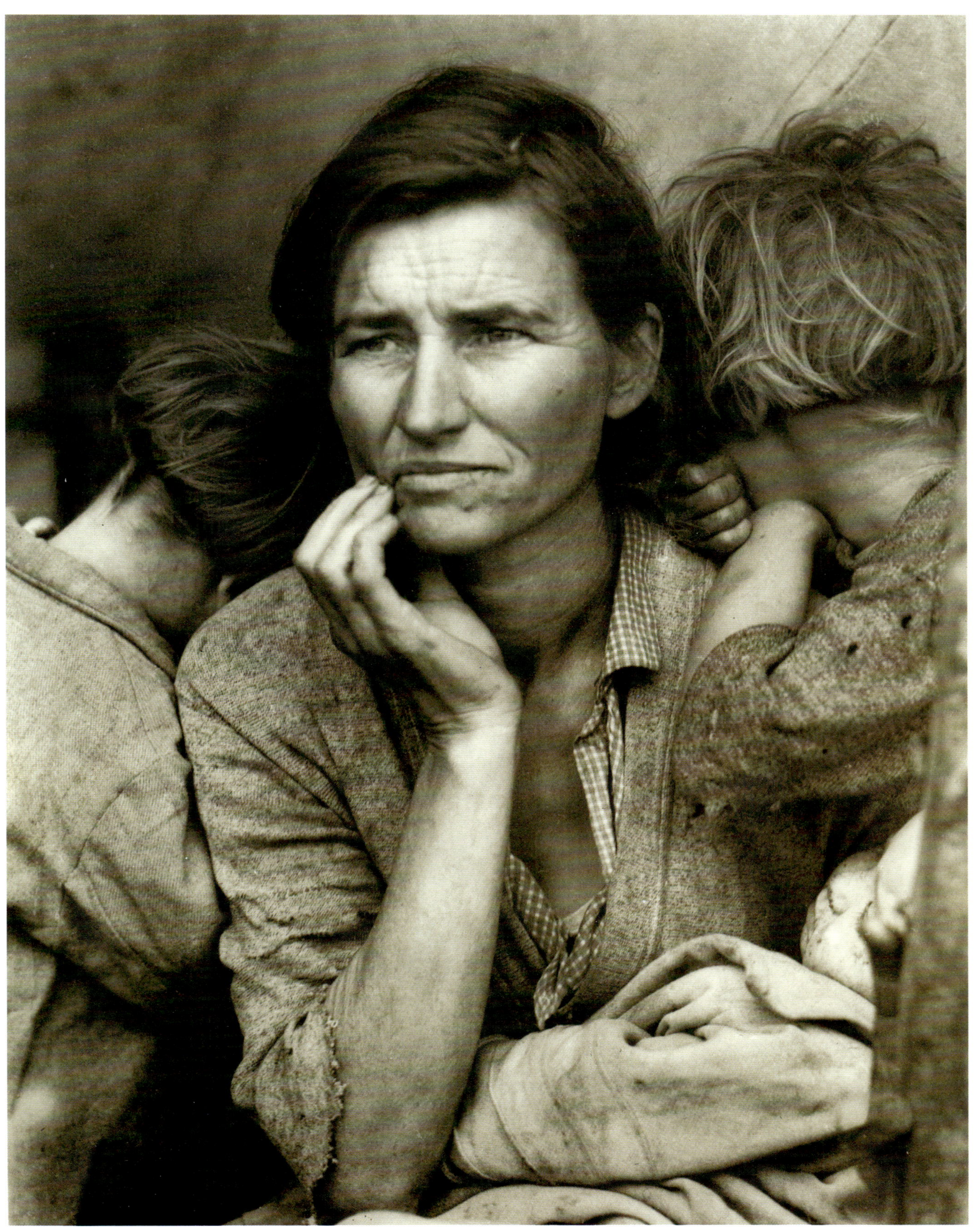

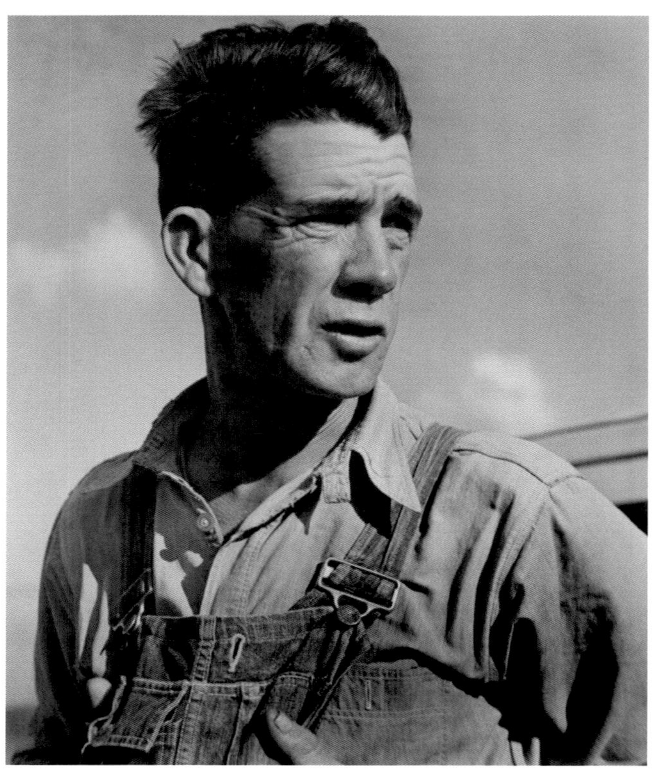

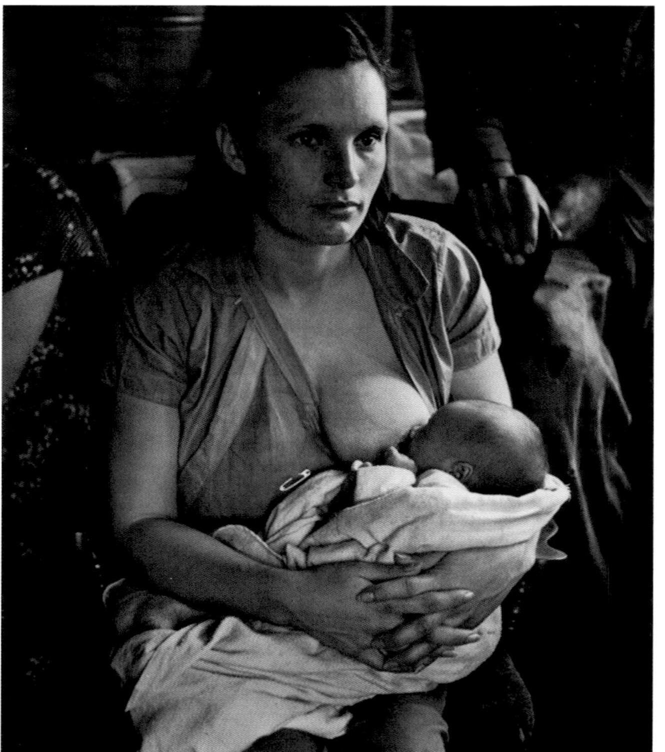

LEFT: Horace Bristol; *Tom Joad* (*Grapes of Wrath* series); gelatin silver print; 1937, printed later; 13⅞ × 11 in.
RIGHT: Horace Bristol; *Rose of Sharon Nursing* (*Grapes of Wrath* series); gelatin silver print; 1937, printed later; 14 × 11 in.
*Bristol invited John Steinbeck to tour the migrant camps with him in 1937 to produce an article for* Life *magazine. After a while, Steinbeck left, deciding to write a novel about the camps:* The Grapes of Wrath. *When the film was made in 1940, Bristol's photos were used as guides. In turn, Bristol applied the names of Steinbeck's characters to the people he had photographed in 1937.*

OPPOSITE: Dorothea Lange; *White Angel Breadline, San Francisco*; gelatin silver print; 1934, printed 1970s; 13¼ × 10v⅛ in.
*This iconic image showing Depression-era homelessness in San Francisco started Lange's transformation from studio photographer to documentary historian.*

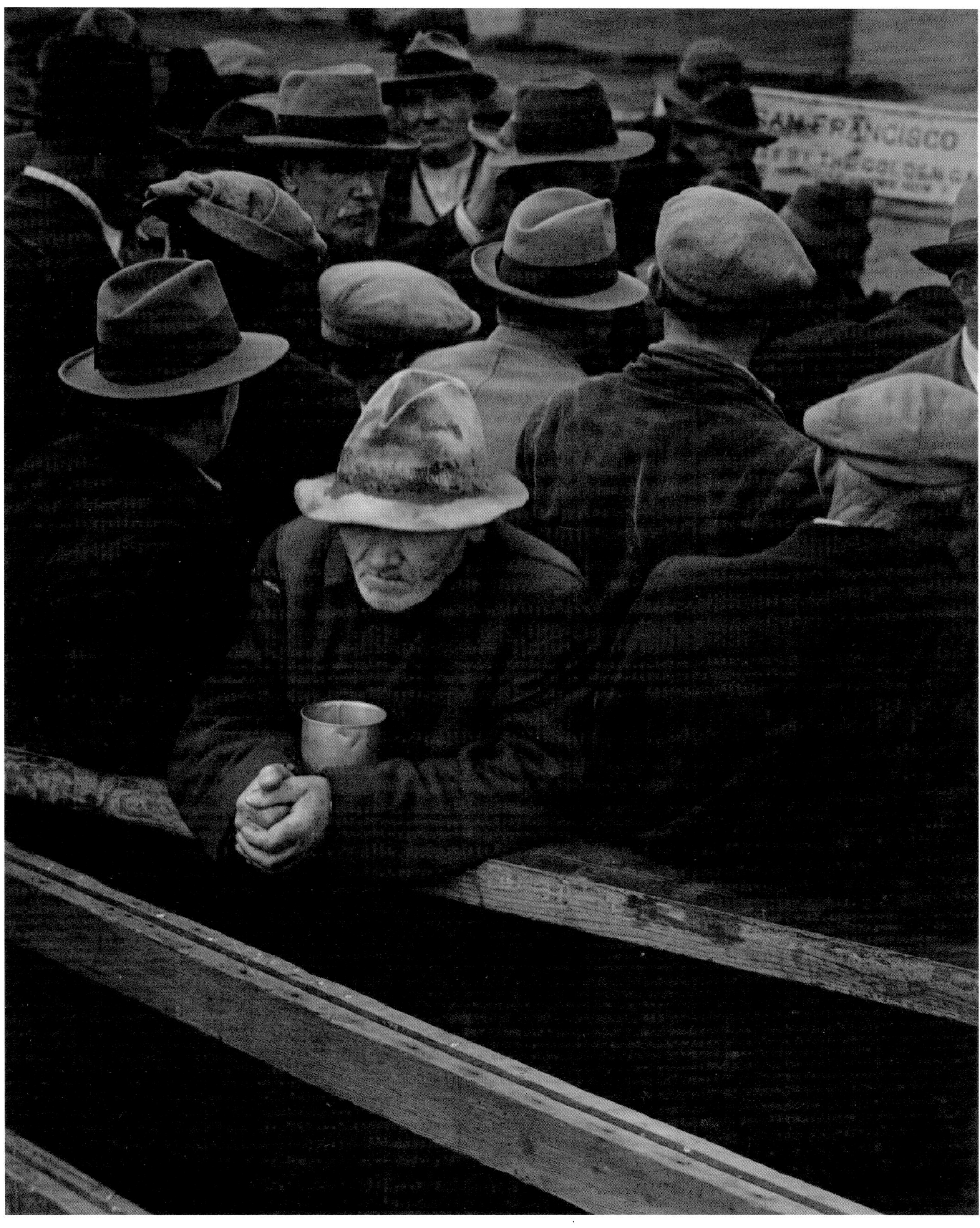

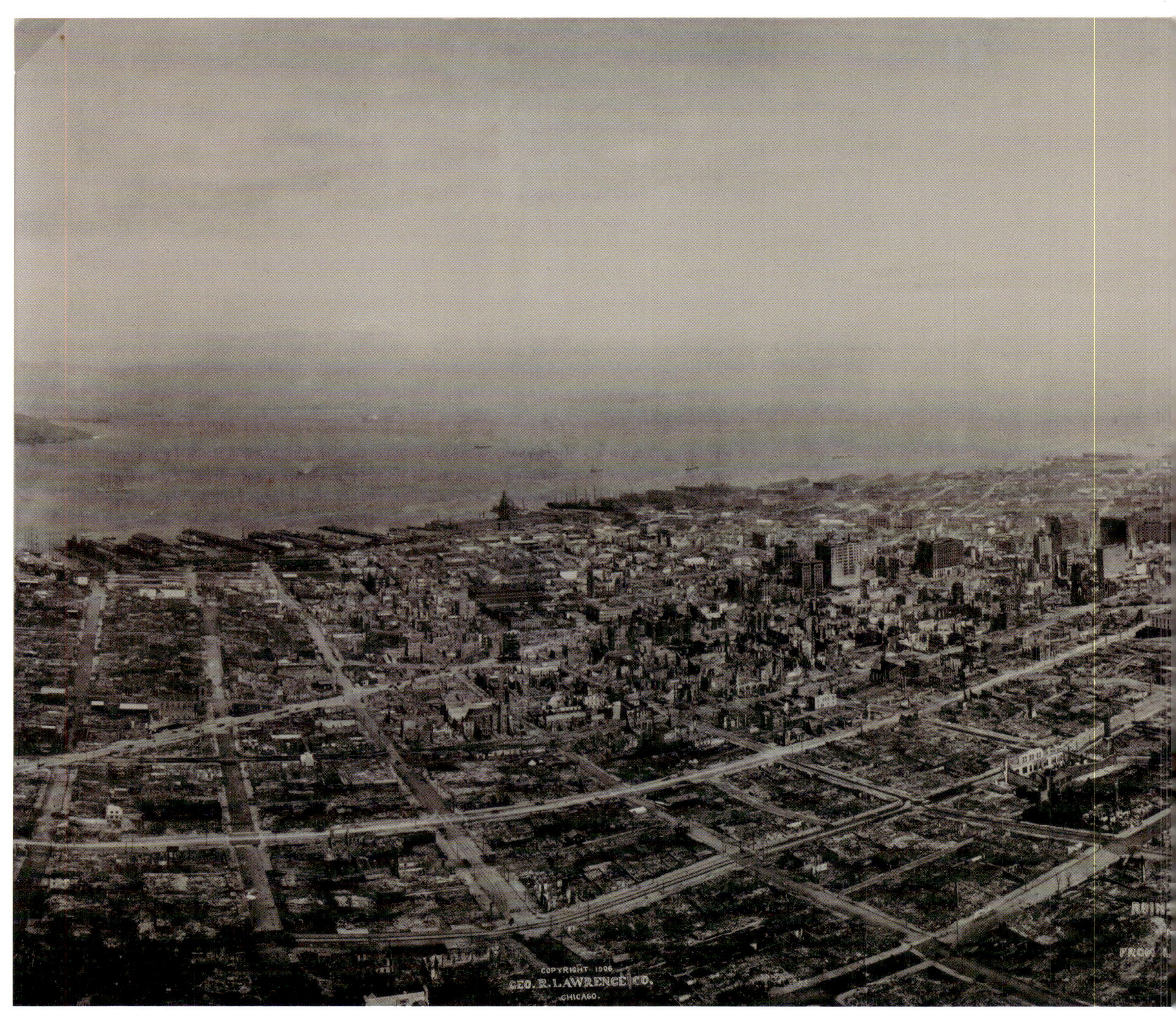
COPYRIGHT 1906
GEO. R. LAWRENCE CO.
CHICAGO.

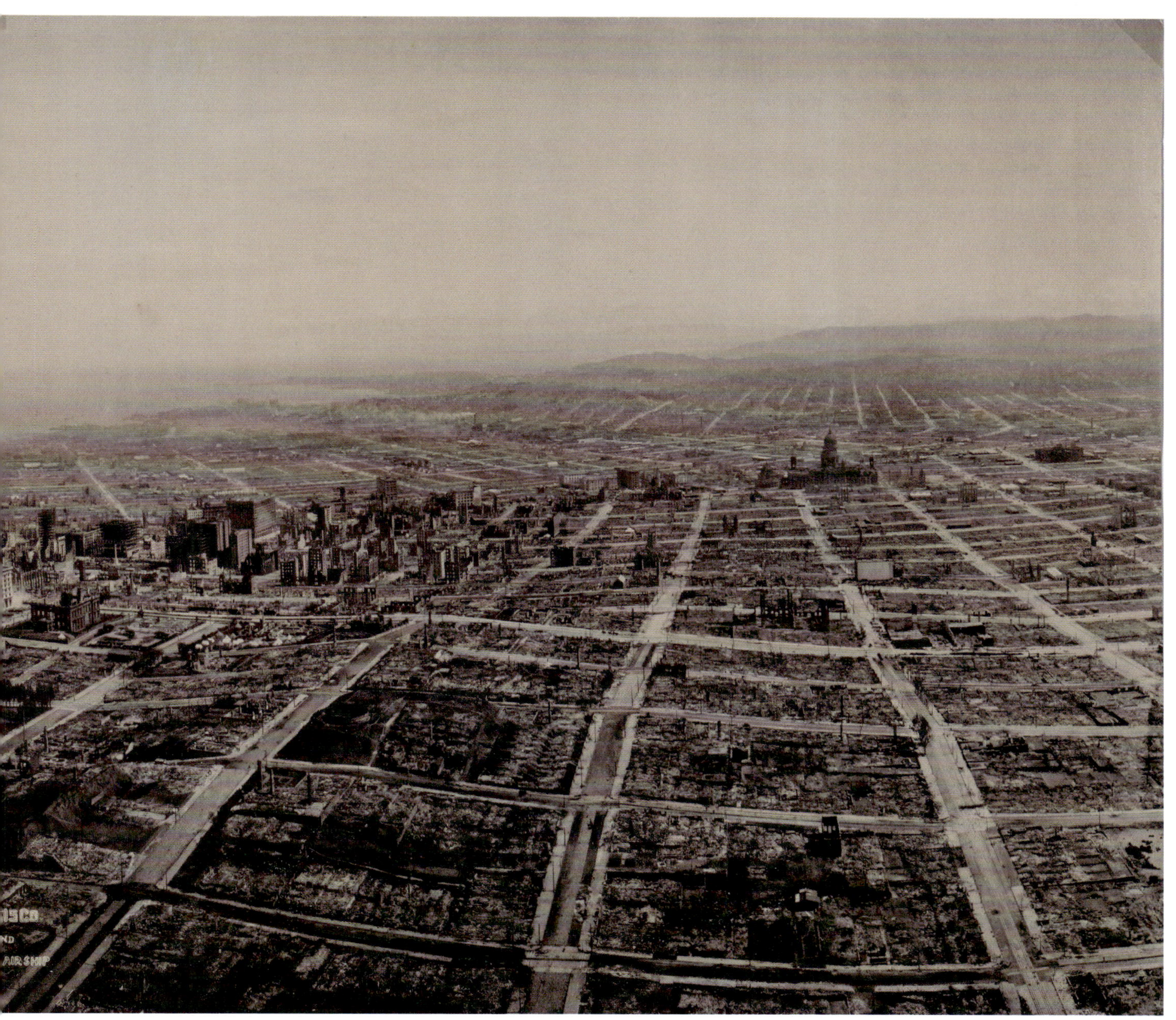

George R. Lawrence; *Ruins of San Francisco*; gelatin silver print; May 29, 1906; 15 × 36¾ in.
*Lawrence made several aerials of the damage in San Francisco using an unmanned balloon. Nob Hill is in the foreground.*

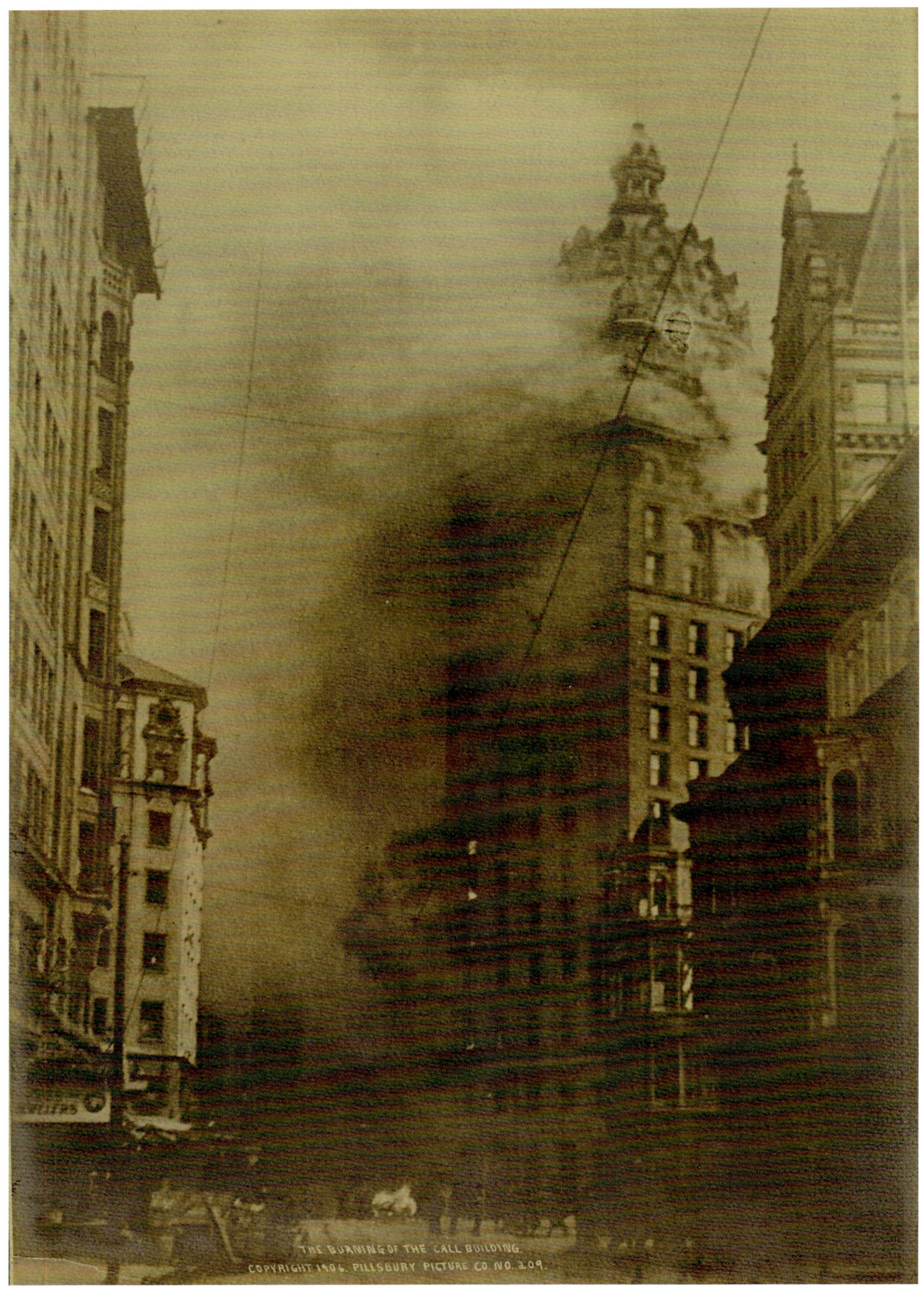
THE BURNING OF THE CALL BUILDING.
COPYRIGHT 1906. PILLSBURY PICTURE CO. NO. 209.

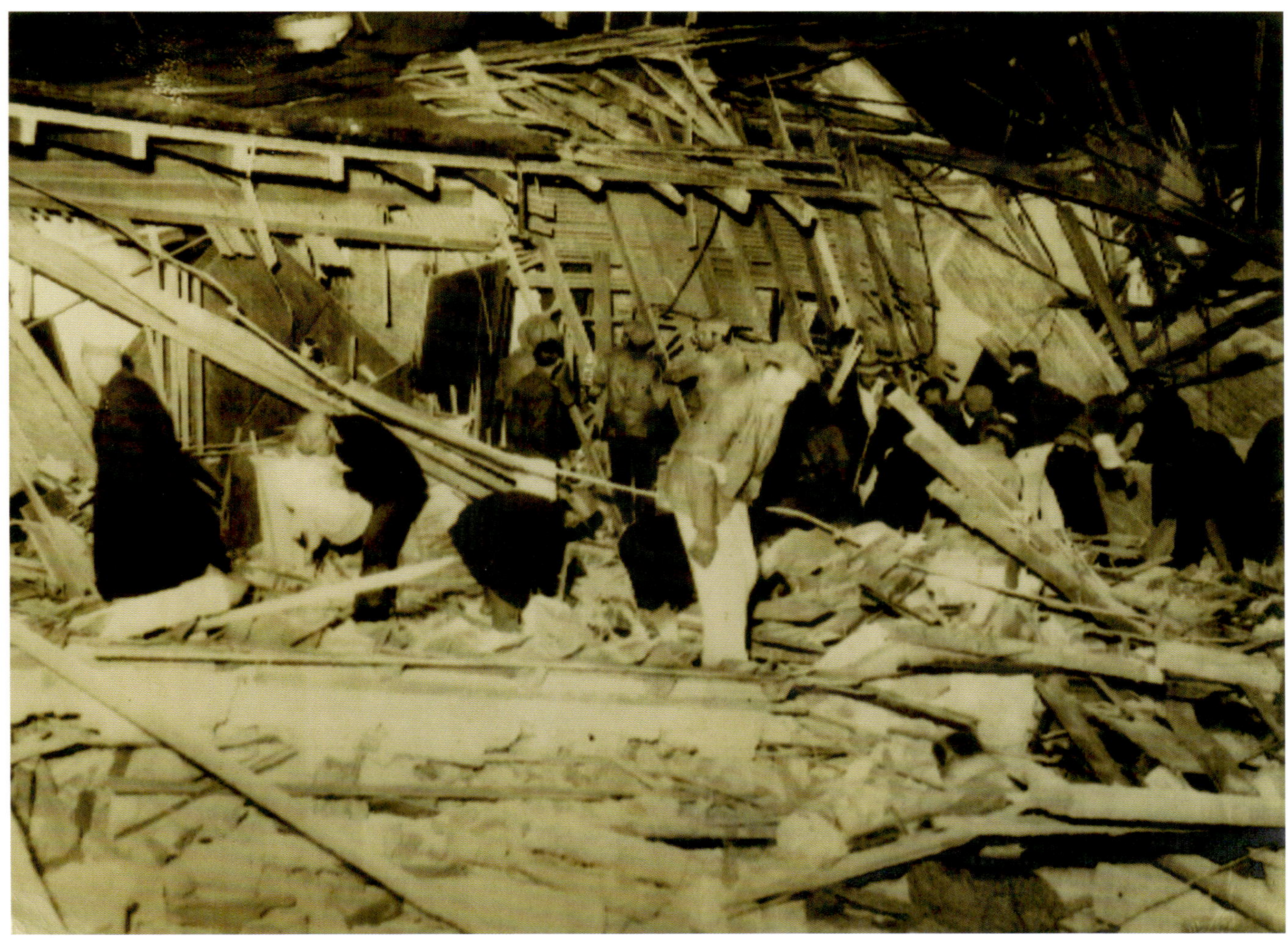

International News Photos; Searching Ruins for Victims of Southern California Earthquake; gelatin silver print; 1933; 6 × 8 in.
*Known as the Long Beach Earthquake, the temblor registered 6.4 magnitude and caused widespread damage, with estimates of fatalities as high as 120 people.*

OPPOSITE: Pillsbury Picture Company; *Burning of the Call Building, San Francisco Earthquake*; gelatin silver print; 1906; 13 × 9 in.
*The greatest destruction came not from the San Francisco Earthquake, but from the fires that followed. Some 500 blocks were leveled and 28,000 buildings destroyed.*

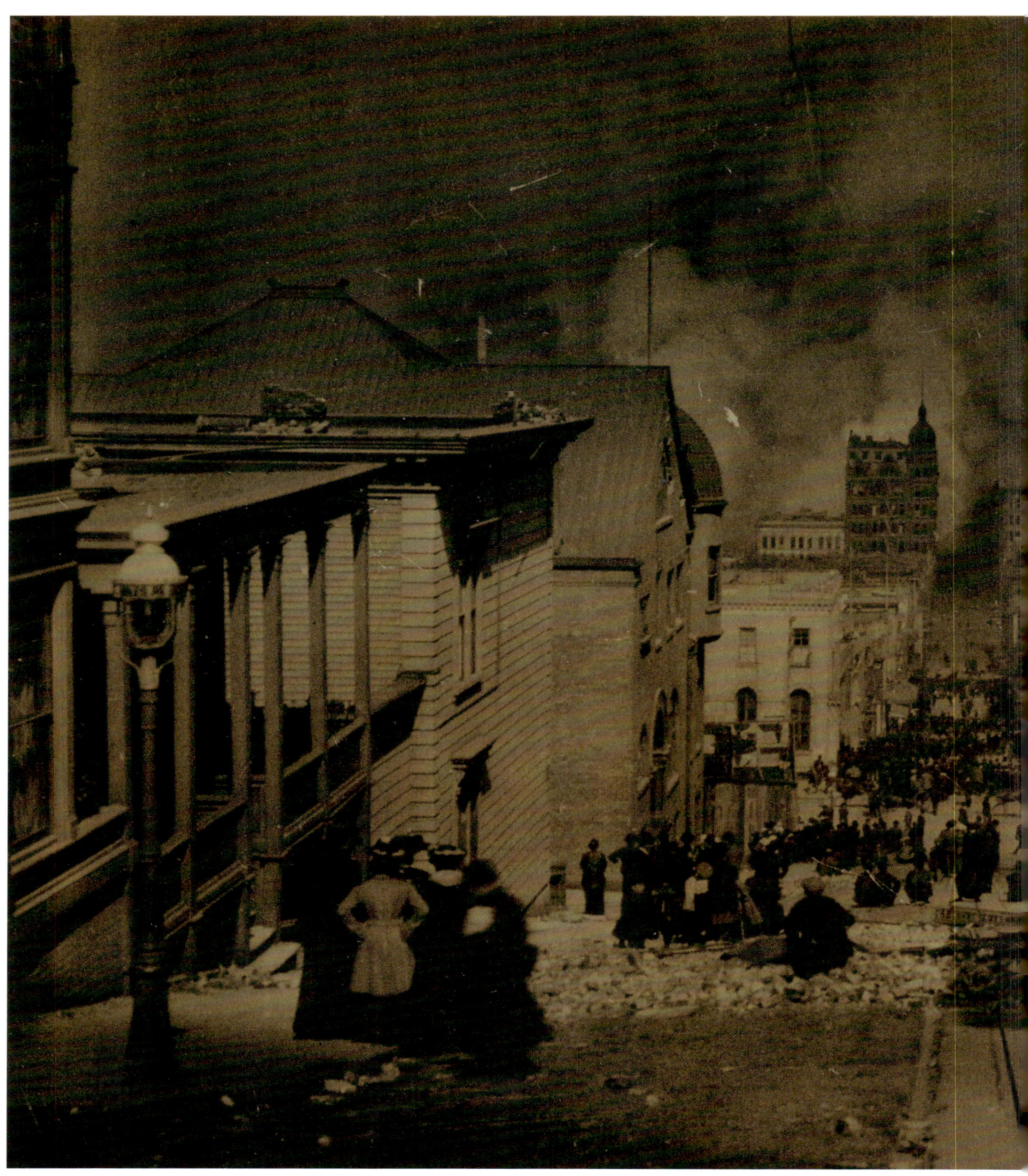

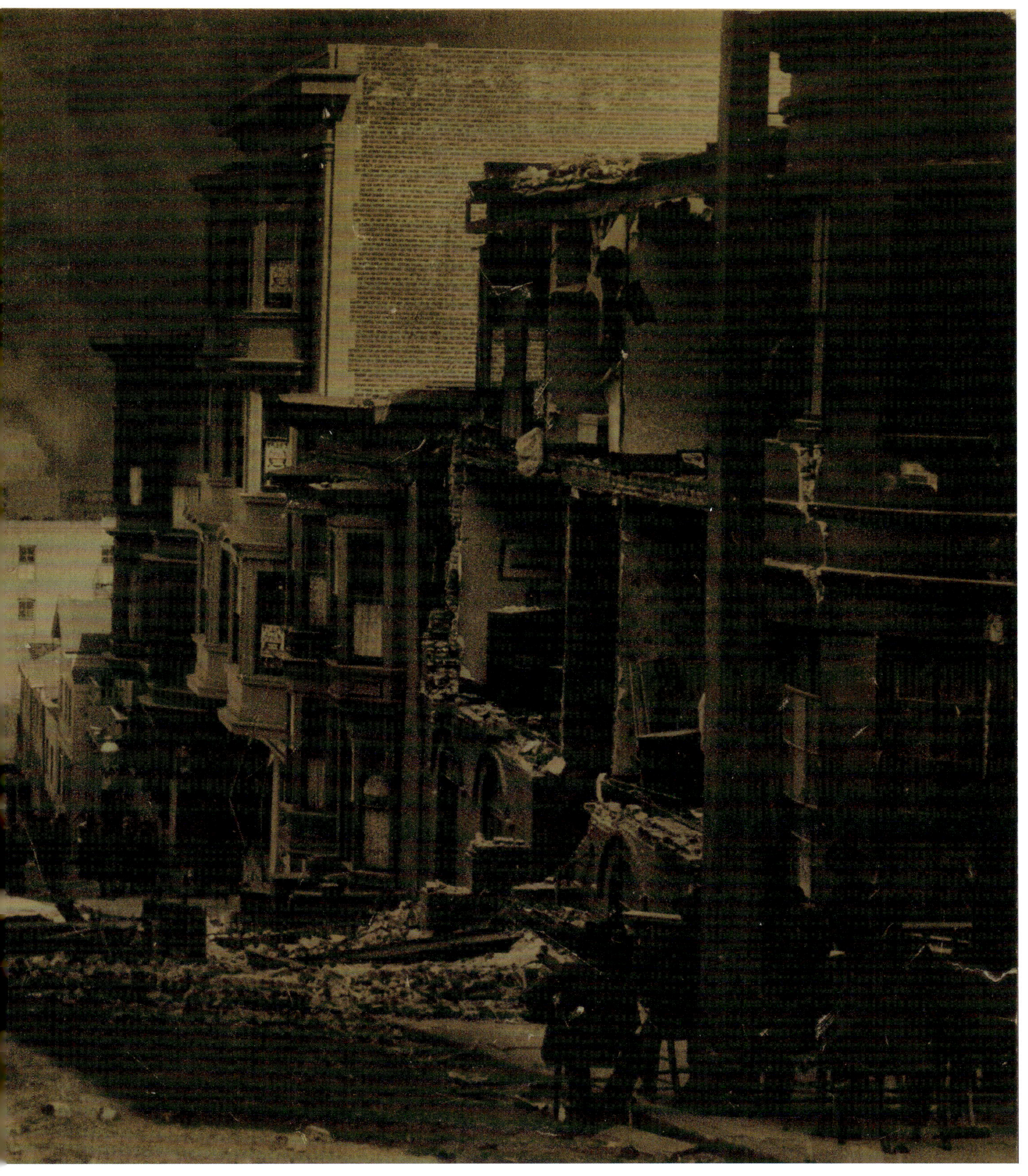

Arnold Genthe; *San Francisco Earthquake, April 18, 1906 (9 am)*; gelatin silver print; April 18, 1906; 6¾ × 12 in.
*After Genthe's studio was destroyed in the earthquake, he ran down the street to the camera store where he purchased supplies, borrowed a camera, and recorded this classic image, in addition to others.*

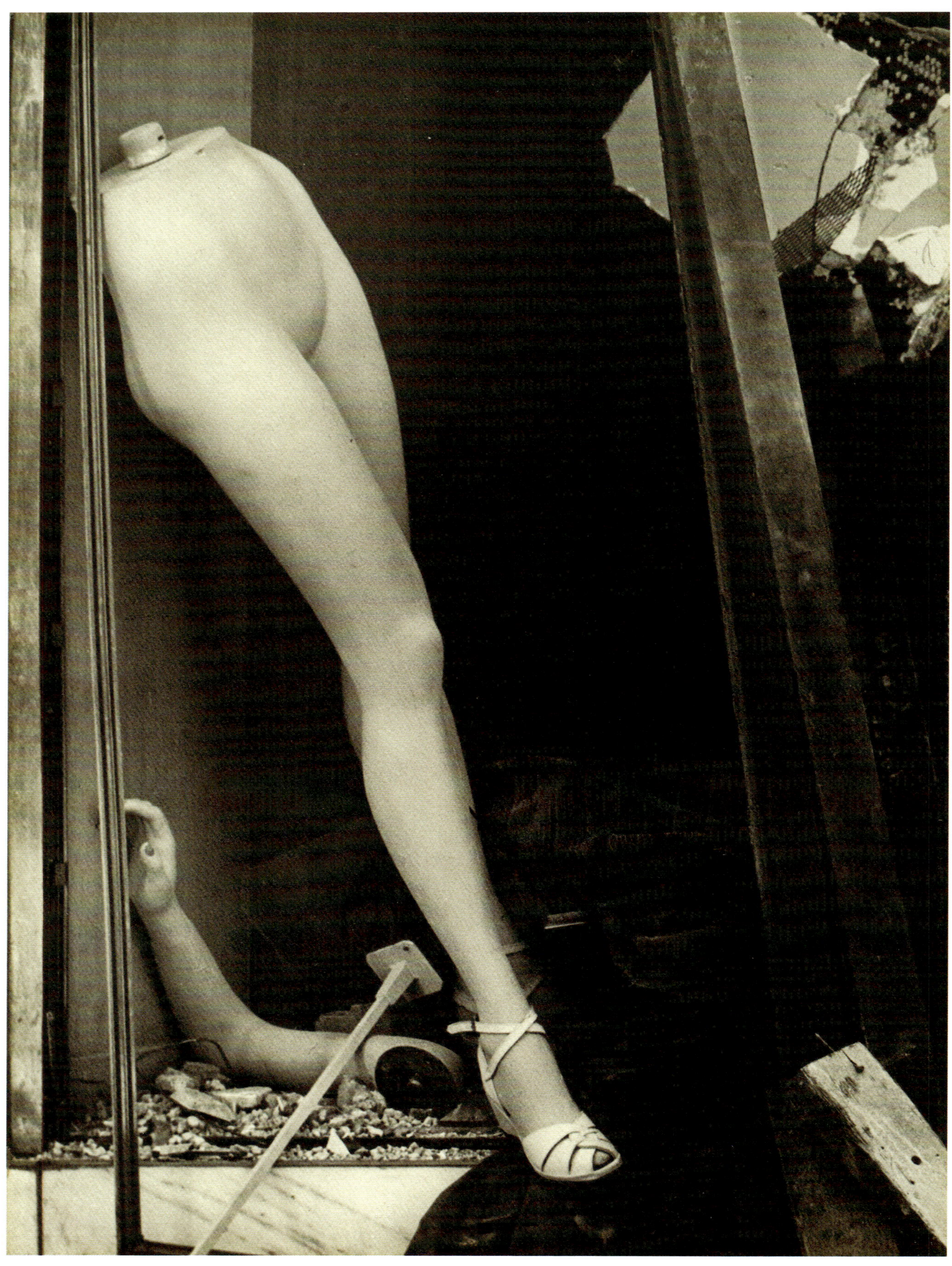

B.G. Stuart; *The Shake Down*; gelatin silver print; 1953; 13½ × 10 in.
*This quake was centered near Tehachapi with a 7.5 magnitude, almost as great as the San Francisco Earthquake of 1906, but in an area with much less population density.*

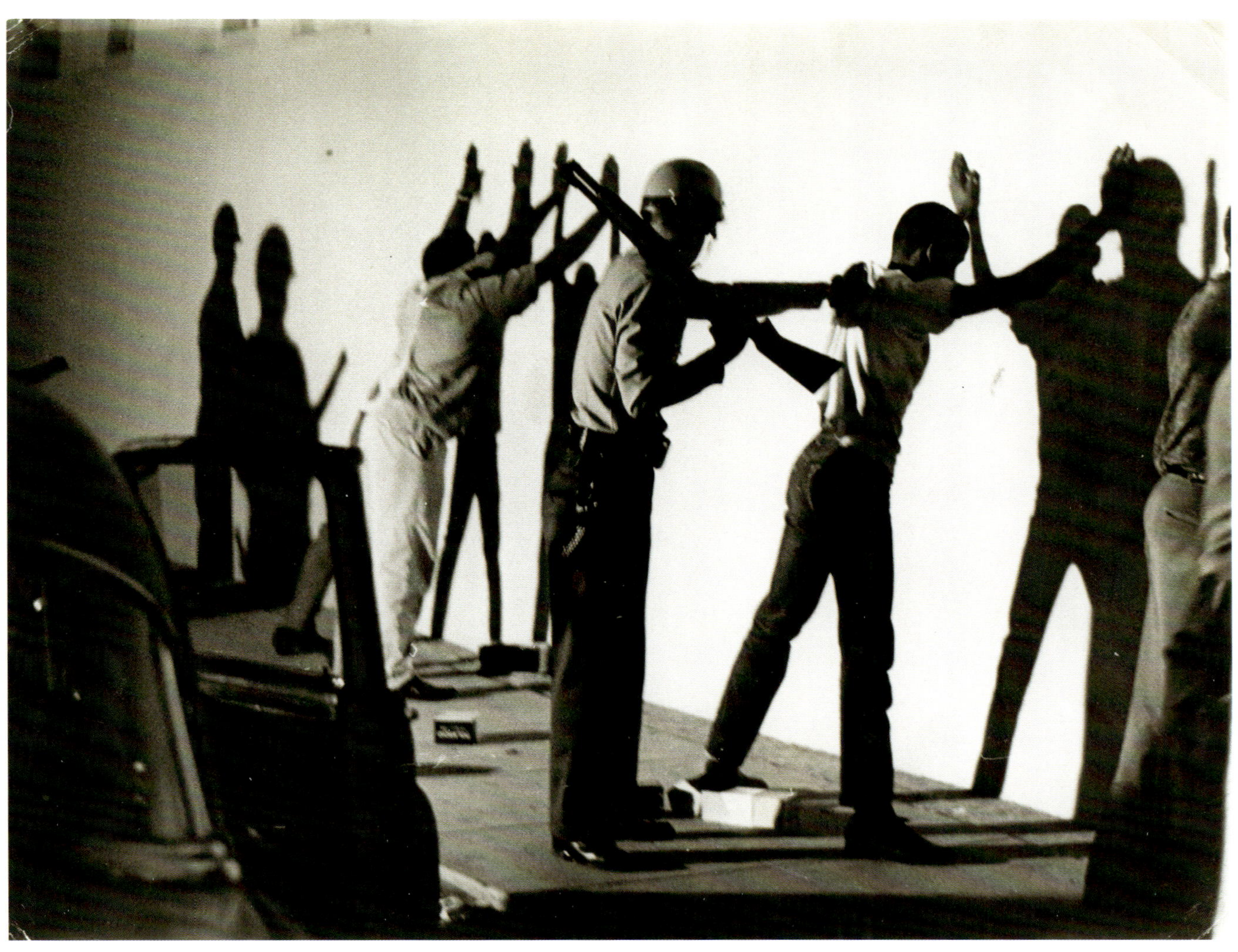

Bud Gray; *Watts Riots, Los Angeles Police Frisk Subjects*; gelatin silver print; 1965; 11 × 14 in.
*Clayton "Bud" Gray worked as a photographer for the* Los Angeles Herald Examiner. *Another of his photographs on the insurrection is in the National Gallery of Art in Washington DC.*

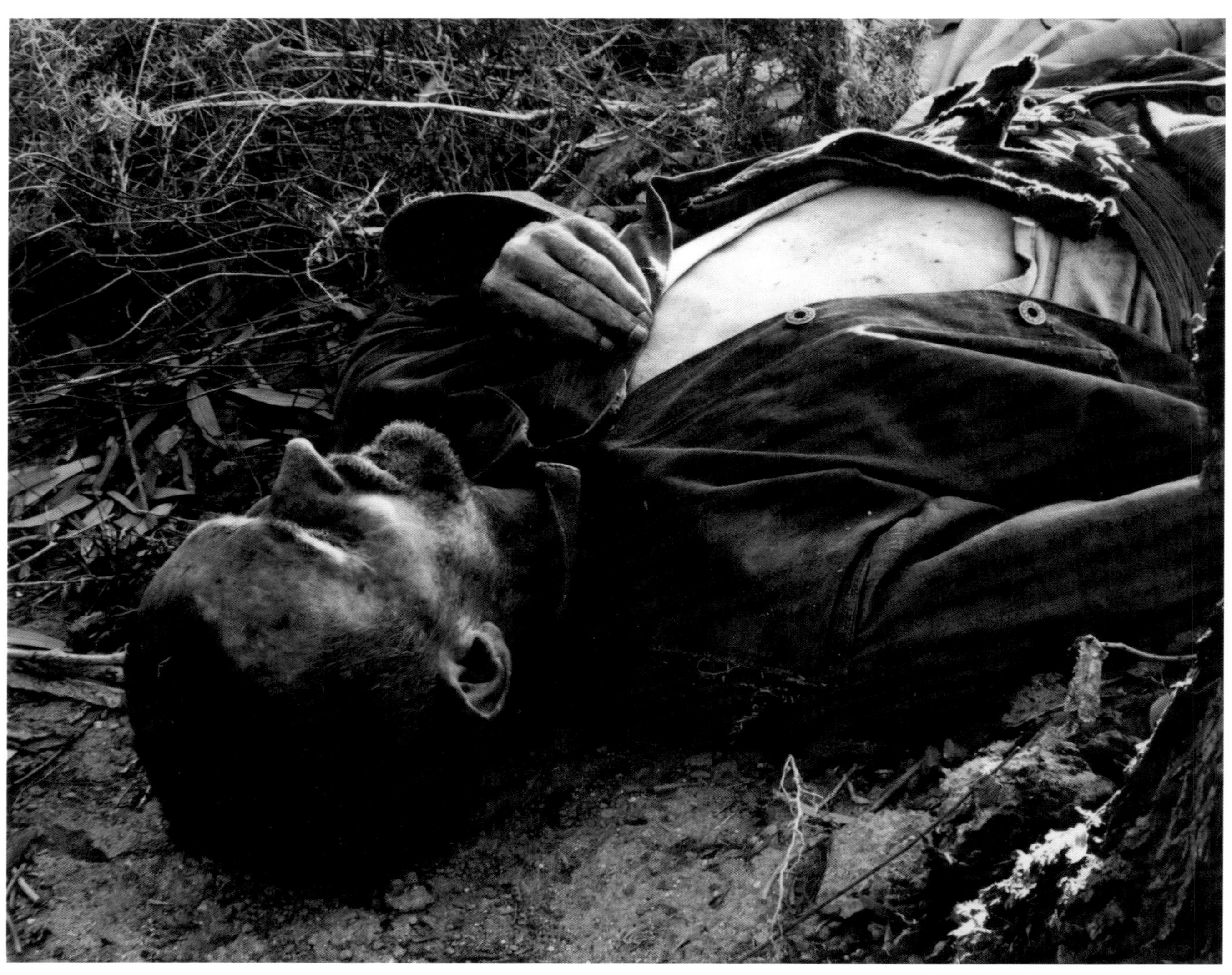

Edward Weston; *Dead Man in Colorado Desert*; gelatin silver print; 1938; 7¾ × 9½ in.
*California's Colorado Desert is a part of the larger Sonora Desert, which encompasses Imperial County, and parts of San Diego, Riverside, and San Bernardino Counties.*

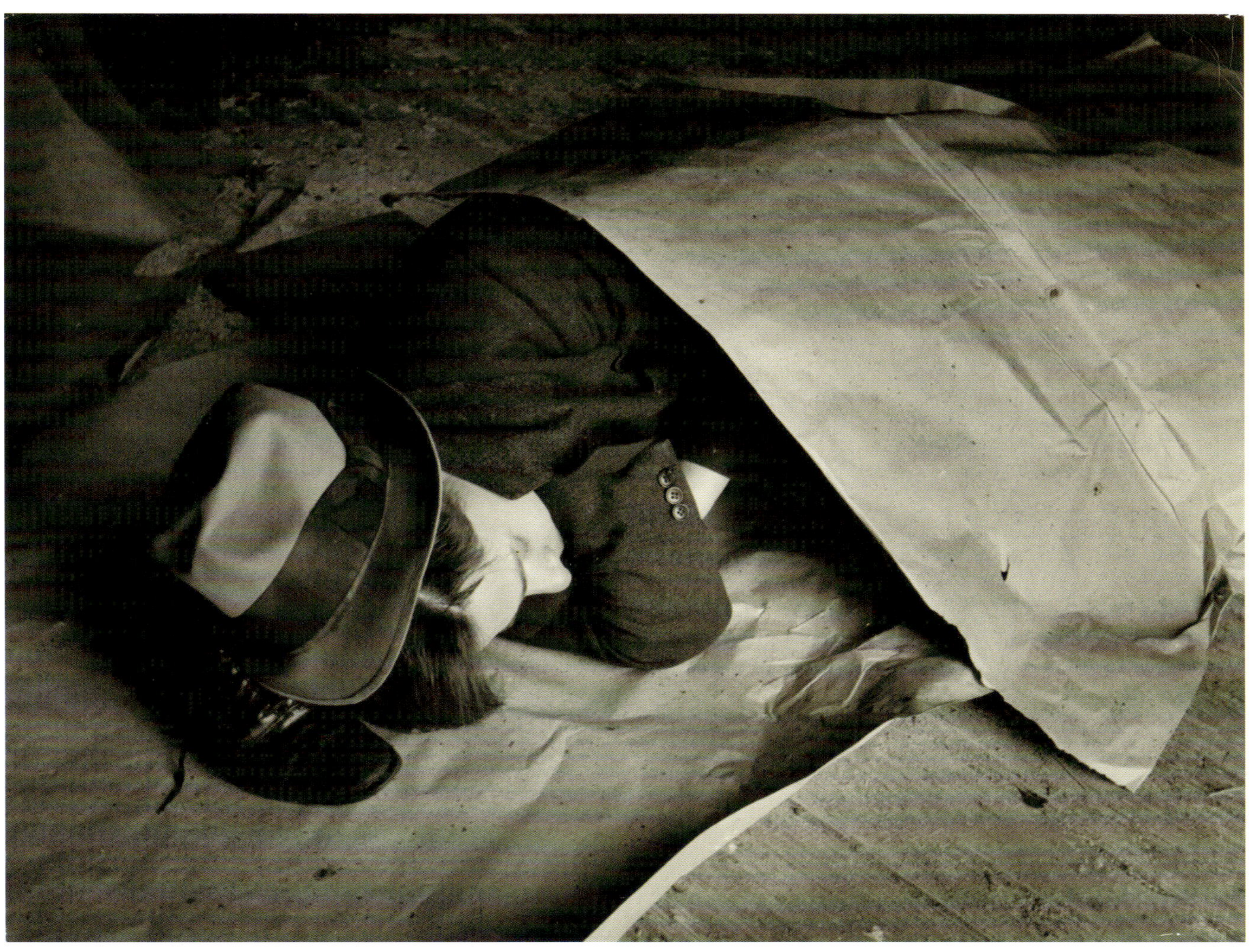

Hansel Mieth; *On the Road to Nowhere, California*; gelatin silver print; 1936, printed ca. 1950; 10 × 12¾ in.
*Mieth, who was married to photographer Otto Hagel, photographed the downtrodden during the Depression in the 1930s, and later photographed Japanese American internees at Heart Mountain, Wyoming.*

Boris Yaro; *Senator Kennedy Lay on the Floor as He Awaited Medical Help for Wounds*; gelatin silver print; 1968; 8⅜ × 7 in.
*Yaro was a staff photographer for the* Los Angeles Times *who attended the Kennedy event that evening, hoping to get a personal photograph. This iconic photograph captured the historic assassination.*

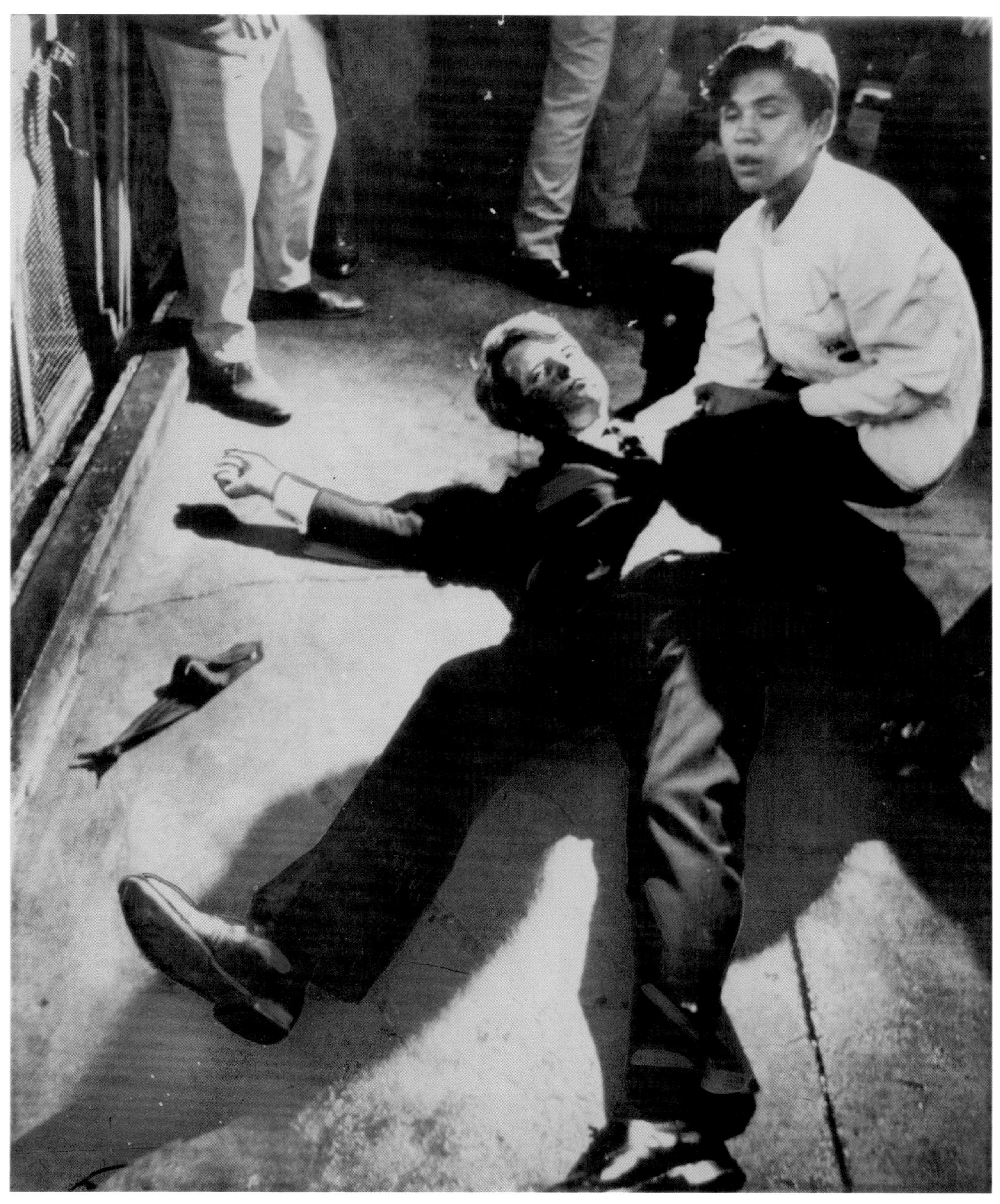

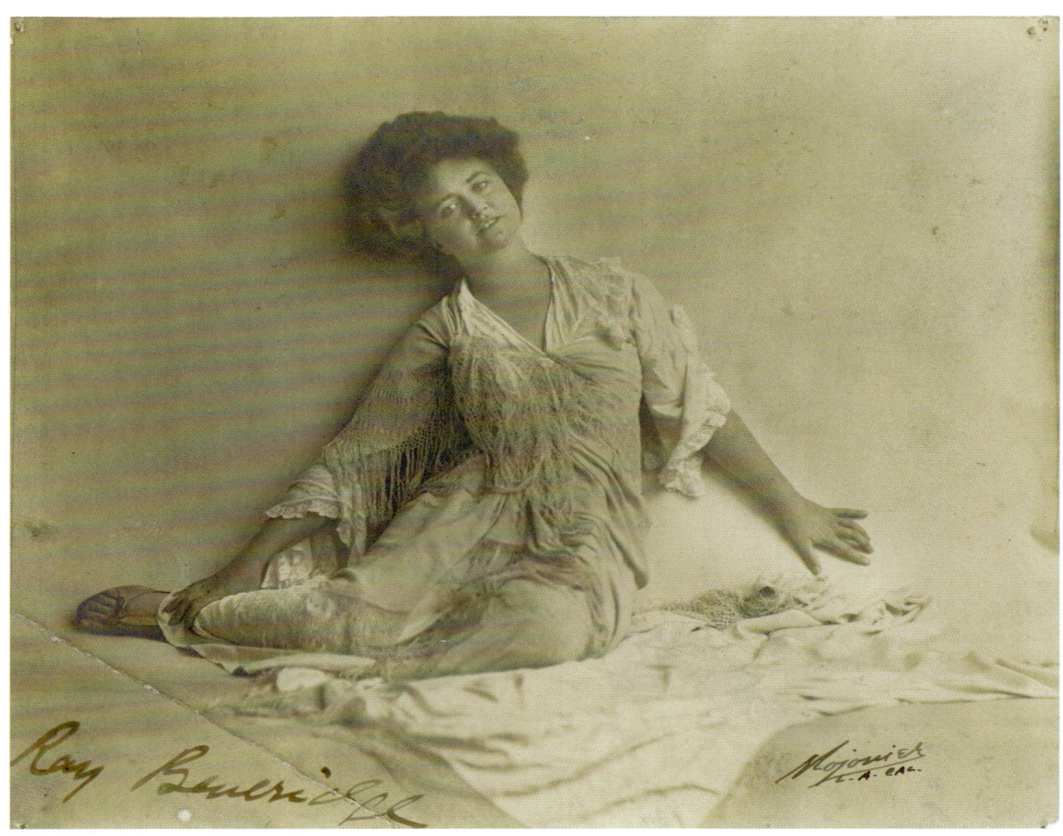


Mojoiner Studio; *Ray Beveridge*; gelatin silver print or platinum print; ca. 1910; 4½ × 5½ in.
*Beveridge, an actress who later became an outspoken racist, lived in Germany, and became an early supporter of Hitler. At the time this image was made, photographer Edward Weston worked for the Mojoiner Studio in Los Angeles. This unorthodox presentation was more characteristic of Weston than a studio photographer.*

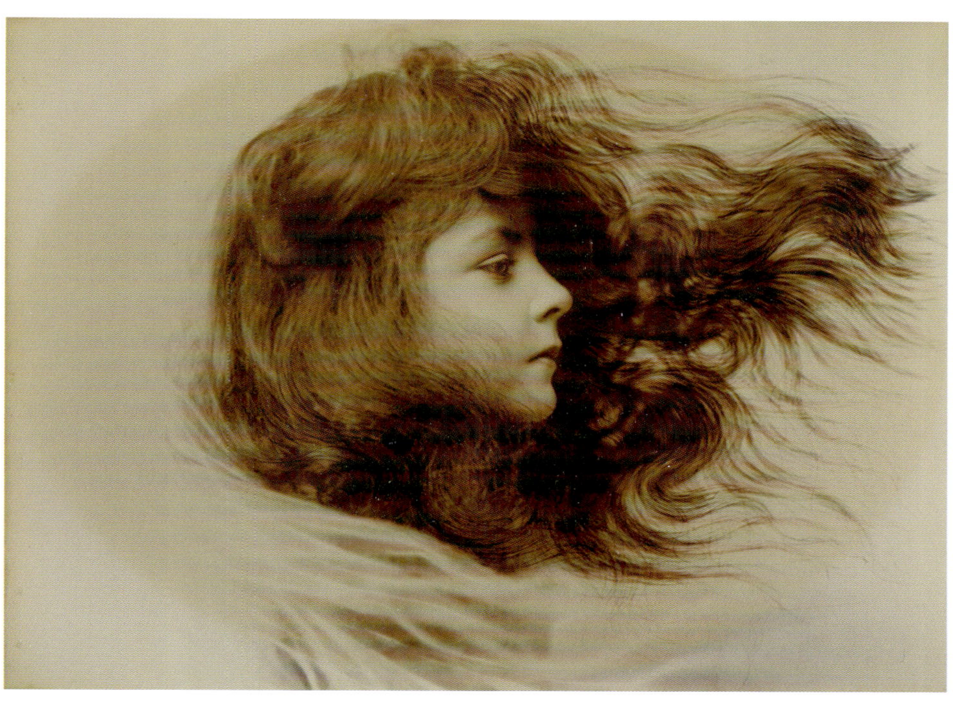

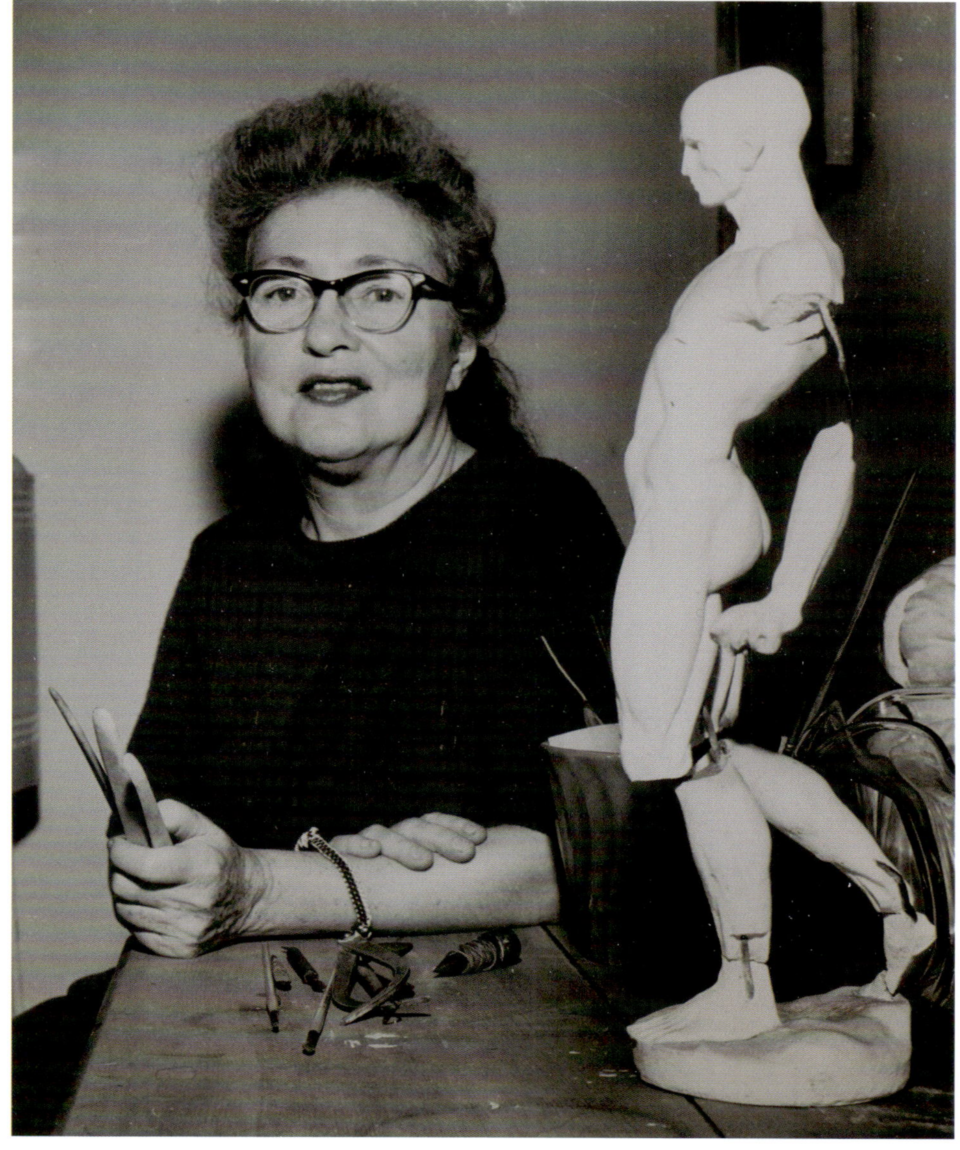

TOP: Unknown Artist; Untitled (Evelyn Nesbit as a teenager); toned silver print; ca. 1900, printed ca. 1930; 12 × 16 in.

RIGHT: Unknown Artist; *Evelyn Nesbit at 70*; gelatin silver print; printed ca. 1960; 8⅜ × 6⅞ in.

*This woman who made ceramics also babysat her grandchildren and lived the last years of her life in Los Angeles. At the beginning of the century, she was a starlet known as "The Girl in the Red Velvet Swing," the Marilyn Monroe of her day. She moved to Los Angeles during World War II to teach ceramics and sculpting and to be close to her son, his wife, and her four grandchildren.*

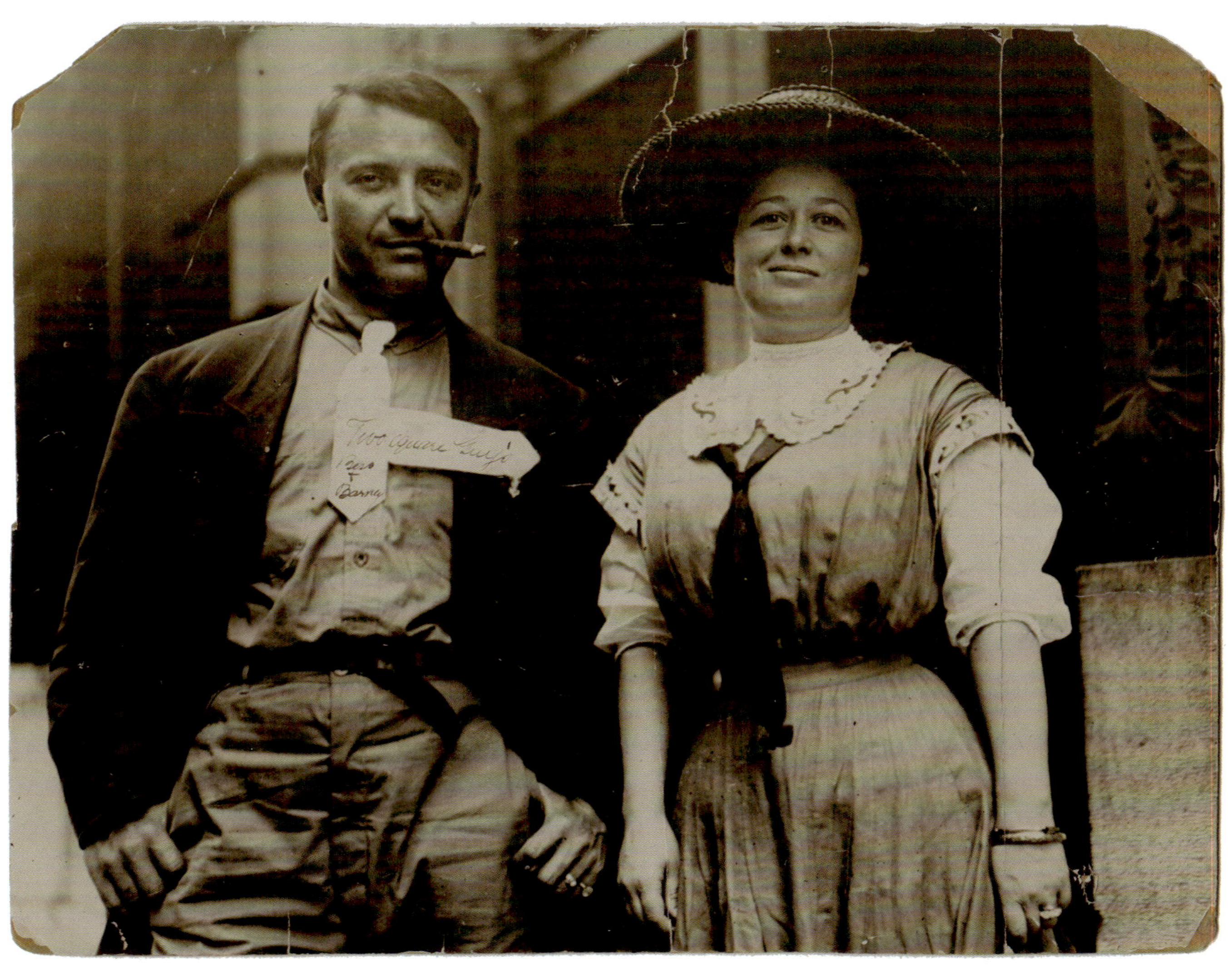


Unknown Artist; *Two Square Guys, Barney and Bess*; gelatin silver print; ca. 1910; $7\frac{7}{8} \times 9\frac{7}{8}$ in.
*Barney Oldfield was a champion race car driver in the early years of the nineteenth century. Legend has it that he loved his wife Bess so much that he married her twice.*

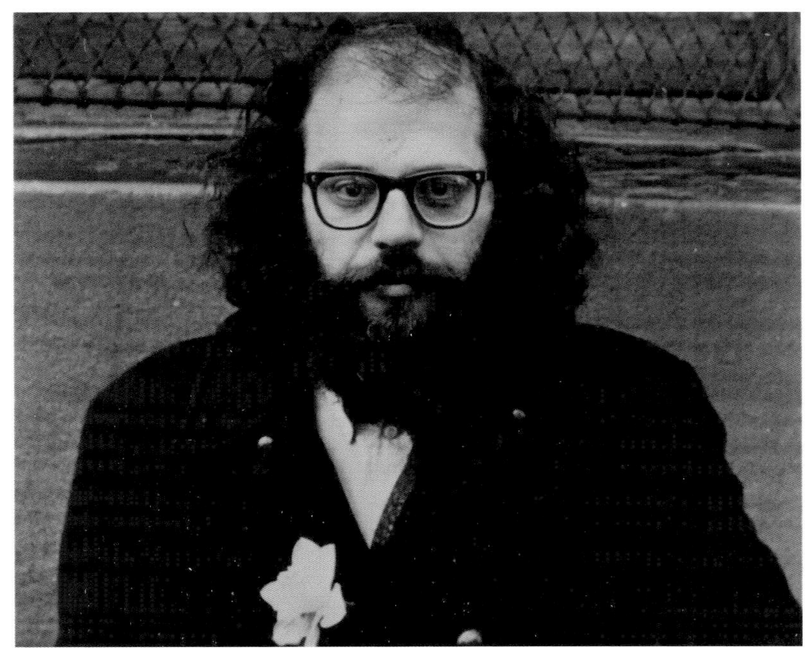

Fred MacDarrah; *Allen Ginsberg at Judson Memorial Church*; gelatin silver print; ca. 1950; 3½ × 4⅛ in.
*Ginsberg, a famous Beat poet, lived in the Bay Area during the 1950s and published his famous poem, "Howl," in 1956.*

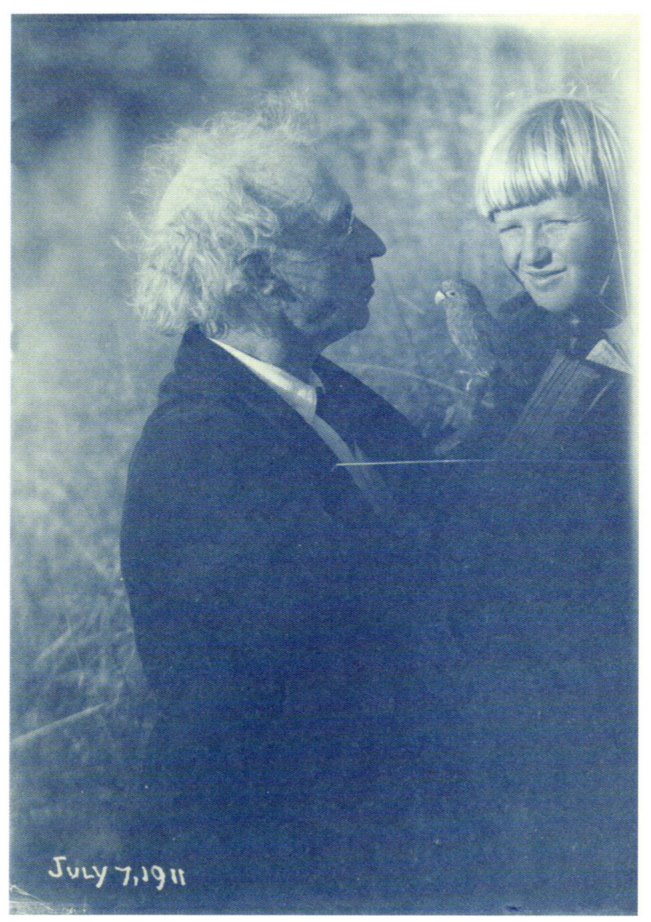


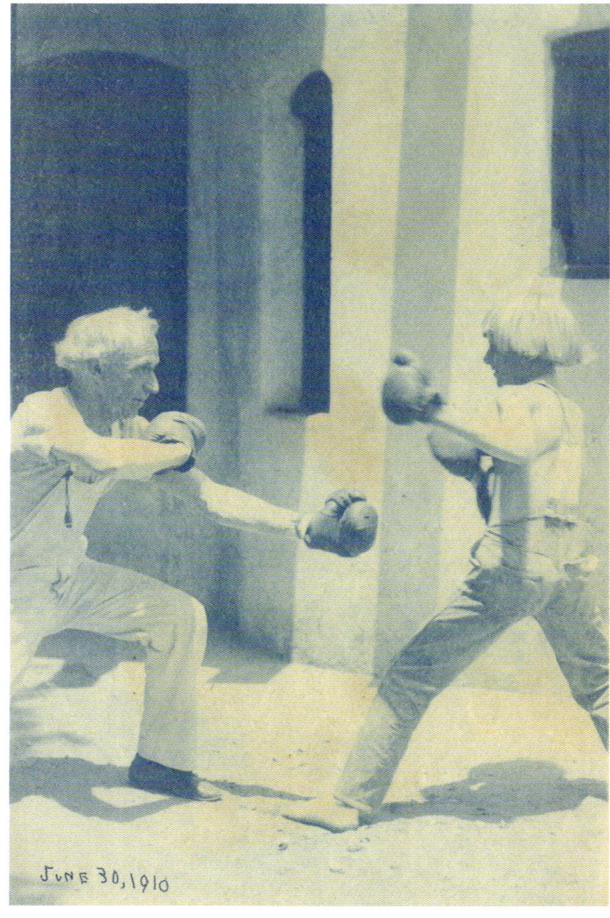


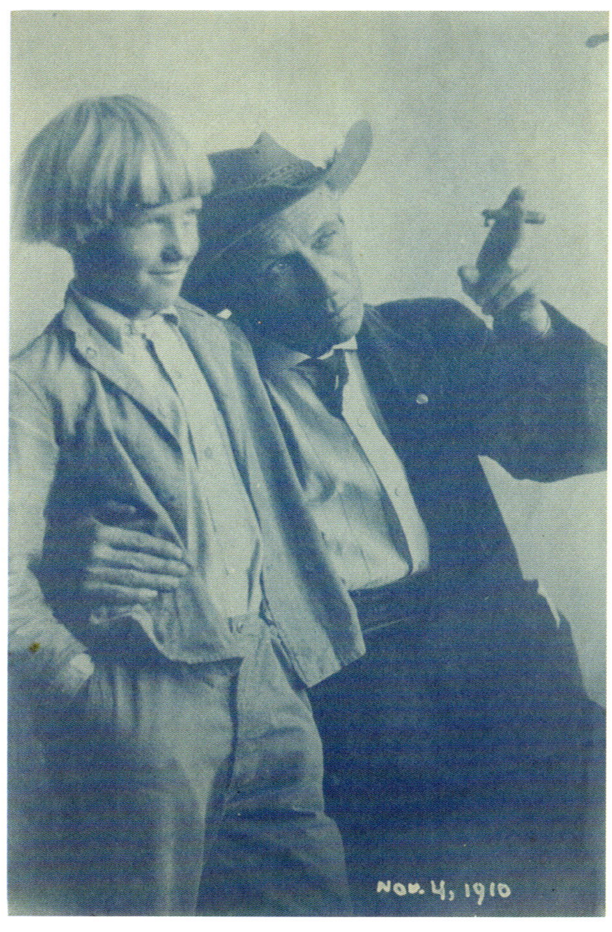


CLOCKWISE FROM TOP LEFT:

Charles Lummis; Untitled (Self Portrait with his son Quimi and a parrot); cyanotype; July 7, 1911; 6¾ × 4½ in.

Charles Lummis; Untitled (Lummis and his son boxing); cyanotype; July 7, 1910; 6¾ × 4½ in.

Charles Lummis; Untitled (Lummis expounding to his son); cyanotype; July 7, 1910; 6¾ × 4½ in.

*A legendary eccentric, Charles Lummis walked from Ohio to California in 1875, was an editor for the* Los Angeles Times, *founded the Southwest Museum, and was head librarian of the Los Angeles Public Library. Most of his photographs are cyanotypes.*

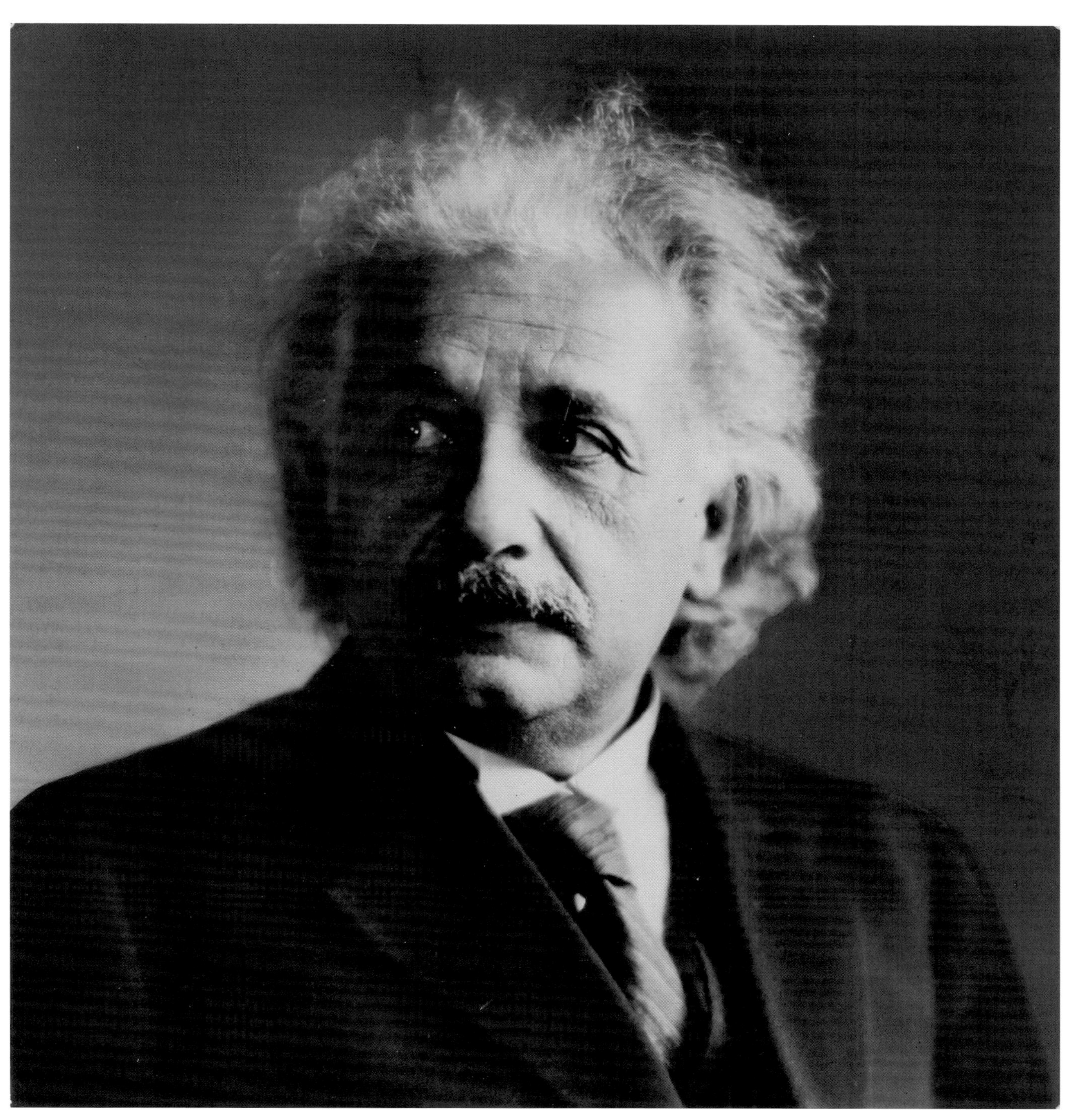

Orrin Turner; *Albert Einstein*; gelatin silver print; September 1932; 7⅞ × 7¼ in.
*Albert Einstein taught at California Institute of Technology in the Pasadena during the winters of 1931, 1932, and 1933.*

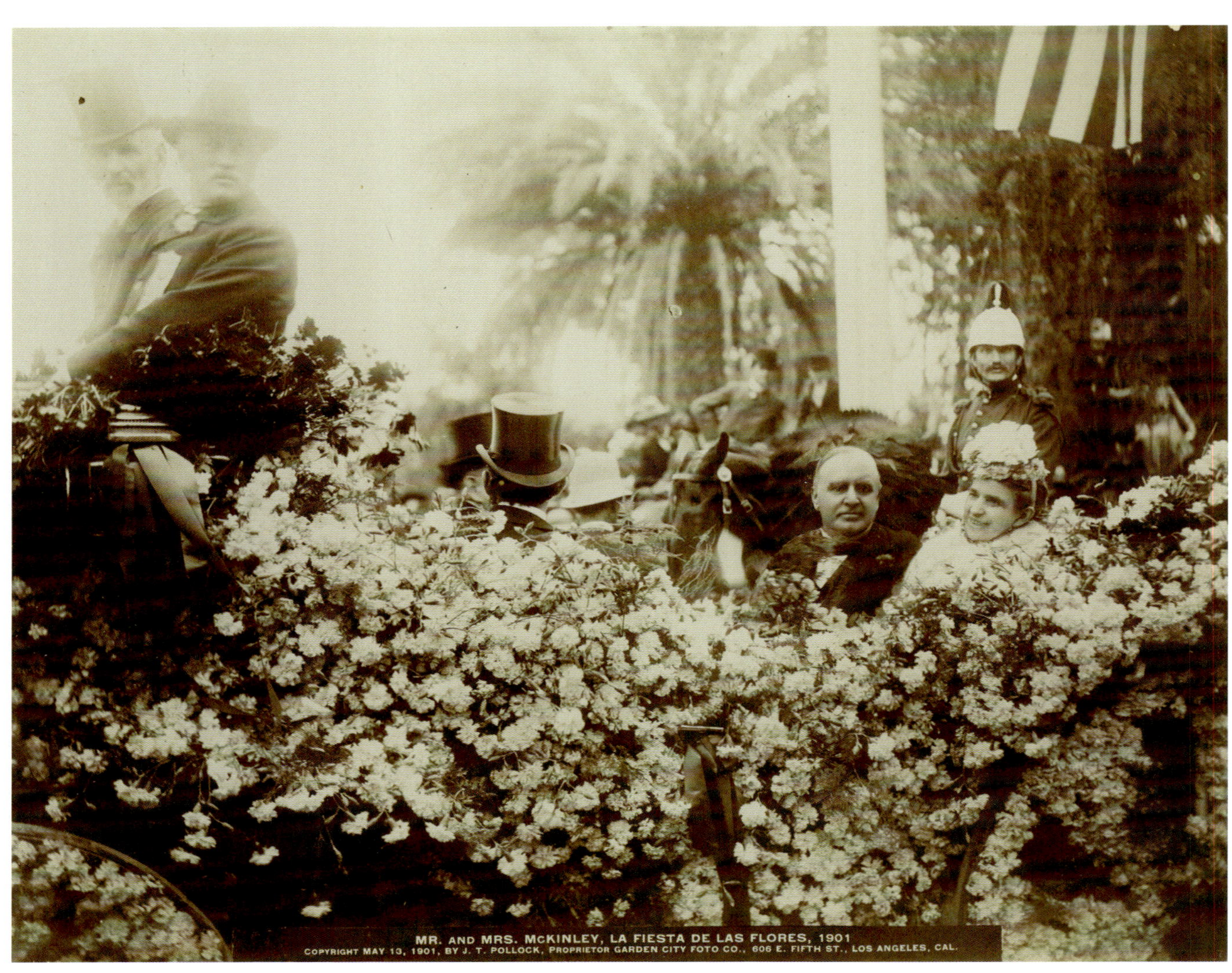


Garden City Foto Co. (James Pollock); *President and Mrs. McKinley at La Fiesta de Las Flores in Los Angeles*; aristotype print; 1901; 10¾ × 13½ in.
*McKinley visited Los Angeles in May 1901 and was assassinated the following September at the Pan-American Exposition in Buffalo, New York.*

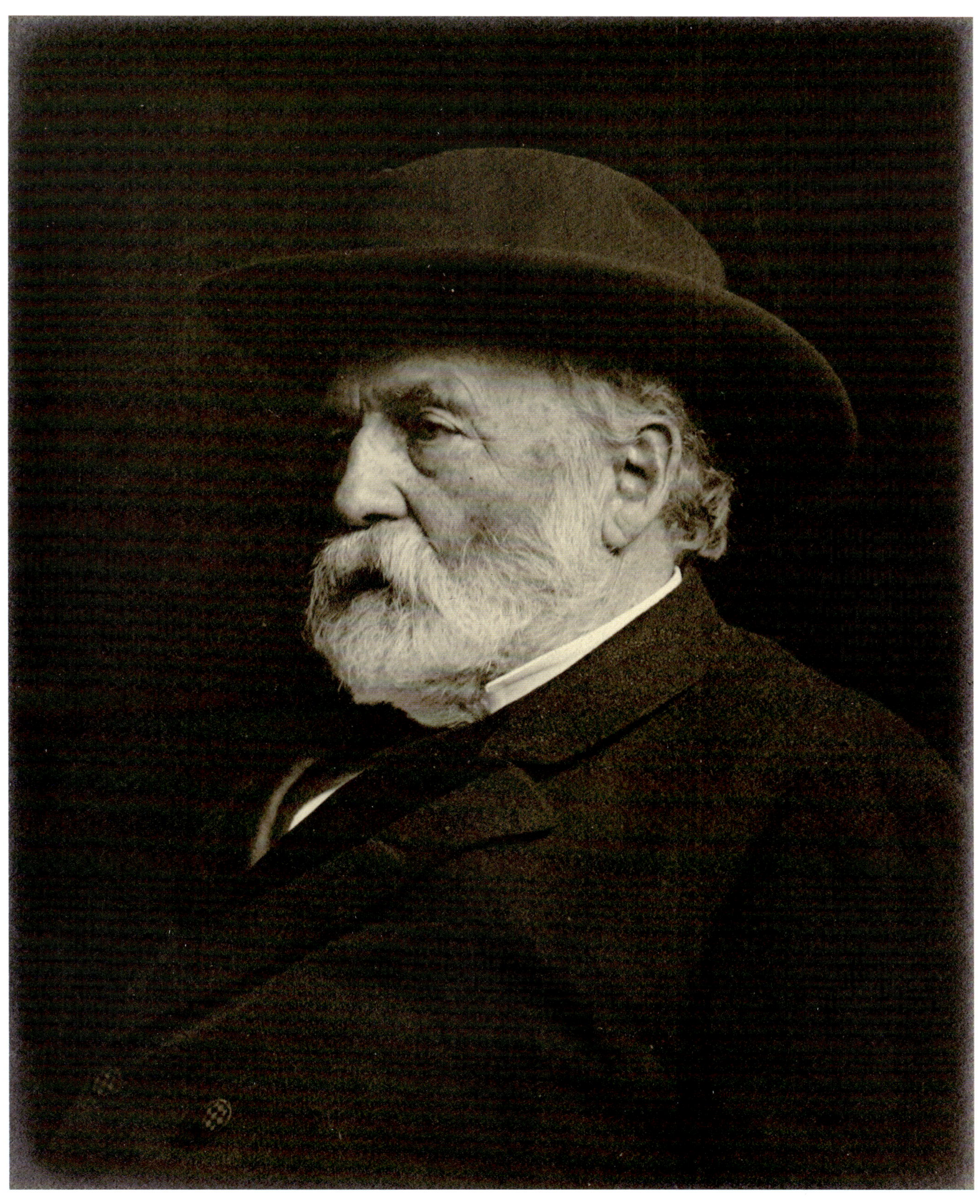

William Keith; *Collis Huntington*; gelatin silver print; ca. 1900; 9½ × 7½ in.
*Known primarily as a painter of large landscapes, Keith made some photographic portraits. Another copy of this photograph is in the National Portrait Gallery in Washington DC.*

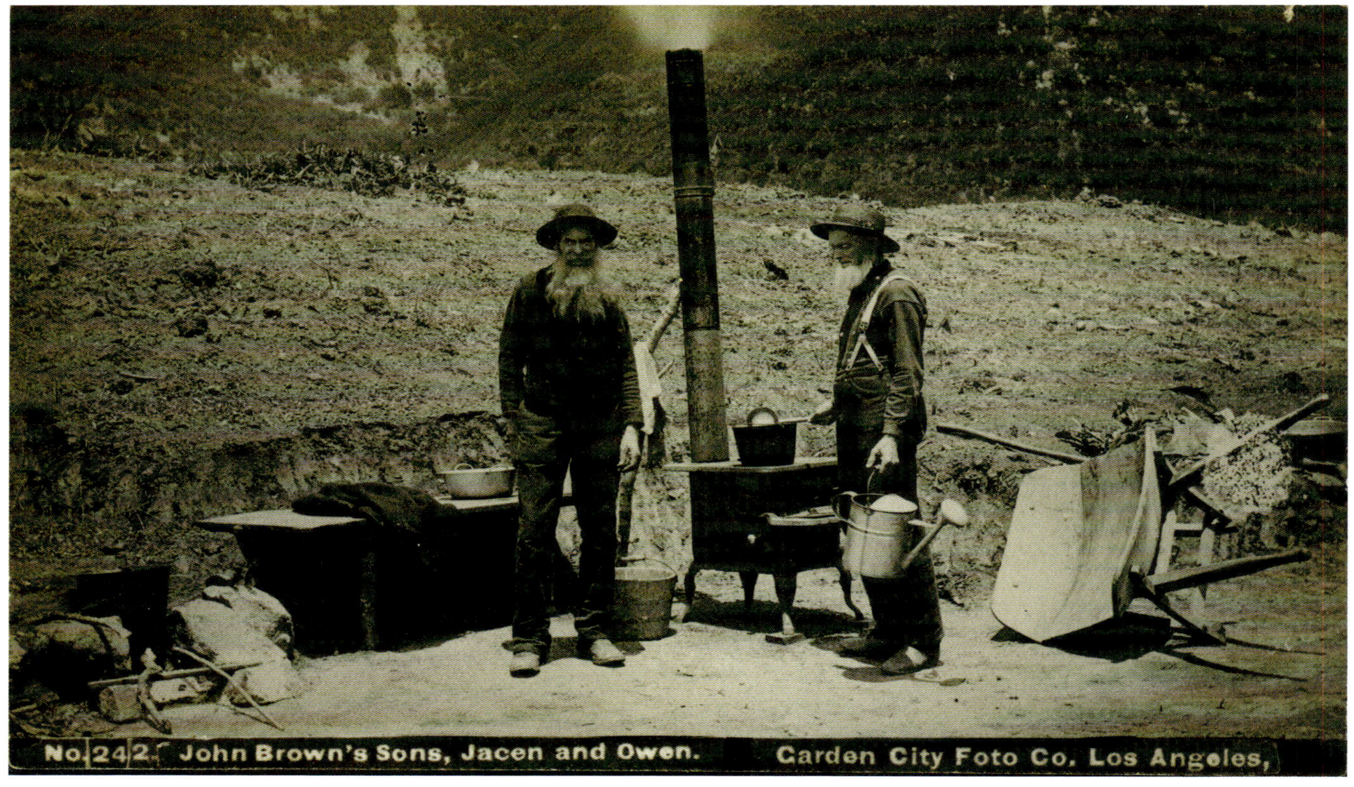


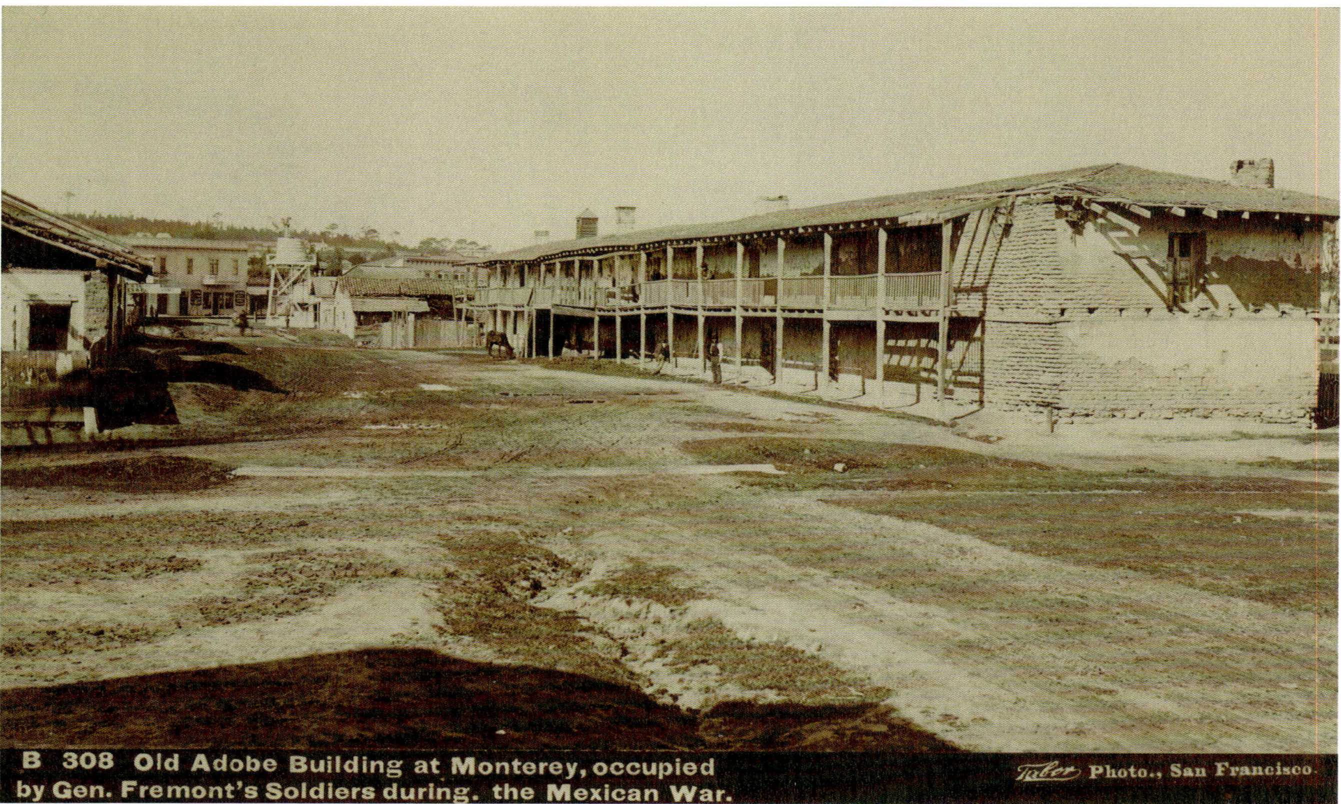


TOP: Garden City Foto Co. (James Pollock); *John Brown's Sons Jason and Owen*; platinum print; ca. 1900; 4 ¼ × 7 ½ in.
*Owen Brown survived the raid on Harper's Ferry, though two of his brothers were killed during the rebellion. Owen and his two brothers lived in the mountains above Pasadena.*

BOTTOM: Isaiah W. Taber; *Old Adobe in Monterey Occupied by Fremont and his Troops During the Mexican-American War*; gelatin silver print; ca. 1890; Mounted: 6 ¼ × 9 ⅛ in. / Paper Size: 4 ⅞ × 7 ⅞ in.
*Fremont and his troops captured Monterey in 1846 without any resistance. Fremont had come to California with secret orders and with the encouragement of the government of the United States. He ended up leading an attack on Mexican rule, which led to California becoming a state in 1850.*

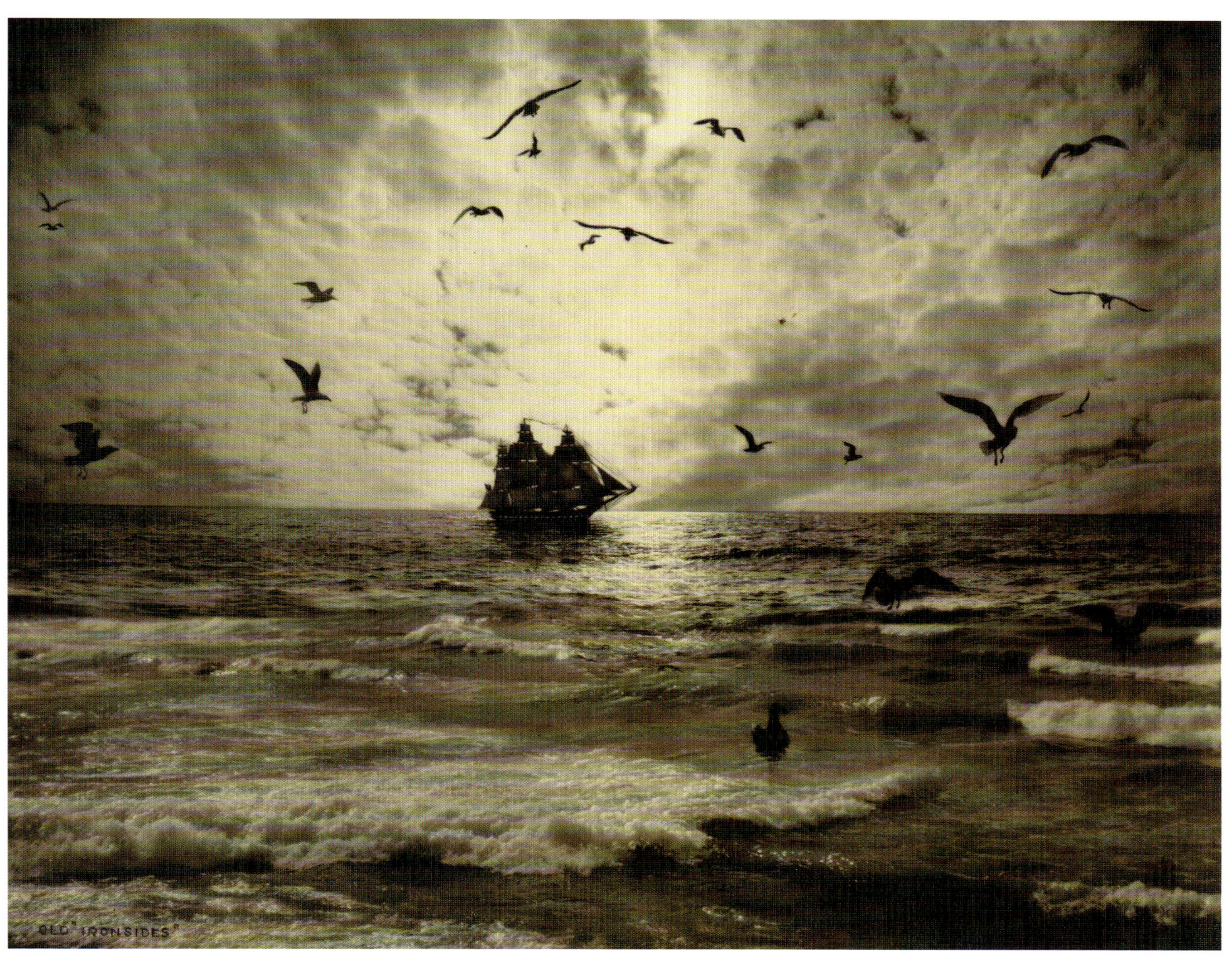


Unknown Artist; *Old Ironsides*; gelatin silver print; 1933; 7½ × 9½ in.
*Also known as the USS* Constitution, *the ship was in the midst of a three-year tour of the nation's coastal cities after its restoration from 1931–1934. Originally launched in Boston in 1797, the USS* Constitution *resides in Boston Harbor.*

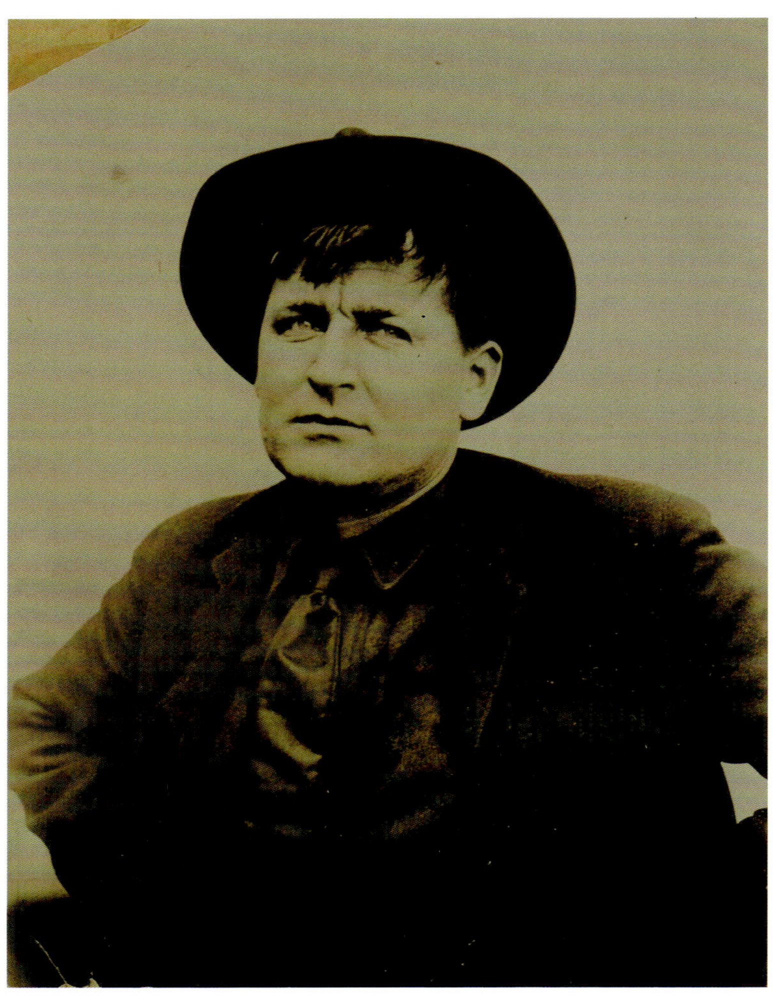

George Bain (attributed); *Death Valley Scotty*; toned gelatin silver print; 1906; 5¼ × 4 in.
*Walter E. Scott, known as Death Valley Scotty, ventured to California to prospect for gold, after performing with Buffalo Bill in a Wild West show. He found backers, including Albert Mussey Johnson, who had built a mansion for himself in Death Valley. Scotty had free use of the house, now a landmark still known as Scotty's Castle.*

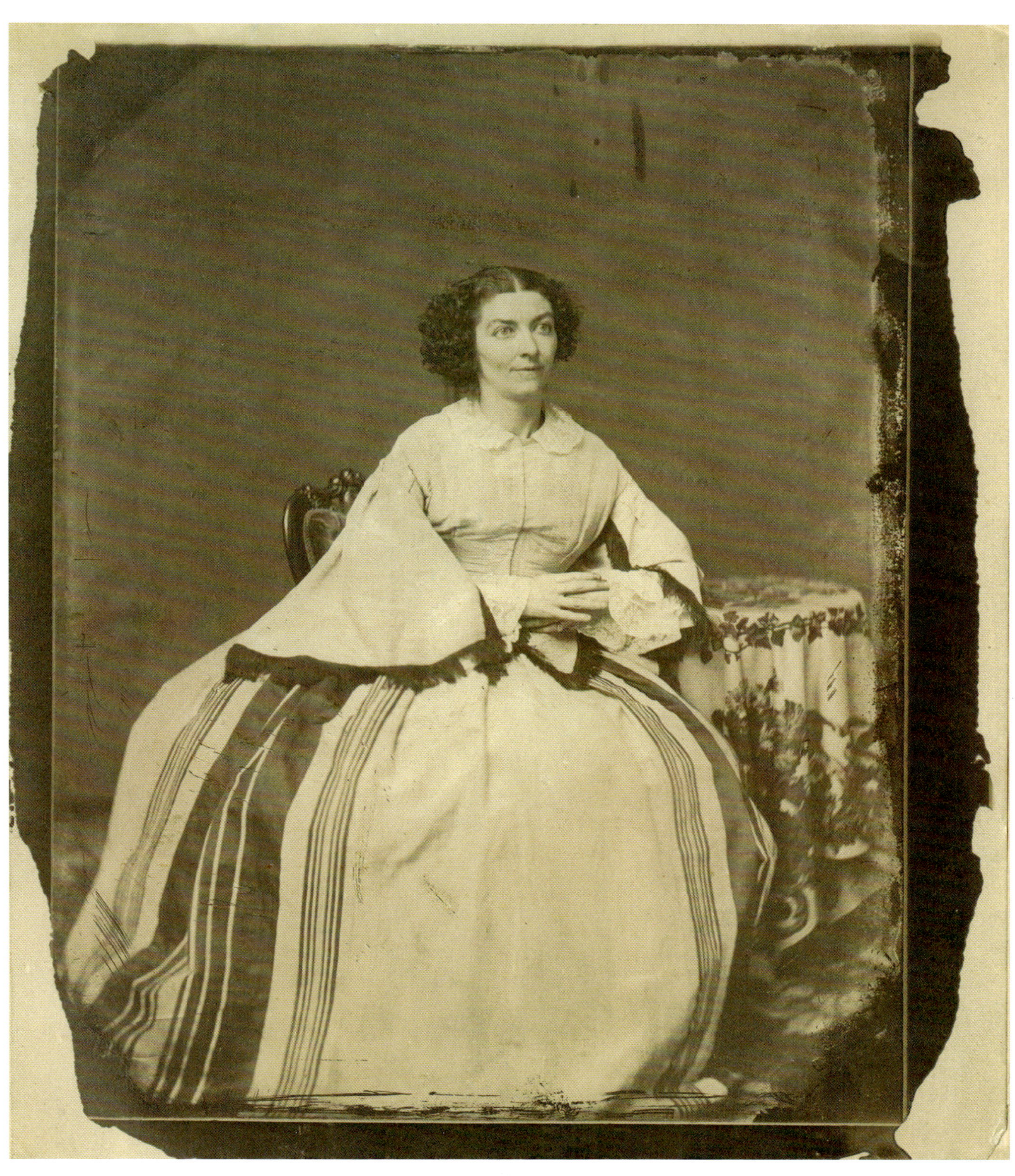

Meade Brothers; *Lola Montez*; salted paper print; ca. 1858; 8½ × 6½ in.
*Lola Montez was of Irish heritage and the toast of Europe as the romantic partner of both King Ludwig I of Bavaria and Franz Liszt. She came to San Francisco in 1853, during the Gold Rush, and performed her famous Spider Dance, lifting her skirts to new heights upon seeing an imaginary spider.*

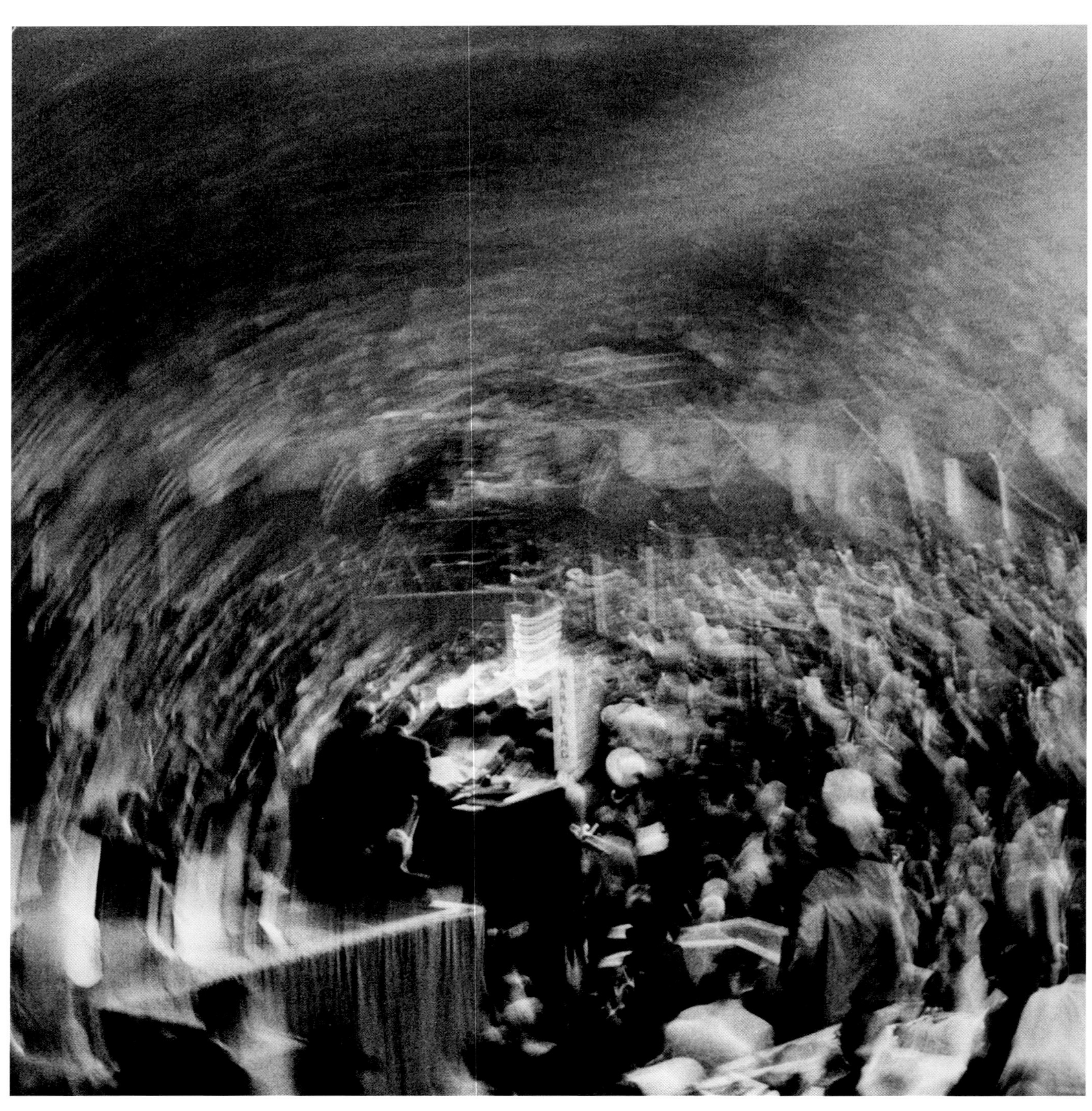

Donald Ross; Untitled (The swirl of the convention, Los Angeles); gelatin silver print; 1960; 16 × 15½ in.
*Delegates to the Democratic Convention nominated John F. Kennedy for president in 1960.*

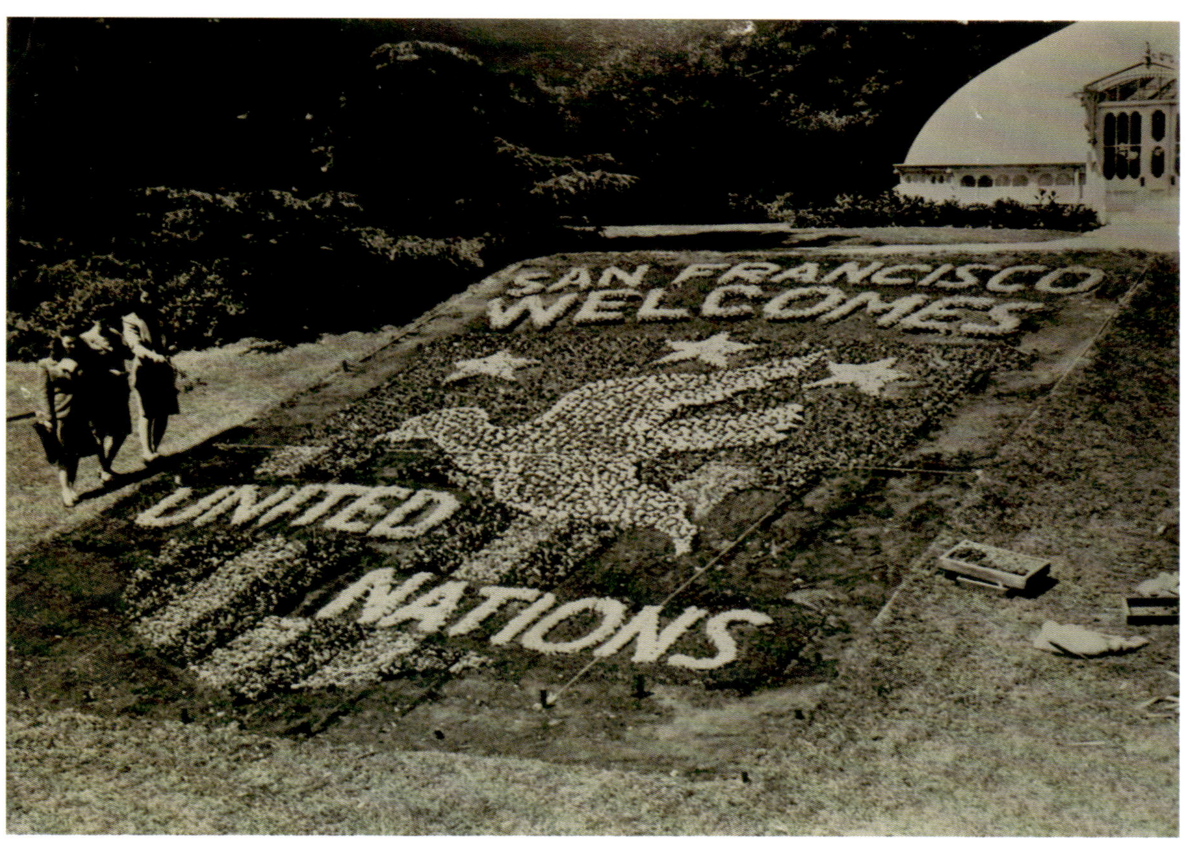


Unknown Artist; *San Francisco Welcomes the United Nations*; gelatin silver print; 1945; 4½ × 6⅛ in.
*Delegates from fifty countries met from April to June 1945 to develop a charter for the United Nations.*

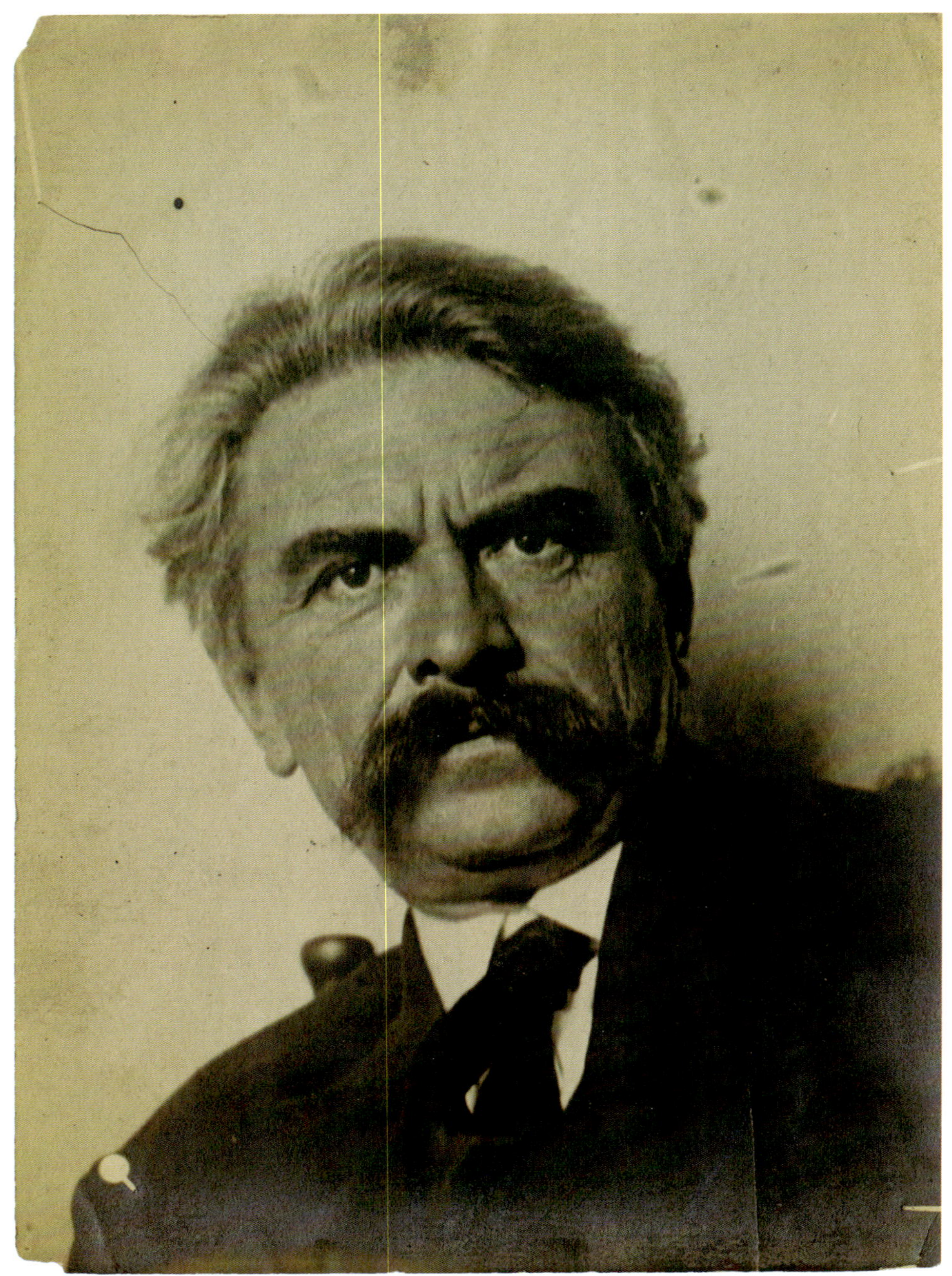

George Bain; *Anton Paul Cherbak, Russian in California*; gelatin silver print; ca. 1915; 7 × 5 in.
*Cherbak published a Russian-language newspaper for the Molokanes, a persecuted Christian sect who emigrated to California. The name is Russian for "milk drinkers," from their habit of drinking milk during Lent.*

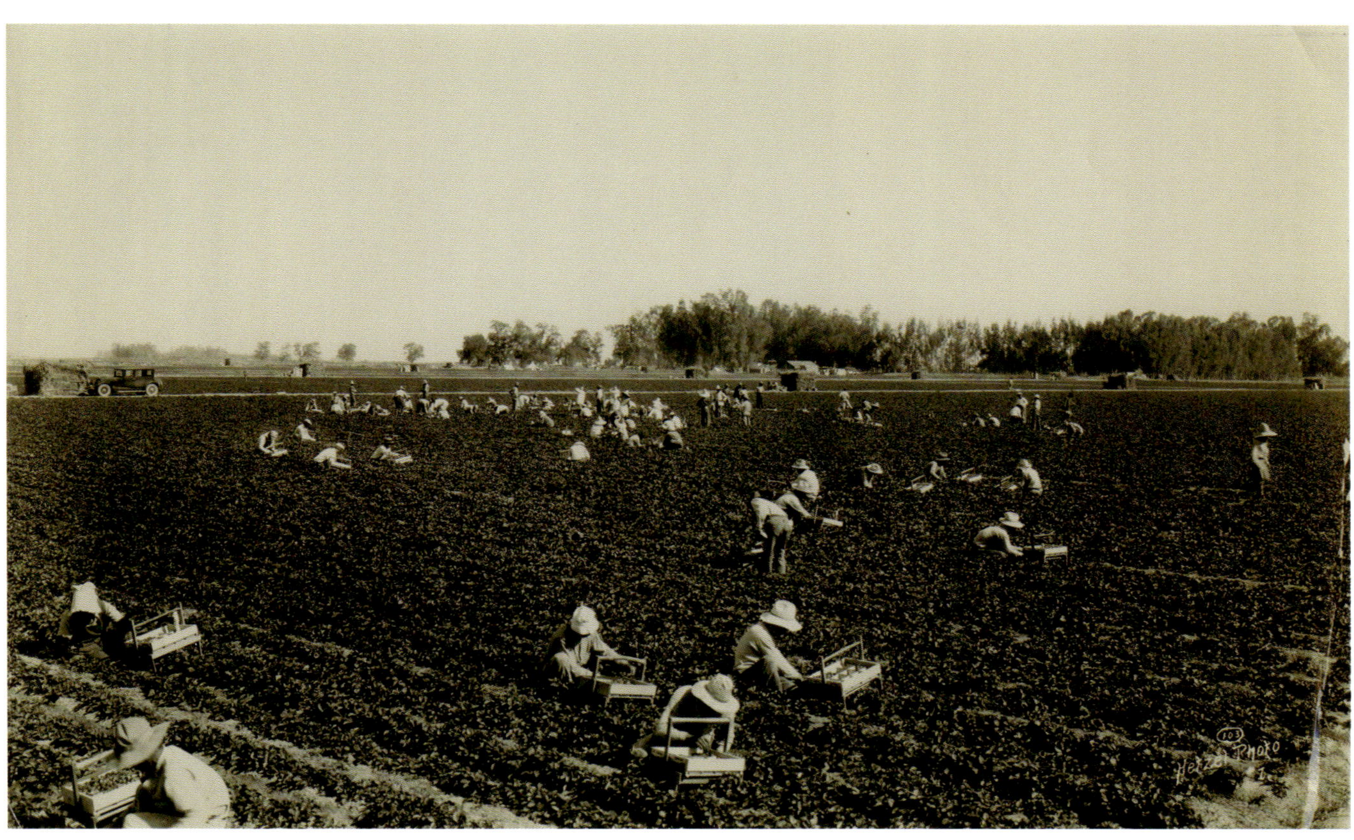


Leo Hetzel; *Strawberries: Harvest in Imperial Valley*; gelatin silver print; ca. 1935; 7 × 10¾ in.
*Many Japanese Americans worked on their own farms until their internment during World War II. Hetzel ran a photography studio in El Centro.*

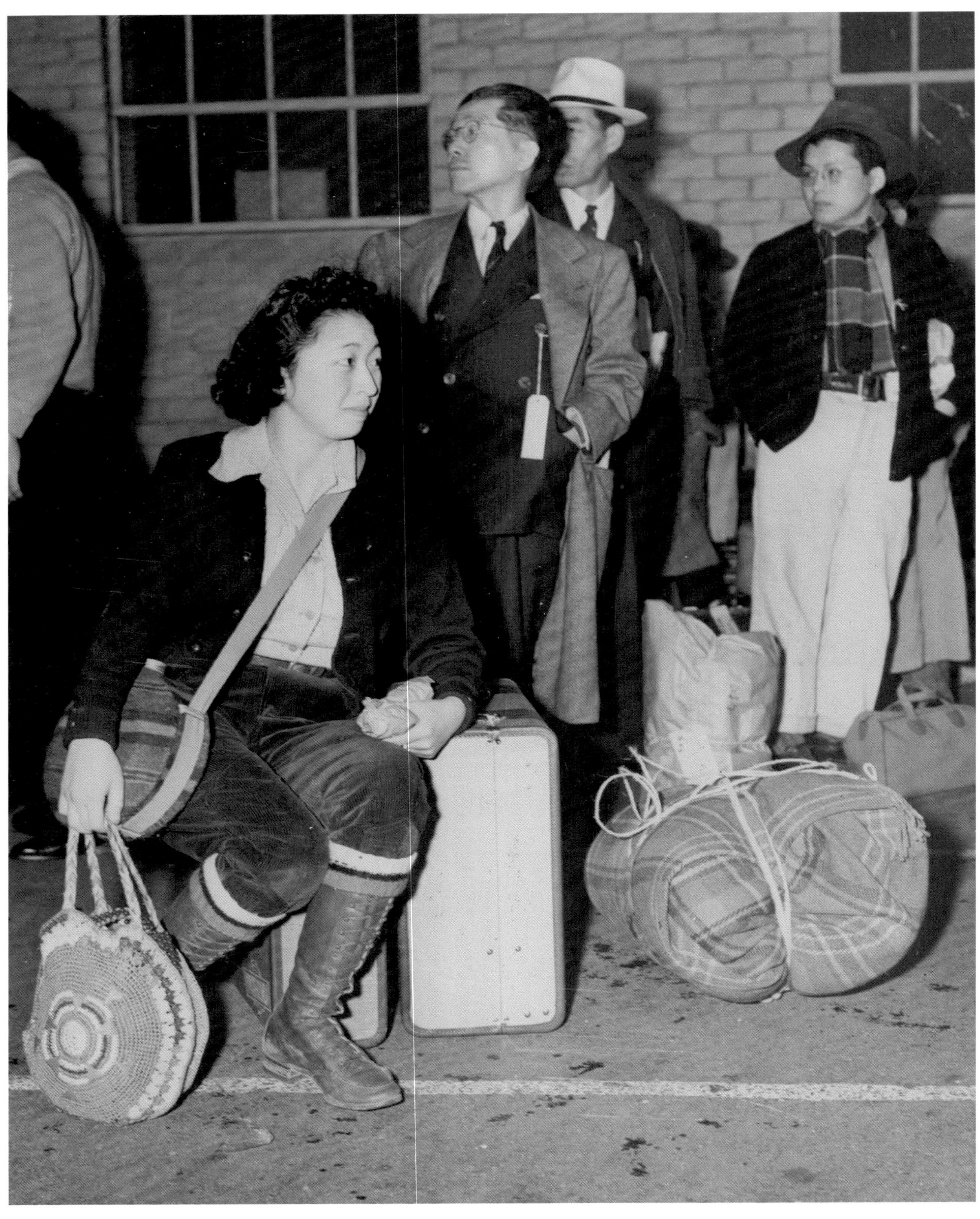

International News Photos; *Harie Shiwo, Los Angeles, Waiting to be Transported to Manzanar*; gelatin silver print; 1942; 8 × 6 in.
*"The young Japanese girl, Harie Shiwo, takes a last look at Los Angeles" read the caption on a picture of Shiwo which was published in both the* Los Angeles Herald *and* Los Angeles Express.

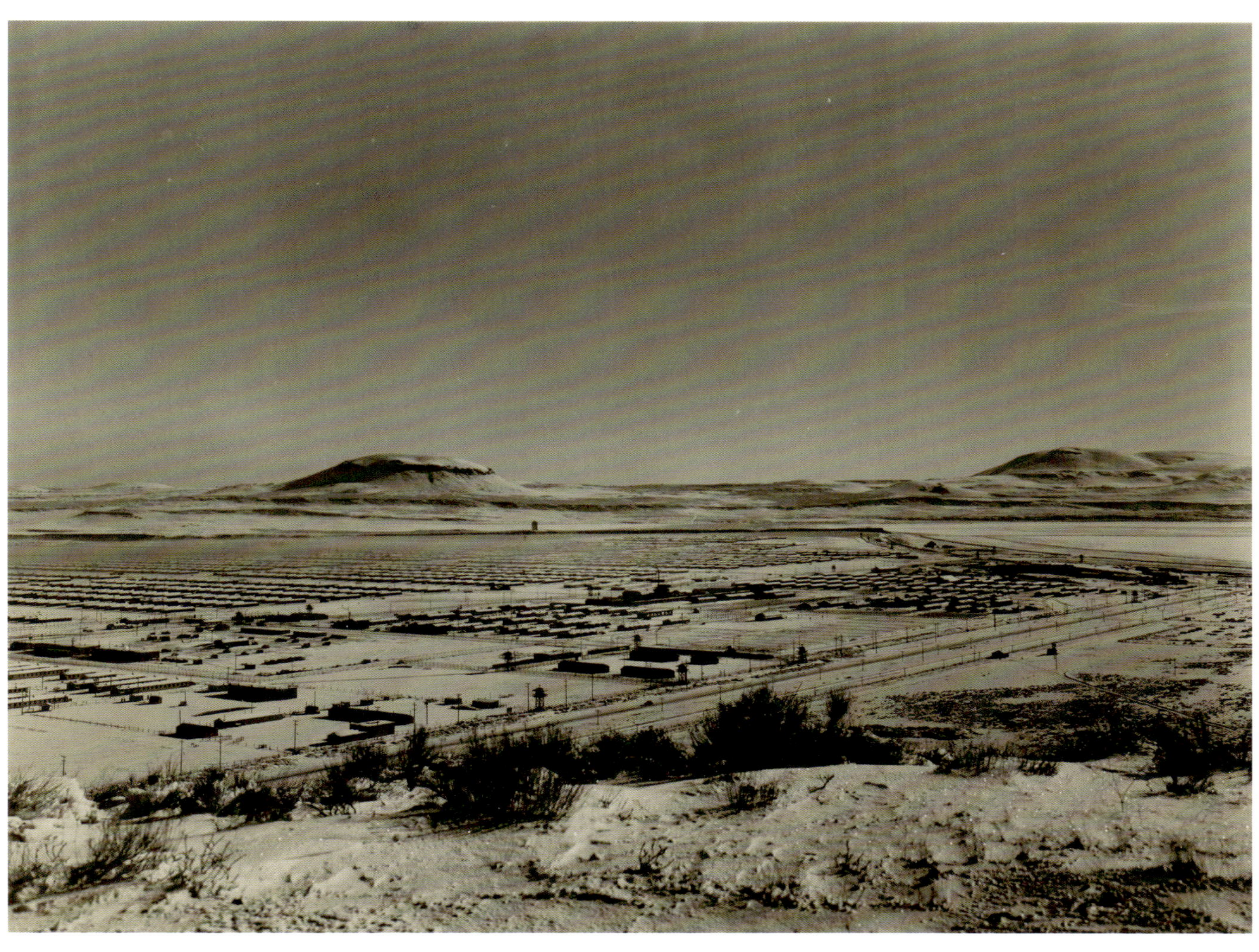

Newlin; *Overview of Tule Lake Camp*; gelatin silver print; ca. 1943; 6 × 8 in.
*Japanese Americans who refused to serve in the US military or take a loyalty oath were sent to Tule Lake. Known as "No-no boys" they had answered "no; no" on those last two questions of a government loyalty form.*

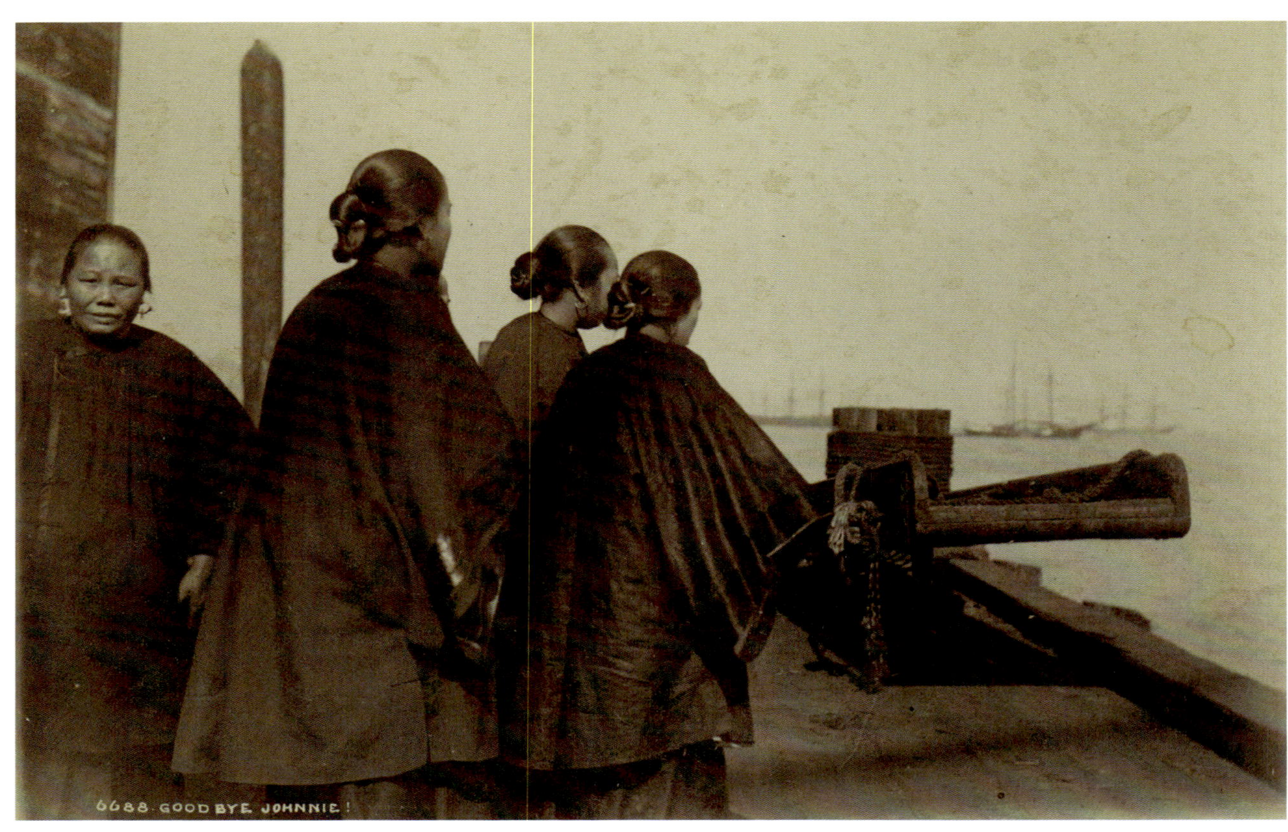


William Henry Jackson; *Goodbye Johnnie*; albumen print; ca. 1880; 4¼ × 6⅝ in.
*William Henry Jackson was a famous Denver photographer who photographed all across the country, including this photograph taken in San Francisco. While his specialty was photographing western landscapes and exploration, this unusual image shows his broad area of interest. He may have had a distribution arrangement with art dealers Chain and Hardy Company.*

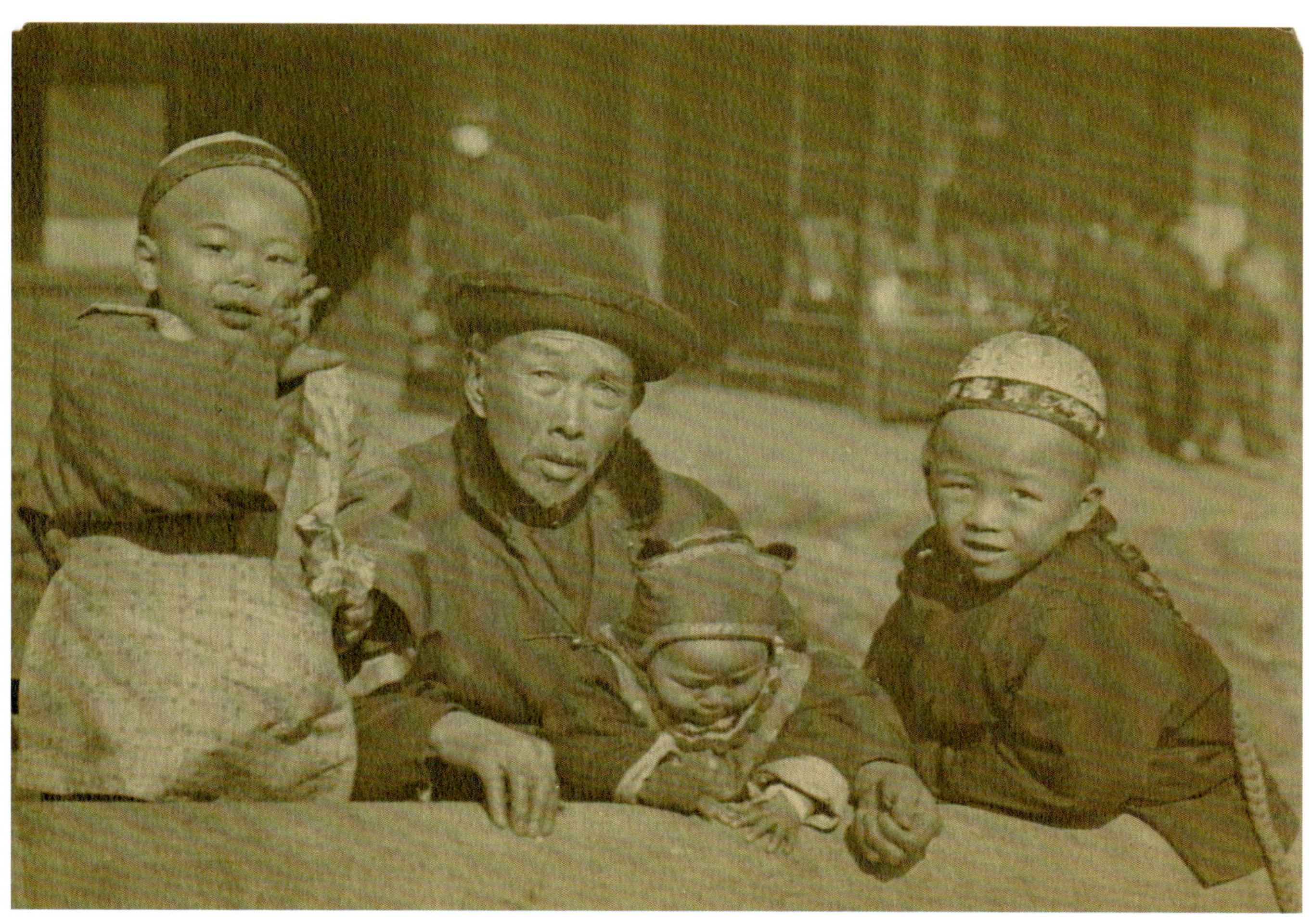

Arnold Genthe; *The Airing* (Chinatown, San Francisco); toned gelatin silver print; ca. 1905, printed ca. 1930; 10⅞ × 13½ in.
*Genthe made a series of photographs of the Chinese community in San Francisco and published the book,* Pictures of Old Chinatown, *in 1908*

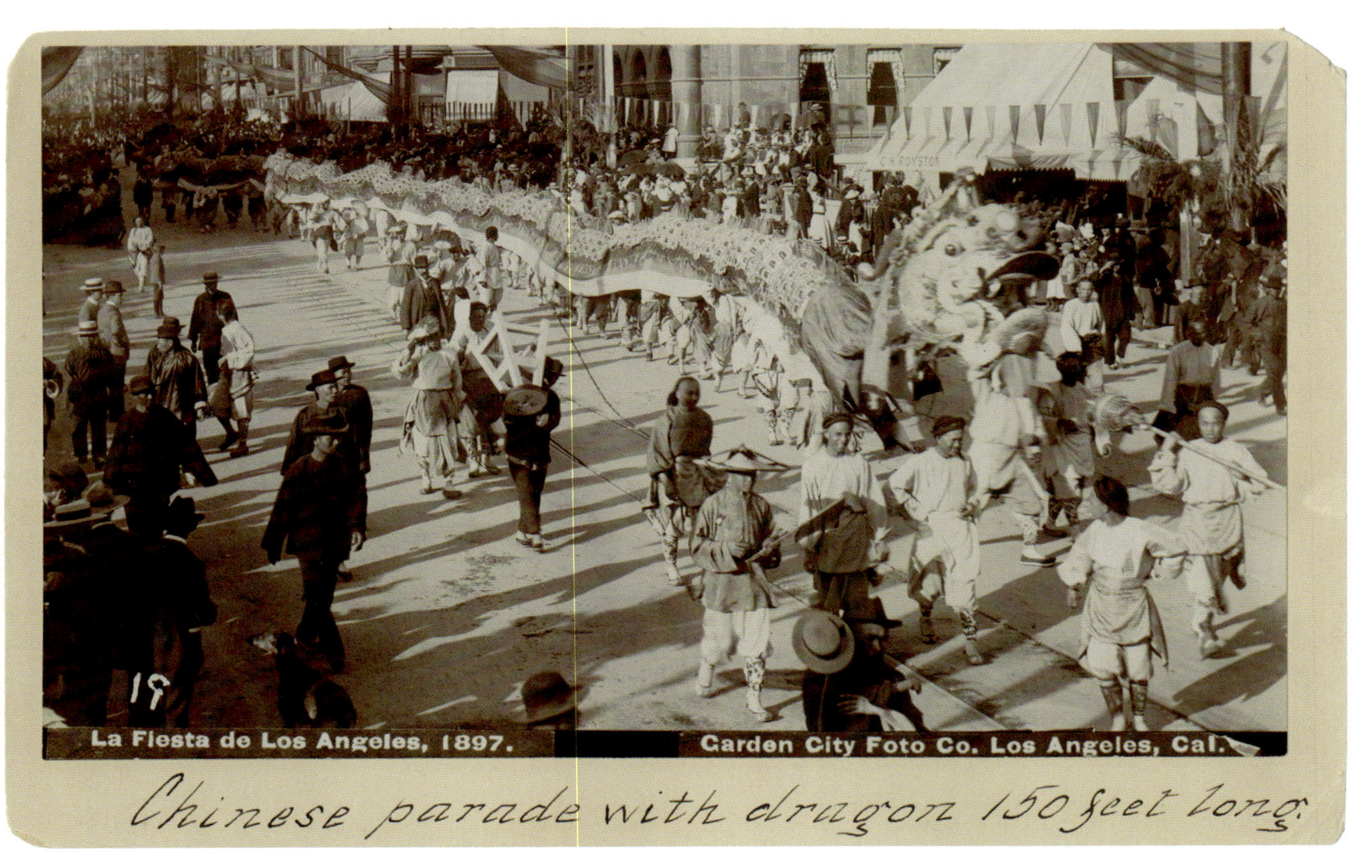


Garden City Foto Co. (James Pollock); *Chinese Parade with Dragon 150 Feet Long*; toned gelatin silver print; 1897; 4½ × 7½ in.
*Part of a multicultural parade and festival that took place in downtown Los Angeles between 1894 and 1916.*

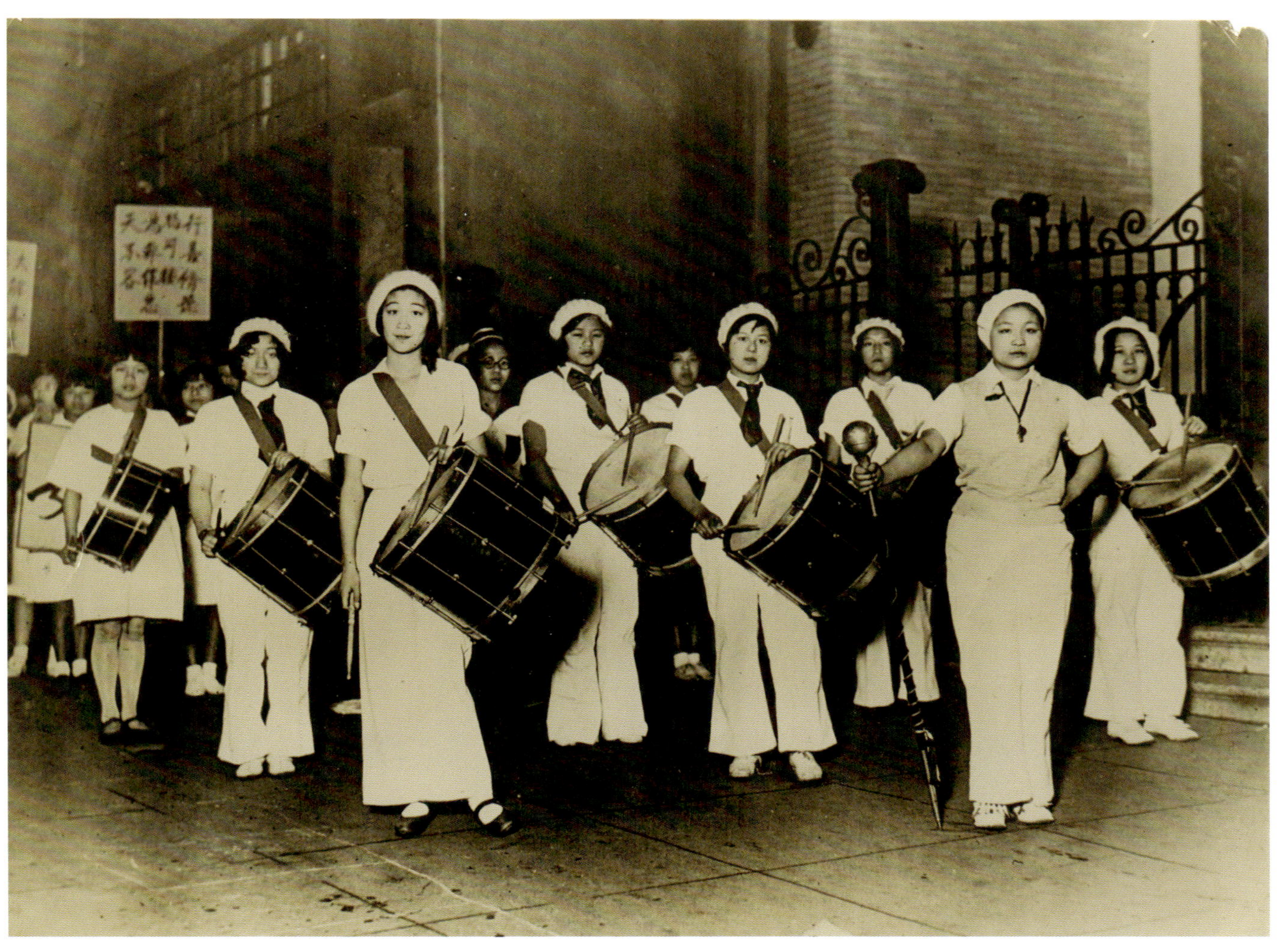

Wide World Photos; *Marching Band, San Francisco*; gelatin silver print; 1928; 6⅞ × 9¼ in.
*The Chinese community in San Francisco became established at the time of the Gold Rush, when more than 24,000 Chinese immigrants escaped from China, came to California to find their fortune, and brought their culture to the city.*

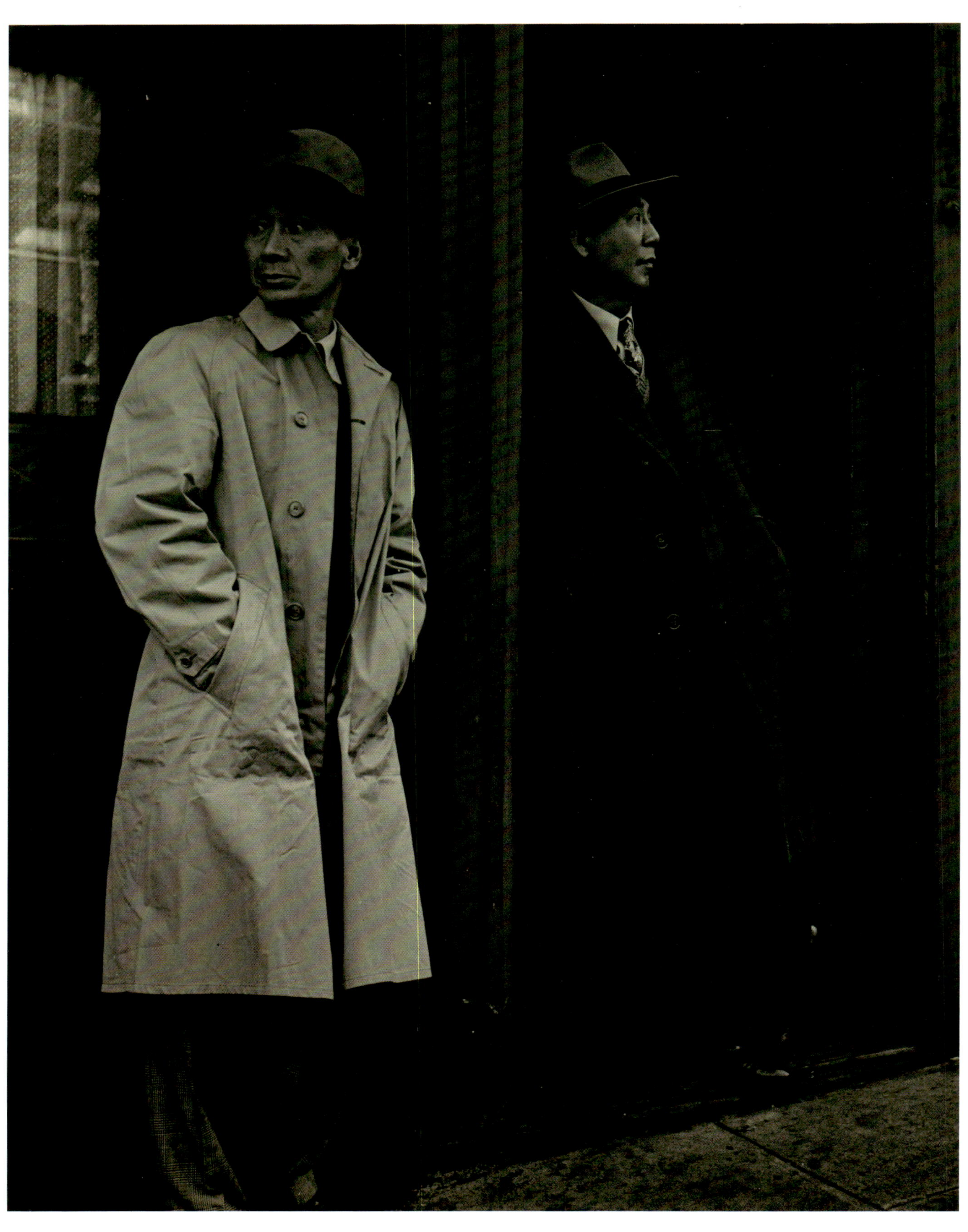

Max Yavno; Untitled (Two men in a doorway); gelatin silver print; 1947; 13 × 10¼ in.
*Yavno published books on San Francisco and Los Angeles and is the subject of a monograph by Ben Maddow. Yavno lived and worked in Los Angeles.*

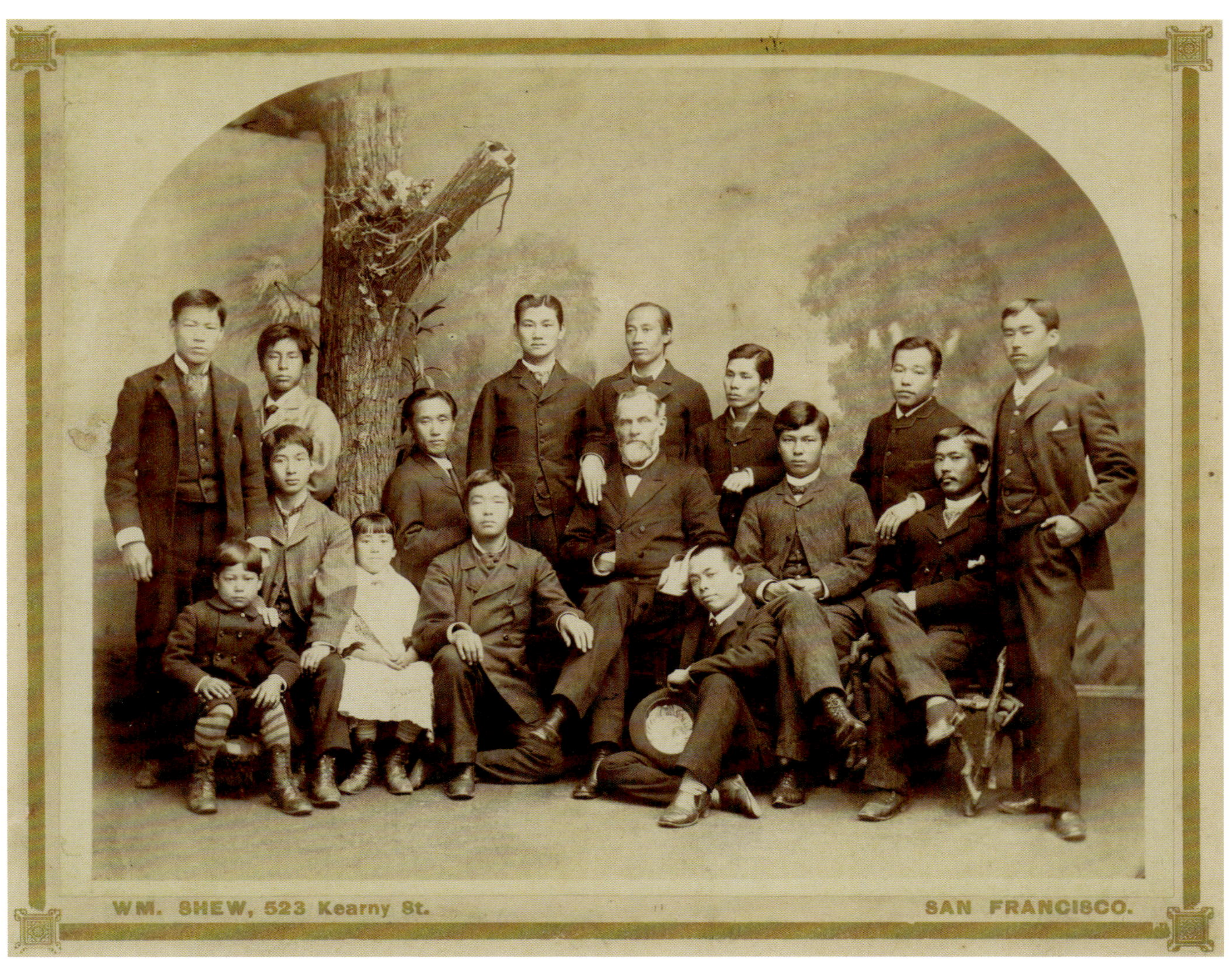


William Shew; Untitled (Self-portrait with group of Chinese immigrants.); albumen print; ca. 1882; 7½ × 9½ in.
*Shew worked with the abolitionist movement in Boston, and then became involved in social issues in San Francisco. This photograph may have been a response to the Chinese Exclusion Act signed into law by President Chester Arthur in 1882, eliminating Chinese citizenship as well as immigration for ten years.*

PART 3: DREAMERS

# DREAMING CALIFORNIA

**by Arthur Ollman**

Those who did well in other nations and other states tended to stay in those places. Of those who didn't, some dreamed of America. Many of these dreams had a more specific focus. America, to hundreds of millions of dreamers, meant California. Some arrived and found what they came for. Some found California a comfortable place to endure not finding it. Refugees from all hemispheres have said that California's physical distance from their torments is a balm.

Some dreamed of peace and safety, some of riches, and others of social reform or of manifesting God's will; some sought adventure, and others wanted to reinvent themselves in a new place. Some sought the ambiguous road of "greater opportunity." It was a fantastic dream that brought most of the '49ers to the arduous and largely unrewarded work of finding gold in the Sierra. A few found a nugget or two. But selling them pants to work in? That was Bavarian Levi Strauss's vein of gold, a mother lode that still produces. The winners are declared geniuses. They dreamed the right path, when no one else did. The losers: fools who should have known better than to follow their dreams.

An anonymous ambrotype of gold miners in the Sierra foothills above Sacramento shows the dirty, unglamorous labor that both successful and unsuccessful miners applied to their dreams of wealth. The brass foil mat, shiny as gold, mocks the rugged misery of the lode miner's life. An image like this would not have been made to show the beauty of the landscape, the portraits of those depicted, or even their energetic efforts.These men were likely formalizing their stake for legal purposes, should ownership someday be challenged by "claim jumpers." For those laborers who had been kidnapped off the streets of China to fill a sailing captain's quota, there were only nightmares in those hills.

If the lure of wealth and opportunity weren't reason enough to inspire migration, then perhaps God's command would do it. A photograph by Richard J. Arnold depicts a statue of Father Junipero Serra standing over the harbor in Monterey, commissioned by Jane Stanford, the wife of Governor Leland Stanford, and sculpted by John Combs in 1891 [Page 138]. When Serra was canonized in 2015, protestors beheaded the statue. It was re-headed in 2017.

The monument shows Serra serenely stepping ashore, in 1770, from his little row boat. His actual arrival was neither serene nor by boat. He had walked hundreds of miles from Baja California, with his retinue, on a near-gangrenous leg. Serra's dream was to follow God's command and convert the indigenous peoples to Catholicism. It was important to the church to wrench children away from tribal families as early as possible, so that the "pagan" culture would have no grip on their souls. Aware that the mother church in Rome had, for centuries, been rife with corruption, Serra believed that the indigenous tribes were uncorrupted, innocent, and ripe for conversion. Forced into slave labor, they were beaten when they resisted.

Many people saw the mistreatment of indigenous people as reprehensible, and sought to create a peaceful coexistence and weigh in on behalf of tribal groups. In 1894, the thirty-six-year-old railroad employee from Illinois, Adam Clark Vroman, opened a bookstore in

Pasadena, California, that also sold photographic supplies. Vroman's Bookstore, pictured in 1908, still thrives today [Page 150]. Mr. Vroman was a passionate photographer of the indigenous people of the Southwest. He surrounded himself with intellectuals, utopian humanists, and social reformers, including some who embraced the dream of ending the racist oppression of American Indians. Vroman's personality was such that tribal people, who had no reason to trust whites, welcomed him. His photographs, some of the most important documentary work on Southwest American Indian life, are dignifying and generous. On his 1894 visit to photograph the snake dance at a Hopi pueblo, a ritual rarely observed by outsiders, Vroman's entourage visited an adobe house. The formal group portrait includes Mr. Vroman, second from the right. Each person is posed as in an individual studio portrait. The rhyming postures and rakishly tilted hats indicate that this grouping was carefully choreographed.

Inevitably, the country was filling up and technology was rapidly shrinking the distance between the coasts. From April of 1860 to October of 1861, the Pony Express operated between Missouri and California, but was not financially viable. In 1861, the first transcontinental telegraph system was completed. One could have an idea in New York and, within minutes, pass that thought to their colleague in San Francisco. In 1869, the railroad across America was completed. A mere seven years later, in eighty-three hours a passenger could ride the rails from coast to coast. Within fifteen years, the very definition of distance changed radically. Easterners have always sought a more intimate relationship with California, and now it was easily accessible.

Once the dream of human flight was accomplished in 1903, flying expanded and intensified. In 1911, William Randolph Hearst offered $50,000 to the first person to fly coast to coast in fewer than thirty days. Cal Perry Rogers took off from Brooklyn, New York, on September 17, 1911. In flight, Rogers looked like a person inserted into a mating pair of large mosquitos. The aircraft was named the Vin Fiz, for a soft drink made by his sponsor. Rogers succeeded in crossing the continent with seventy-five stops, largely for repairs, sleep, and sixteen crashes, one of which is seen here. It took him forty-nine days—too late for his reward. Fifty thousand people watched him land on the sand at Long Beach, and he taxied into the surf [Page 175]. A year later, at the age of thirty-three, he died in a crash in the same area. There are no hard lines between dreamers, adventurers, and lunatics.

The majestic Sierra, the vertiginous cliffs of Big Sur, the heaven-bound redwoods, the gnarly surf, the deadly desert, glorious Golden Gate, impregnable Alcatraz, lustrous Hollywood, the fecund Central Valley, the soothing climate, the economic juggernaut . . . California's gravitational pull on the dreamers of the world is as potent as ever. But urban traffic, the suburban sprawl, the cost of living, lengthening fire seasons, crippling droughts, and the looming Damocles of the "Big One" are the nightmares that buzz-kill runaway dreams. But even now, in engineering, science, technology, and the arts, dreamers remain California's greatest propellant.

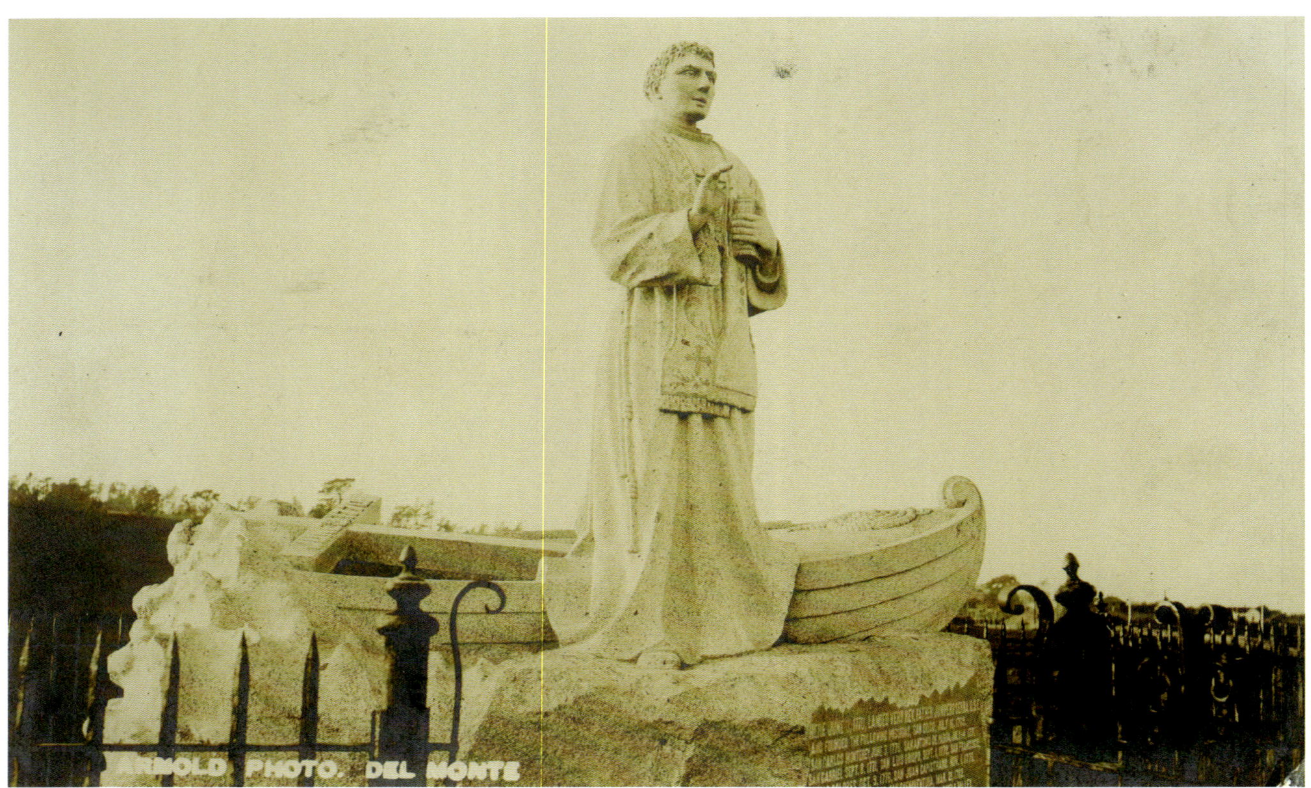


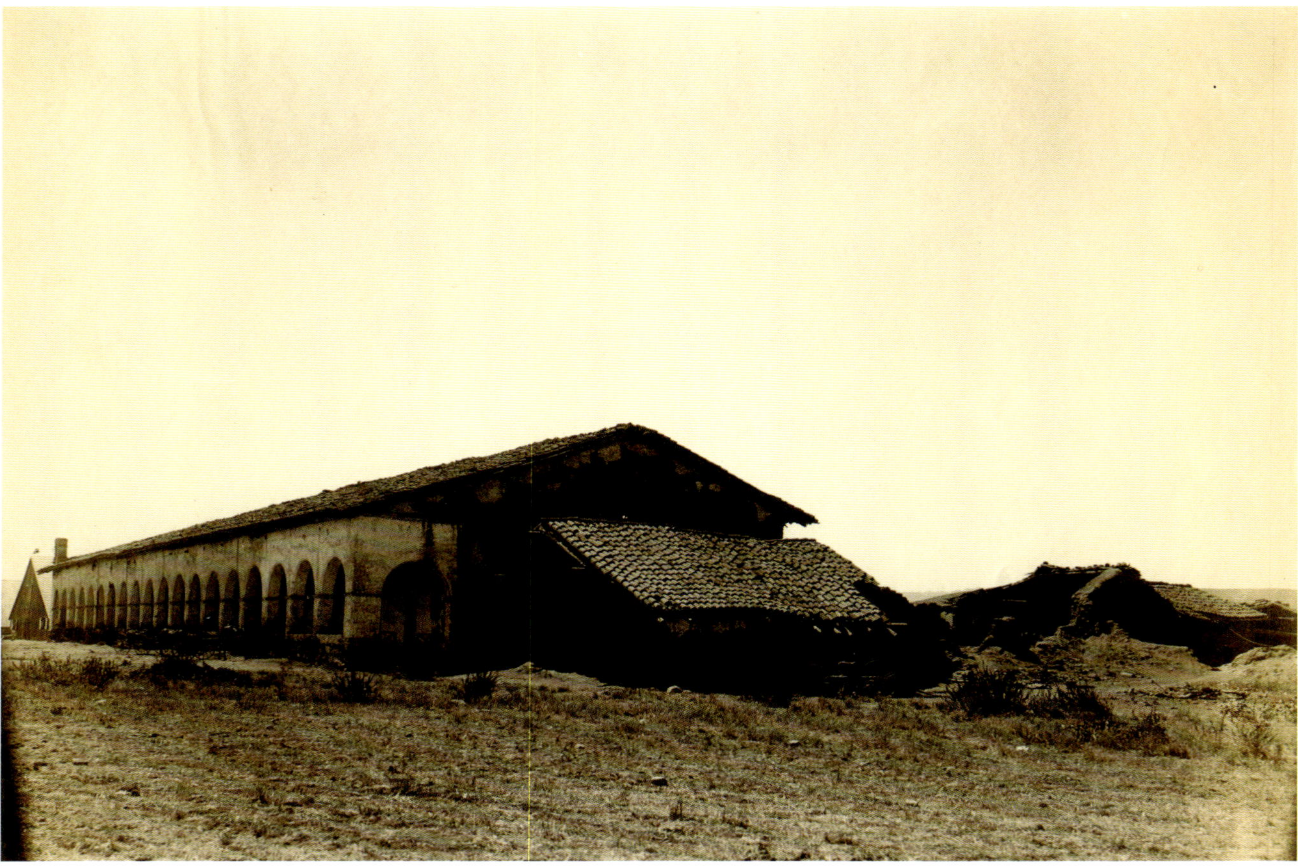

TOP: Richard J. Arnold; *Father Junipero Serra*; gelatin silver print; ca. 1900; 5 × 8 in.
*Serra dreamed of a series of missions that would convert the indigenous tribes to Catholicism, a practice that led to exploitation and death for many of the peoples of California and Baja.*

BOTTOM: Adam Clark Vroman (Attributed); Untitled (San Fernando Rey de España Mission); salted paper print; ca. 1904; 6½ × 9¼ in.
*Vroman and Charles Lummis were involved in a project to rebuild decaying missions around the turn of the century.*

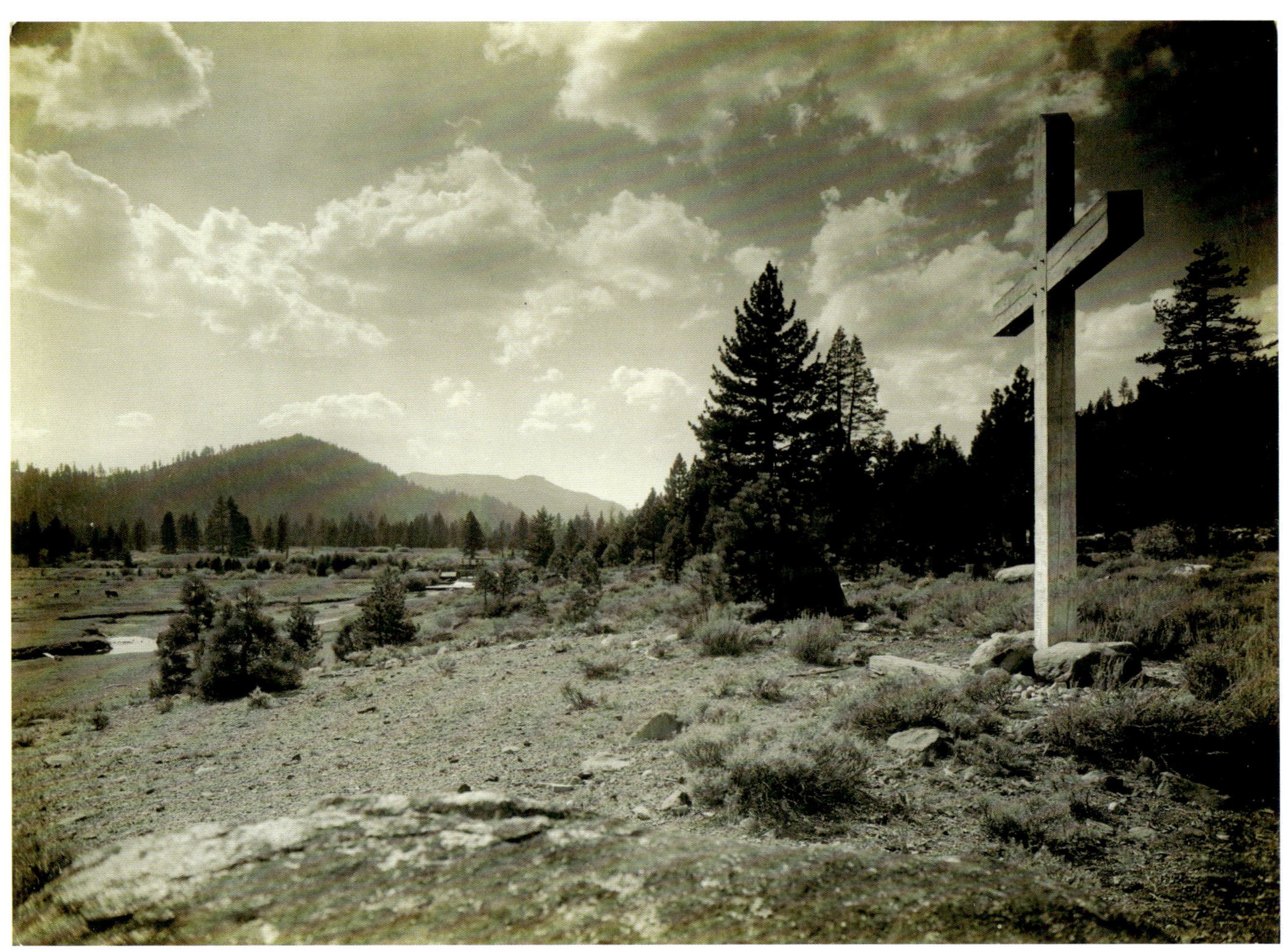

Unknown Artist; *Donner Lake*; gelatin silver print; ca. 1920; 6¼ × 8⅜ in.
*The cross has deteriorated, been rebuilt, and moved many times. The Donner party was snowed in at what is now known as Donner Pass during the winter of 1846.*

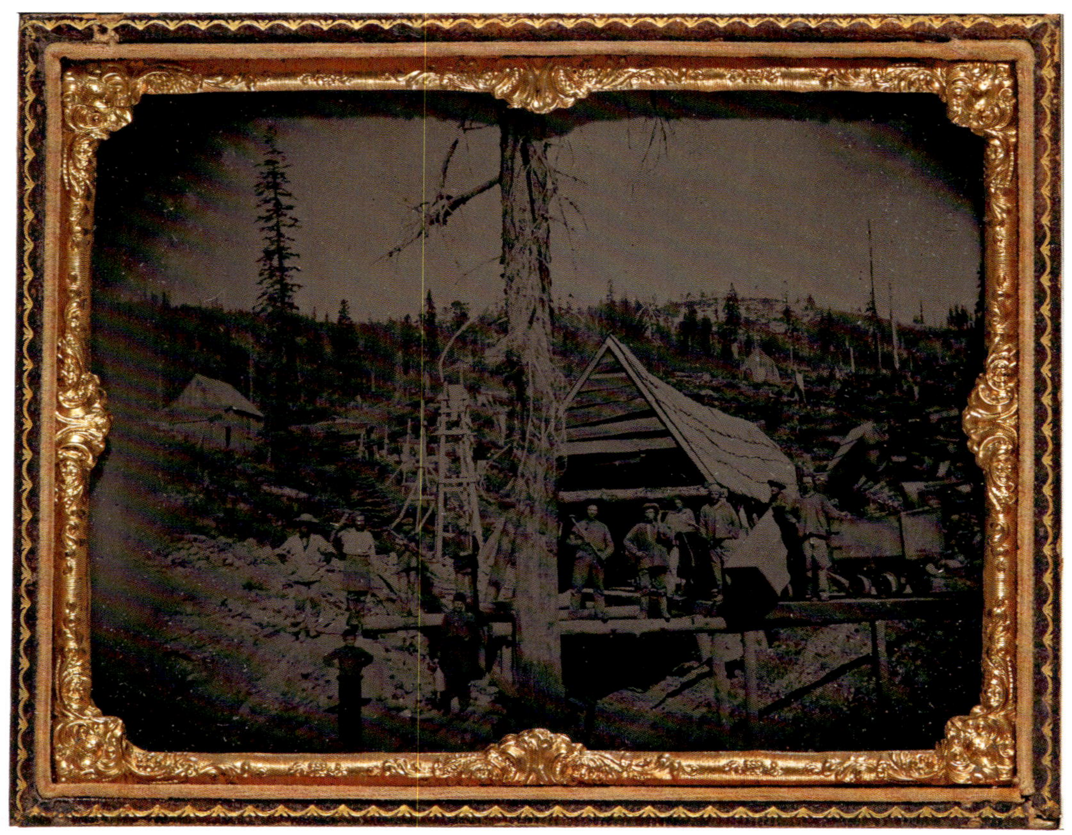

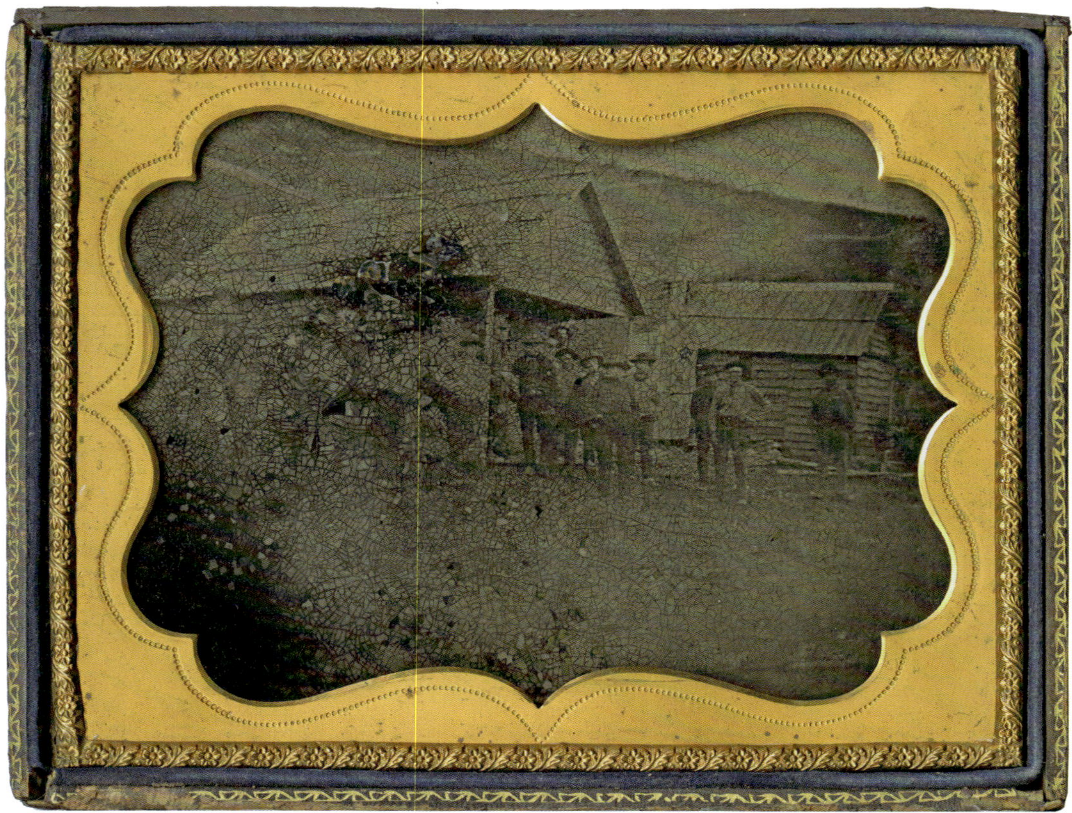

TOP: Unknown Artist; Untitled (Miners during the Gold Rush); ambrotype; ca. 1850; 4¼ × 5½ in.
*Gold Rush photographs brought many prospectors to the gold fields in search of instant wealth.*

BOTTOM: Unknown Artist; Untitled (William Pitt's cabin in Diamond Springs.); ambrotype; ca. 1855; 4¾ × 6 in.
*Pitt wrote a friend not to come west to California, though he said he was getting by okay, and complained about those who gambled away their profits from diggings.*

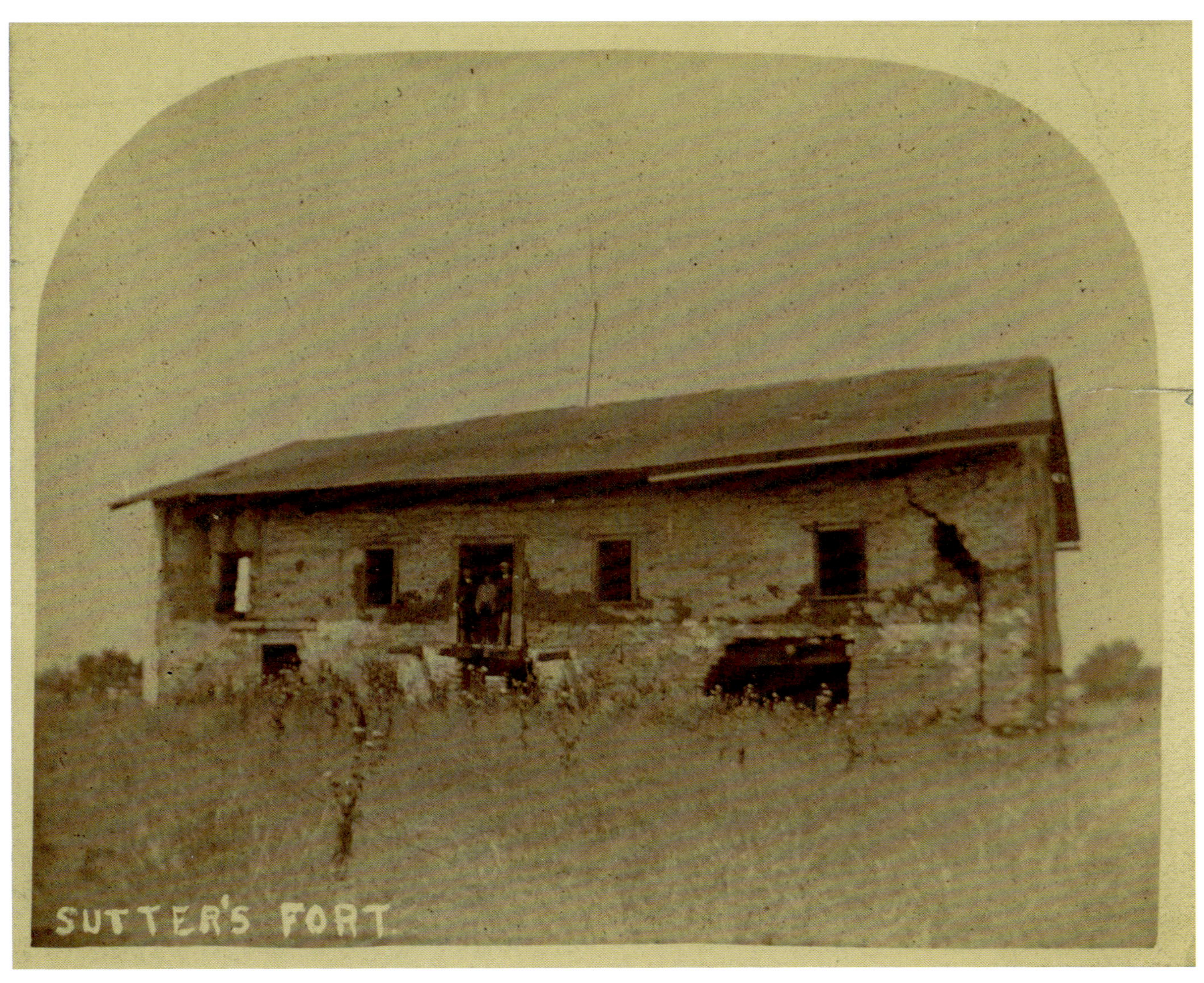


Unknown Artist; *Sutter Ruins*; albumen print; ca. 1890; 3⅞ × 4½ in.
*Sutter's Fort is where John Marshall discovered gold in 1848. Sutter was among the richest men in California when gold was discovered, but the gold seekers trampled his land and crops, leading him into bankruptcy.*

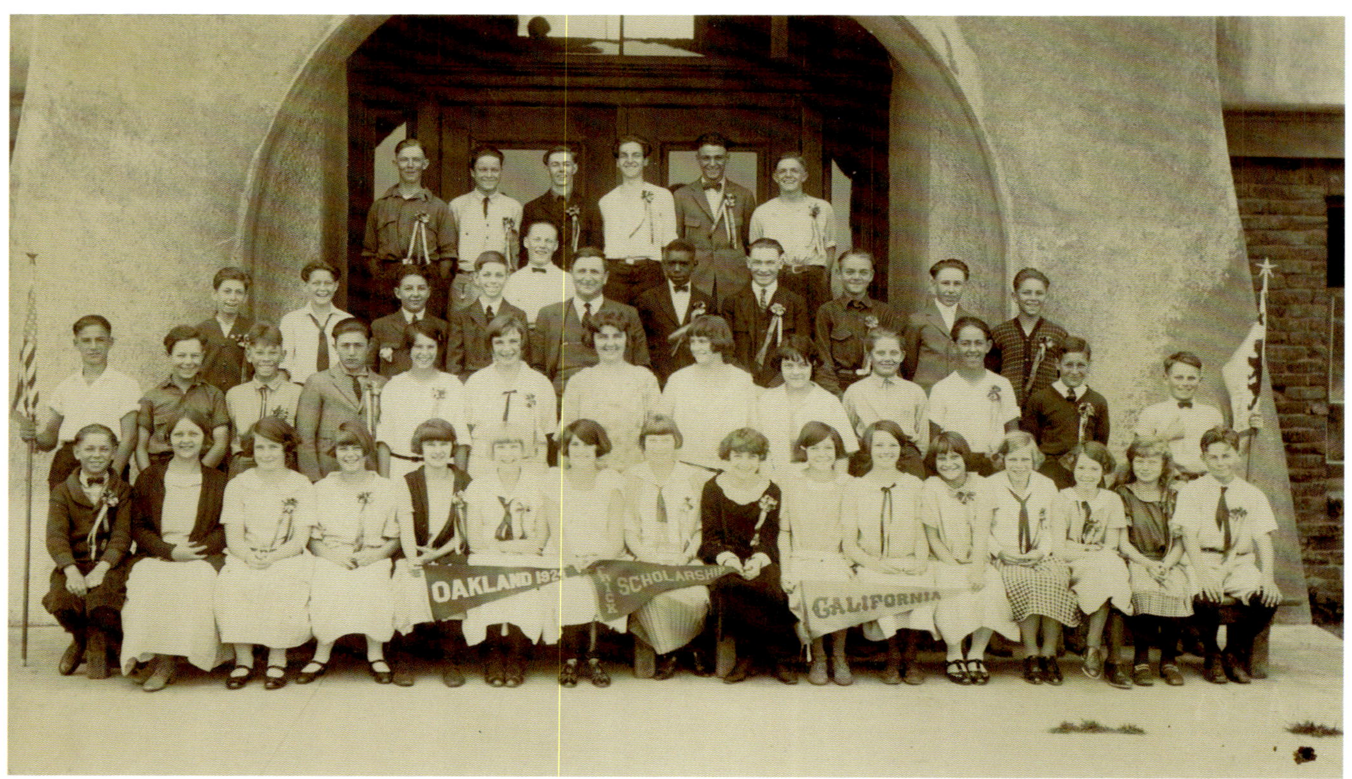


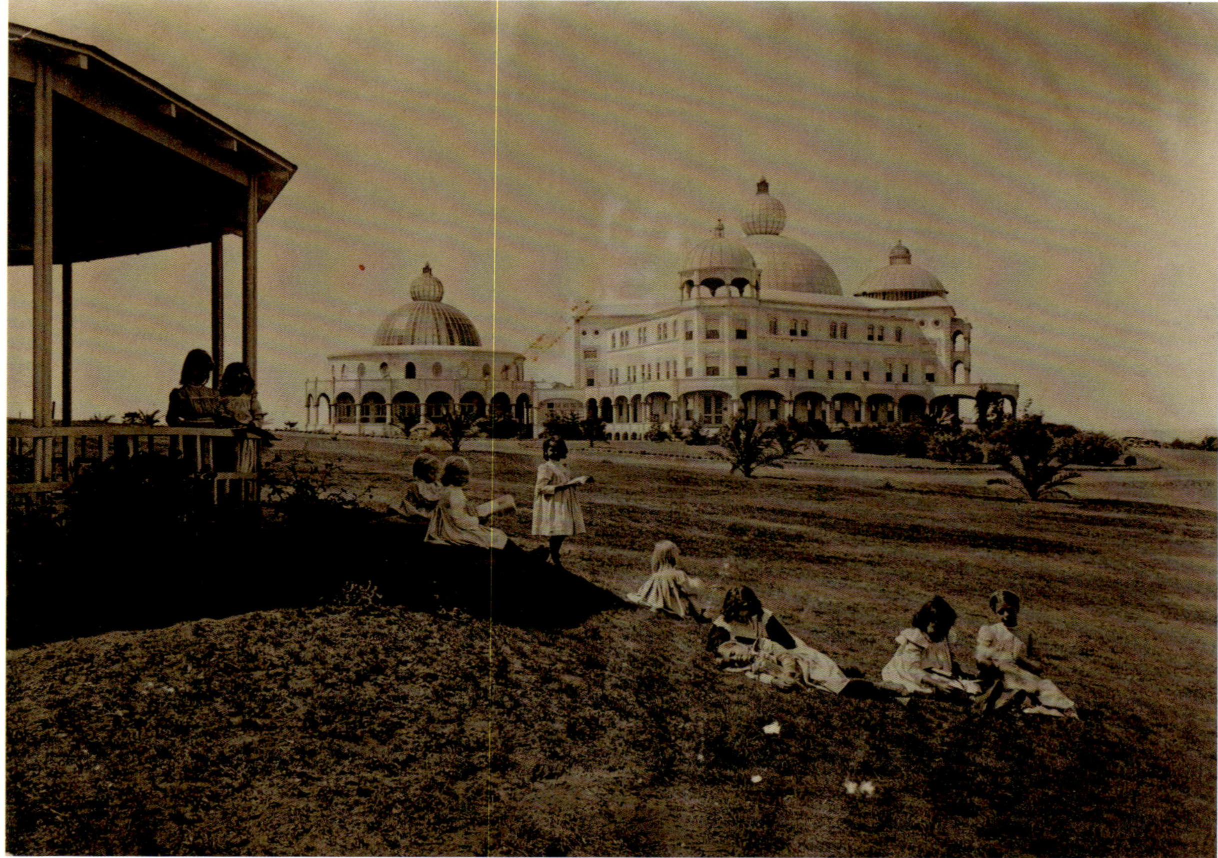

TOP: Hugo Weitz; *Frick Scholarship Oakland, California*; gelatin silver print; 1924; 4½ × 7¾ in.
*Frick, originally built in 1909, became a middle school in 1923 and now serves disadvantaged students as the Frick Impact Academy.*

BOTTOM: Unknown Artist; *Theosophical Society Center at Point Loma, San Diego*; platinum print; ca. 1905; 5½ × 7⅞ in.
*An educational center for the Theosophical Society under the direction of Katherine Tingley, the facility was known as "Lomaland." The buildings burned down in 1952.*

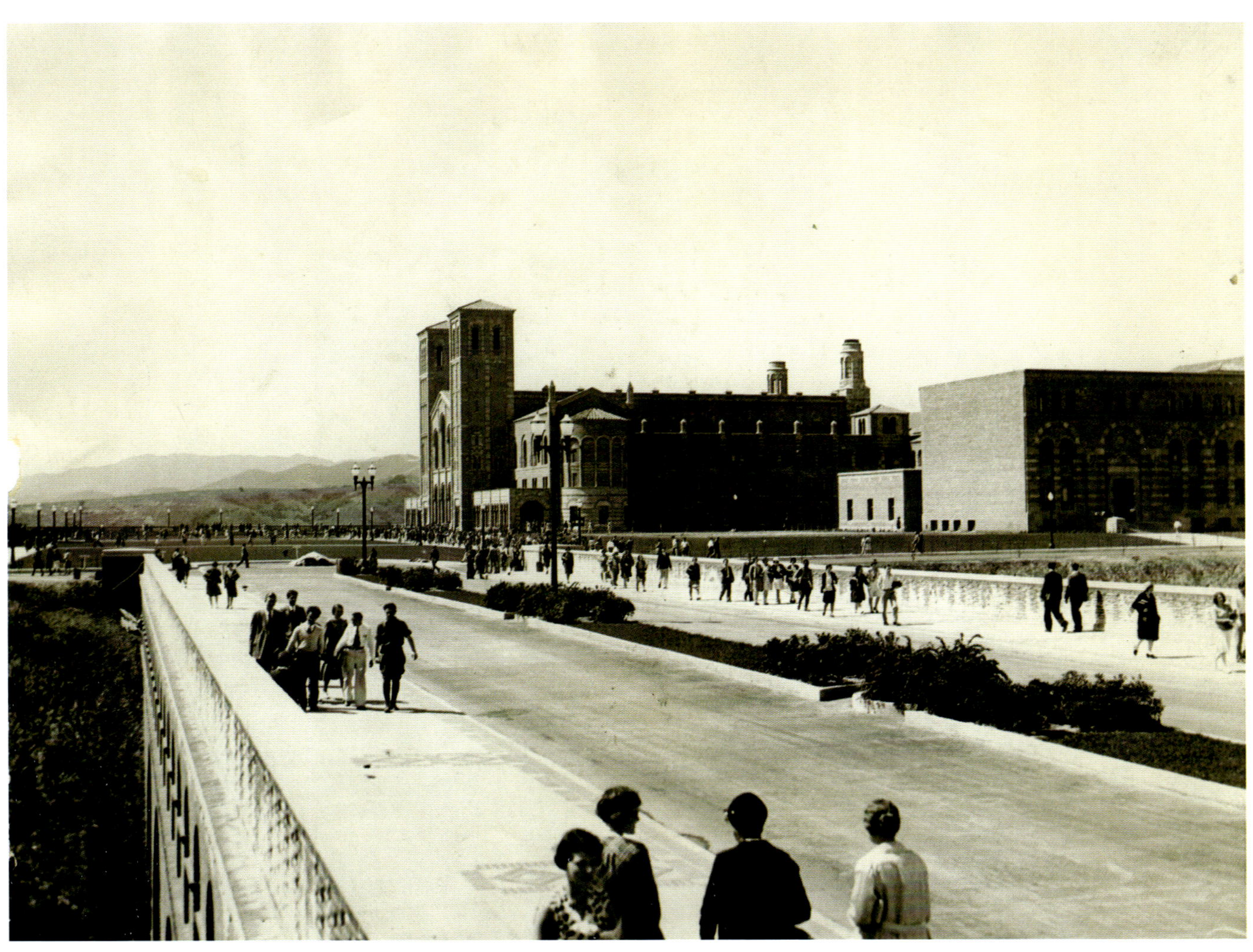

Seidman Photo Service; *New University of California Building in Westwood*; gelatin silver print; ca. 1930; 7⅞ × 9¾ in.
*UCLA was accredited in 1919 and moved to its Westwood campus in 1930. It is considered one of the top public universities in the country.*

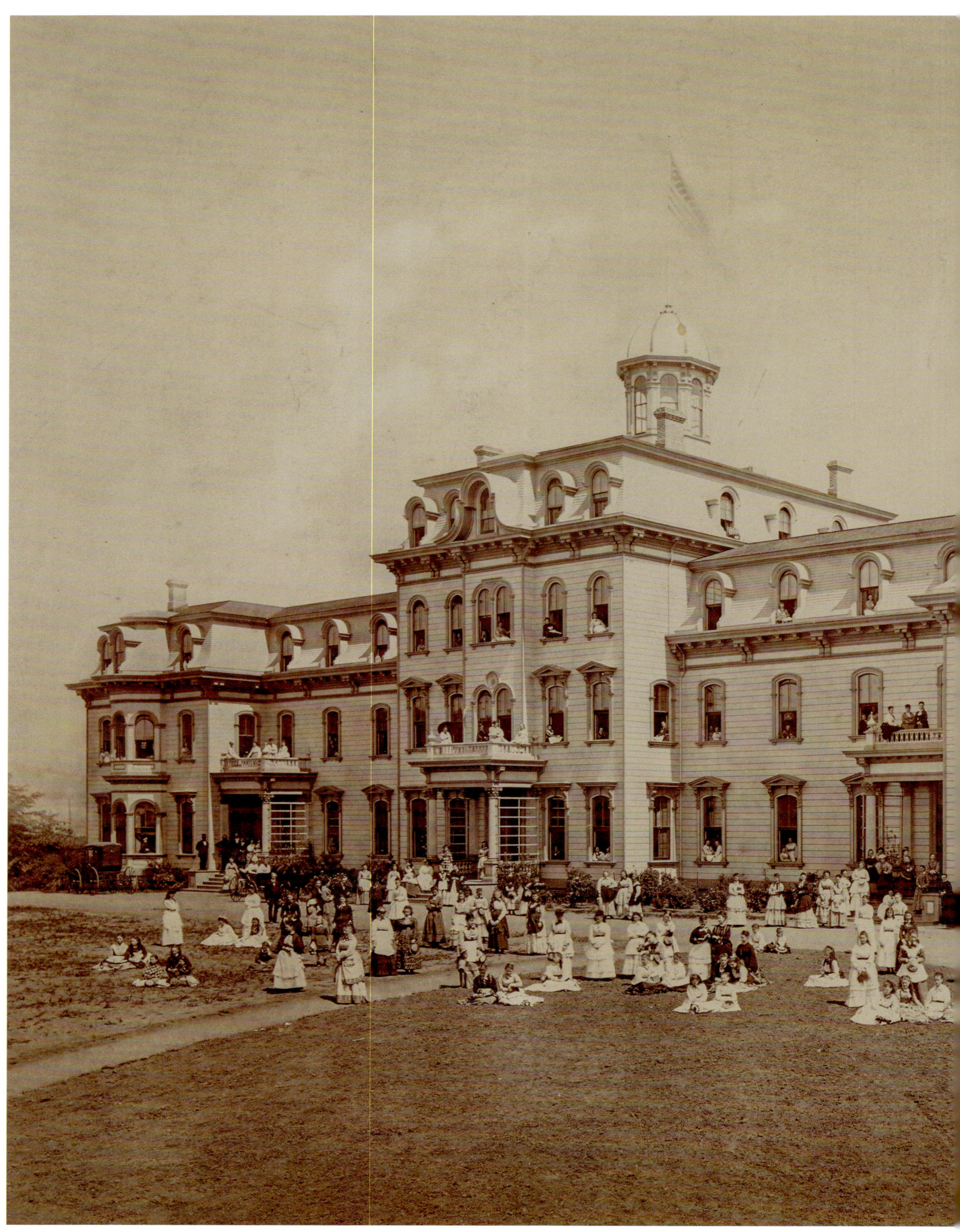

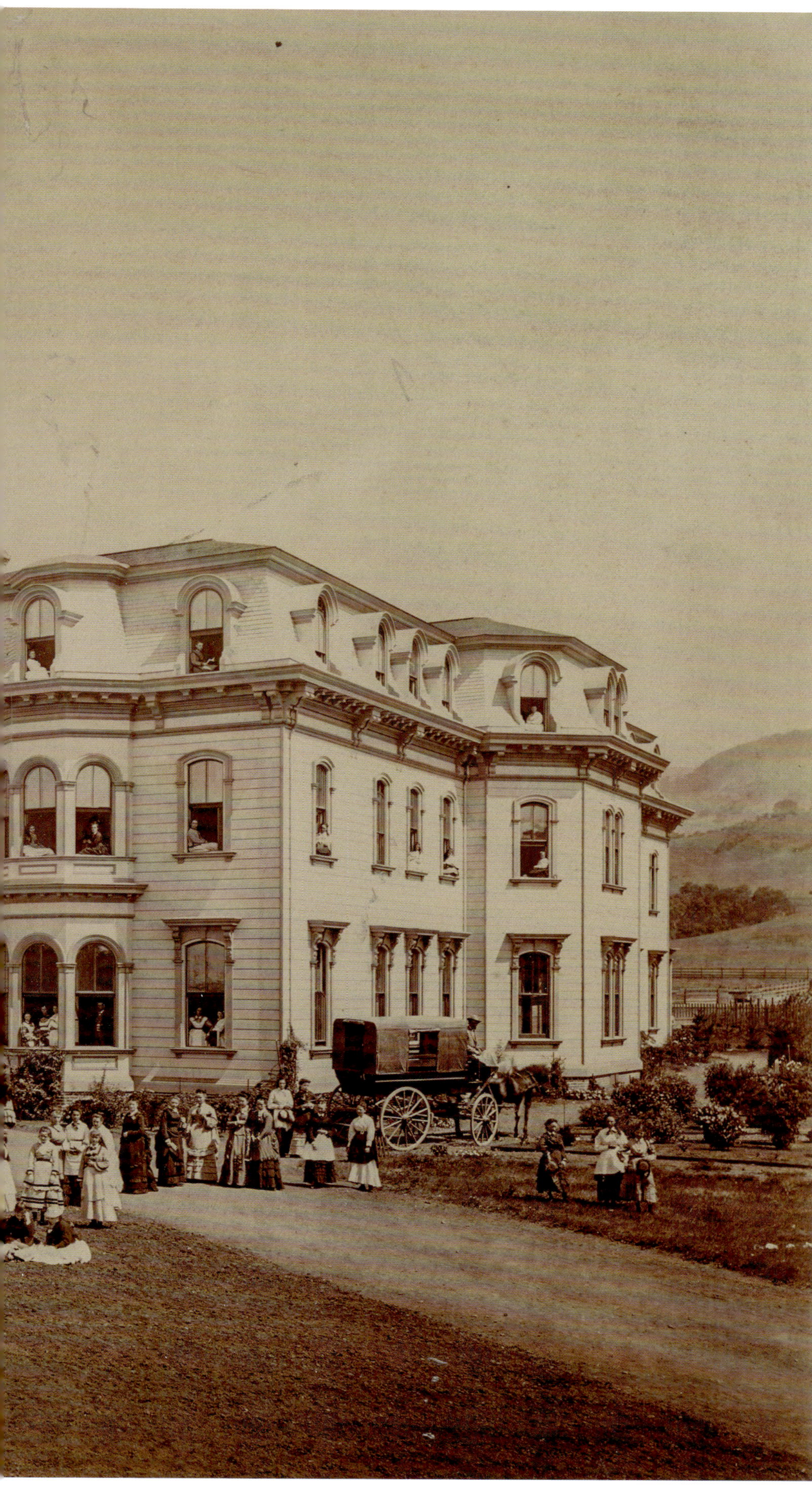

Eadweard Muybridge; Untitled (Mills College, new campus, Oakland Hills); albumen print; 1872; 17 × 21 in.
*Mills Seminary moved to this location in 1871 from Benicia, in Solano County, the year before this photograph was taken. The Millses, who founded the school, were missionaries who believed in equal education for women.*

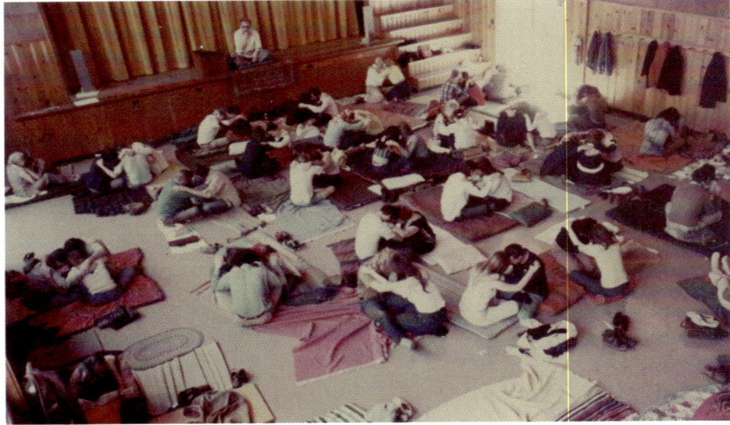

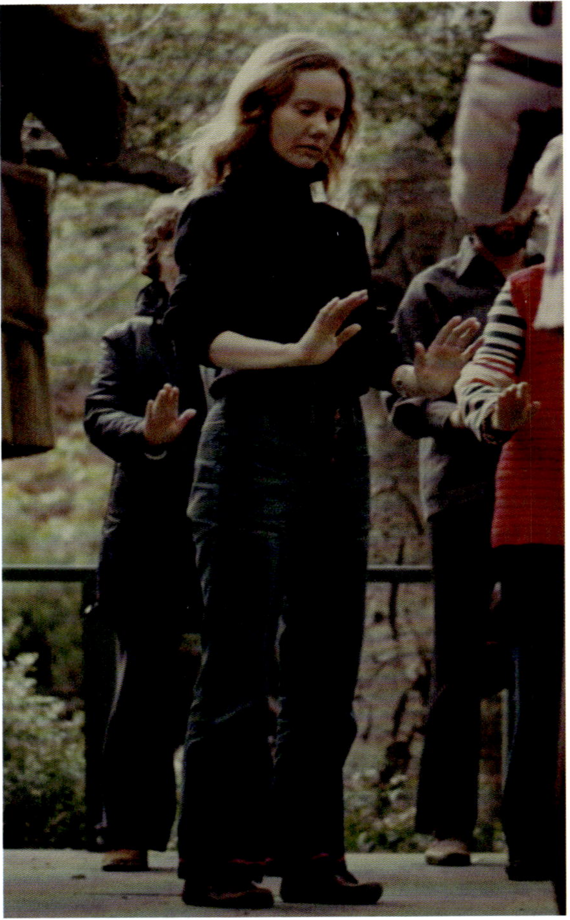

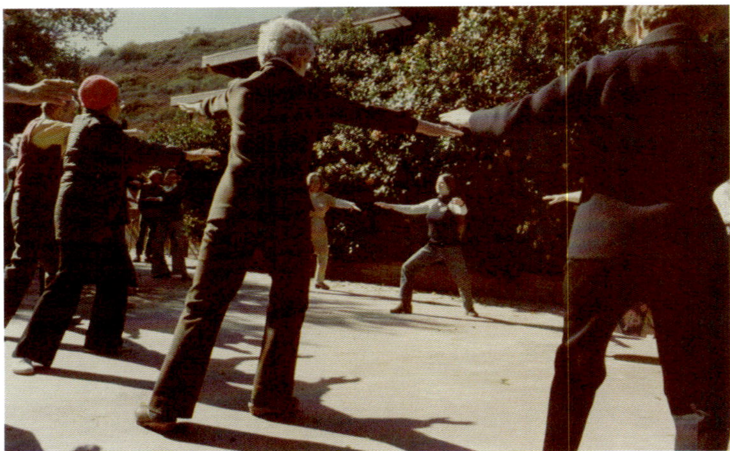

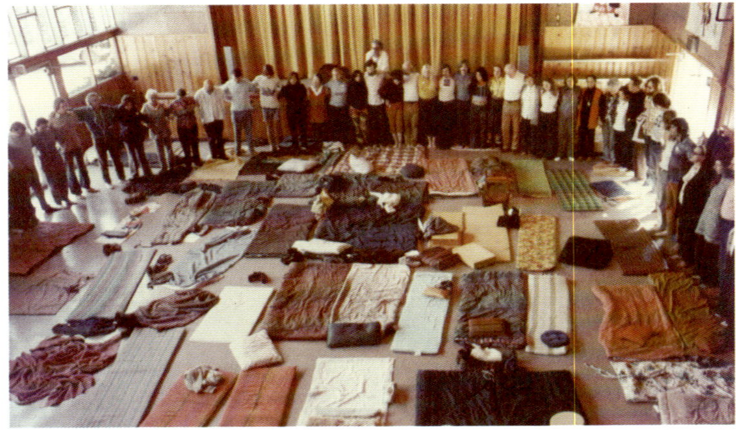

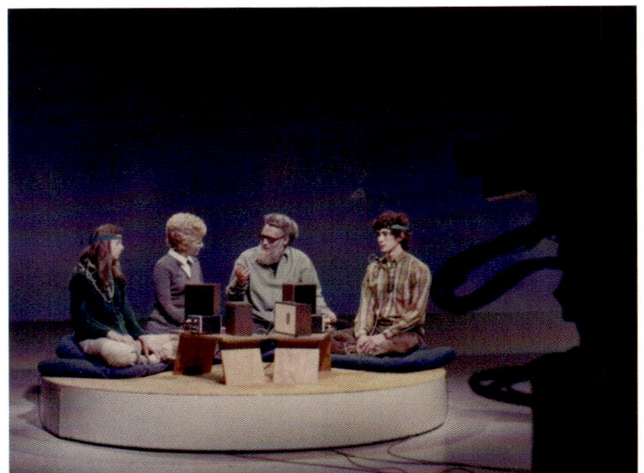

LEFT COLUMN, TOP TO BOTTOM:
Unknown Artist; Untitled (Exercises for enlightenment, Topanga); chromogenic print; ca. 1960; 7⅝ × 4¾ in.
Unknown Artist; Untitled (Exercises for enlightenment, Topanga); chromogenic print; ca. 1960; 7⅝ × 4¾ in.
Unknown Artist; Untitled (Exercises for enlightenment, Topanga); chromogenic print; ca. 1960; 7⅝ × 4¾ in.

RIGHT COLUMN, TOP TO BOTTOM:
Unknown Artist; Untitled (Exercises for enlightenment, Topanga); chromogenic print; ca. 1960; 7⅝ × 4¾ in.
Unknown Artist; Untitled (Exercises for enlightenment, Topanga); chromogenic print; ca. 1960; 7⅝ × 4v¾ in.

*California was a center for such activities as EST, communalism, transcendental meditation, and alternative religious practices, particularly at centers like Moonfire Ranch in Topanga, Esalen in Big Sur, and the San Francisco Zen Center.*

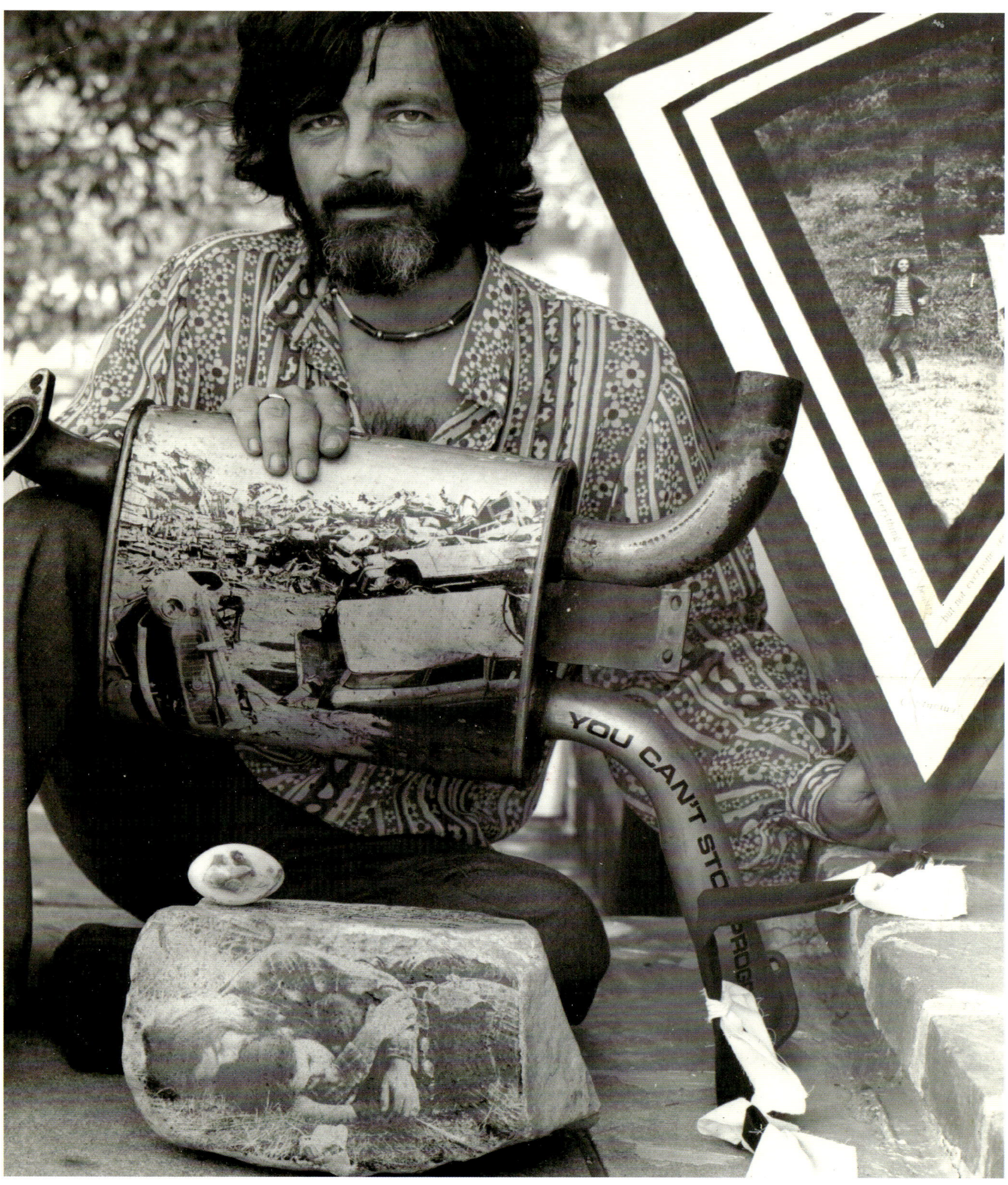


*Unknown Artist; Untitled (Jay Thompson); gelatin silver print; ca. 1965; 9 × 7½ in.*
*Jay Thompson, a photographer who photographed the hippie movement, is depicted here.*

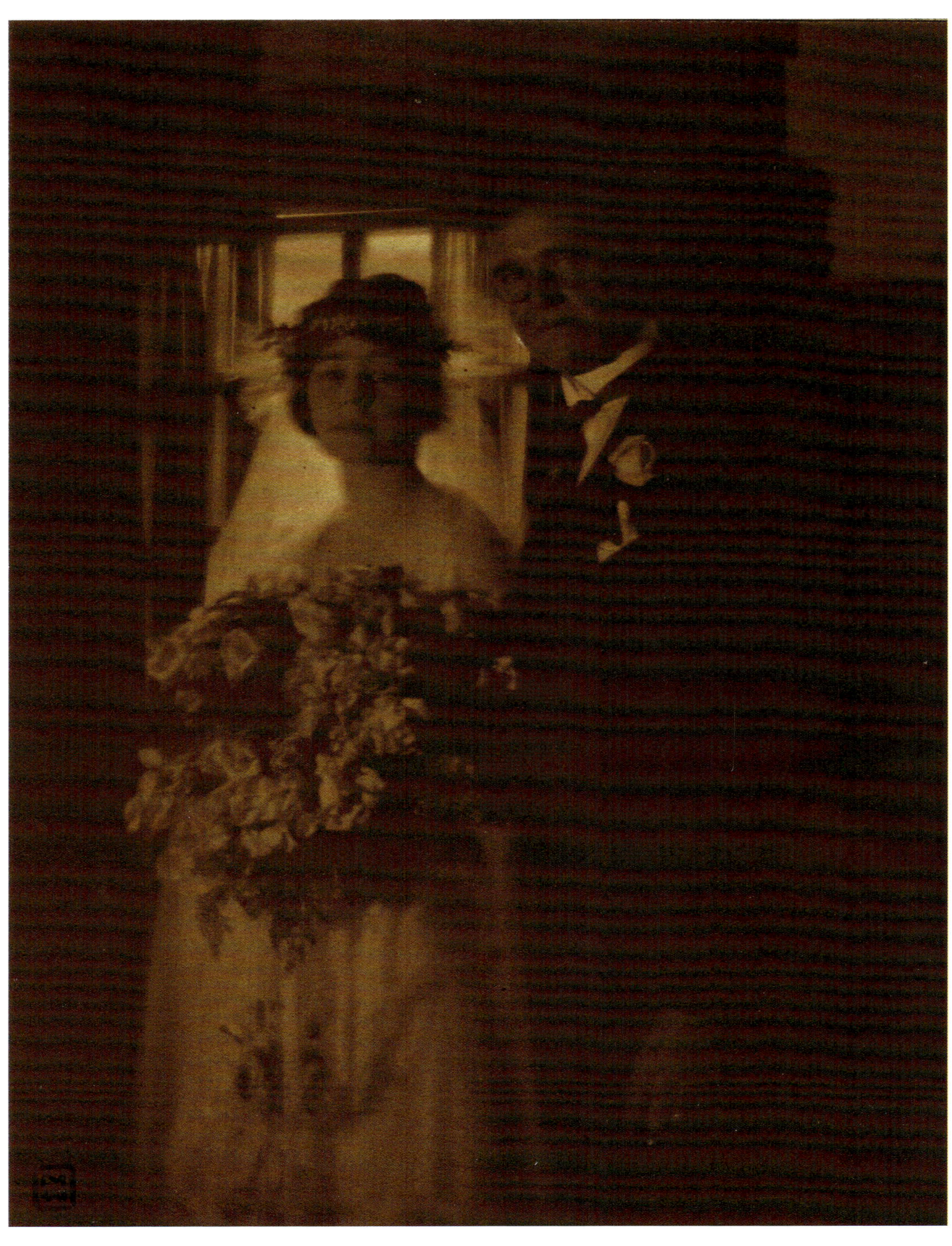

Mabel Watson; Untitled (Wedding of Karl and Ethel Struss); gum platinum print; 1923; 7½ × 5⅞ in.
*Mabel Watson was a pictorial photographer who worked in Pasadena. Karl Struss was a famous still photographer in New York before coming west to work as a cinematographer in silent films. He, along with Charles Rosher, won the first Academy Award for cinematography in 1929 for the film* Sunrise. *Ethel Struss was an artist who studied etching with Paul Landacre.*

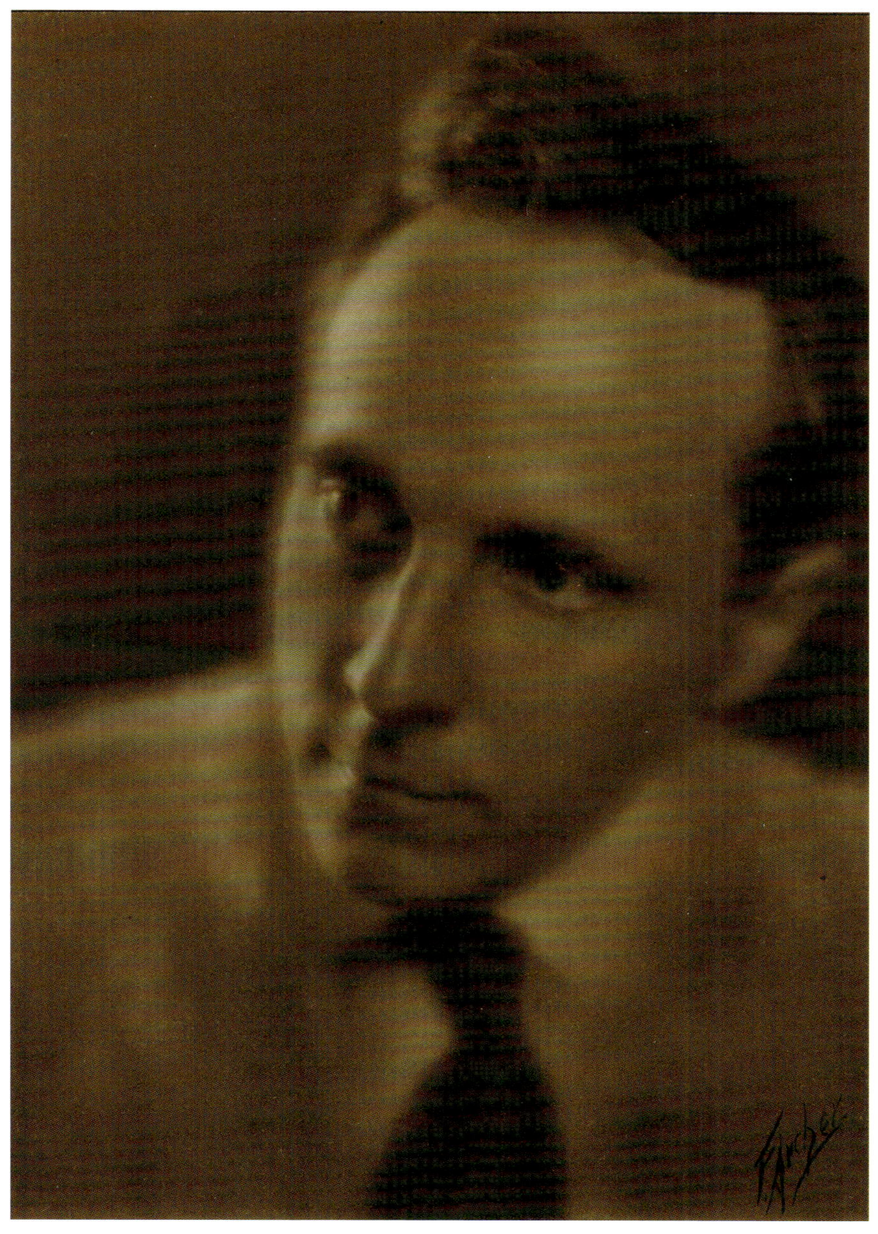

Fred Archer; Untitled (Portrait of Edward Weston); palladium print; 1916; 6½ × 4½ in.
*A reproduction of this image was published in* Photo-Era, *June 1916.*

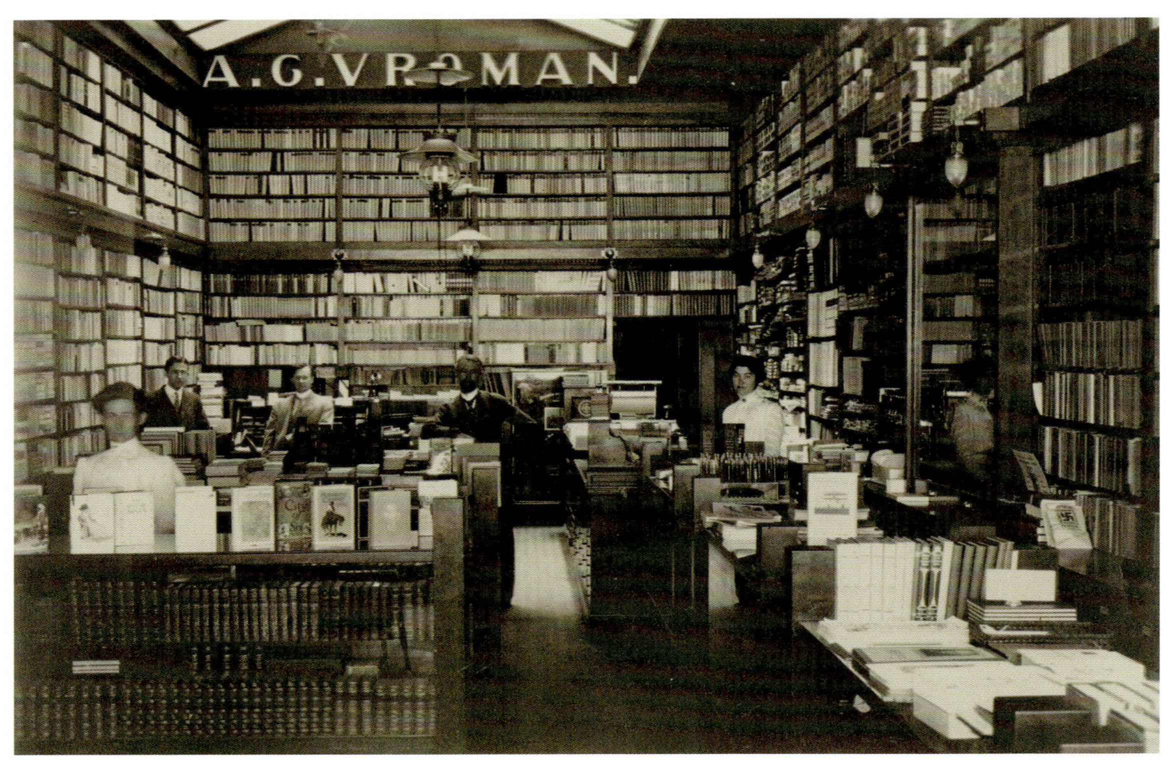


Adam Clark Vroman; *A Pasadena Bookstore*; platinum print; ca. 1908; 4 × 6 in.
*Vroman's is still a popular Pasadena bookstore, more than a hundred years after this photo was taken.*

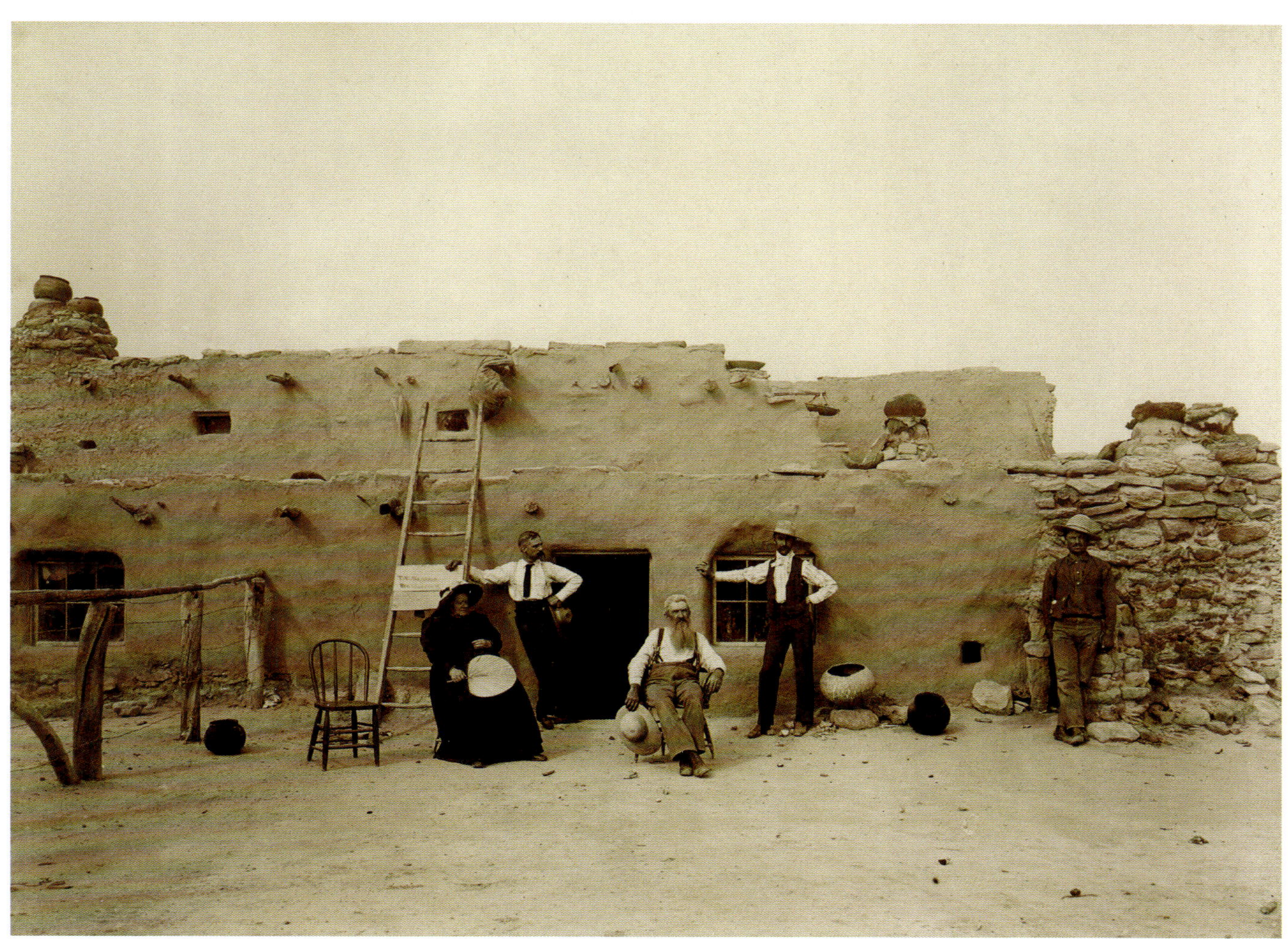

Adam Clark Vroman; *Our Home on the Mesa*; aristotype print; 1895; 6 ¼ × 8 in.
*Shown in "The Photograph and the American Dream," an exhibition at the Van Gogh Museum in Amsterdam, co-curated by the author. Taken on Vroman's first trip to visit and photograph the Hopi.*

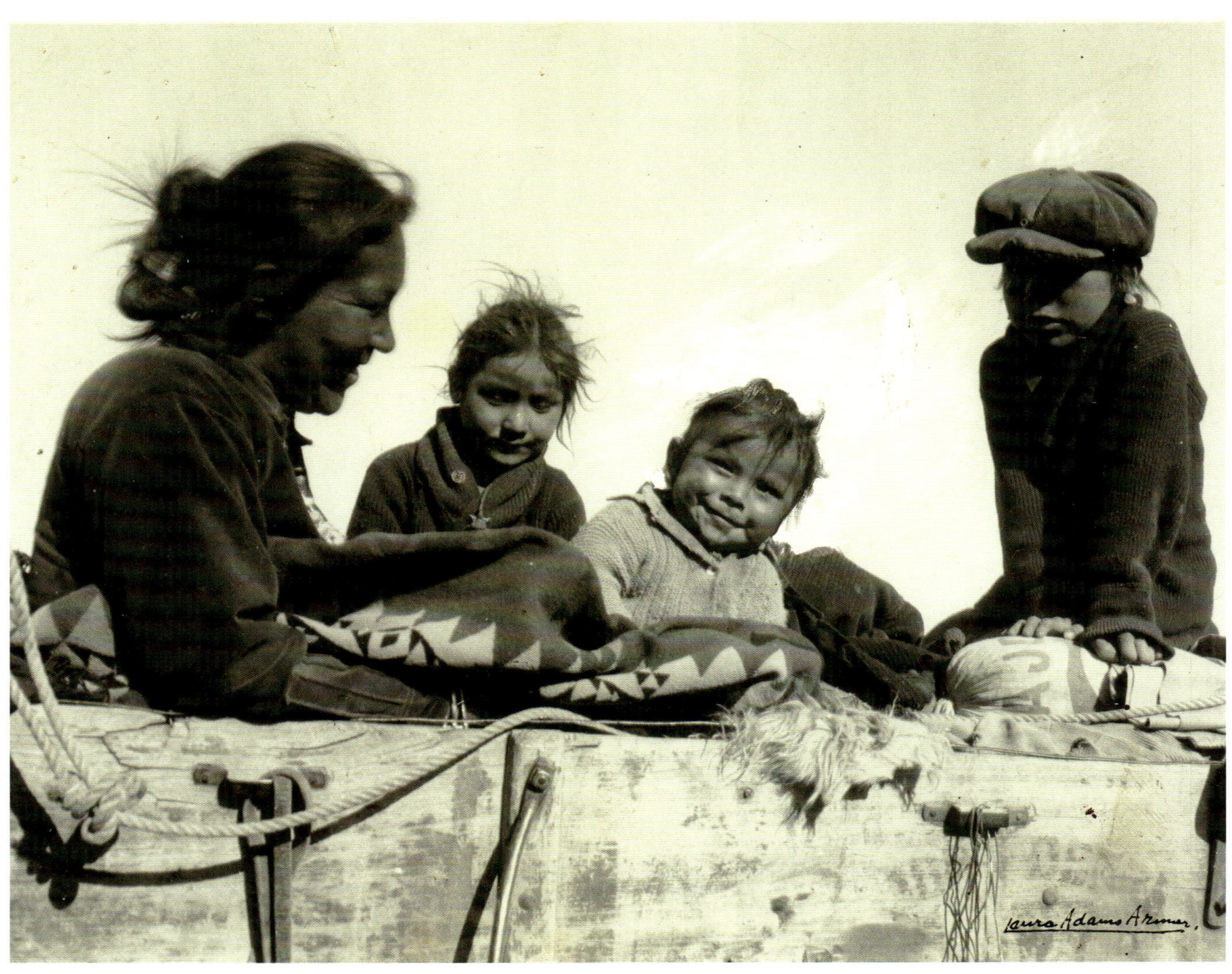


Laura Adams Armer; *There Were Many Little Children in Every Wagon*; gelatin silver print; ca. 1920; 7 ⅜ × 9 ¼ in.
*Armer, a Bay Area writer and photographer, wrote children's books, which she illustrated with her own photographs. The best known was* Waterless Mountain.

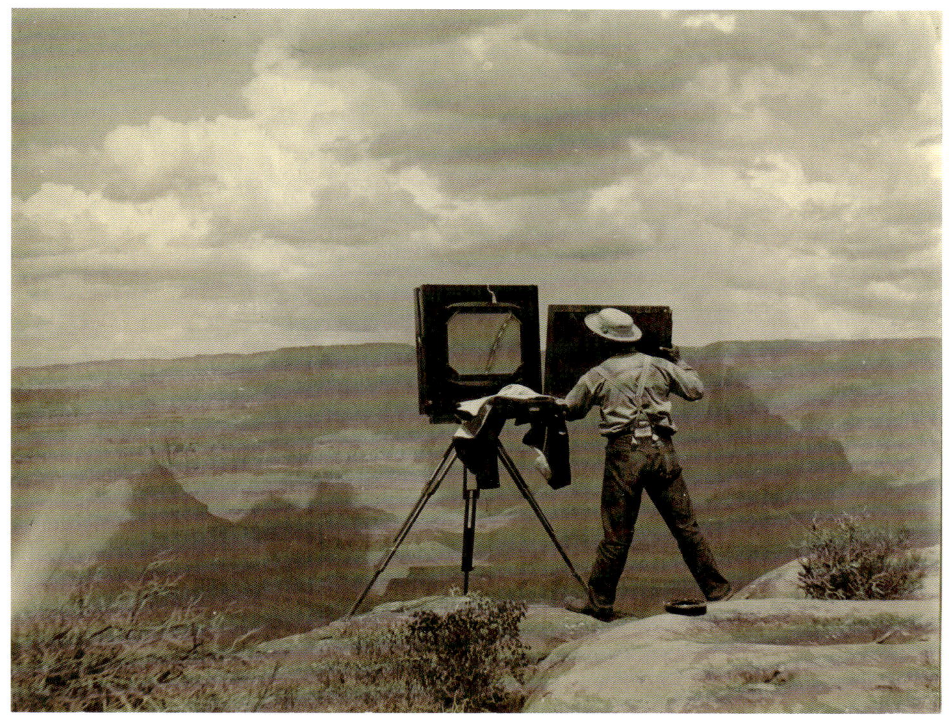

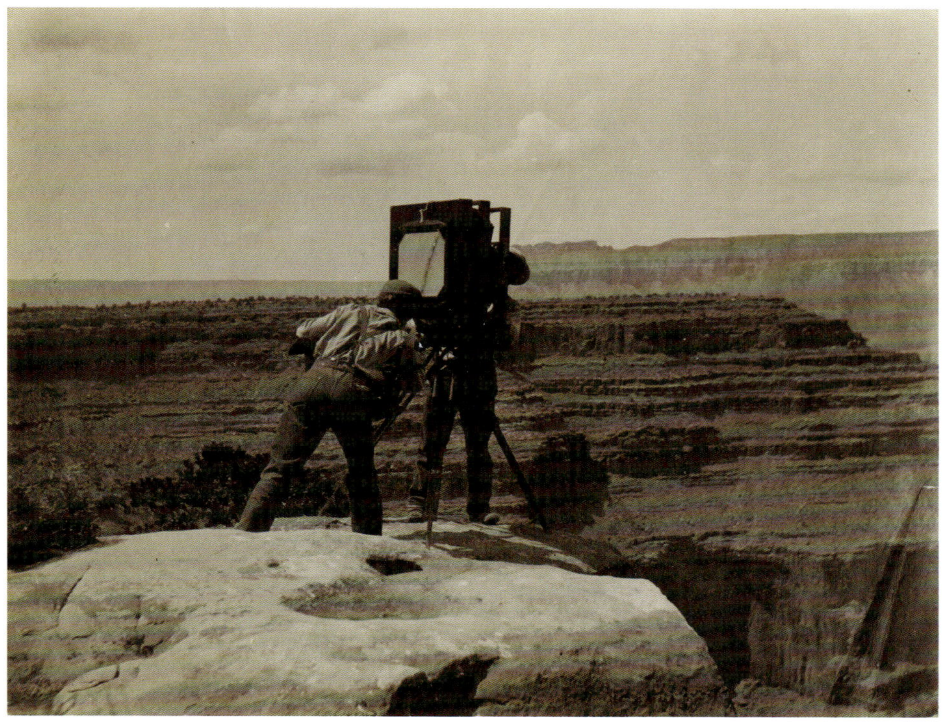

TOP: Henry Peabody; Untitled (Photographing the Grand Canyon); toned silver print; ca. 1900; 3⅝ × 4⅞ in.
BOTTOM: Henry Peabody; Untitled (Photographing the Grand Canyon); toned silver print; ca. 1900; 3⅝ × 4⅞ in.
*Peabody was a Pasadena photographer who photographed the West and once worked with photographer William Henry Jackson.*

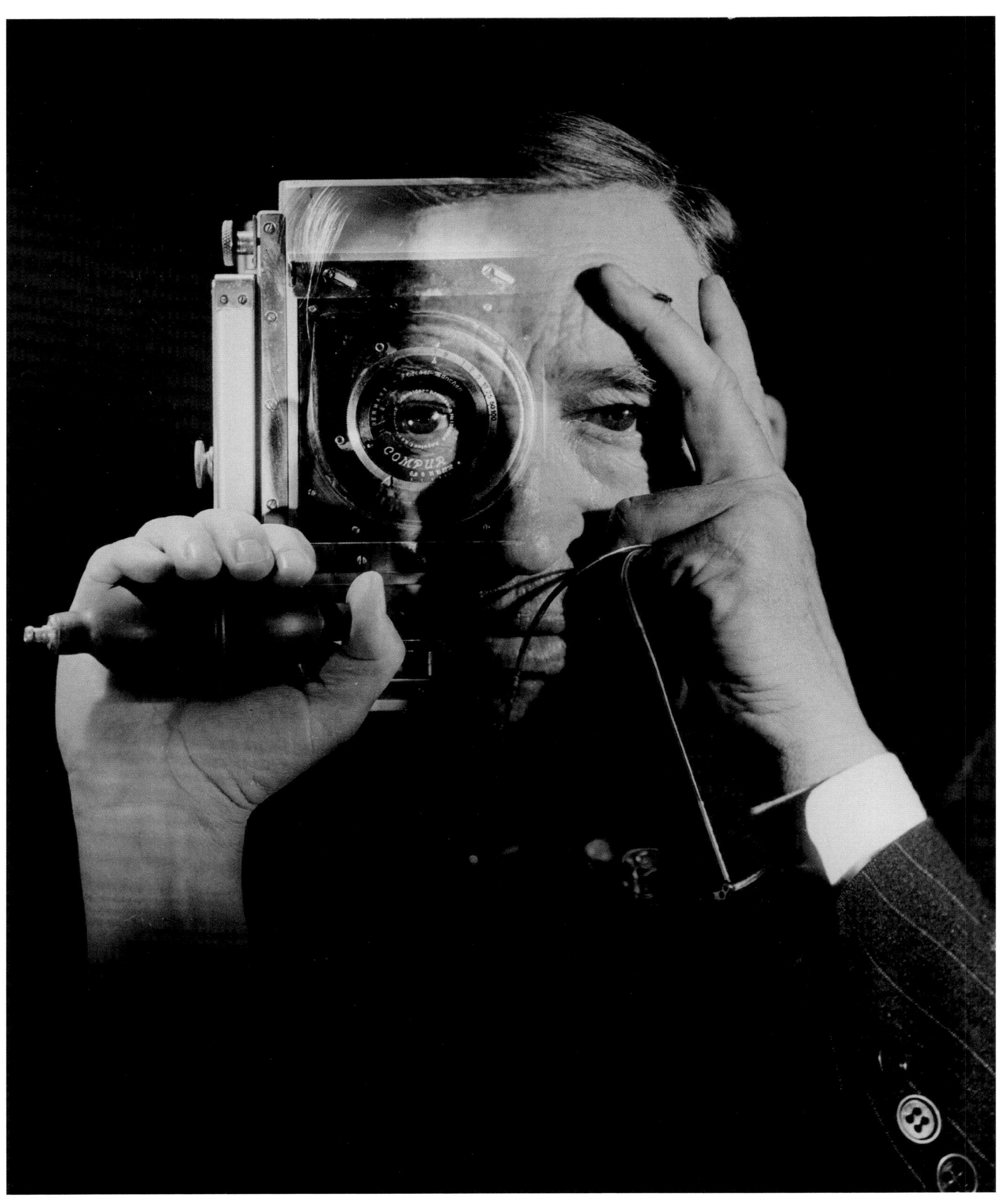


Fred Archer; Untitled (Self-portrait); gelatin silver print; ca. 1946; 15¼ × 12½ in.
*Archer taught at Art Center School. He is also known for developing the zone system with Ansel Adams, used in highlighting elements in landscape photography.*

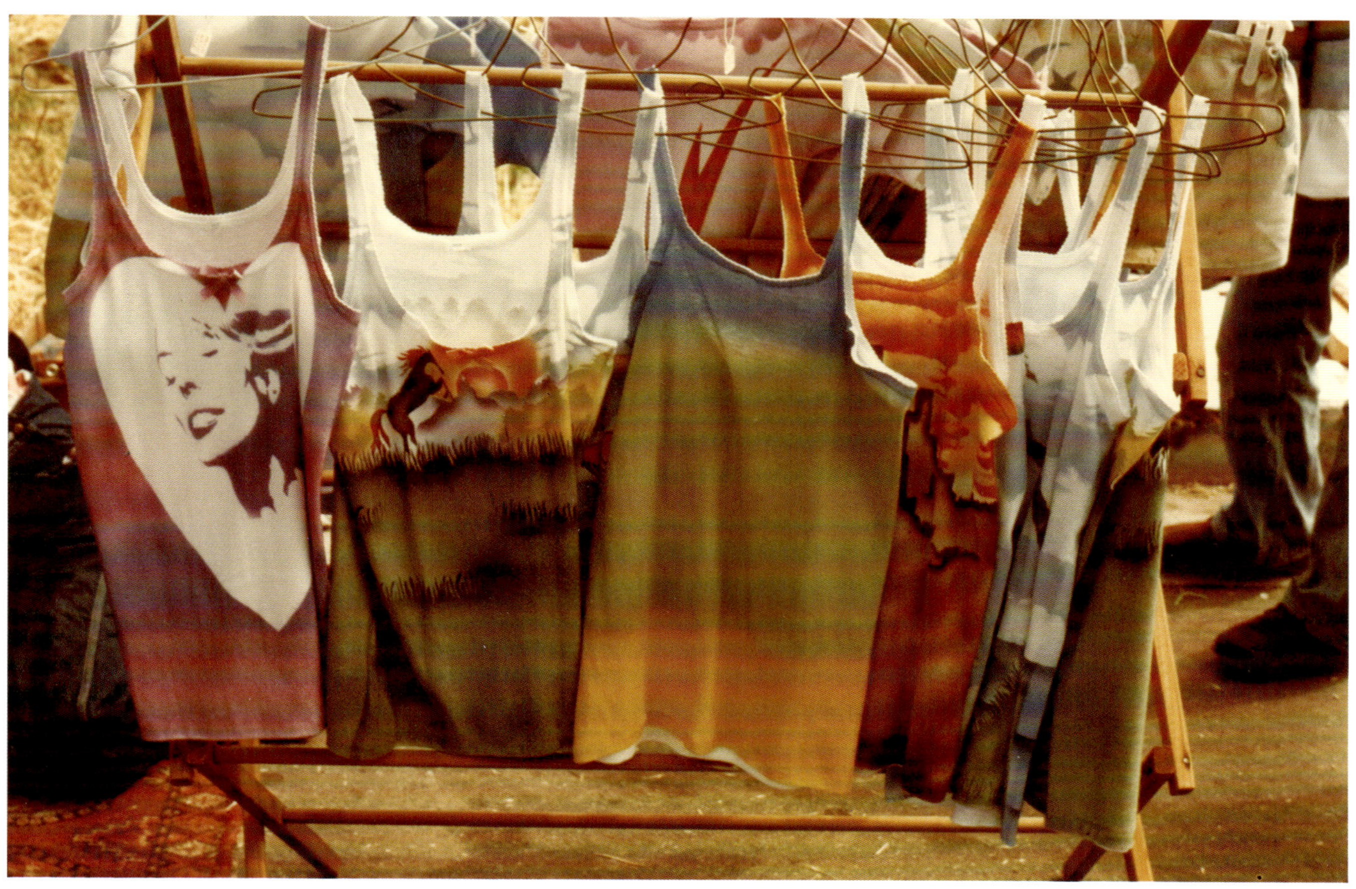

Marion Post Wolcott; *Tie-Dye for Sale in Isla Vista*; chromogenic print; ca. 1960; 6⅜ × 9½ in.
*Wolcott, best known for her work for the Farm Security Administration during the Depression, took photographs around California in the 1960s.*

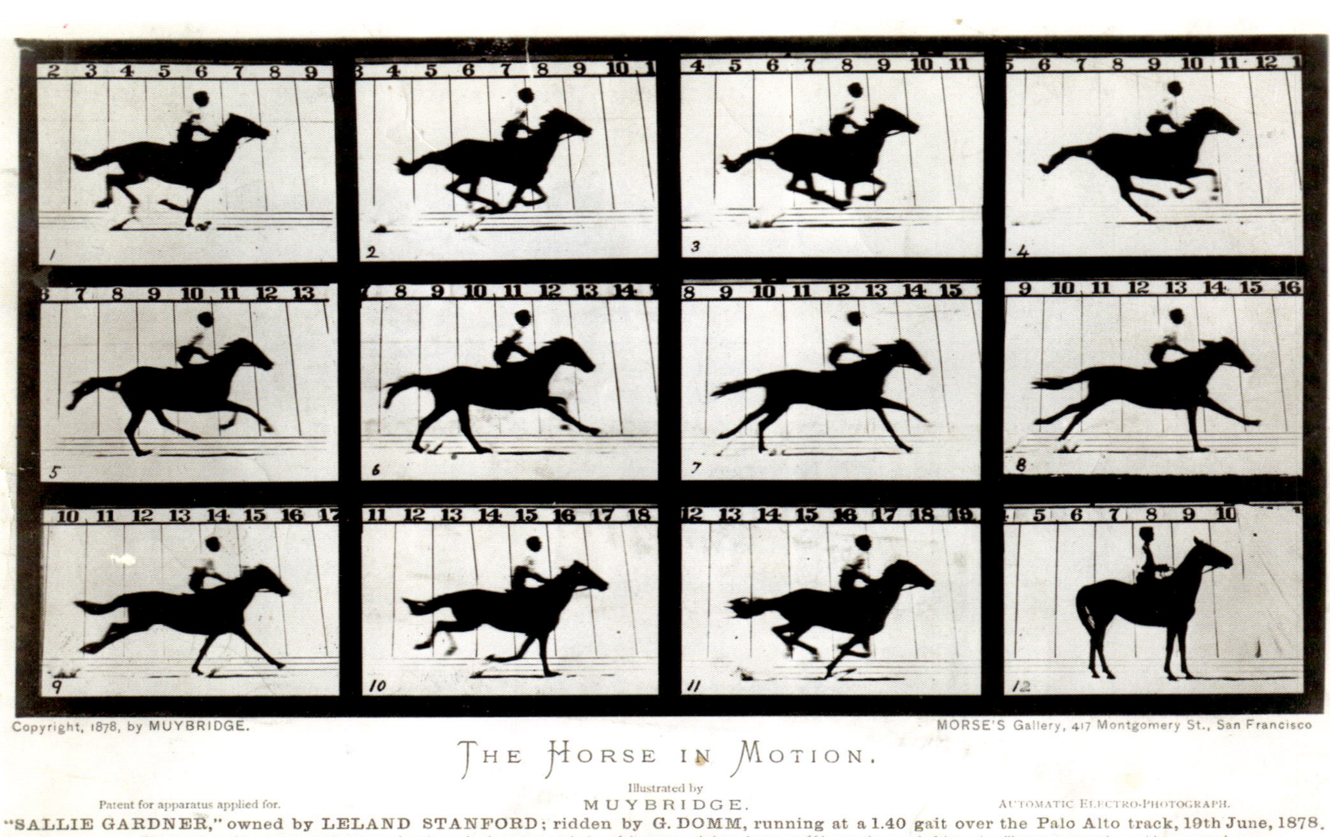


Eadweard Muybridge; *The Horse in Motion, Sallie Gardner*; gelatin silver print; 1878, printed later; 8⅛ × 10 in.
*In 1872, at the request of Leland Stanford, Muybridge set up a series of cameras side-by-side to prove whether a horse ran with all four feet off the ground. Muybridge attached a string to each camera, then ran each string across the track, so that the movement of the horse's feet would prove out Stanford's theory.*

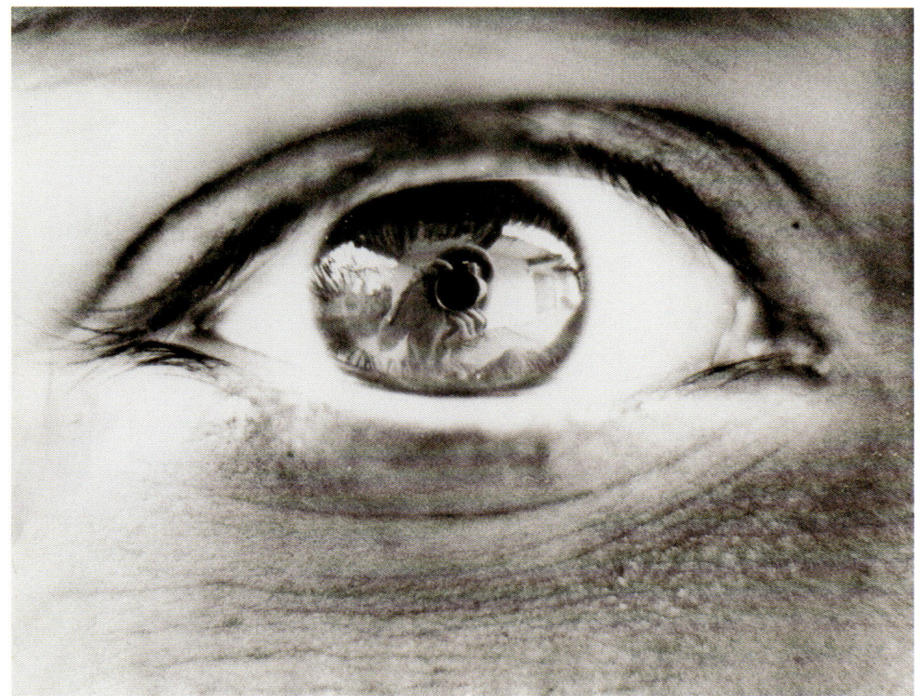

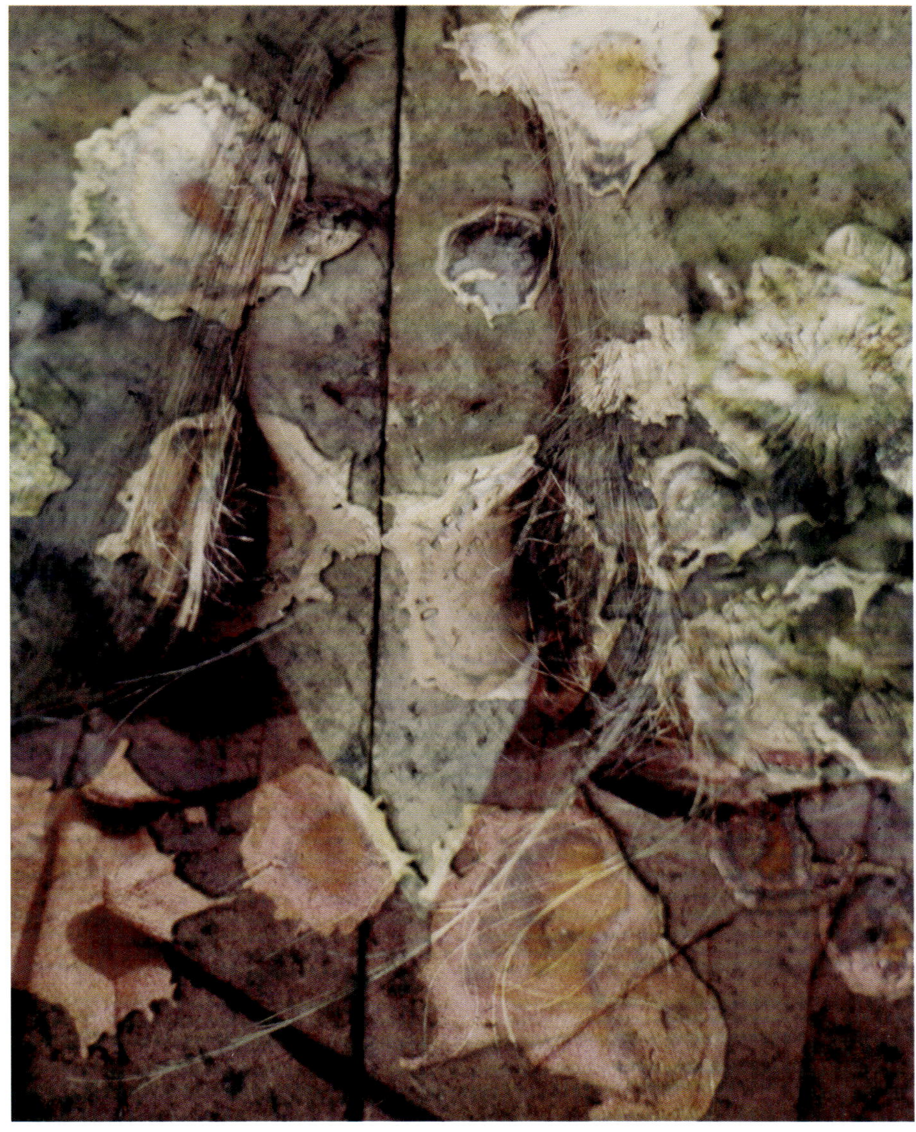

TOP: Kali Archibald; *The Eye is a Photographer*; gelatin silver print; 1968; 8 × 10 in.

BOTTOM: Kali Archibald; *Hip-Girl-Red Coat-Sand*; gelatin silver print; ca. 1960; 9½ × 7½ in.

*Kali Archibald's papers and photographs are at Emory University. In the 1960s, she lived and worked out of Palm Springs, California. Her given name was Joan M. Yarusso. In 2021, her work was featured in an exhibition at Staley-Wise Gallery in New York.*

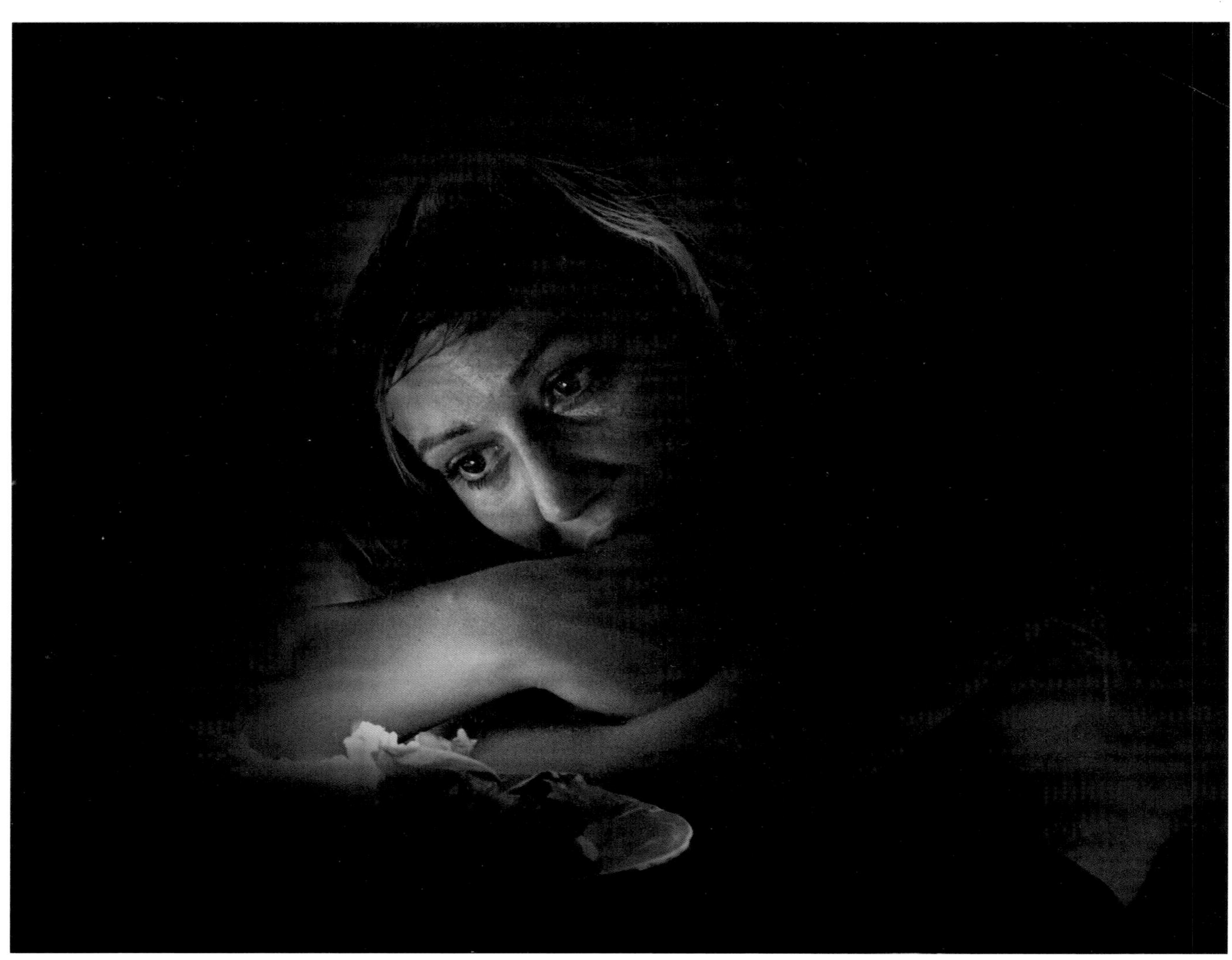

Wynn Bullock; Untitled (Dreaming); gelatin silver print; ca. 1960; 7½ × 9 ⅜ in.
*While we don't know the nature of this woman's dreams, we know California is a place that has drawn dreamers from all over the world.*

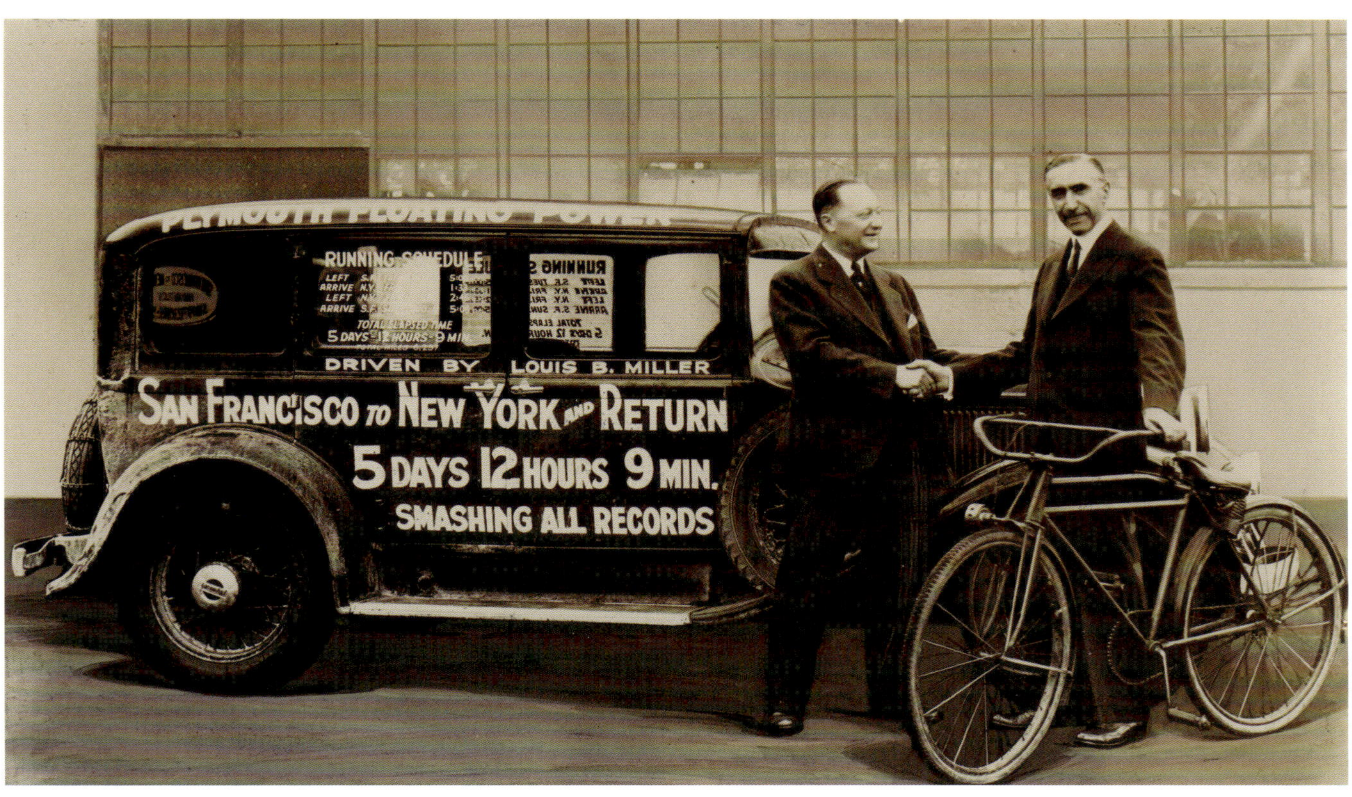


Unknown Artist; L.B. Miller, *Driver of the Record-Breaking Transcontinental Plymouth*; toned silver print; 1931; 5½ × 9¼ in.
*Miller drove his Plymouth from San Francisco to New York and back in five days, twelve hours, and nine minutes.*

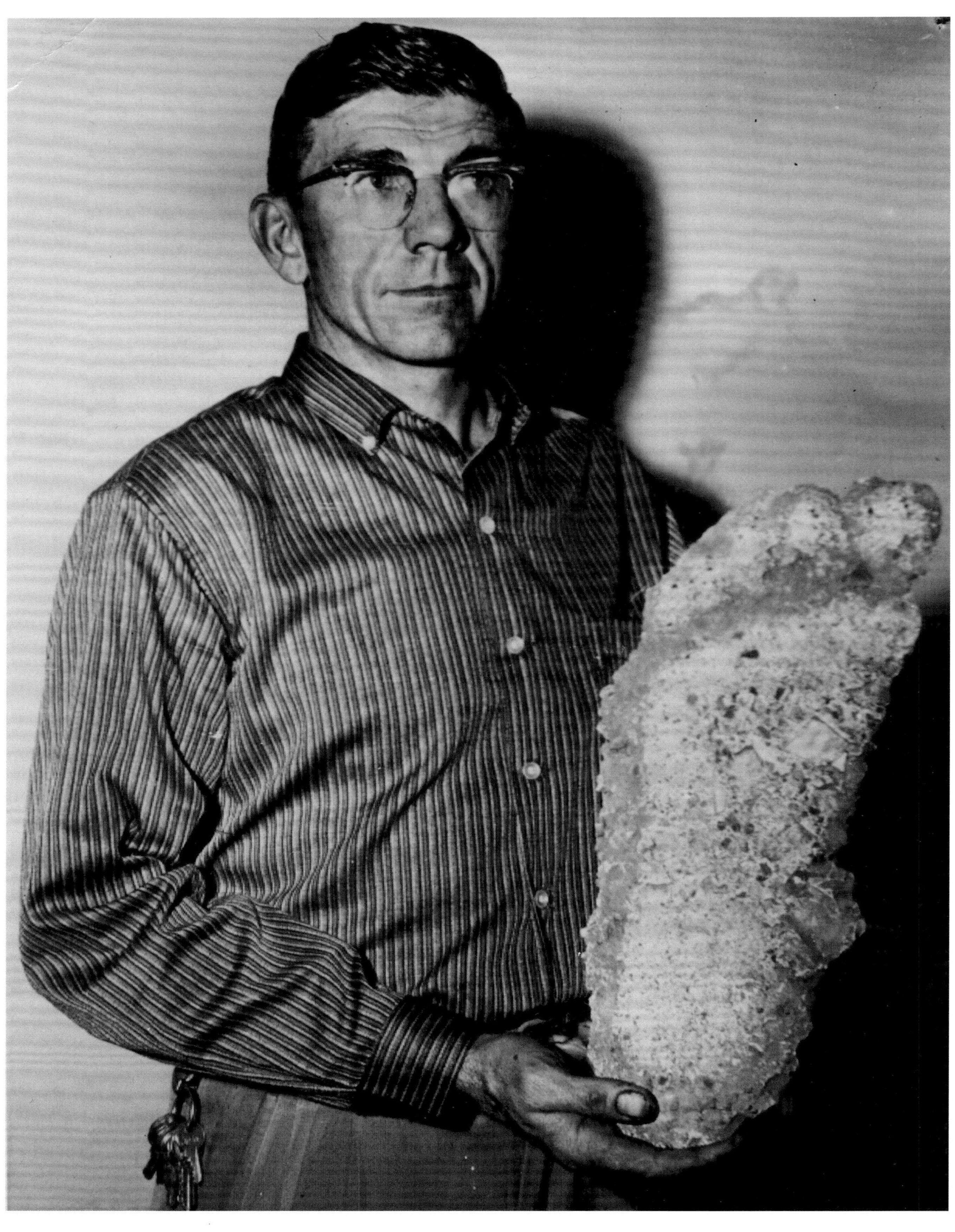

AP Wire Photo; *"BIGFOOT" REAL Plaster Cast of a Footprint 16-Inches Long*; gelatin silver print; 1958; 9¼ × 5½ in.
*Bigfoot is the California version of the Loch Ness monster. There were many sightings of Bigfoot in the Northern California woods, and Gerry Crew's plaster cast of "Bigfoot" joined in the fun.*

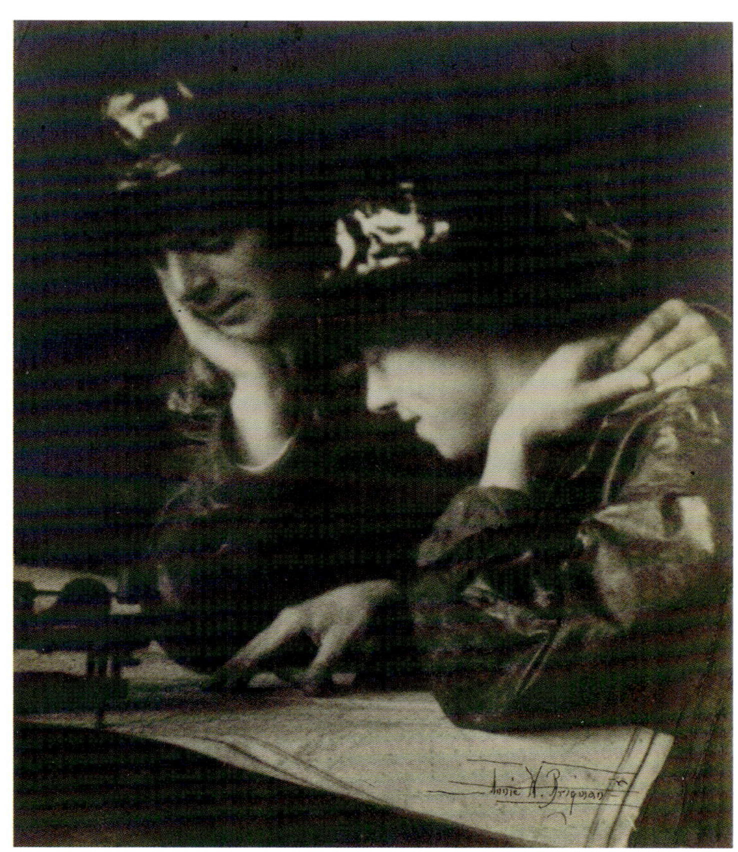

Anne Brigman; Untitled (Jack and Charmain London); gelatin silver print; ca. 1910; 4½ × 3¾ in.
*Jack London, a brilliant writer, also ran for mayor of Oakland. Annie Brigman was an outstanding Bay Area photographer whose work was published in* Camera Work *magazine.*

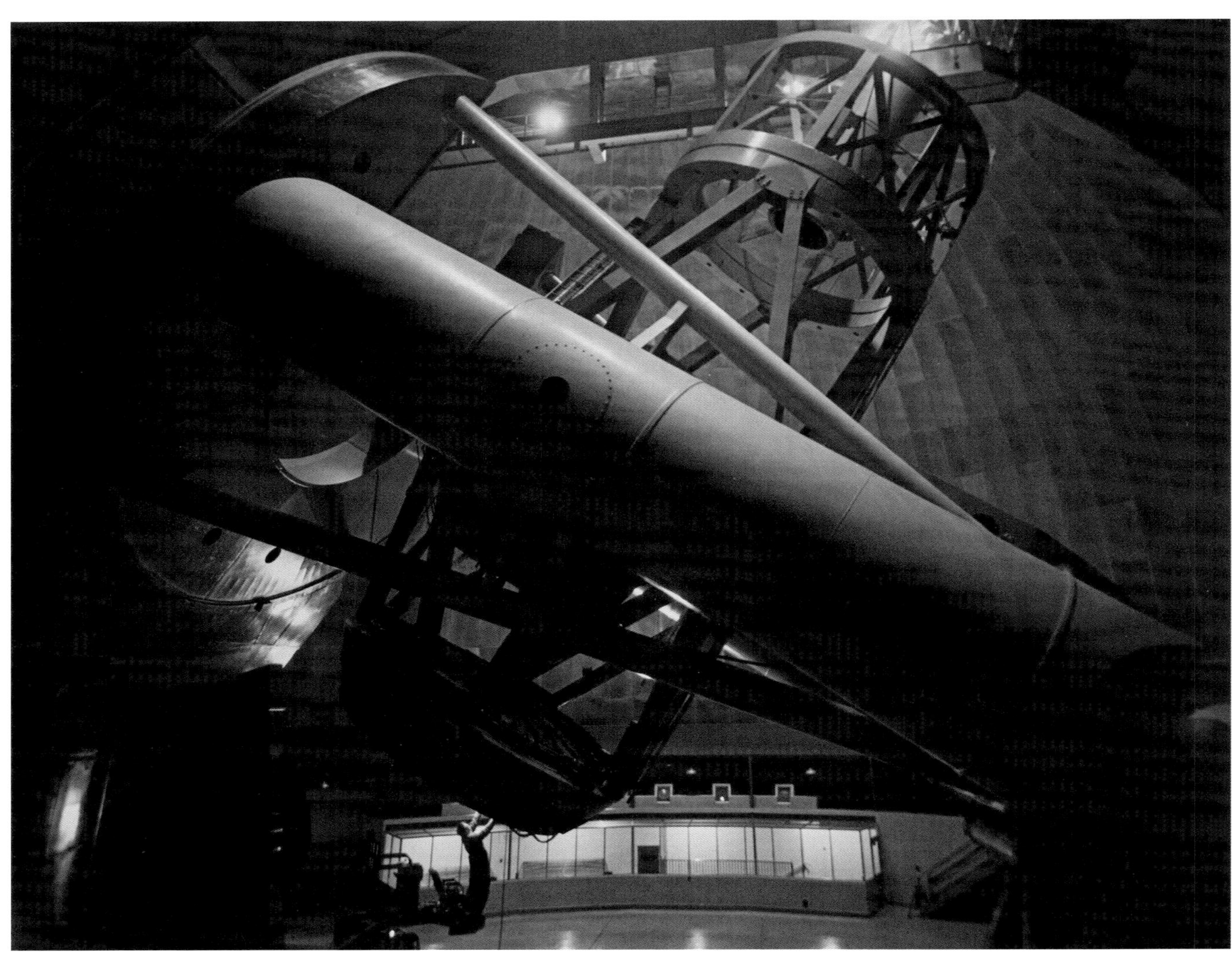

Will Connell; *Hale Telescope*; gelatin silver print; ca. 1950; 15½ × 19⅝ in.
*Astronomers dreamed of better understanding the universe. George Hale championed building Palomar Observatory in San Diego County, where the 200-inch Hale telescope is housed.*

OPPOSITE TOP: Unknown Artist; *Giant Telescope at Lick Observatory*; albumen print; 1886; 8 × 10 in.
OPPOSITE BOTTOM: Isaiah W. Taber; *James Lick Tomb Beneath Telescope, Lick Observatory*; albumen print; ca. 1890; 9 × 11¼ in.
*James Lick was once the richest man in California. He made his money investing in property during and after the Gold Rush. Prior to his death, he wanted to build a series of monuments to himself, but the famous California geologist, George Davidson, talked Lick into using his money to benefit science and the common good. When Lick died in 1876, some of his wealth was used to construct Lick Observatory near San Jose. Once it was completed, in accordance with his wishes, his body was moved and entombed beneath the giant telescope.*

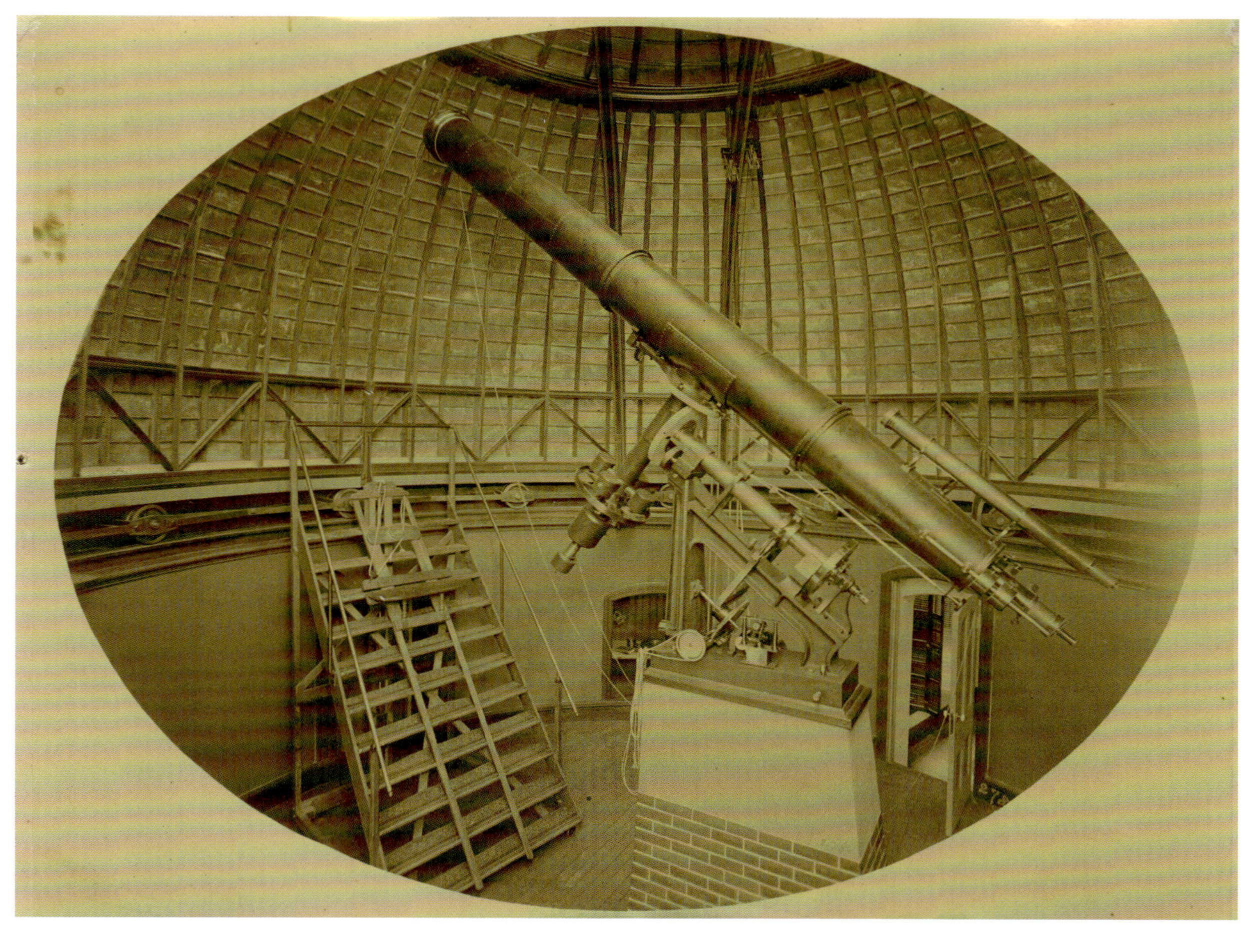

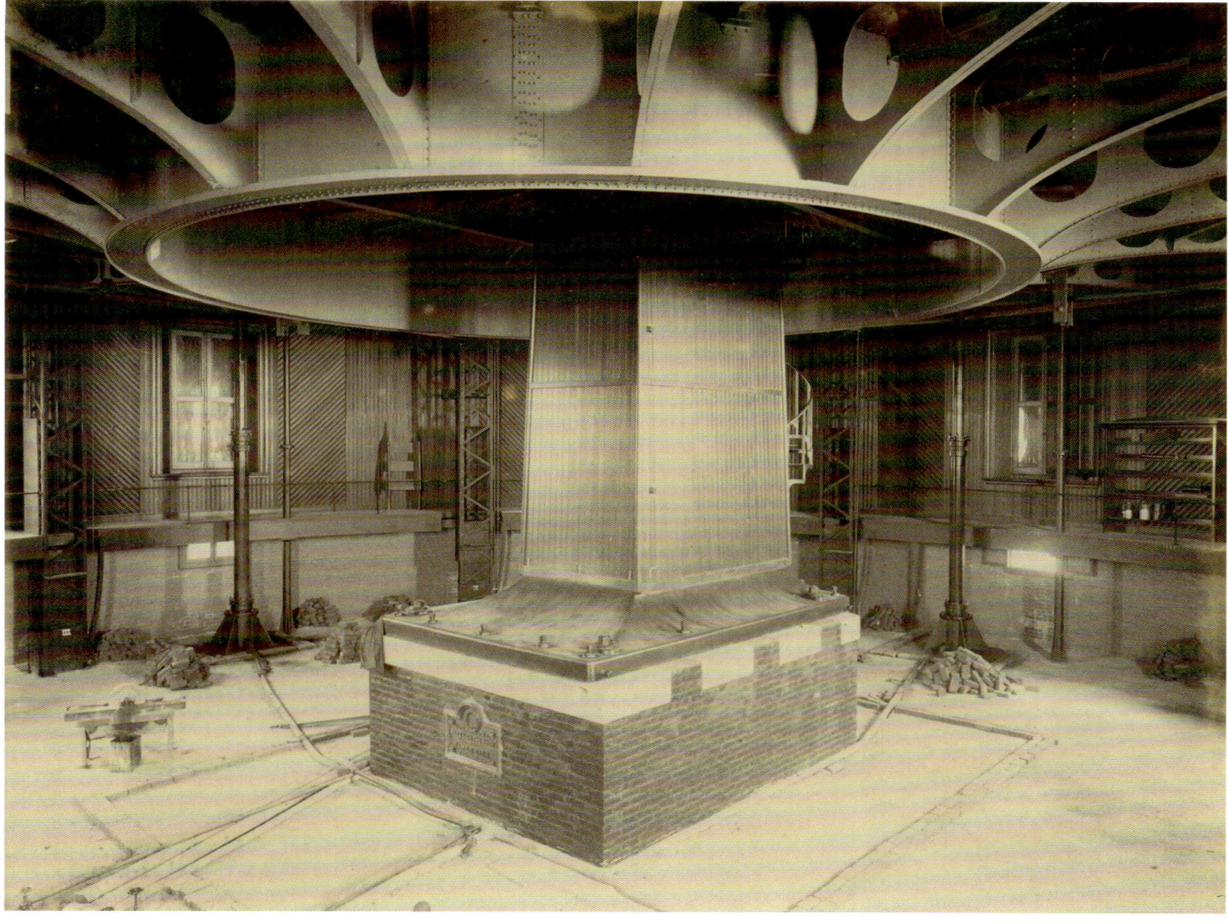

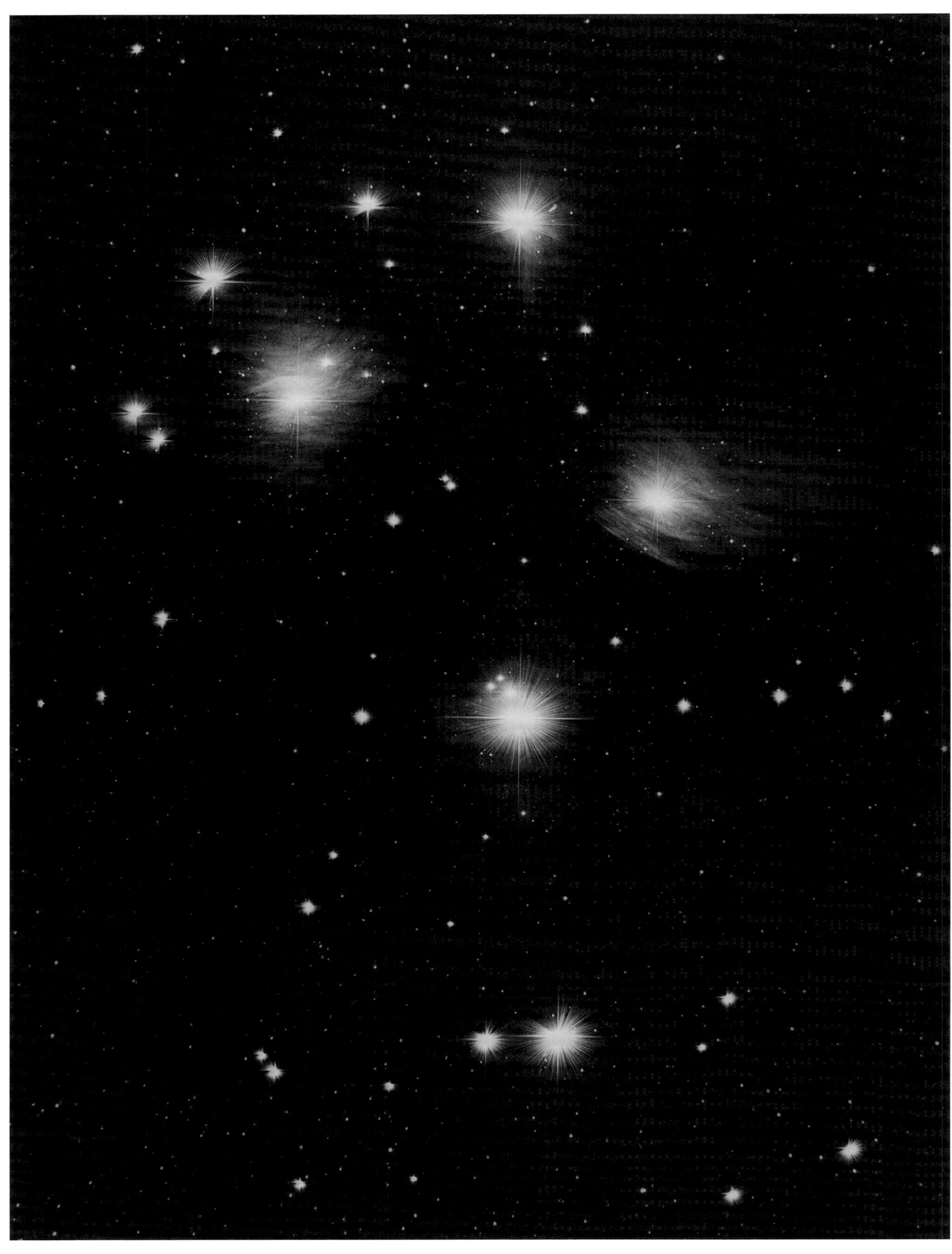

Palomar Observatory, print attributed to Ansel Adams; *Pleiades Constellation*; gelatin silver print; 1955; paper size: 19¼ × 14¼ in. *Exhibited on Panel 14 in the exhibition* This is the American Earth, *shown at Yosemite in 1955.*

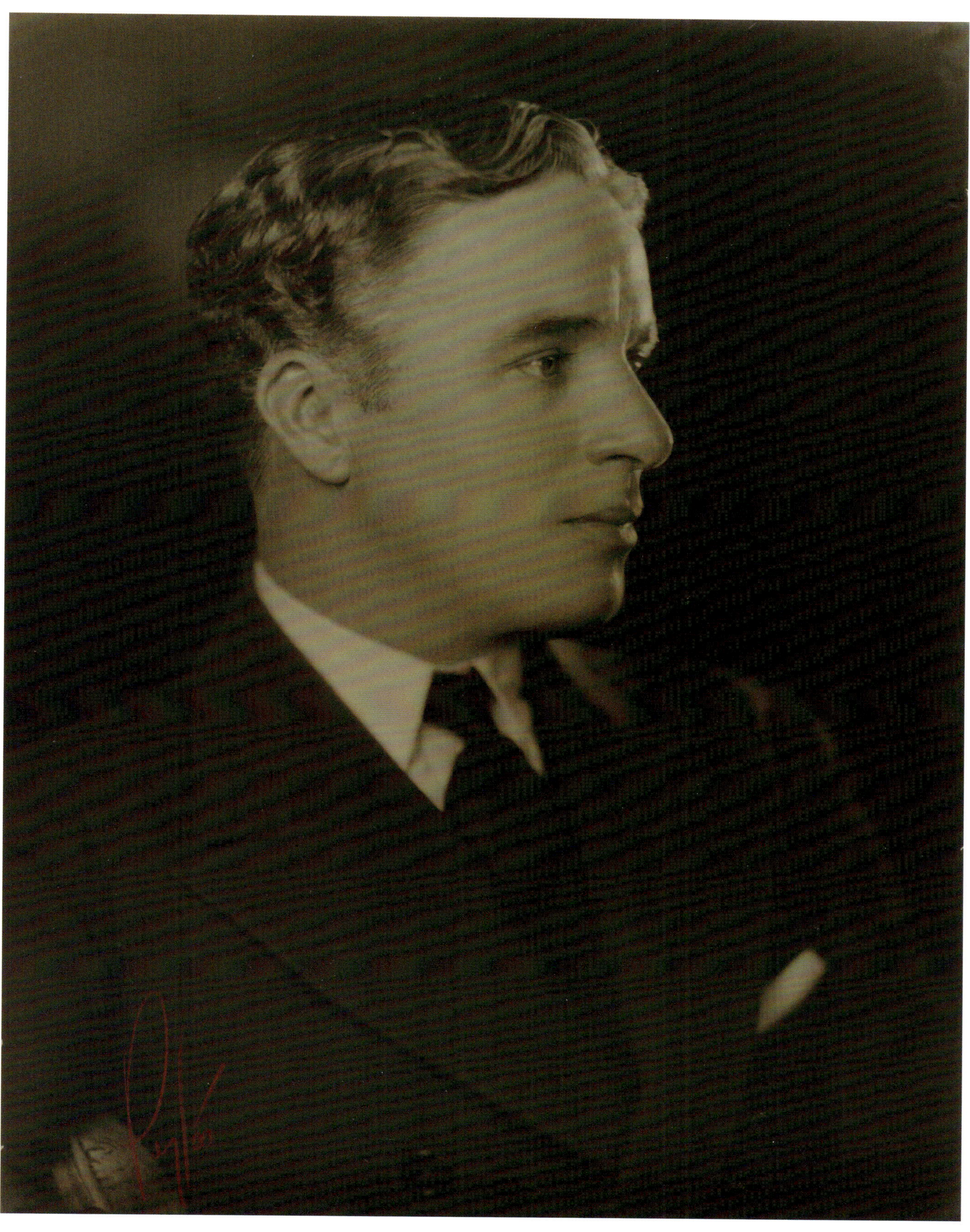

Homer Peyton; *Charlie Chaplin*; toned gelatin silver print; 1929; 13½ × 10½ in.
*Payton worked with Benjamin Strauss in their Kansas City studios from 1903 to 1929. Together they photographed many of the most important people in the arts. After they separated and sold their business to their employees in 1929, Peyton set up a studio for a few months in Hollywood.*

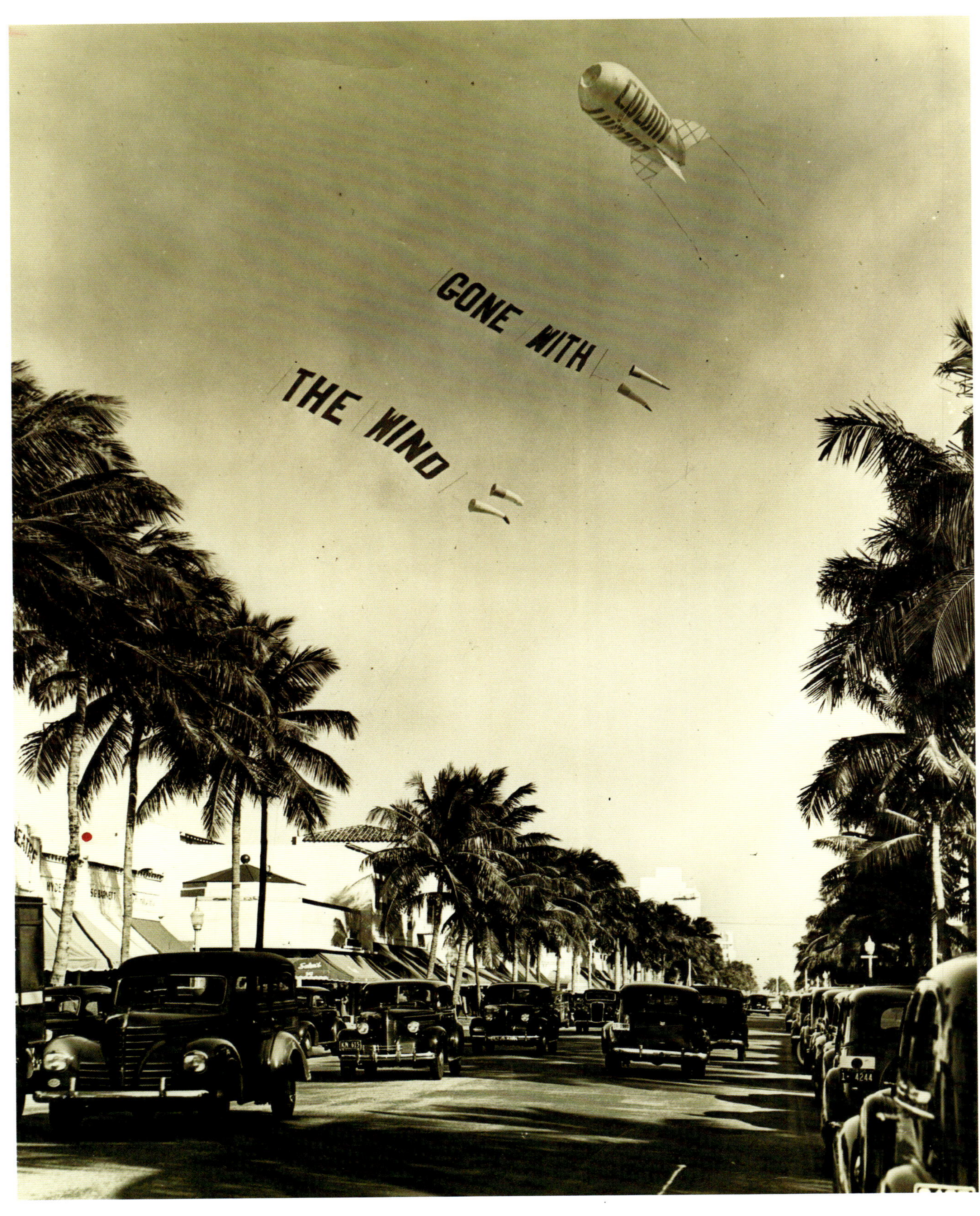


Unknown Artist; *Gone with the Wind*; gelatin silver print; 1939; 9½ × 7¾ in.
*This image may have been taken in Venice, California.*

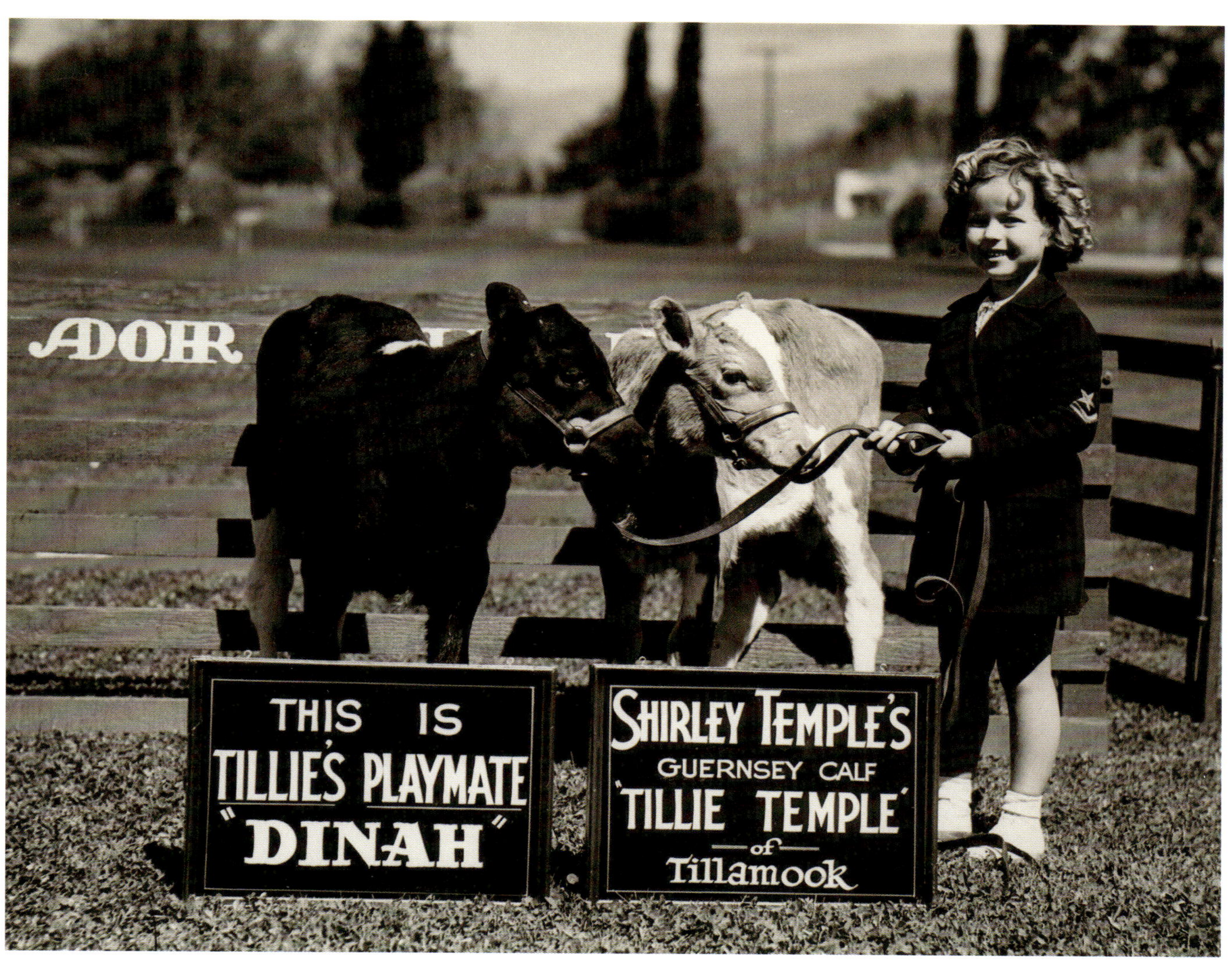


Frank Judson; Untitled (Shirley Temple for Adohr Farms); gelatin silver print; ca. 1936; 7½ × 9½ in.
*Judson was part of the famous Los Angeles family of craftsmen that ran Judson Studios since 1897.*

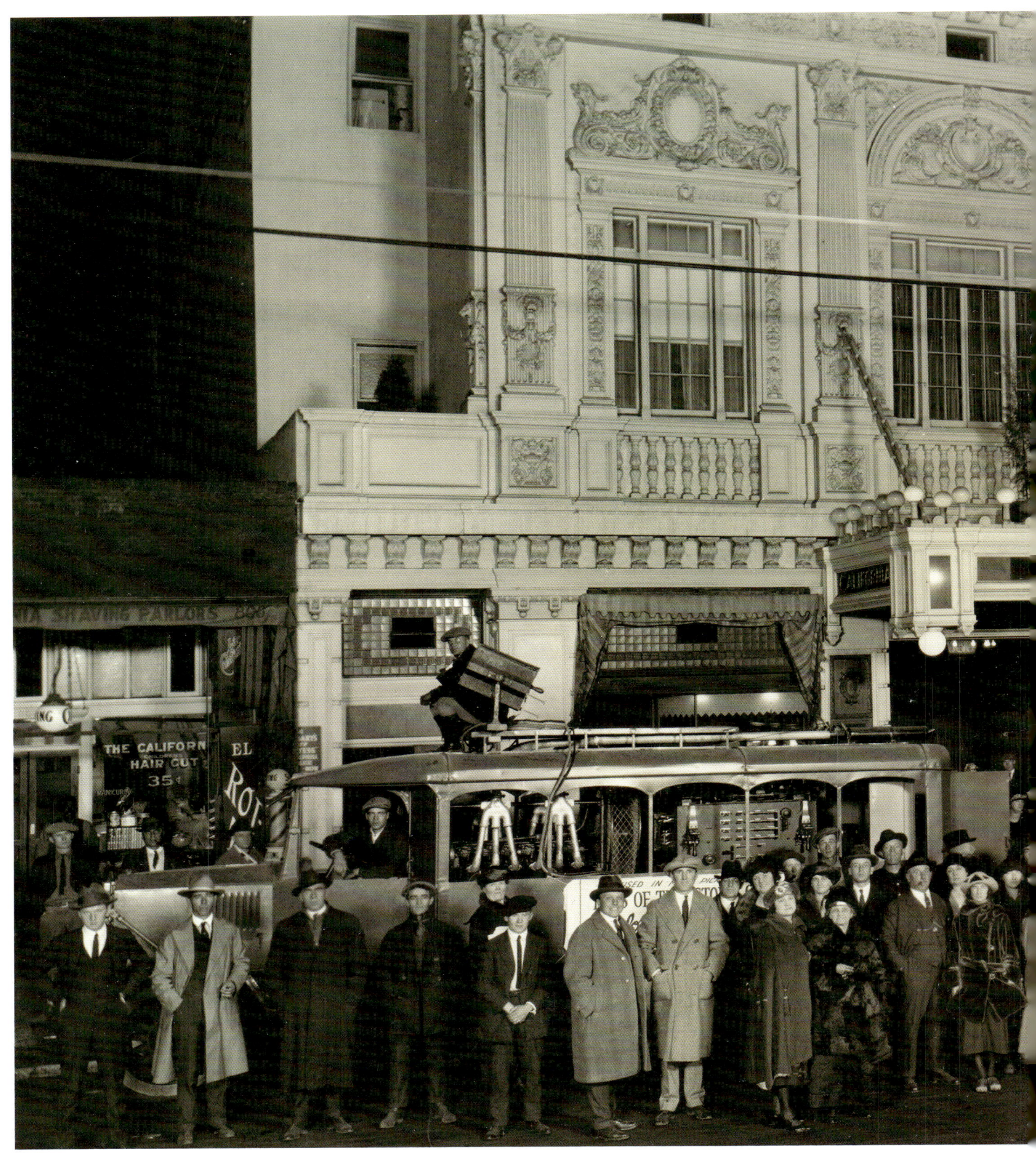
SHAVING PARLORS 808
THE CALIFORN
HAIR CUT
35¢

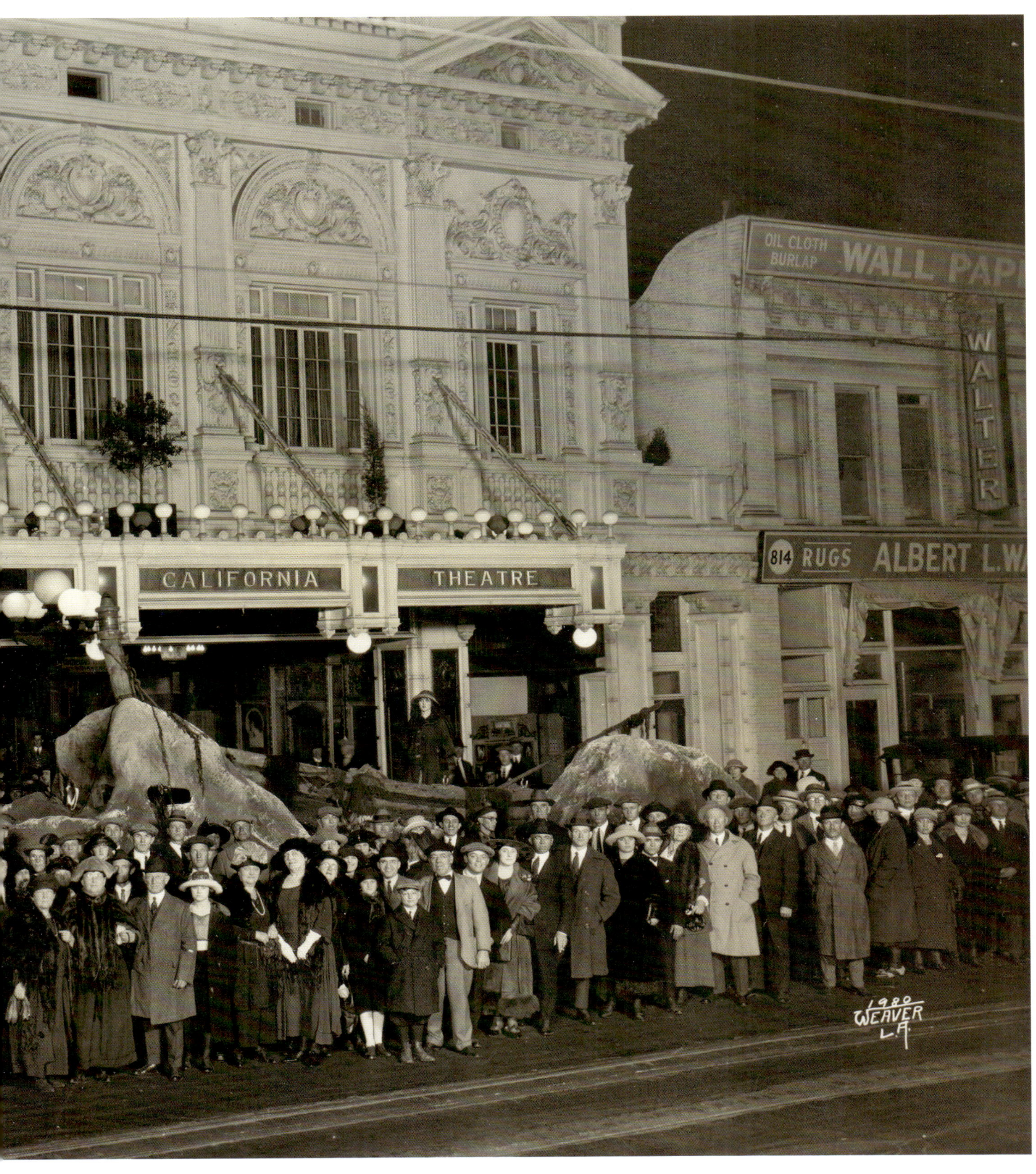


Miles F. Weaver; *The California Theatre*; gelatin silver print; 1918; 9¼ × 17 in.
*From its 1918 opening, the California Theatre evolved from a movie theater with vaudeville acts, to a Spanish-language theater, to a Pussycat Theater showing pornography. The California Theatre's arc reflected the changes that took place in downtown Los Angeles across the twentieth century.*

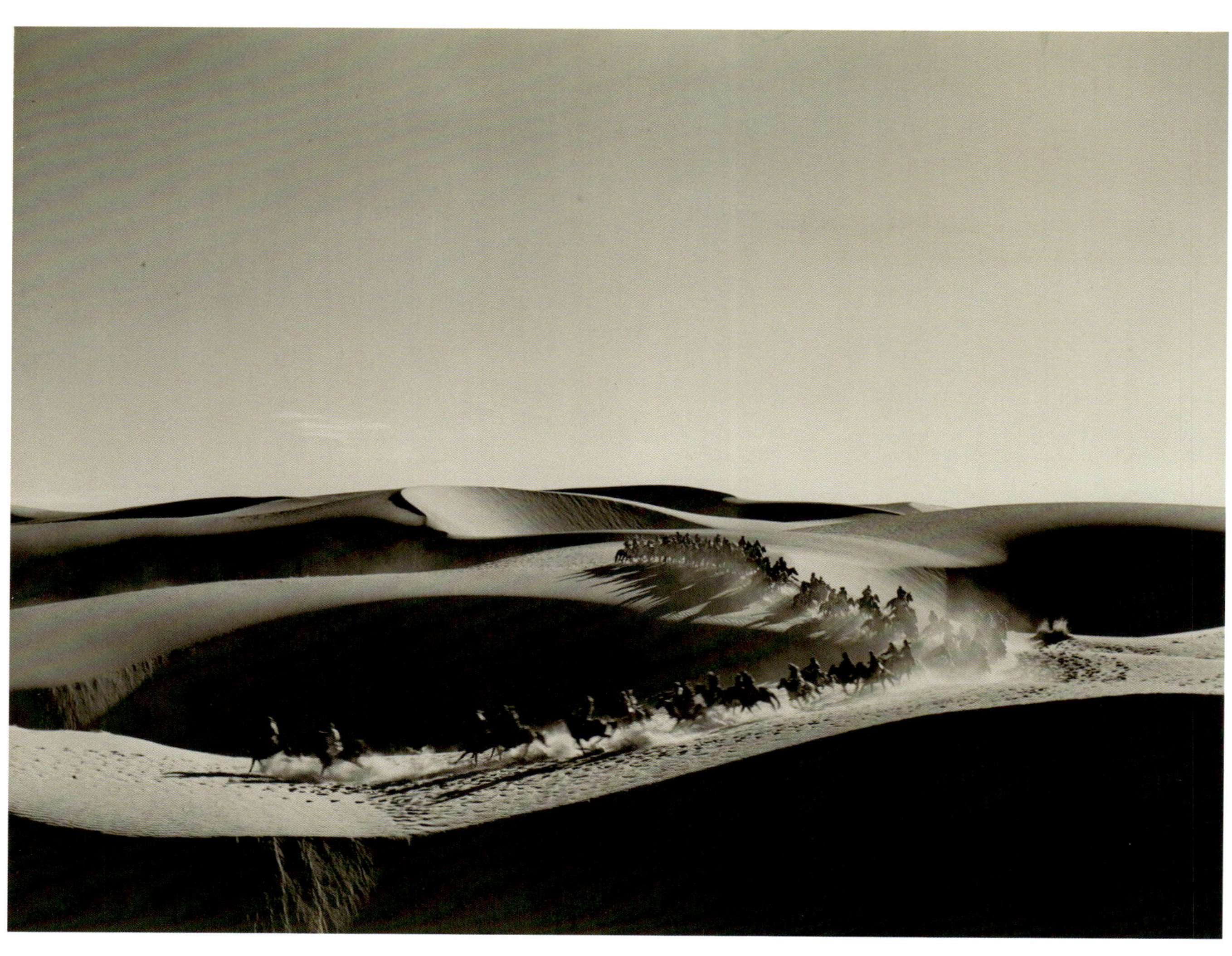

Mack Julian; Untitled (Desert film scene); gelatin silver print; ca. 1940; 10¼ × 13¼ in.
*Possibly a still from* The Charge of the Light Brigade.

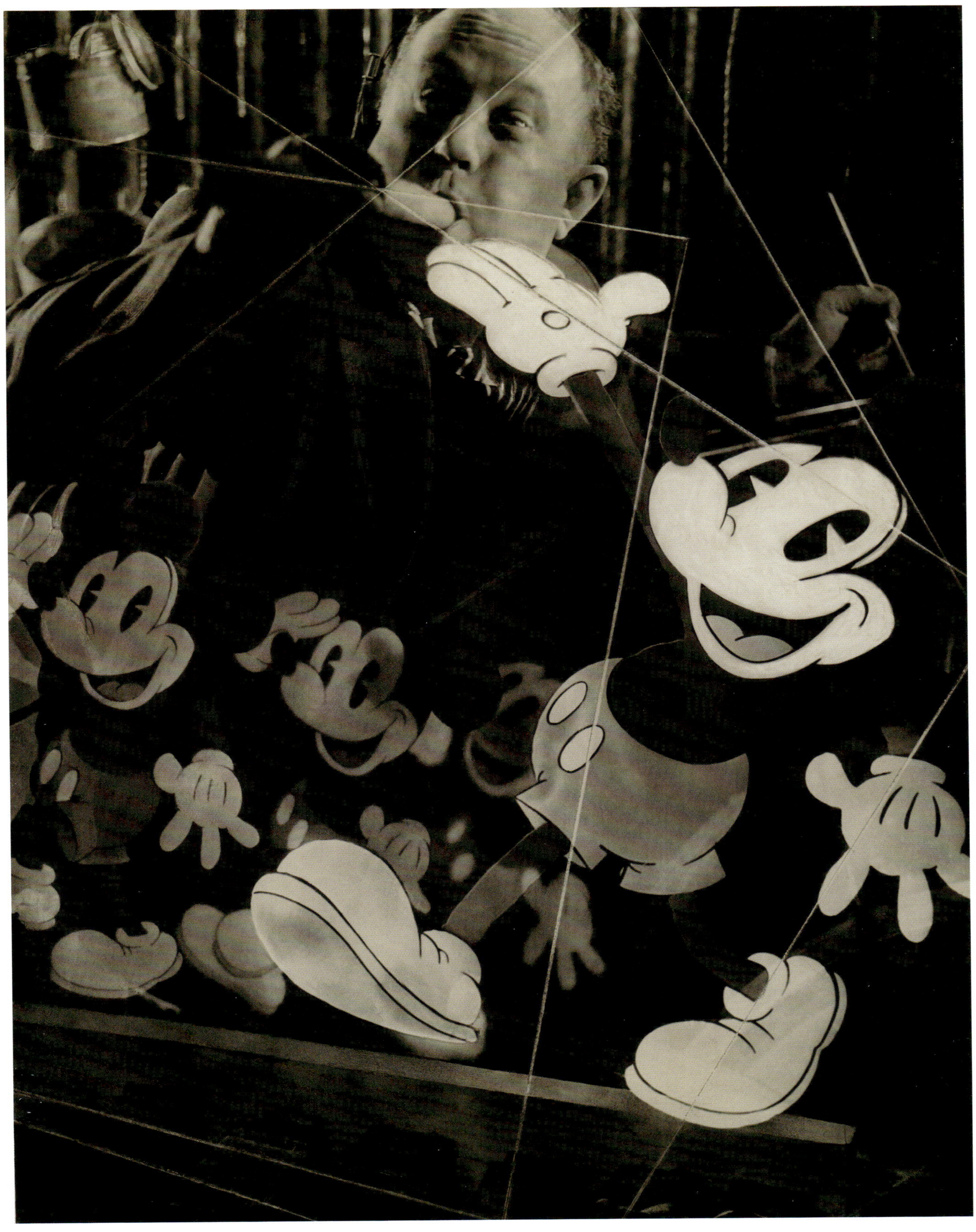

Will Connell; *Cartoon* (*In Pictures* series); gelatin silver print; 1936; 13¾ × 10⅝ in.
*Connell's* In Pictures, *a satire on Hollywood, managed to get him barred from the studios.*

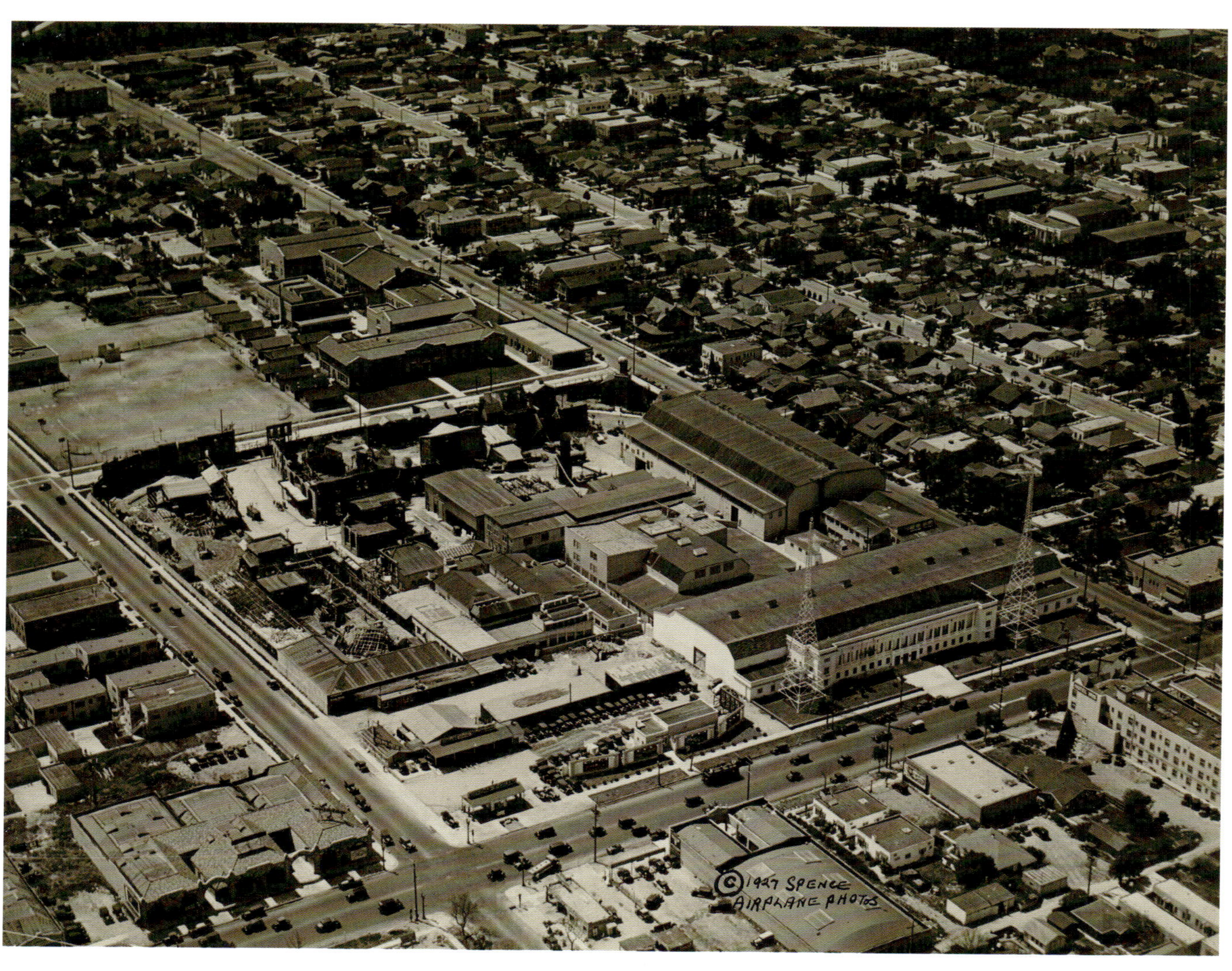


Spence Airplane Photos; *Warner Bros.*; gelatin silver print; 1927; 7½ × 9½ in.
*Aerial photographs have greatly added to our understanding of the topography of the Earth; the earliest were taken a few short years after the first flight in 1903.*

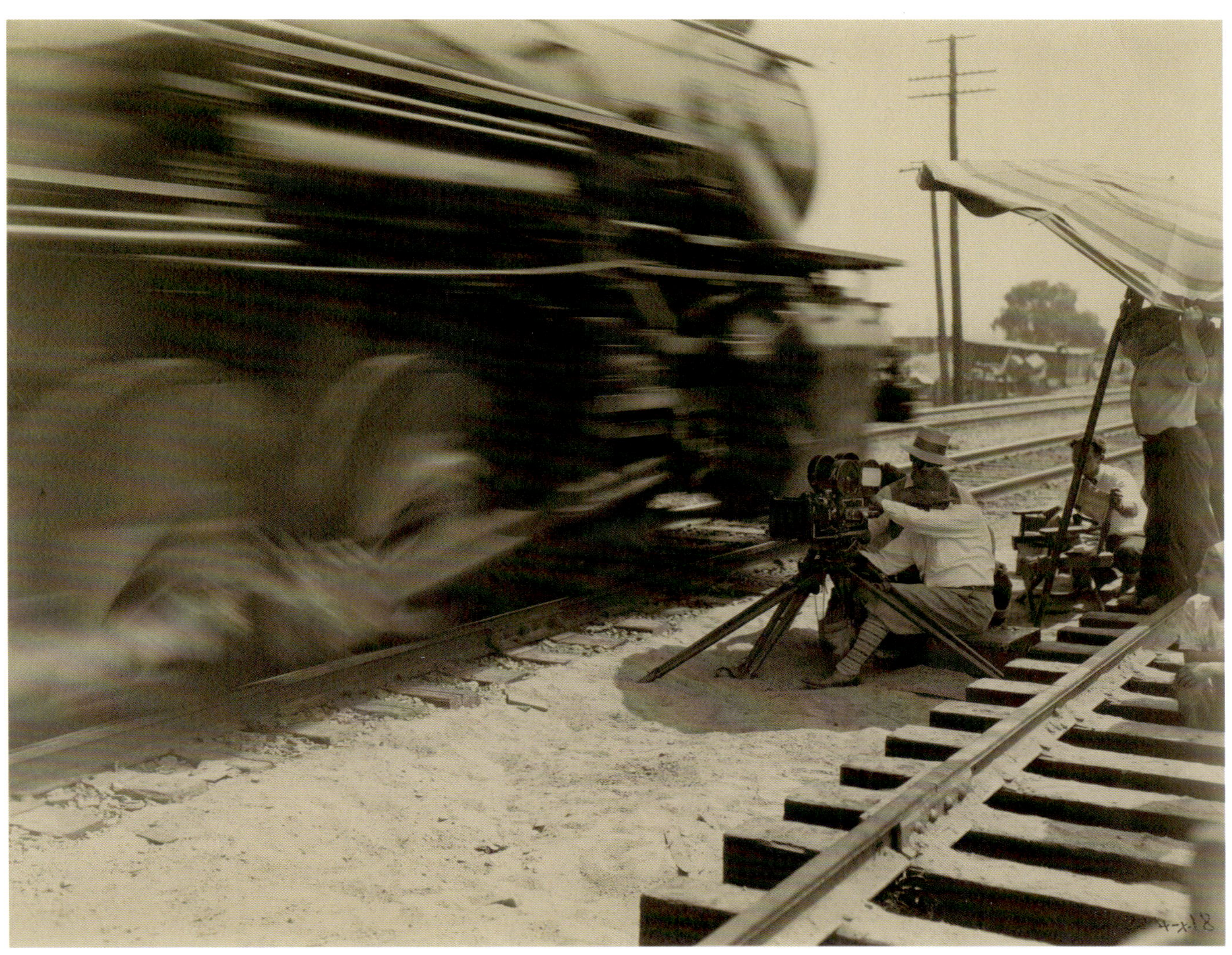

Unknown Artist; Untitled (Crew filming a speeding train); gelatin silver print; ca. 1920; $7\frac{1}{4} \times 9\frac{1}{8}$ in.
*Most likely taken for publicity purposes, this photograph captures the realism films strived to achieve during the silent film era.*

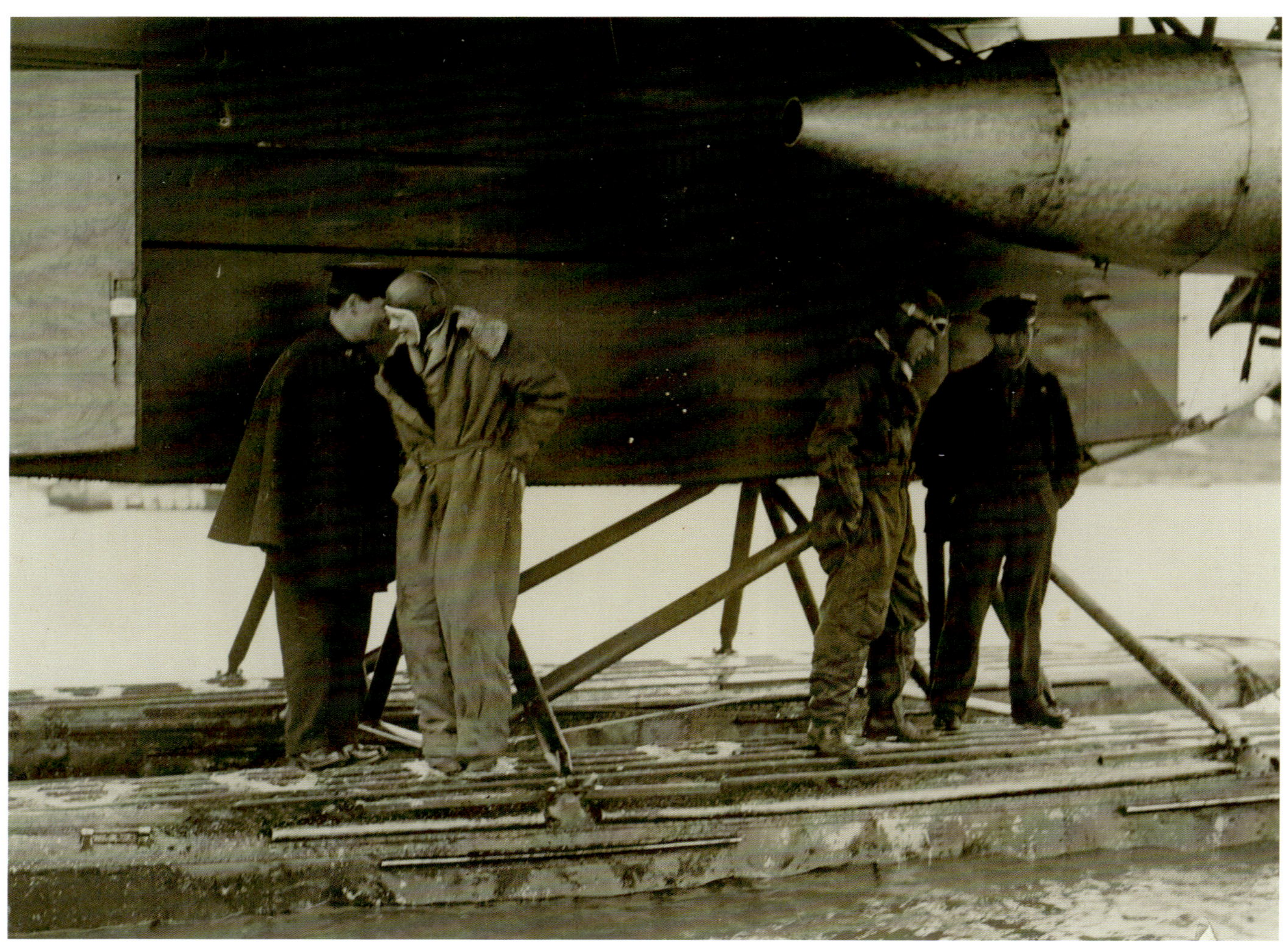

London Times; *Amelia Earhart, Post-Atlantic Flight*; gelatin silver print; June, 1928; 6 × 7⅞ in.
*Earhart is seen here with the pilot and the mechanic at Burry Port in Wales after being towed from the harbor where they landed. Just two miles apart, Burry Port and the South Wales village of Pwll have a running argument as to where she first landed on the flight. Earhart moved to California and set many records before disappearing on a flight around the world in 1937.*

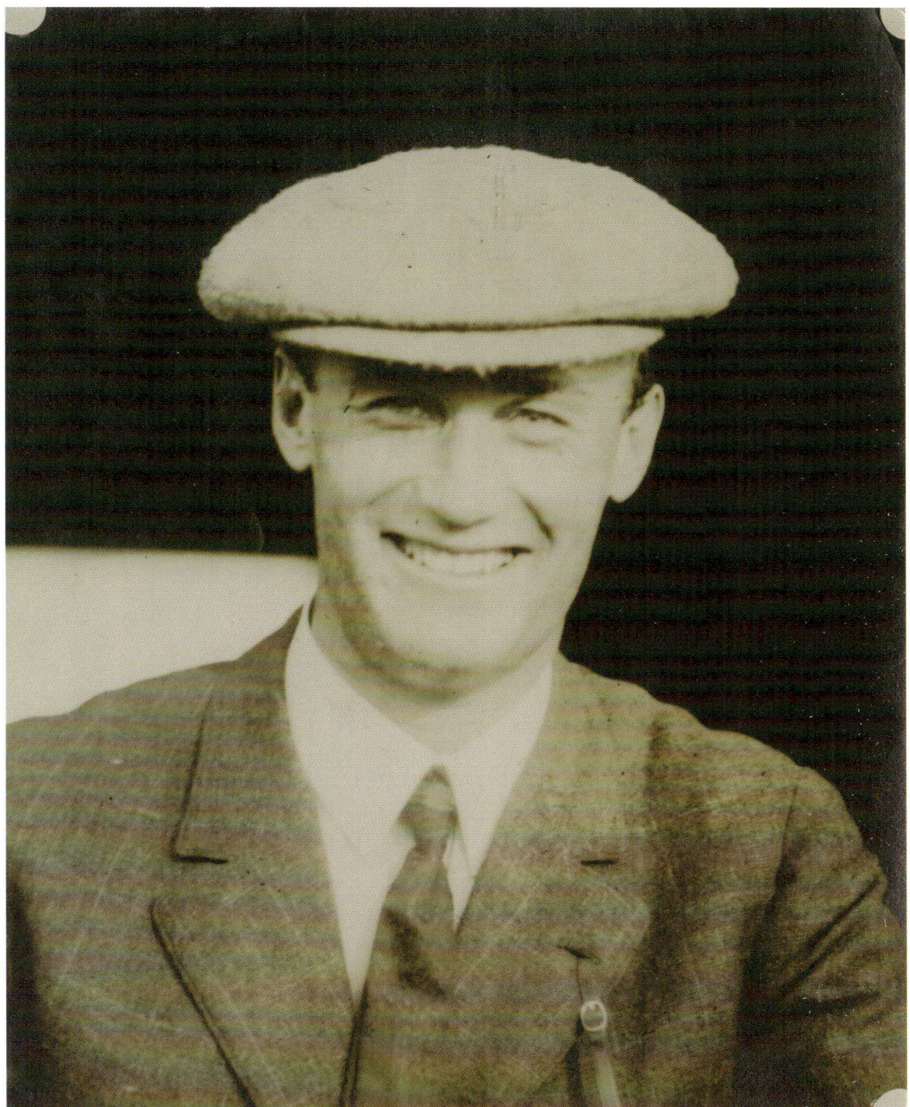

TOP: Unknown Artist; *Cal Rodgers*; gelatin silver print; 1911; 9½ × 7½ in.

BOTTOM: Unknown Artist; *Compton* (Vin Fiz crashes); gelatin silver print; 1911; 7¾ × 9¾ in.

*Rodgers landed in Pasadena on November 10, 1911, some forty-nine days and at least twelve crashes after he began his cross-country flight. On the last stretch, from Pasadena to Long Beach, he crashed in Compton, sustaining injuries and setting him back a month before he reached the Pacific. A few months after coming to California, while flying exhibitions at Long Beach, he flew into a flock of birds that caused his plane to crash, and he perished.*

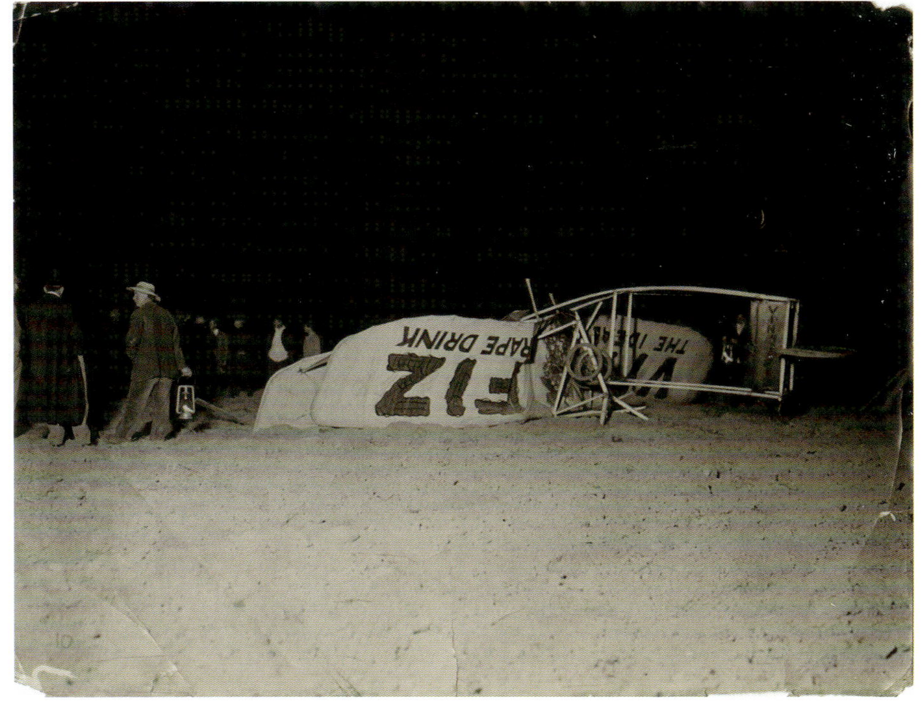

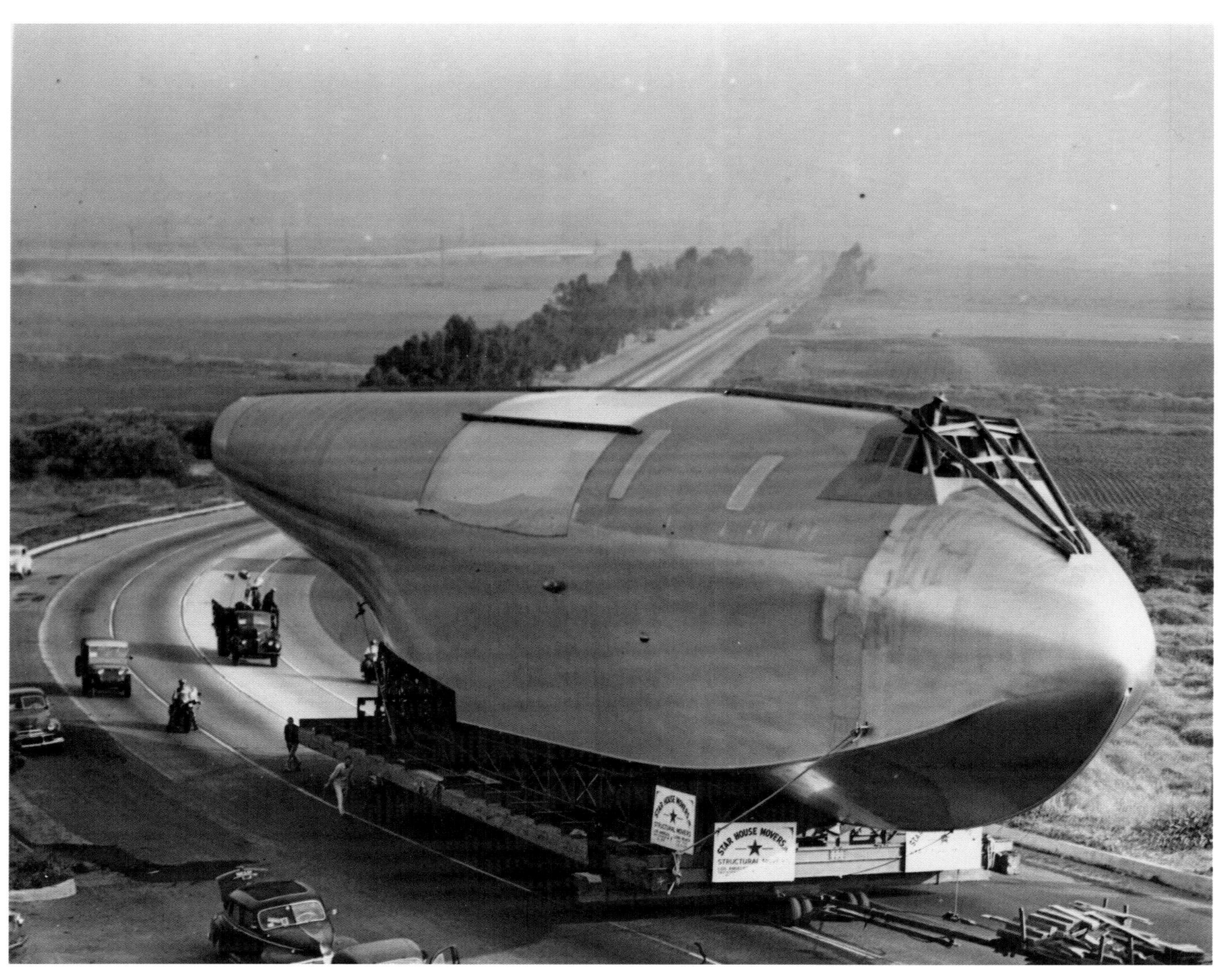


Acme News Photos; Untitled (Hull of *Hercules*, the "Spruce Goose"); gelatin silver print; 1946; 7¾ × 9⅜ in.
*The movement of the largest wooden aircraft ever built,* H-4 Hercules *(called the "Spruce Goose" because spruce was used in its construction) from its hangar in Culver City to Long Beach created quite a spectacle as Howard Hughes's giant airship passed through Los Angeles streets. It is currently housed at the Evergreen Aviation and Space Museum in McMinnville, Oregon.*

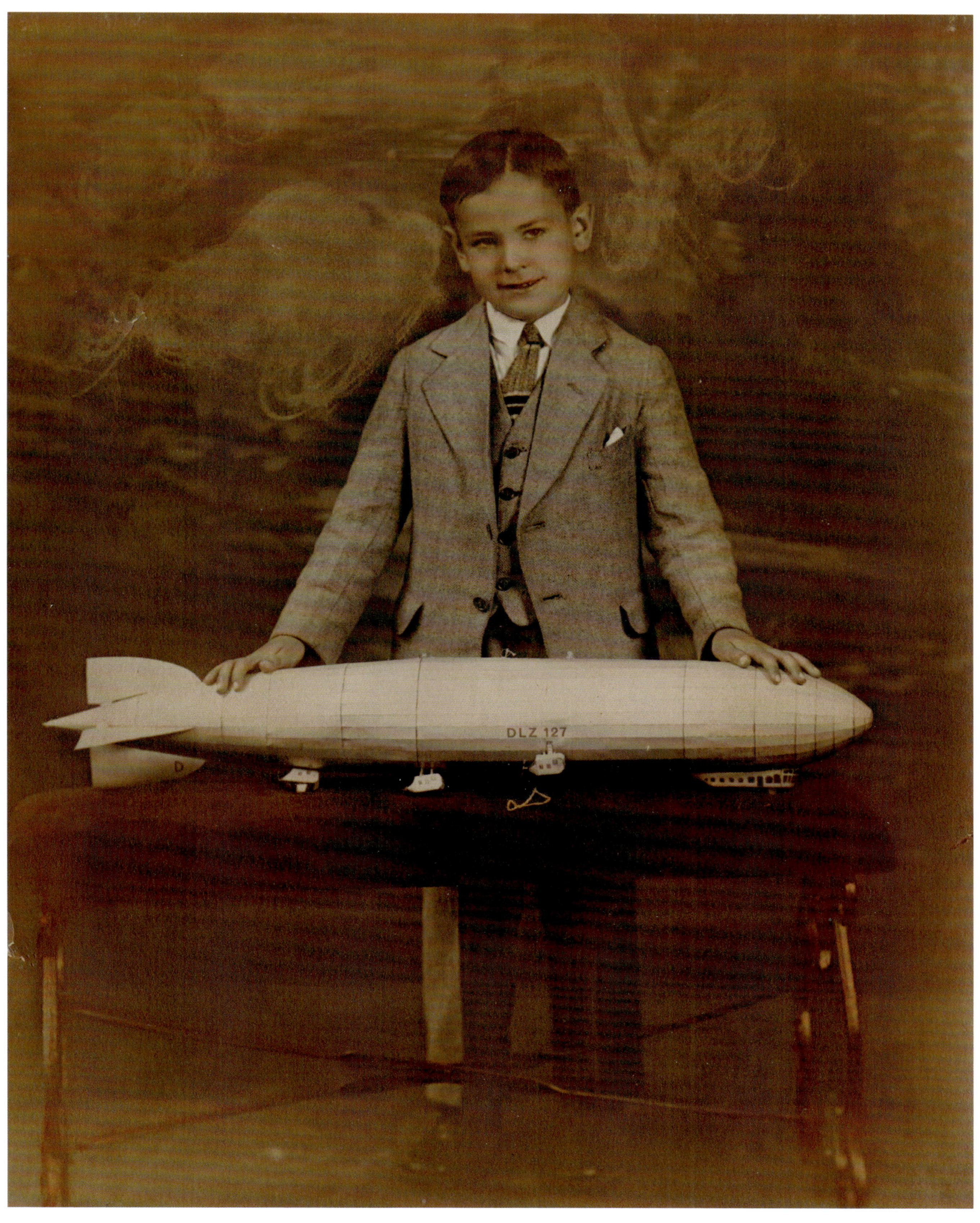


Unknown Artist; *Carl Groth with his Model of the Graf Zeppelin*; hand-colored gelatin silver print; 1929; 9¾ × 7¾ in.
*Groth's uncle had this replica of the* Graf Zeppelin *made in Germany, and it was flown to San Francisco to present to Groth on the* Graf Zeppelin.
*Six-year-old Groth's photo appeared on the front page of the* Oakland Post-Enquirer *on August 30, 1929.*

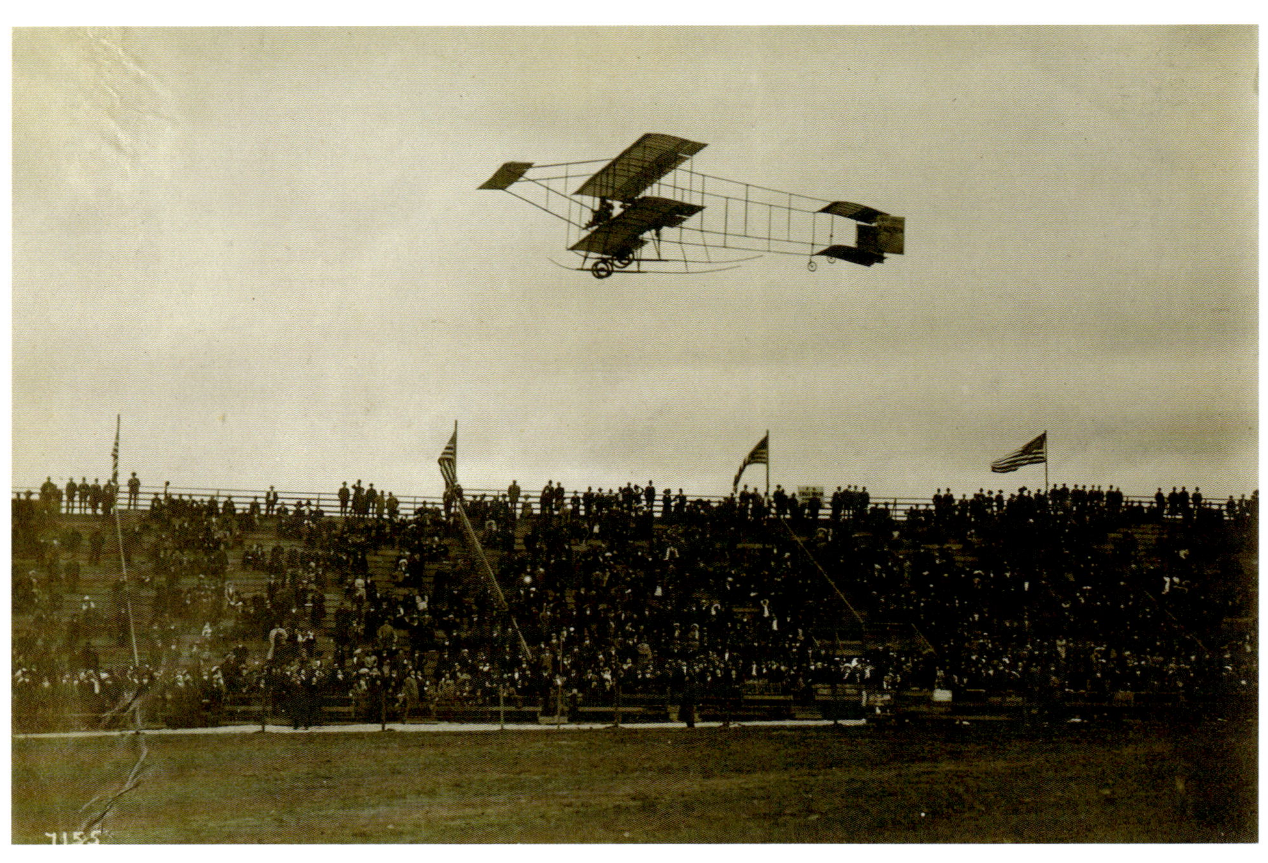

Roy Knabenshue; *Paulhan* (Dominguez Hills Air Meet); gelatin silver print; 1910; 4½ × 6½ in.
*Knabenshue flew his dirigible over the first air meet in the United States and took photographs from the air as well as on the ground. The meet lasted ten days.*

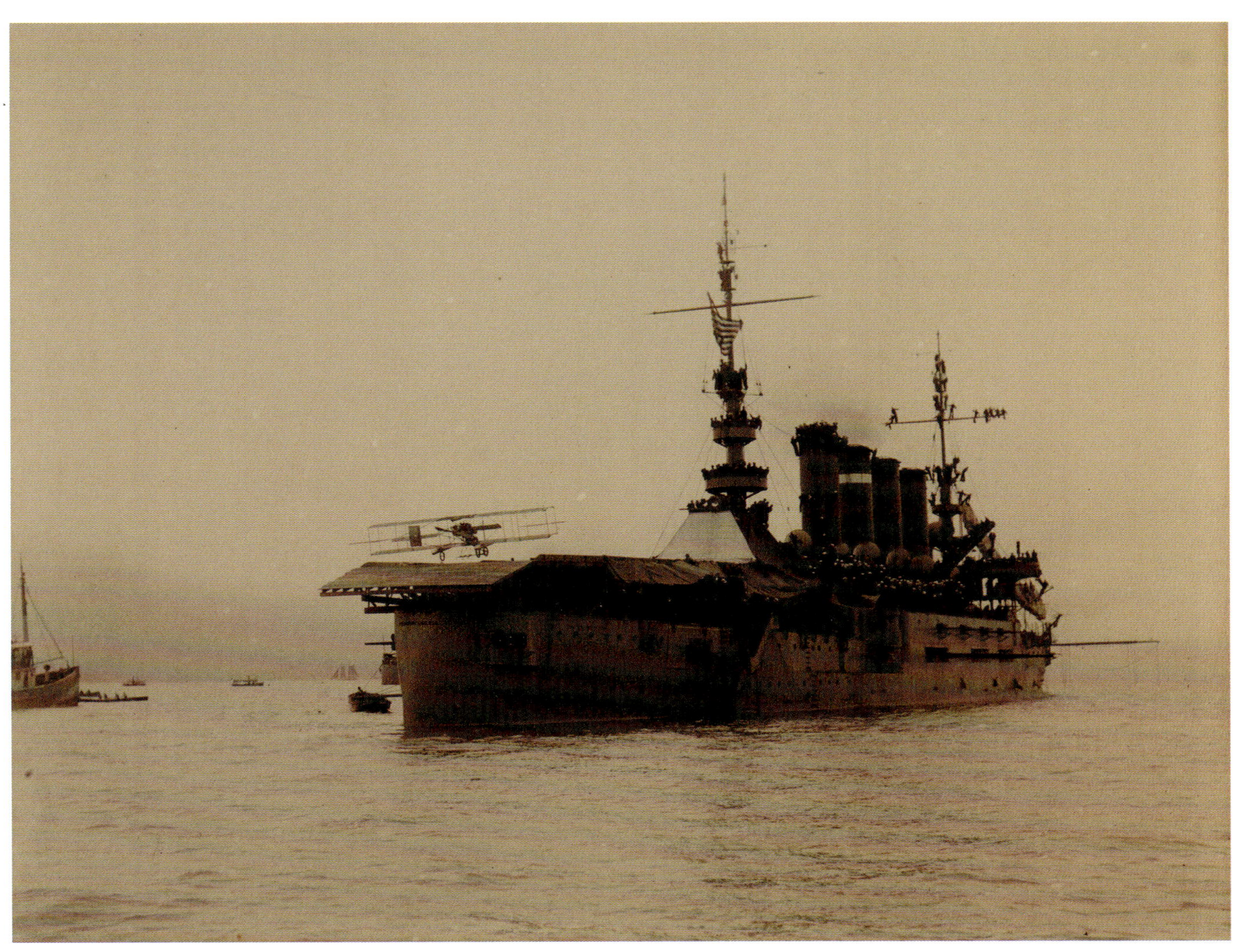

Unknown Artist; Untitled (Eugene Ely arriving on deck of Pennsylvania); toned gelatin silver print; 1911; 15¾ × 20⅛ in.
*Ely flew from Tanforan Racetrack on the San Francisco peninsula to make the first landing on the deck of a ship on January 18, 1911.*

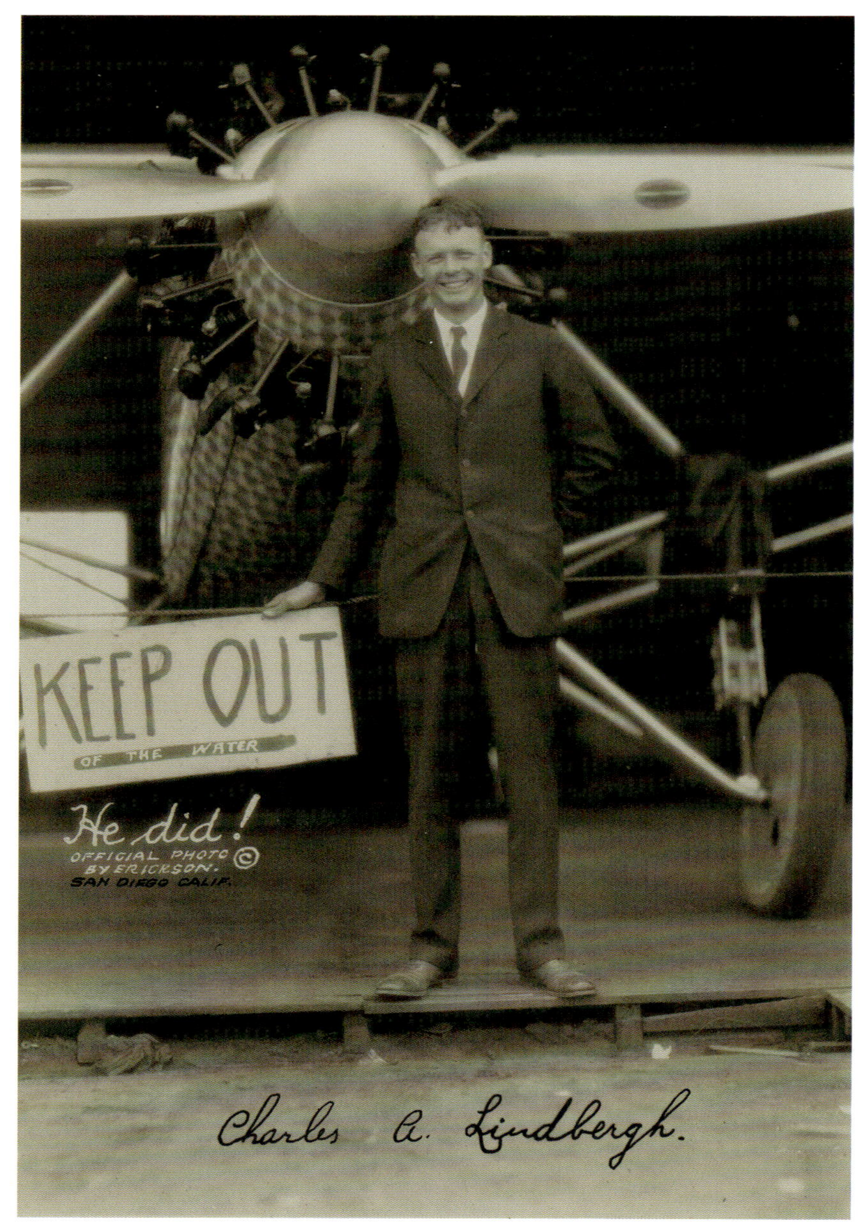


Augustus William Ericson; *Keep Out of the Water* (Charles Lindbergh); gelatin silver print; 1926; 6½ × 4⅜ in.
*Lindbergh is standing in front of the* Spirit of St. Louis *holding a sign saying "Keep out of the water." The plane was built for Lindbergh by Ryan Airlines in San Diego.*

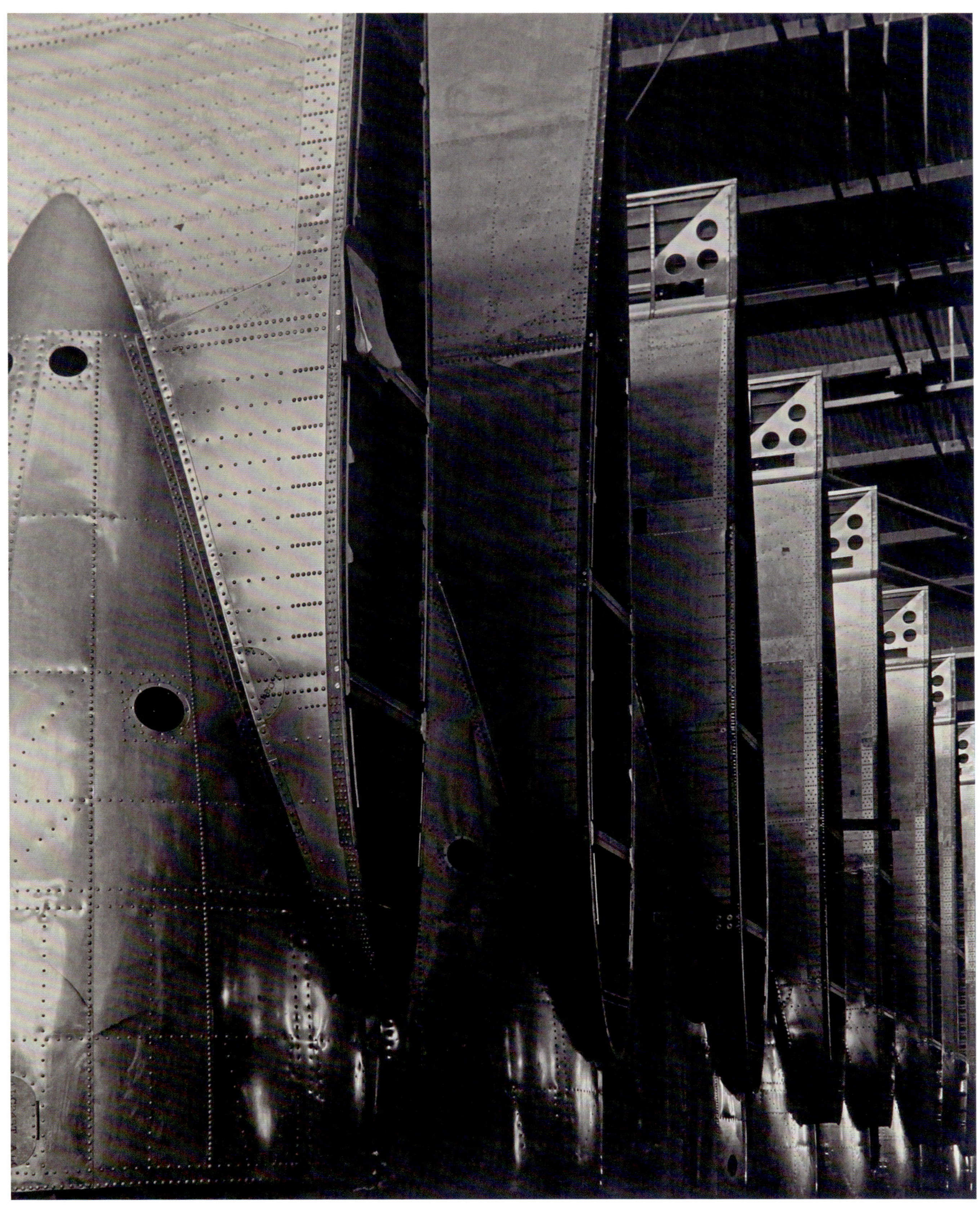

Will Connell; Untitled (Airplane wings at Douglas factory); gelatin silver print; ca. 1950; 19⅛ × 15⅛ in.
*Douglas Aircraft Company was a large airplane manufacturer originally based in Santa Monica. California was long known as one of the world's major hubs of airplane construction.*

PART 4: PROMOTING CALIFORNIA

## SELLING THE DREAM

**by Jim Farber**

Her name was Kitty Tatch, a vivacious, independent-minded young woman who found work in the late 1880s as a waitress at the Sentinel Hotel, high atop Glacier Point in Yosemite National Park. A bit of a daredevil, Kitty became a star when she was photographed by George Fiske perched on a jutting block of granite called Overhanging Rock, two thousand feet above the valley floor—and a few feet from eternity [Page 189].

It was a bright, sunny day in 1900 when Tatch, dressed in a full skirt and pert little hat, strode onto the rock and proceeded to dance for the camera, producing a series of death-defying kicks. After the photographs were reproduced as postcards, Tatch would recreate her perilous feat for tourists, then autograph her postcard. It was exactly the type of clever photography-driven marketing that helped transform California from a brawling gold rush frontier into one of the world's great tourist destinations.

To attract tourism is to create a heightened sense of expectation, and a desire in the would-be visitor to share the experience. In this regard, photography has played an essential role, particularly with the multiple generations of photographers who have focused their lenses on Yosemite. This tradition began in earnest in 1861, with a series of large format images of the valley's imposing granite cliffs and cascading waterfalls created by Carleton Watkins—photographs that played a crucial role in expanding public knowledge of the valley and influencing President Lincoln to designate Yosemite as America's second national park [Page 28].

In the 1930s, a young photographer named Ansel Adams went to work for the Curry Company and Yosemite National Park, essentially as a publicity photographer. His primary assignment was to take pictures that would attract potential visitors to the park by depicting its natural wonders and seasonal entertainments, particularly in winter. While Adams was compiling this large body of publicity work, he captured a moment that juxtaposed the massive face of Half Dome with the park's skating rink, just as a pair of graceful ice skaters were at the apex of a perfectly executed spin. The image would later be prominently featured in *The Four Seasons in Yosemite National Park: A Photographic Story of Yosemite's Spectacular Scenery*, published in 1936. Today there is no single individual, with the possible exception of John Muir, whose name is more closely associated with Yosemite than Ansel Adams.

Marketing the California myth, however, meant concealing the dark side of the Golden State's history, whether it was the devastation wrought upon the land by the rampage of the Gold Rush, or the systematic removal and genocide enacted on the indigenous peoples. In Yosemite, indigenous survivors were displayed for tourists as novelties, as they were for the Panama-California Exposition of 1914 [Page 192]. California blatantly promoted its agricultural bounty with fantastical postcards showing fruit so big it had to be loaded on flatcars, while ignoring the treatment of the migrant workers that picked the crops. It was fine to promote the Mexican heritage of Olvera Street, Grant Avenue's Chinatown, or Little Tokyo as tourist destinations, as long as you avoided mentioning California's long history of overt racism toward Hispanics, the Chinese, and Japanese Americans.

While the Gold Rush made San Francisco the golden gateway to California, the emergence of Los Angeles as a glittery tourist mecca took a good deal longer. Before the transcontinental railroad was completed in 1876, Los Angeles was little more than a dusty desert community on the ocean, bordered by mountains. There was no navigable waterway, no natural harbor, no reliable source of fresh water, and no valuable natural resource except the black goo called oil, which was initially seen to have no value beyond greasing wagon wheels.

What Los Angeles did possess was idyllic weather and a lot of open space. And at a time when America was experiencing a boom in health-related tourism, Los Angeles suddenly became a desirable place to visit and potentially live. Of those early days it was said, they sold the sunshine and threw in the land for free. As the rail lines of the Pacific Electric Railway were extended to reach one development after another, the patchwork quilt of Los Angeles communities began to take shape.

The abundance of sunshine and land also attracted a band of pioneering moviemakers anxious to find space and plenty of daylight to make their "flickers." Their discovery of both in Los Angeles gave the city a new identity, signaling the birth of the Hollywood dream factory and its larger-than-life movie stars.

With its proximity to the ocean and its ever-rolling waves, it was inevitable that California developed a thriving beach culture. By the 1920s, there were bath houses and amusement parks from San Francisco to San Diego, a phenomenon captured by the thriving indoor Sutro Baths near the Cliff House in San Francisco [Page 202].

L.A. had seen its share of ostrich farms, alligator farms, and a farm owned by the Knotts family known for its fried chicken and jam. But it was the opening of "The Magic Kingdom," Disneyland, on July 17, 1955, that changed the world of family entertainment/tourism in California forever. What began as 160 acres of bucolic orange groves in a little-known town called Anaheim became "the happiest place on Earth." In 2019, Mickey Mouse greeted 18.67 million visitors to the park.

As the wealth of California developed, so did its cultural institutions. Great private art collections (along with estates to house them) were created by business tycoons like Henry Huntington, J. Paul Getty, and William Randolph Hearst, whose hilltop Hearst Castle on California's Central Coast remains one of the state's most frequently visited attractions.

If there was a motto for California's growth into a multi-billion-dollar-a-year center for tourism, it might be: Eureka, we found it! I wonder what Kitty Tatch would think of the legacy she helped found? What would she see today from her lofty perch: a world suffering from the effects of climate change or a future where, on a clear day, you can see forever? Like Kitty, we all seem to be standing on a tipping point.

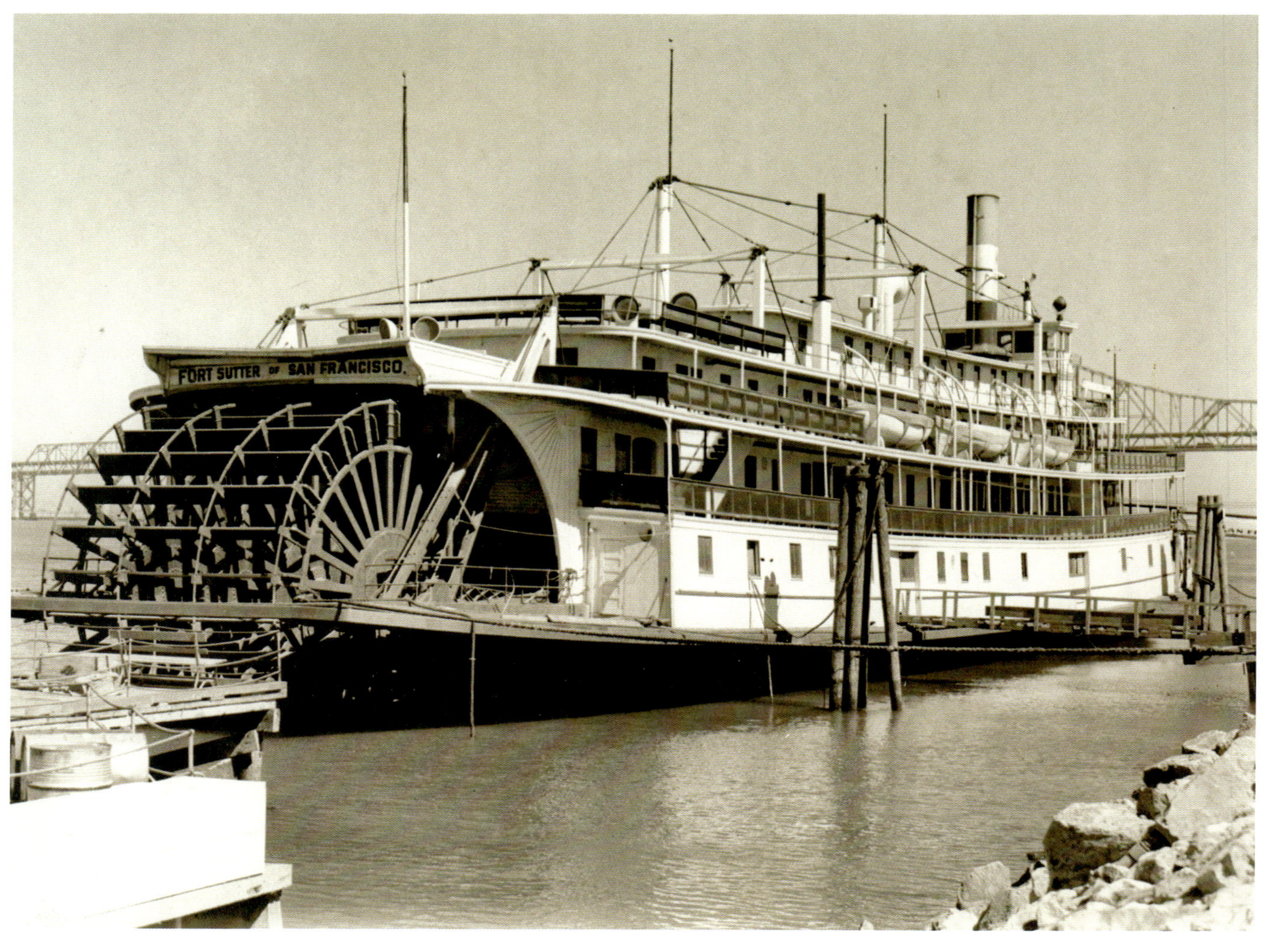


Unknown Artist; *Fort Sutter–San Francisco*; gelatin silver print; ca. 1930; 10½ × 12¾ in.
*The* Fort Sutter *sailed San Francisco Bay and the Sacramento River. The riverboat was built in 1912 with fifty-nine staterooms and 110 berths. It was destroyed by fire in 1959.*

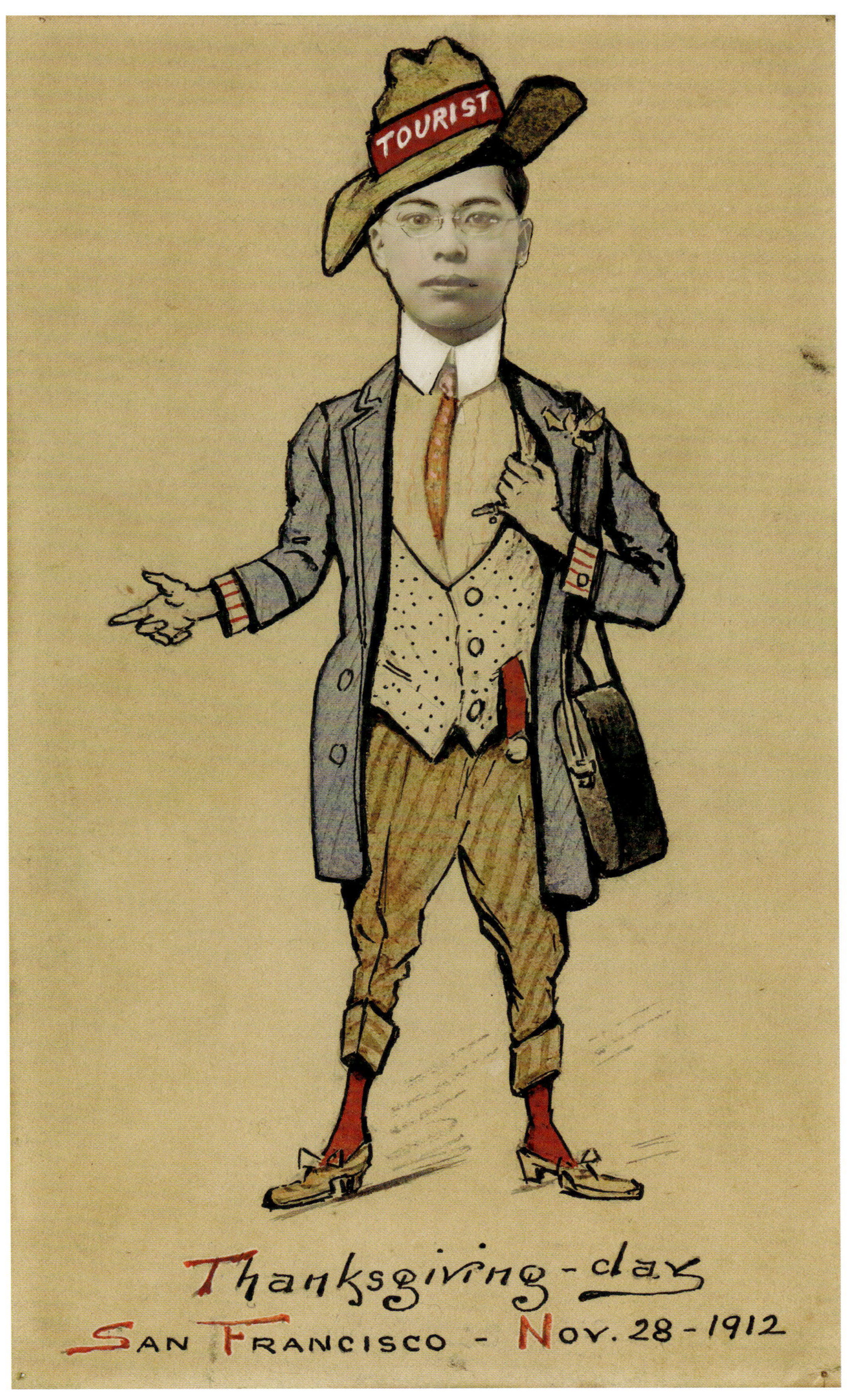


Unknown Artist; *Thanksgiving Day, San Francisco*; gelatin silver print and drawing; 1912; 9½ × 5½ in.
*This tourist made an unusual reminder of his Thanksgiving visit to San Francisco.*

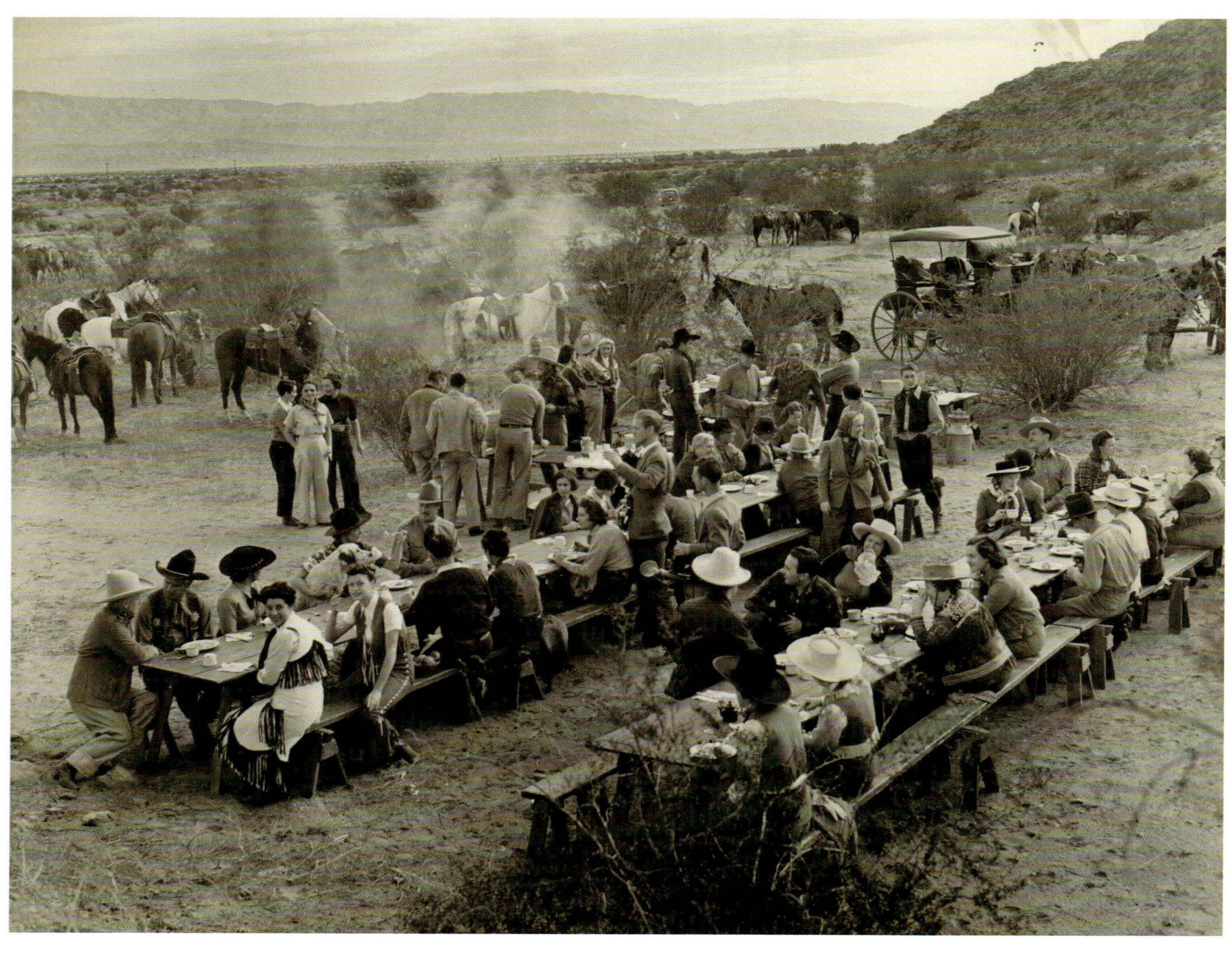

Acme Art Photo; *Sunrise Desert Ride and Breakfast, Palm Springs*; gelatin silver print; 1938; 6¾ × 8½ in.
*An early version of the dude ranch brought visitors to the desert community of Palm Springs.*

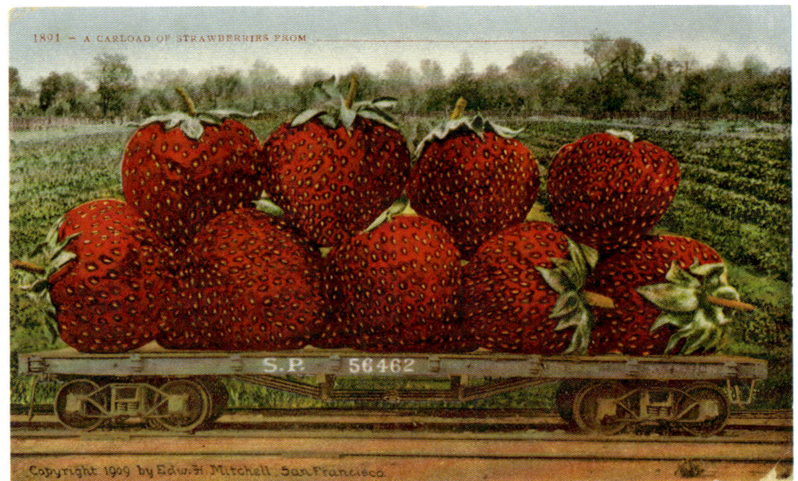


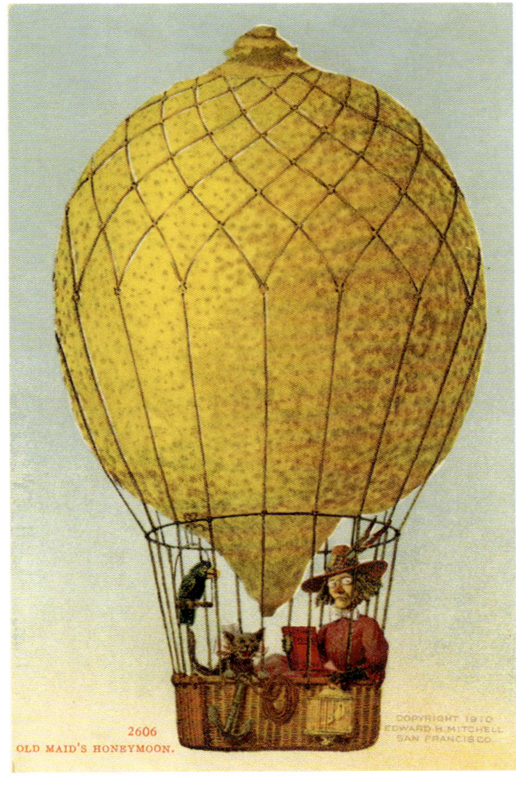


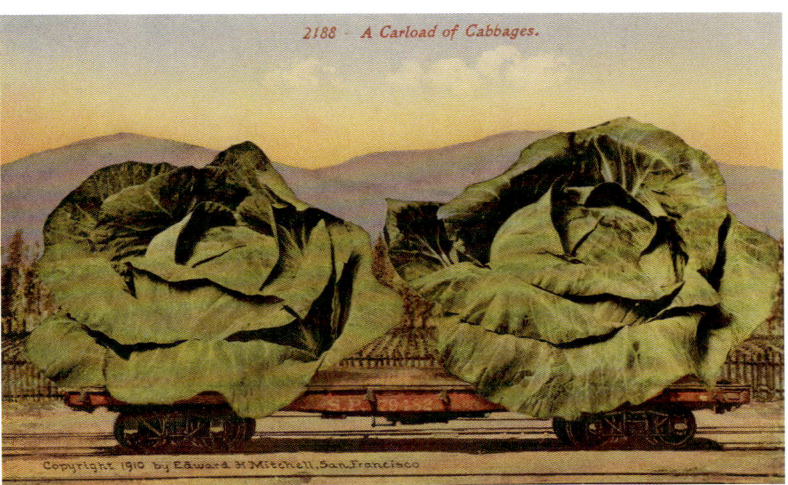


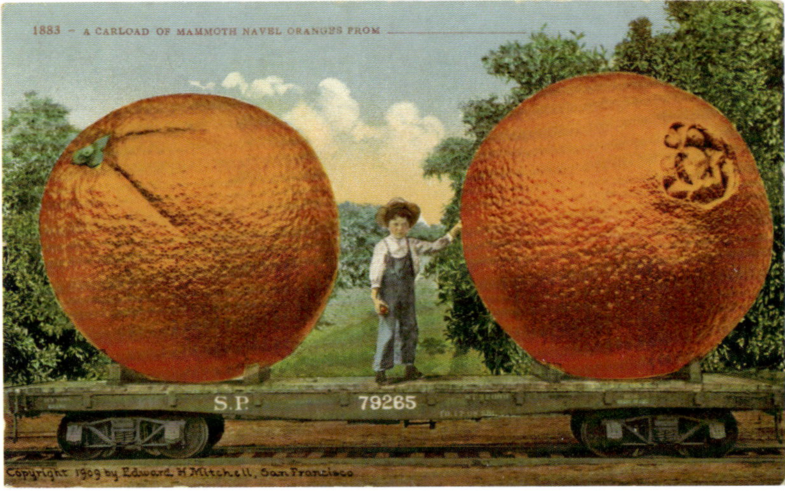


CLOCKWISE FROM TOP RIGHT:
Edward H. Mitchell; *Carload of Strawberries*; colored photolithograph; 1909–1910; 3½ × 5½ in.
Edward H. Mitchell; *Carload of Cabbages*; colored photolithograph; 1909–1910; 3½ × 5½ in.
Edward H. Mitchell; *A Carload of Mammoth Navel Oranges*; colored photolithograph; 1909–1910; 3½ × 5½ in.
Edward H. Mitchell; *A California Honeymoon*; colored photolithograph; 1909–1910; 5½ × 3½ in.
*Propaganda for California agriculture, in the tourist-friendly form of postcards to send home to envious friends and family.*

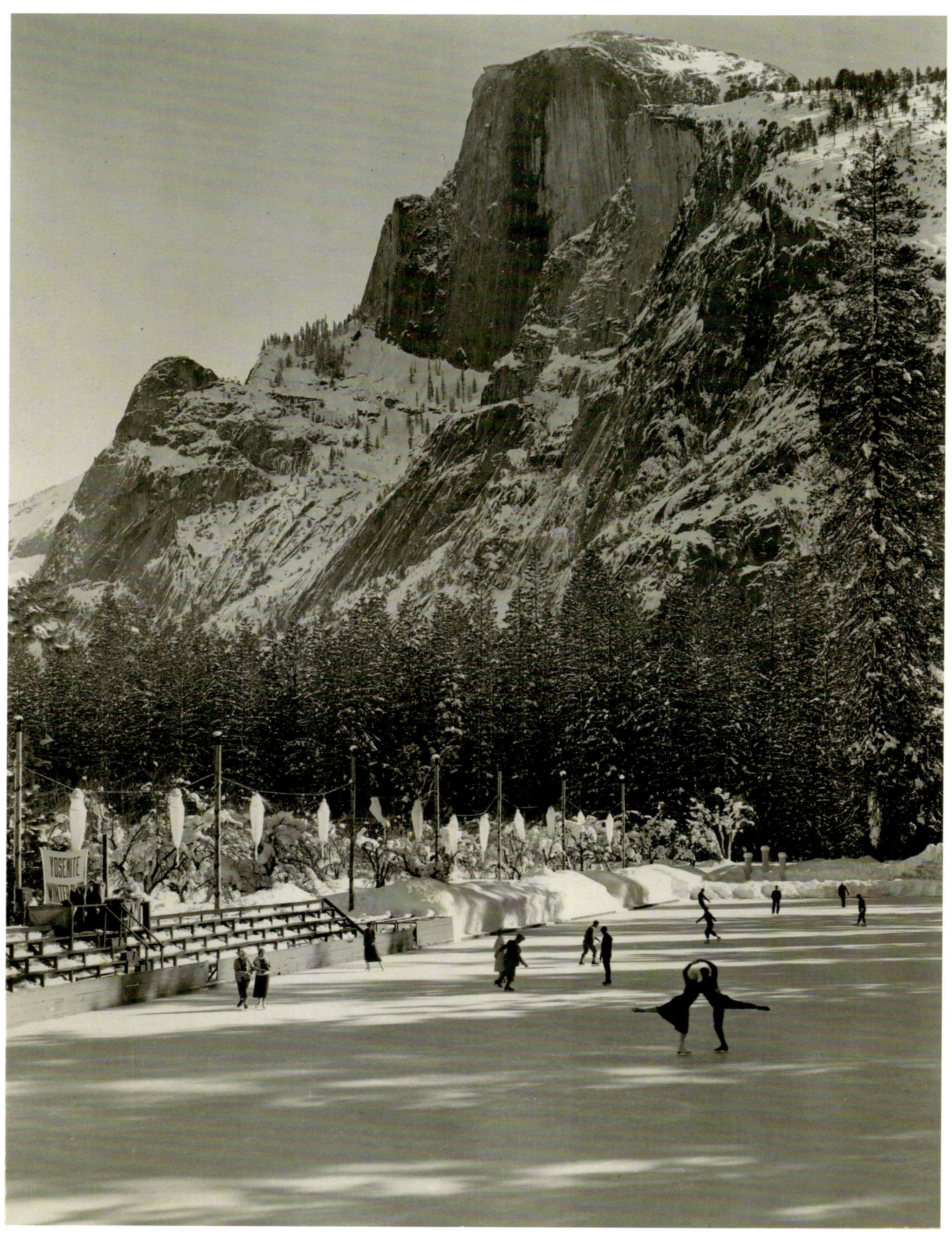


Ansel Adams; *Skating, Plain and Fancy*; gelatin silver print; ca. 1935; 8¼ × 6⅛ in.
*Adams made a series of photographs of winter in Yosemite in the 1930s.*

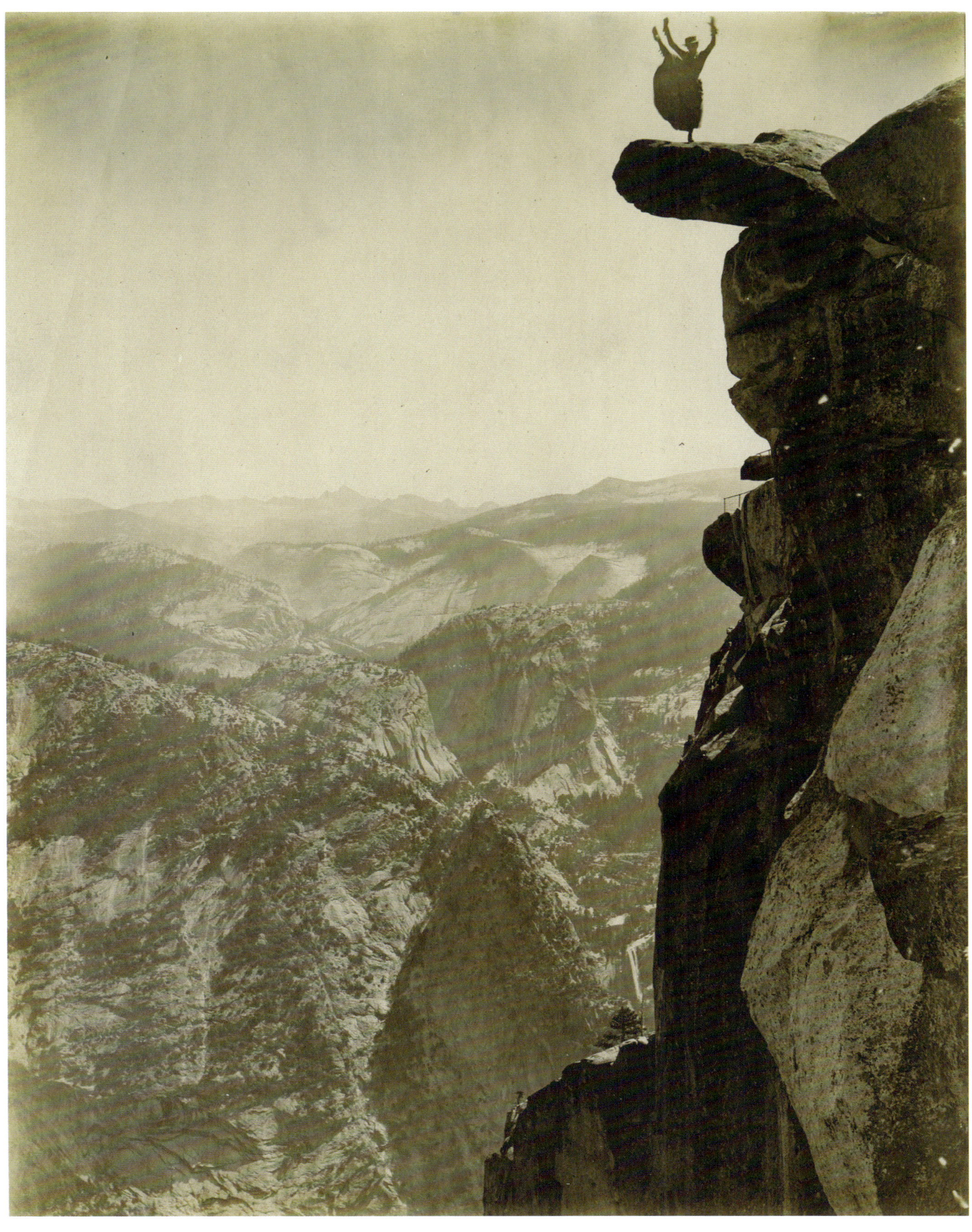

George Fiske; Untitled (Kitty Tatch dancing on Overhanging Rock, Yosemite); gelatin silver print; ca. 1905; 9½ × 7½ in.
*A variant of a photograph of two dancers on Overhanging Rock shown in Hickman and Pitts* George Fiske Yosemite Photographer. *Kitty Tatch was a maid and waitress at the Sentinel Hotel in Yosemite at the turn of the twentieth century.*

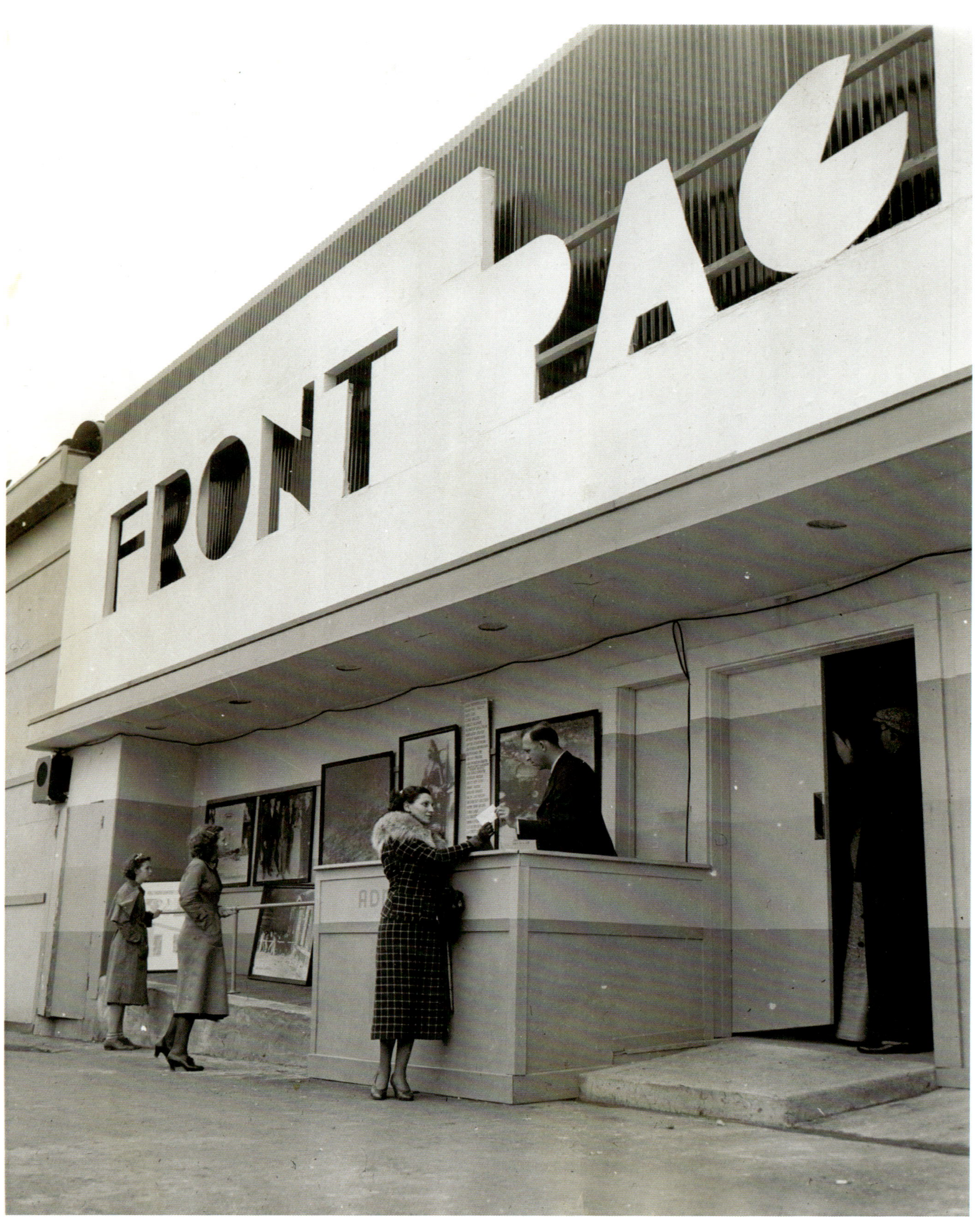


Unknown Artist; Untitled (Front Page building, San Diego Exposition); gelatin silver print; 1936; 8½ × 6⅝ in.

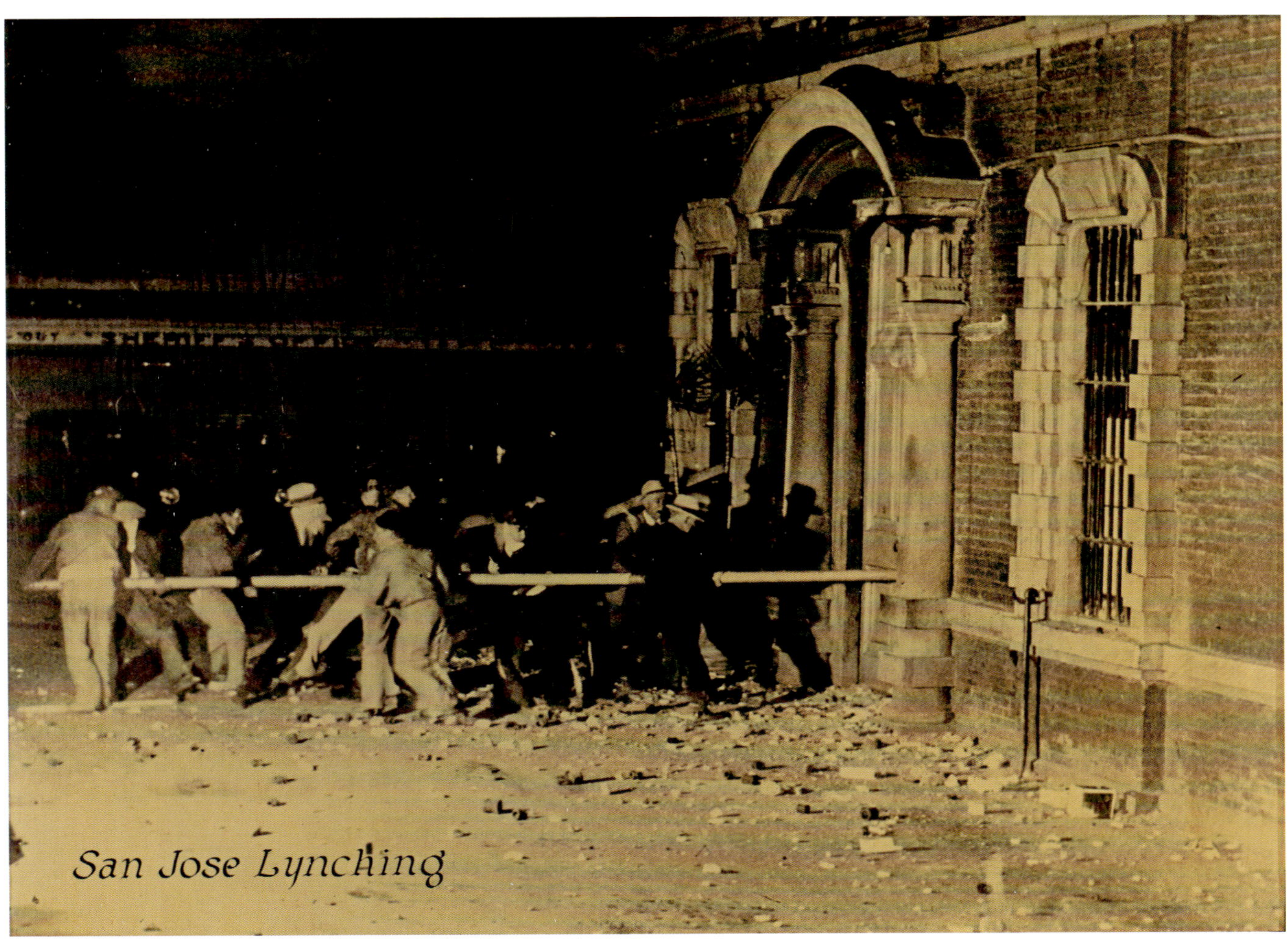


Unknown Artist; *San Jose Lynching*; gelatin silver print; 1933, printed 1936; 29 × 40 in.
*This photograph was used as one of several outside attractions for the Front Page exhibition in the* Fun Zone *at the San Diego Exposition in 1936. A mob broke into the Santa Clara County Jail where they dragged out two suspects in a kidnapping/murder and hanged them before a trial. California's Governor James Rolph Jr. said he would pardon any of the mob arrested, but none were prosecuted. Governor Rolph died of a heart attack the following year. A panel of photographs depicting the break-in and lynching was shown inside the exhibition.*

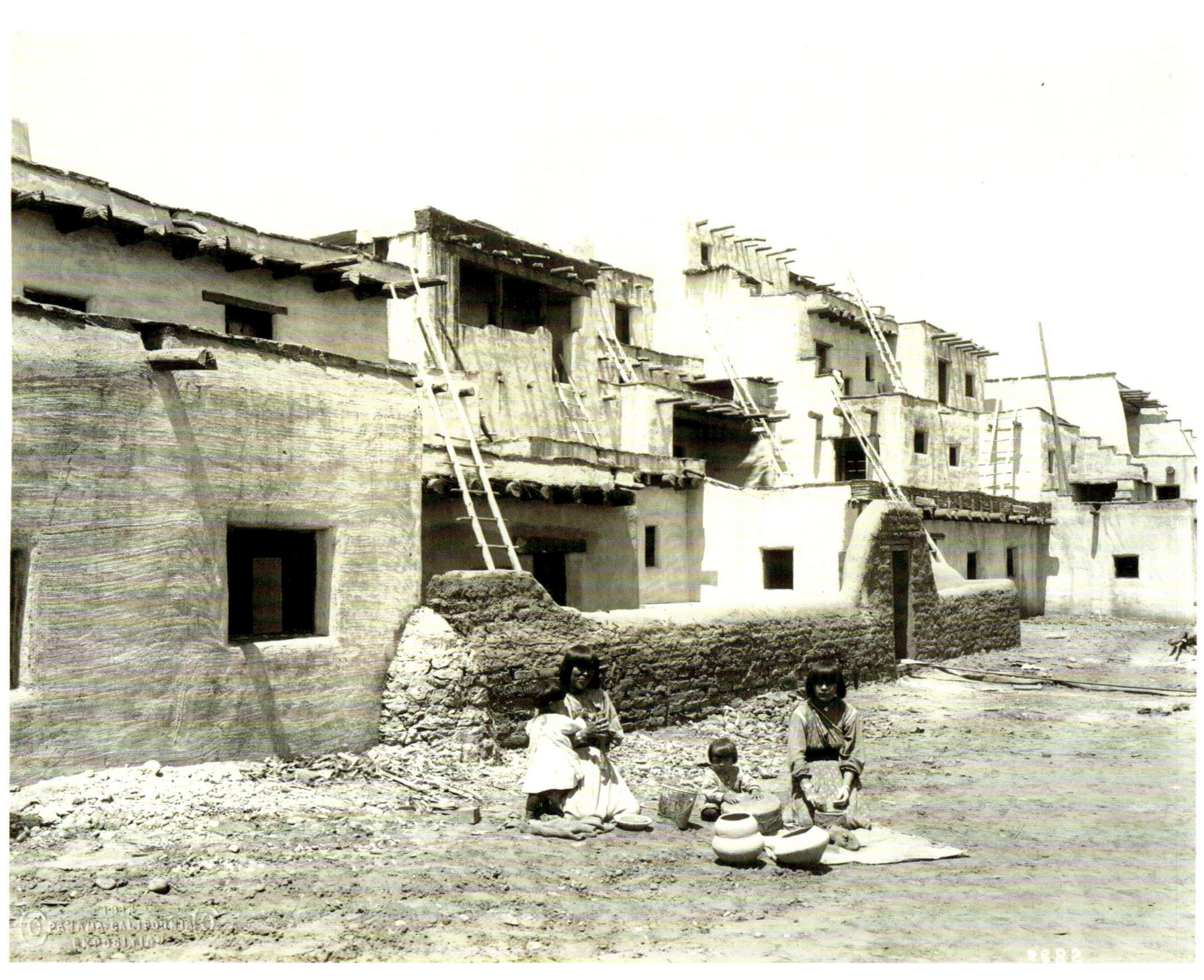

Unknown Artist; *In the Painted Desert, San Diego Exposition, Pottery Making*; gelatin silver print; 1914; 7½ × 9⅜ in.
*As part of the Panama-California Exposition, Indigenous people were displayed as objects of curiosity.*

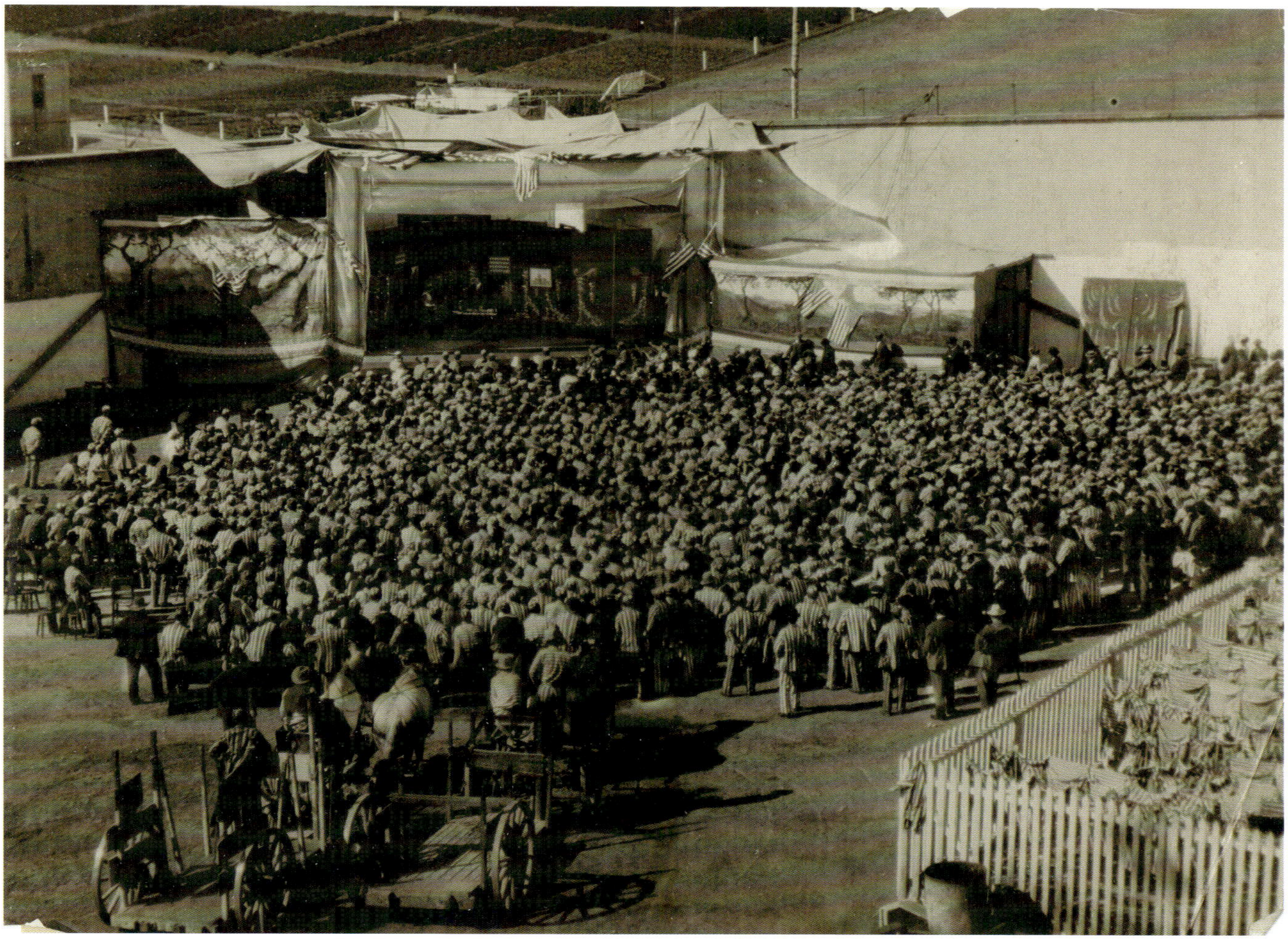

TOP: Unknown Artist; *3000 Convicts in San Quentin Watching Presentation in Prison Yard of "Alias Jimmy Valentine," a Play Dealing with Convict Life and Redemption*; gelatin silver print; 1911; 6⅛ × 8¼ in.

RIGHT: Unknown Artist; *The Theatre*; photo-illustrated magazine cover; January 1912; 13½ × 9½ in.
*This photo is reproduced in* Theatre Magazine *for January 1912 along with an article by Ella Bennett titled "Convicts See a Play of Convict's Life."*

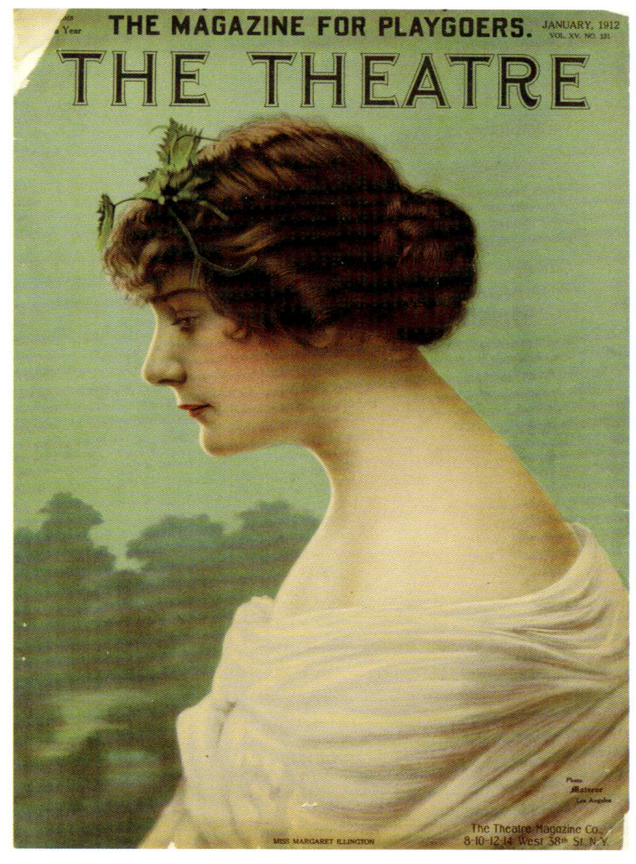

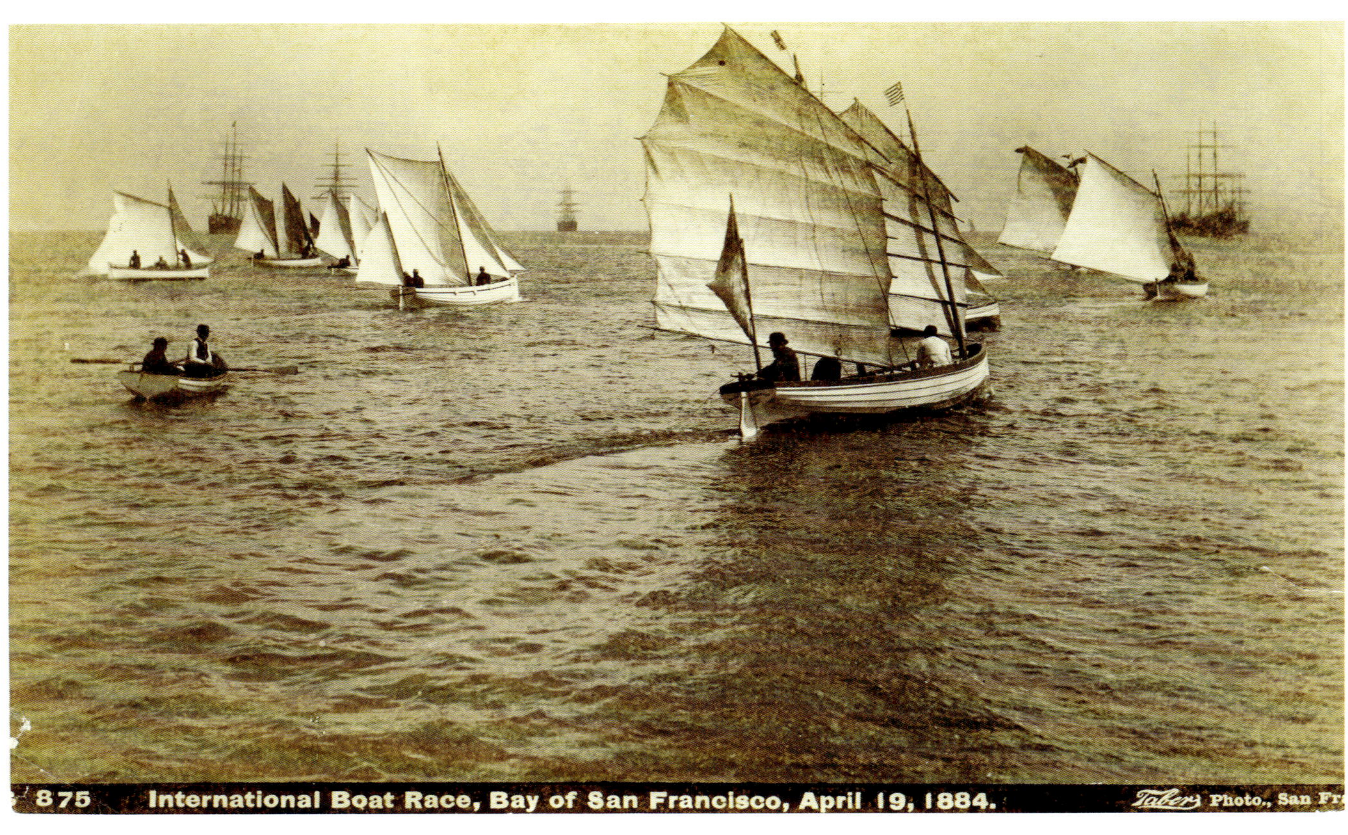


Isaiah W. Taber; *International Boat Race, Bay of San Francisco*; albumen print; April 19, 1884; 4½ × 7¾ in.
*This image was chosen for the dust jacket of* Taber: A Photographic Legacy 1870–1900 *published in 2004.*

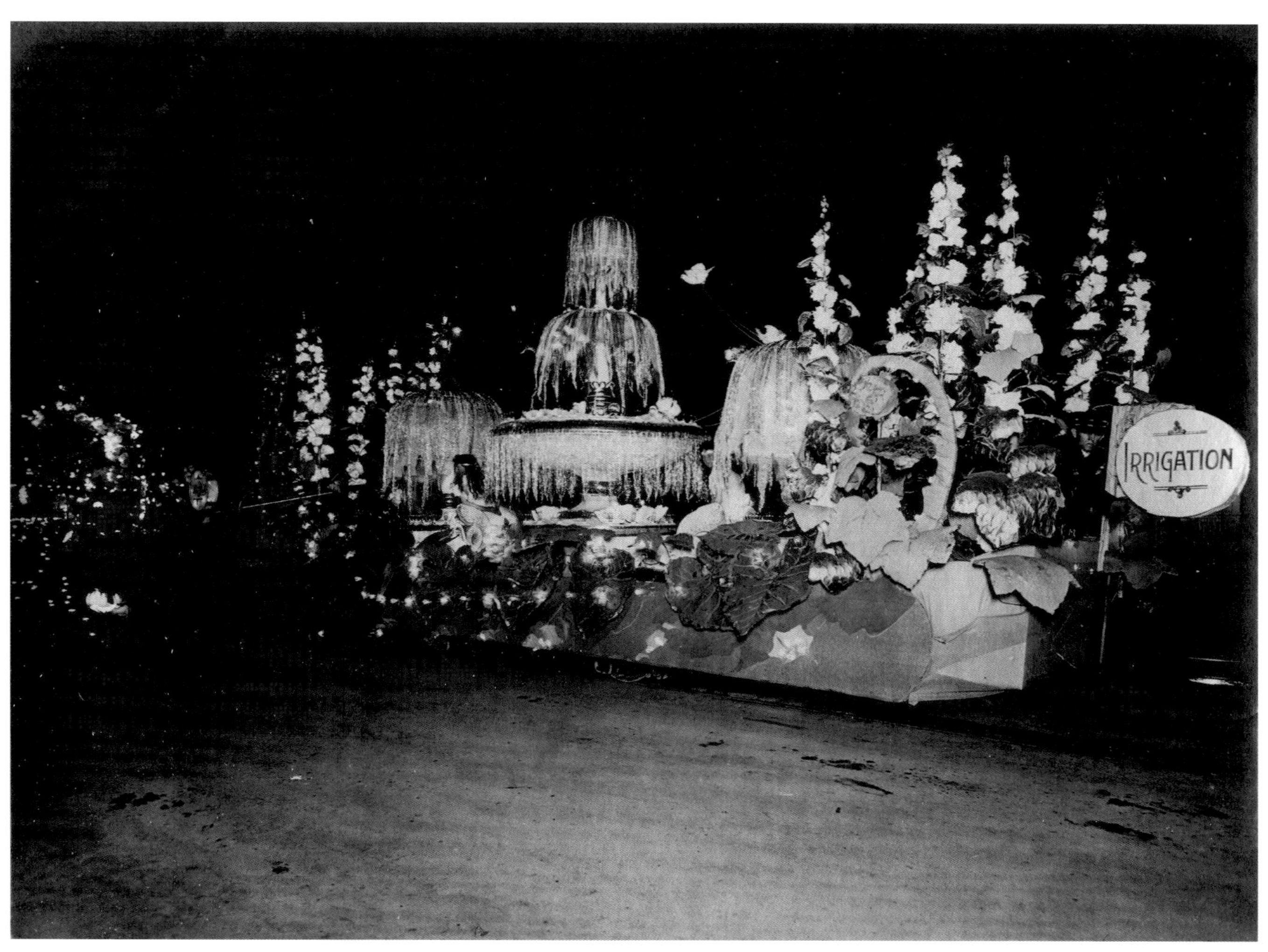


Unknown Artist; *The Electrical Parade*; gelatin silver print; ca. 1915; 6 × 8 in.
*Trolley cars, like this one decorated as an irrigation float, ran along the tracks through Los Angeles.*

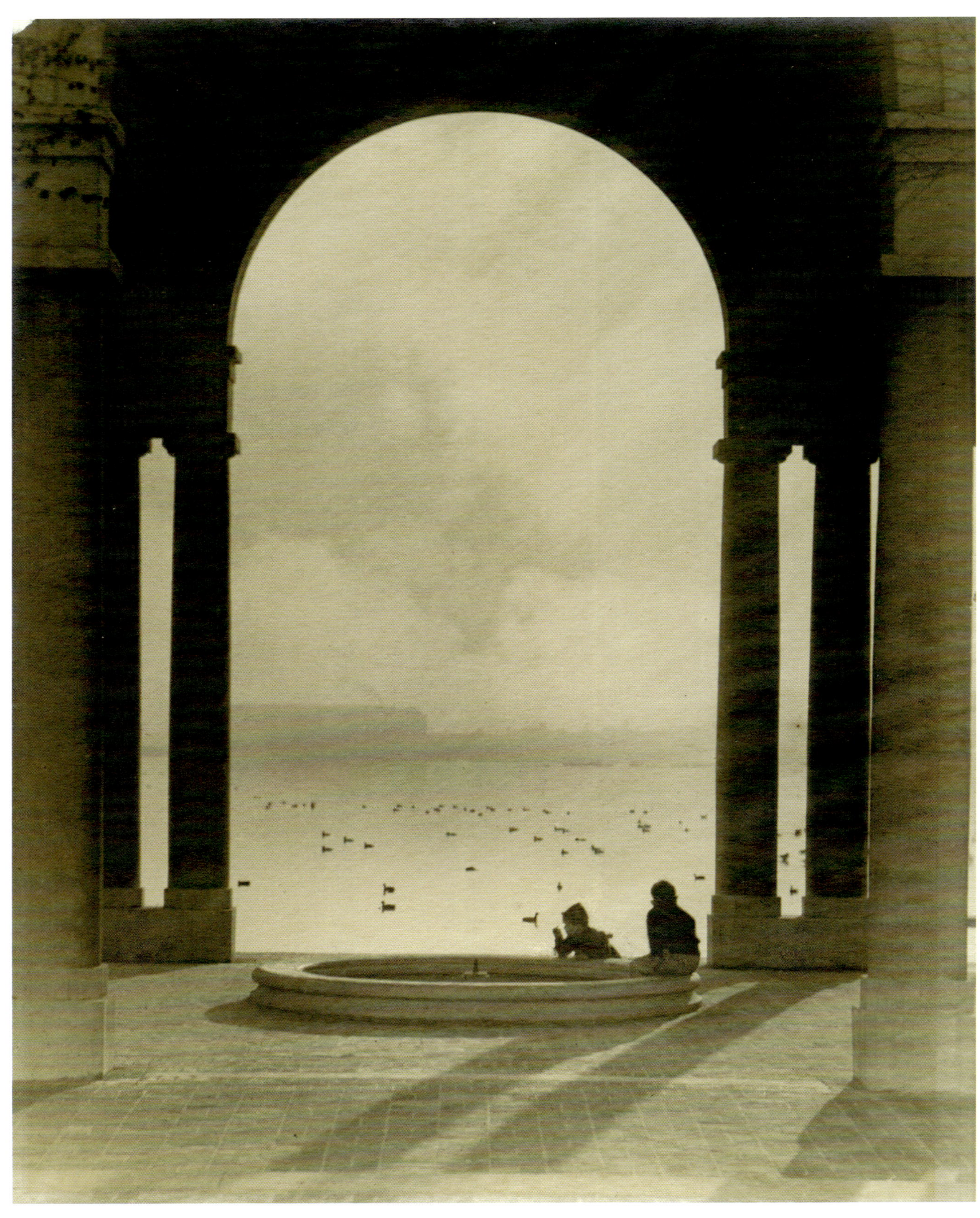

Henry Hussey; *Tranquility, Lake Merritt, Oakland*; toned gelatin silver print; 1924; 12⅝ × 10 in.
*Exhibited at the Salon of Photography, Camera Pictorialists of Los Angeles. Lake Merritt, named after Dr. Samuel Merritt, who donated the land in 1869, has always been a popular recreation area for East Bay Area residents.*

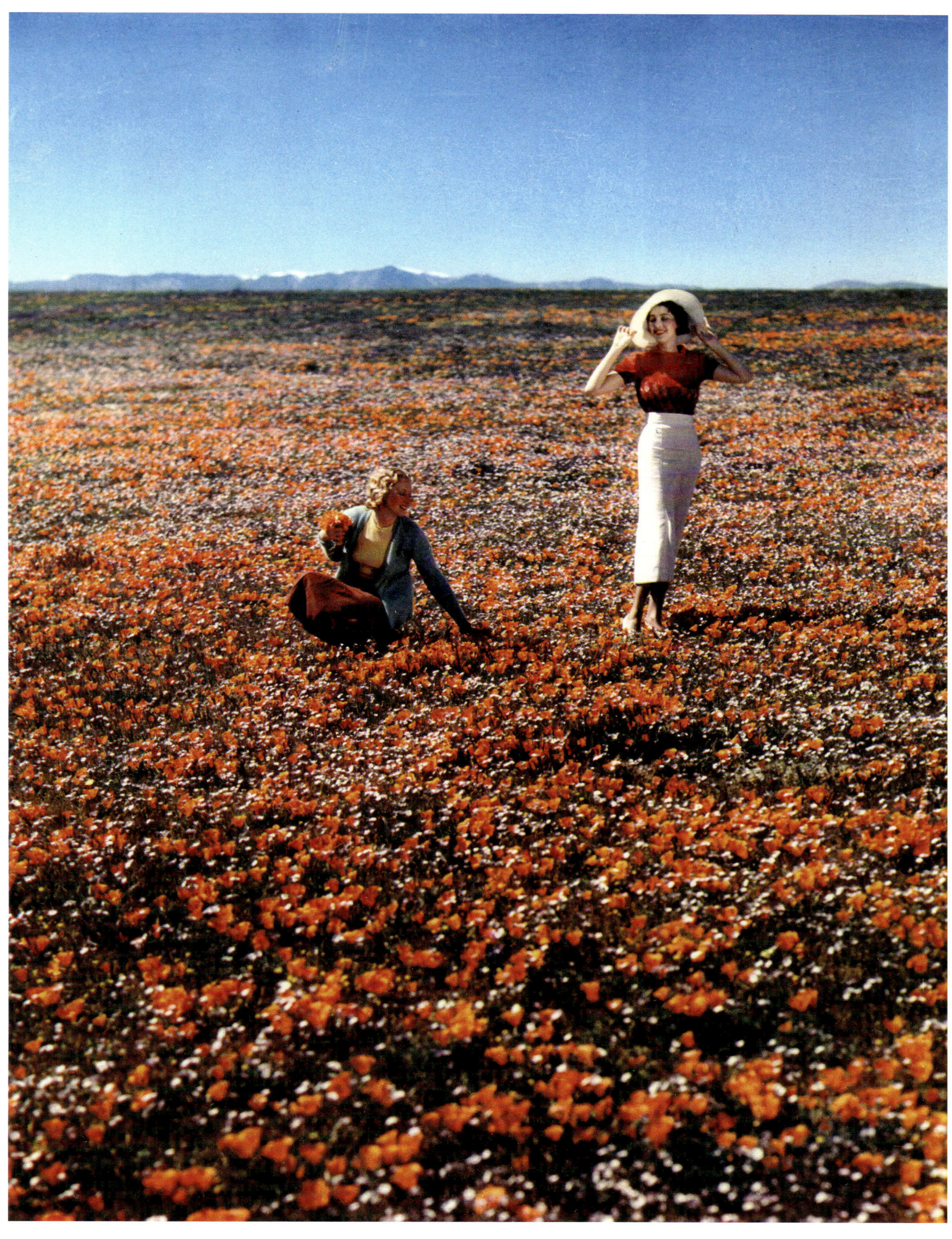

James N. Doolittle; *In the Poppy Fields*; tri-color carbro print; ca. 1936; 13 × 9½ in.
*Doolittle was one of the few photographers working with color printing in the 1930s. He taught at Art Center School in Los Angeles.*

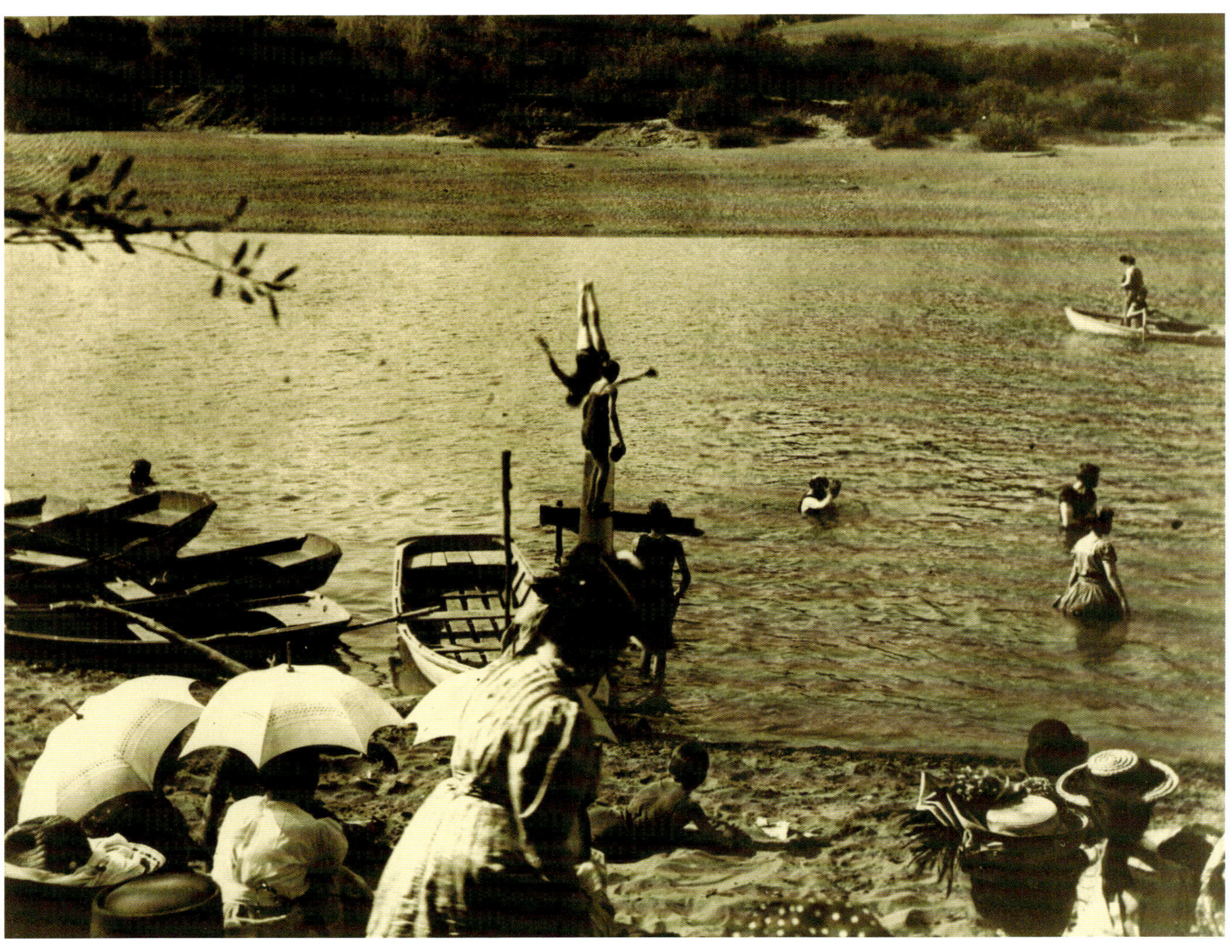

Harry Smith; Untitled (Diving on the Russian River); palladium print; ca. 1900, printed 1980; 10½ × 13½ in.
*Smith, a Danish American amateur photographer working in San Francisco at the turn of the century, recorded events of daily life as well as the aftermath of the San Francisco Earthquake.*

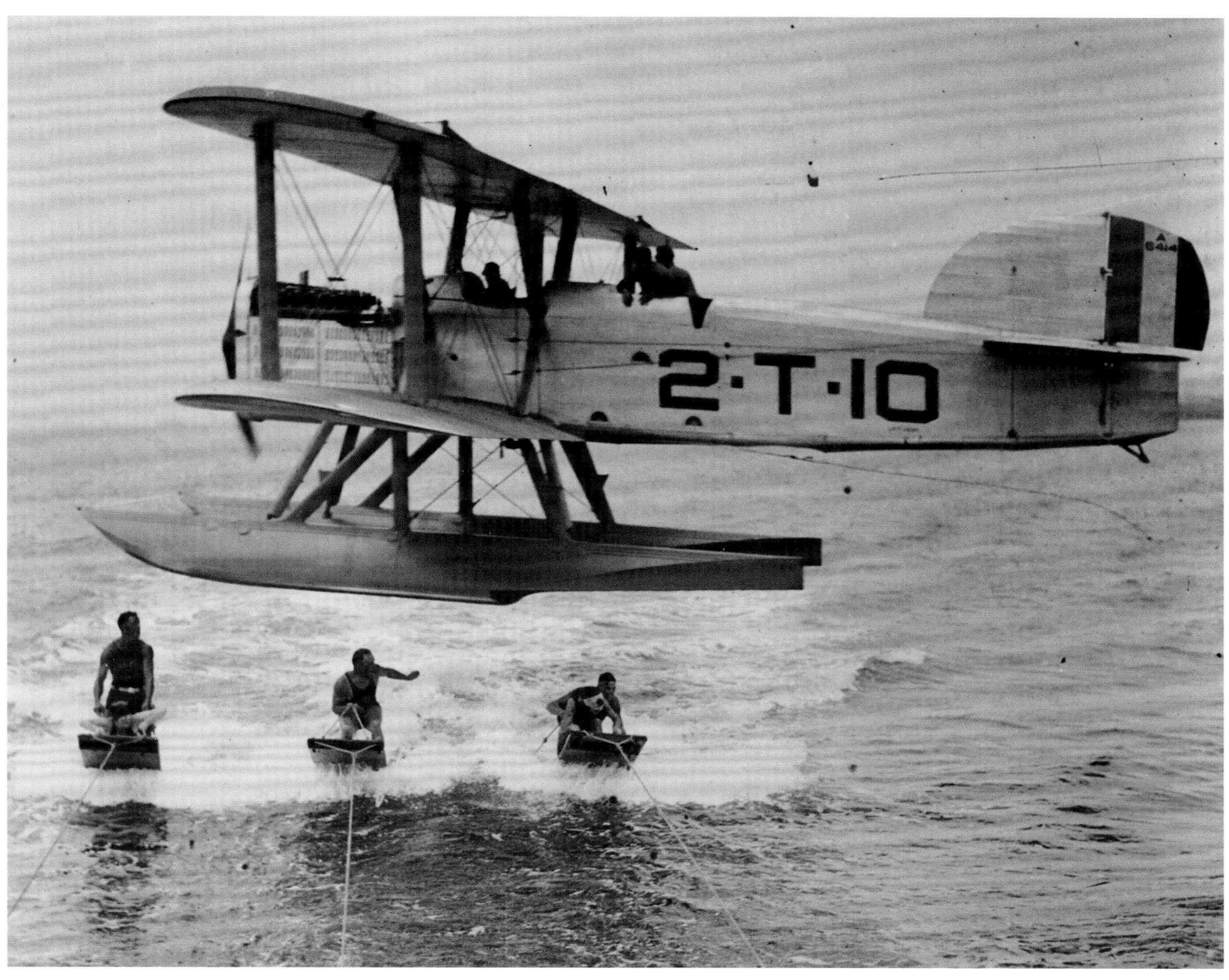


Harry Bishop; *Low Bridge, San Diego*; gelatin silver print; ca. 1930; 15½ × 19¼ in.
*Water sports and aviation were both popular in San Diego thanks to the mild climate.*

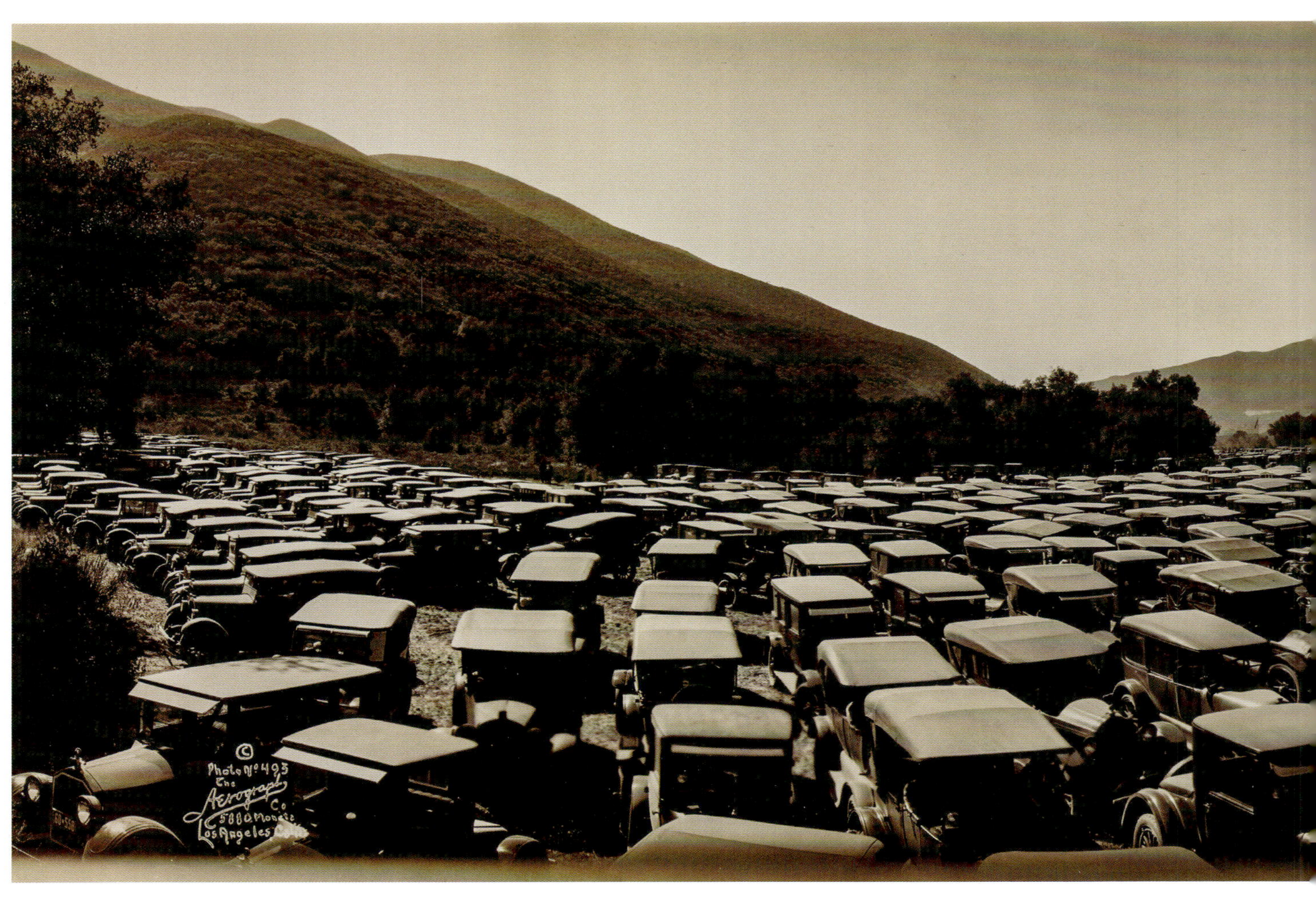
©
Photo No 493
The
Aerograph
Co
Los Angeles

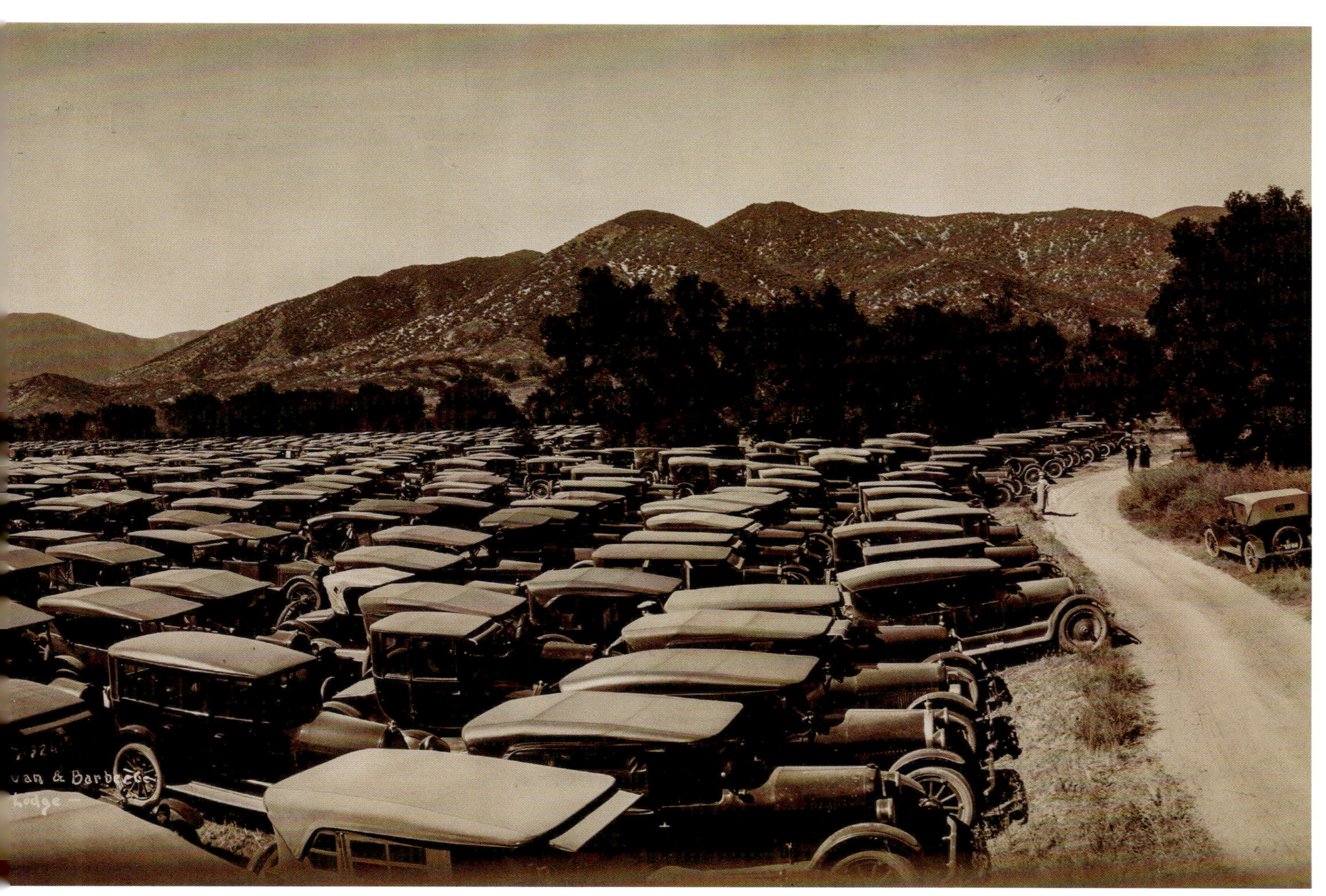

Aerograph Company Los Angeles; Untitled (KHJ Caravan and barbecue La Joya Ranch); gelatin silver print; 1924; 9 × 27⅛ in.
*Salsbury, an Australian world traveler, invited all of Southern California to his 1,100-acre estate called La Joya Lodge for a barbecue and entertainment promoting the use of radio. Sixty thousand people showed up in more than fifteen thousand cars after the invitation was extended over KHJ radio station. This panorama image captured only a small portion of the cars parked for the event.*

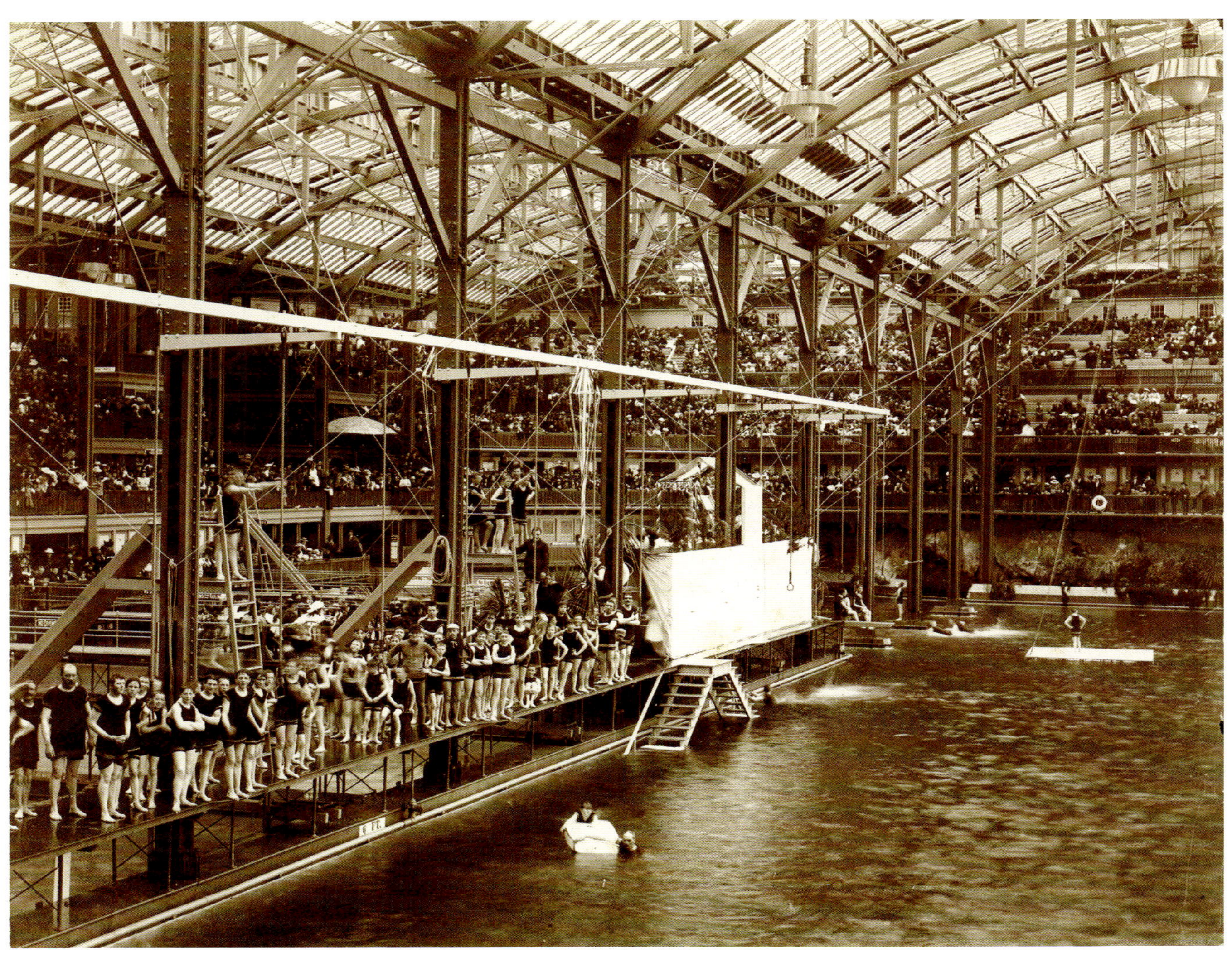

William C. Billington; *Sutro Baths in Sutro Heights, San Francisco*; aristotype print; ca. 1890; 7⅞ × 9½ in.
*The Sutro Baths was a popular gathering place for locals for decades. The massive bathhouse covered three acres and was constructed in 1894.*

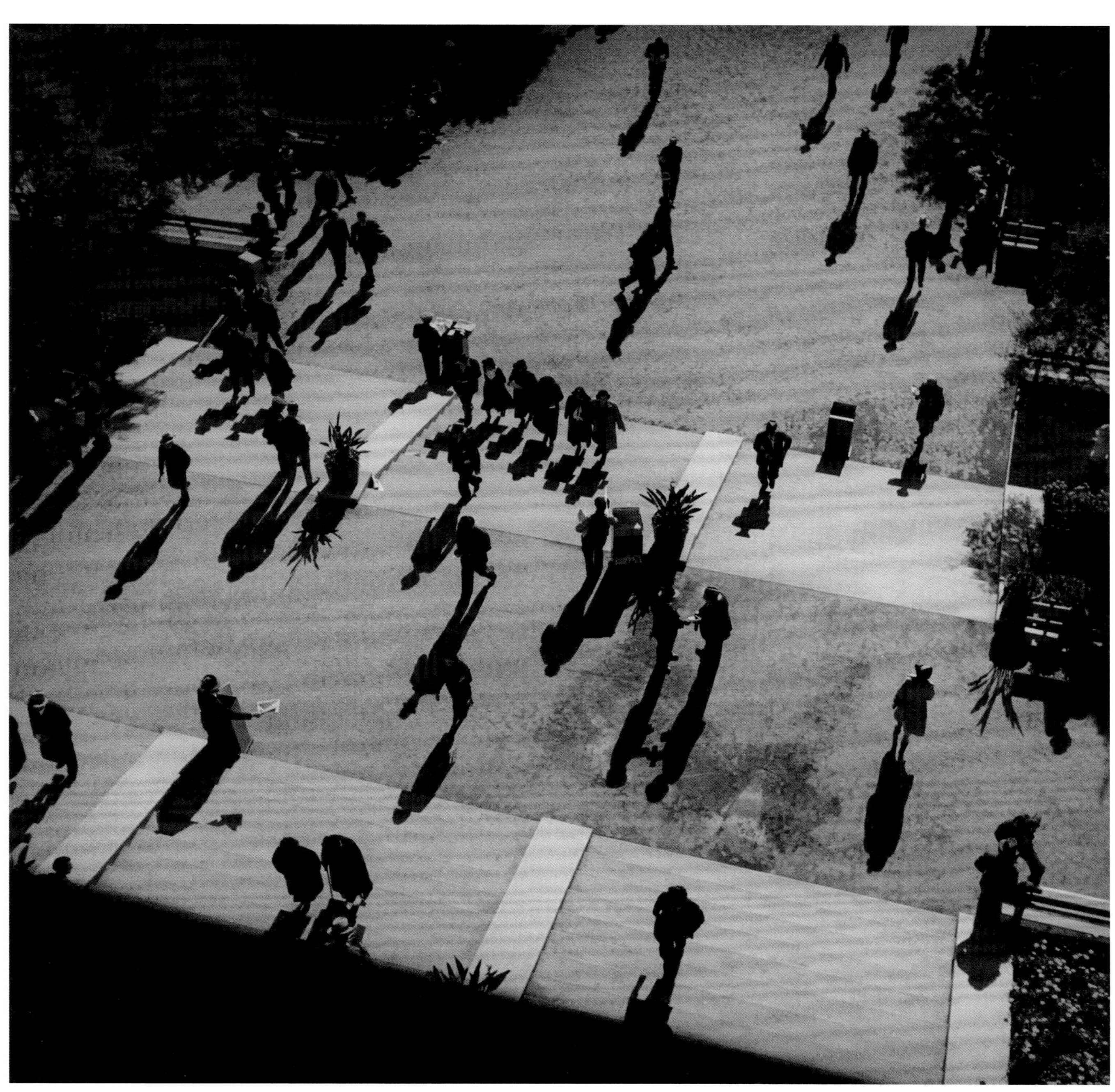

Julius Shulman; *Santa Anita Racetrack*; gelatin silver print; 1938; 15⅞ × 16 in.
*Originally opened by "Lucky" Baldwin in 1907, the Santa Anita Park race track opened at a new location on December 25, 1934. Shulman became a leading architectural photographer whose images are archived at the Getty Research Institute.*

Carleton E. Watkins; *Frank Mayo*; albumen print; ca. 1870; 20⅜ × 16¾ in.
*Frank Mayo is shown here dressed as Davy Crockett. Crockett died at the famous battle of the Alamo in 1836. Fifty years later he had become a legend.*

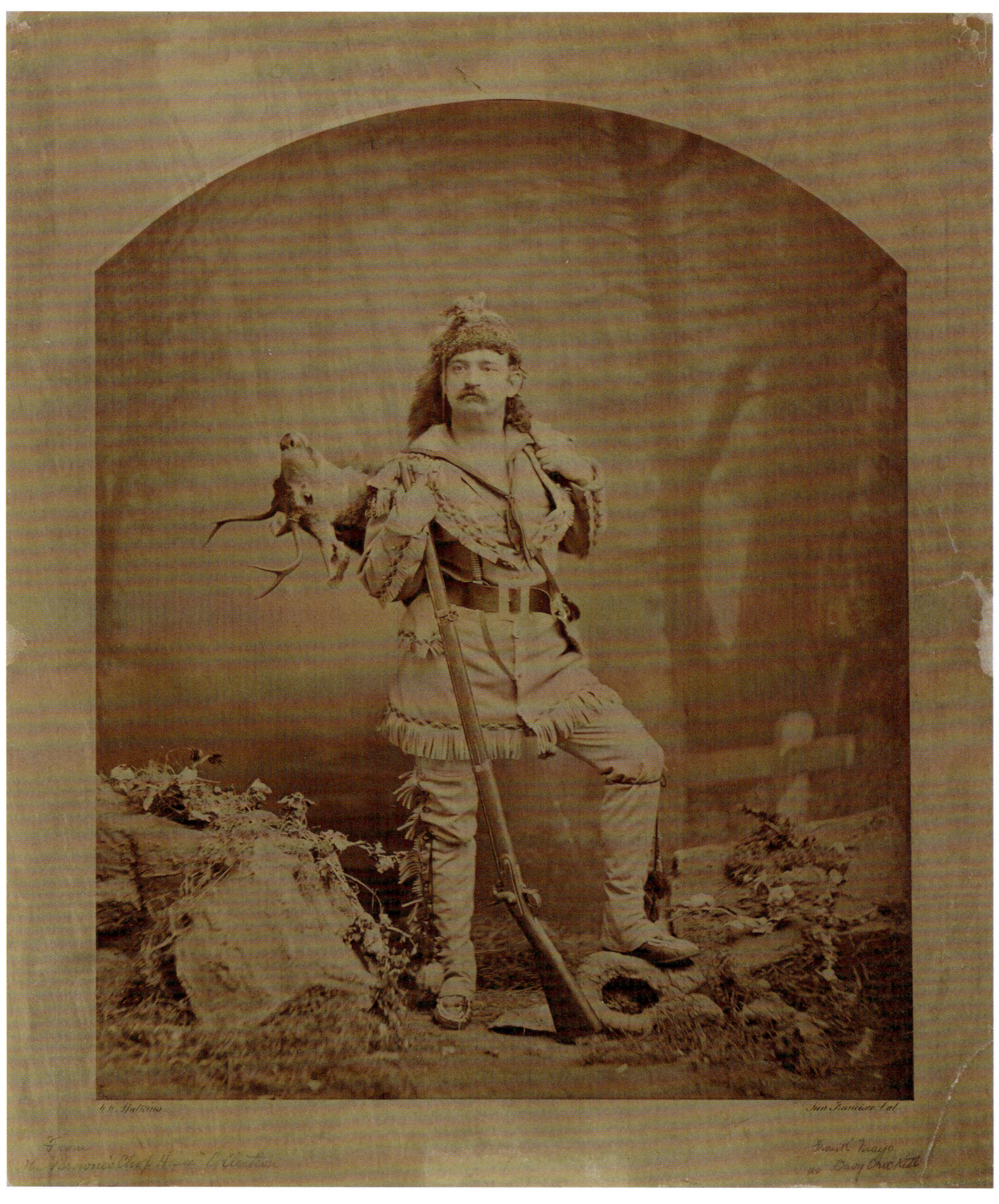
San Francisco Cal.
Frank Mayo
as Davy Crockett

# ACKNOWLEDGMENTS

This book came about as my collection of California photographs grew. So many tales and images populated the story of California from the Gold Rush onward that I began to think of the state as a separate country. But to dream about a book is a beginning; then comes the necessary hard work and collaboration with others to bring the project to fruition.

As the book evolved, discussions with my wife Mus, my lawyer—and fellow collector—Michael Whalen, and friends such as Dennis Reed, Jonathan Spaulding, and Jim Farber, led to the shaping of the sections in the book. The contributors gave the book a flavor I could not have done myself: The fascinating and personal foreword by Lynell George; the timely poem about water by California poet Suzanne Lummis; and the essays by Arthur Ollman, former director of the Museum of Photographic Arts in San Diego; Catherine Gudis, associate professor of history at the University of California, Riverside; Jonathan Spaulding, former head of exhibitions at the Autry National Center; and Jim Farber, an independent writer, critic, and collector.

I owe much to the staff of Angel City Press who brought the book together. Terri Accomazzo, executive editor, asked the right questions and offered many important suggestions, as did publisher Paddy Calistro. Scott McAuley developed a database that made corrections easy. As she designed the book, Amy Inouye worked diligently to ensure it reflected my vision. As a group their dedication and enthusiasm for the project kept me moving ahead.

Others helped me realize my dream of creating an exhibition from my personal California collection titled *California Stories*, differing from but complementing *A Country called California*. Sheila Bergman, executive director of UCR ARTS worked through pandemic delays and rescheduling to bring the exhibition to the California Museum of Photography in Riverside. Leigh Gleason, director of collections and Rita Souther, exhibitions manager, both used their expertise to guide the project toward its realization. Matthew Clouse, museum registrar, spent endless hours developing a checklist and scanning photographs for the exhibition and book. Every time a problem appeared, Matthew was there to solve it. Timothy LeBlanc did the hard work of framing and preparing the images for the exhibition. And finally, guest curator Dennis Reed organized the layout of the exhibition, wrote the captions, and worked closely with me on the choice of material.

Thank you to each and all!

**Stephen White**
November 2021

## ABOUT THE CONTRIBUTORS

Author **Stephen White** has been a gallery owner, collector, curator and historian of photography since he opened a gallery in Los Angeles in 1975. He has been collecting photographs related to California's growth and development over the past twenty-five years and has more than one thousand images that tell the visual story of California from the nineteenth century forward. He has published several catalogues to accompany major museum traveling exhibitions he previously curated or co-curated and has written extensively on every aspect of photography history and contemporary photography.

**Lynell George** is an award-winning Los Angeles-based journalist, essayist and author. A former staff writer for both *Los Angeles Times* and *L.A. Weekly*, George explores social issues and human behavior in her work, as well as urban histories, visual art, music and literature. She is the author of three books of nonfiction: *No Crystal Stair: African Americans in the City of Angels* (Verso), *After/Image: Los Angeles Outside the Frame* (Angel City Press) and her most recent, *A Handful of Earth, A Handful of Sky: The World of Octavia E. Butler* (Angel City Press).

**Suzanne Lummis** is a poet who edited the anthology *Wide Awake: Poets of Los Angeles and Beyond*, which *Los Angeles Times* named one of the ten best books of 2015. Her poems have appeared in *Ploughshares*, *Spillway*, *Hotel Amerika*, *Plume*, *New Ohio Review*, *The American Journal of Poetry*, and *The New Yorker*. Her most recent collection *Open 24 Hours* was published by Lynx House Press. Lummis was a 2018/19 COLA (City of Los Angeles) fellow.

**Jonathan Spaulding** is an independent curator and author based in Southern California. He formerly served as chief curator of the Autry Museum of the American West and Director of the Seaver Center for Western History Research in the Natural History Museum of Los Angeles County. He is the author of *Ansel Adams and the American Landscape: A Biography* (University of California Press, 1995), among other works.

**Catherine Gudis** is a professor of history and director of the Public History Program at the University of California, Riverside, where she holds a Pollitt Endowed Term Chair for Interdisciplinary Research and Learning in the Humanities and Social Sciences. Currently, she also serves as scholar-in-residence at Los Angeles Poverty Department's Skid Row History Museum & Archive. Her research, writing, and public and environmental humanities projects explore how public space is privatized, landscapes are racialized, and inequalities of access are contested, with a geographical focus on California.

**Arthur Ollman** is a lifelong exhibiting photographer, and founding director of the Museum of Photographic Arts who has curated more than one hundred exhibitions, many traveling world-wide. Emeritus professor and former director of the School of Art and Design at San Diego State University, he has written or contributed to twenty-five books in photography. For six years, he was the president of the board of the Foundation for the Exhibition of Photography, based in Paris and Lausanne, a non-profit organization that produces unique and influential photography exhibitions, and circulates them around the world.

**Jim Farber** was born in Los Angeles in 1946 into a family with deep roots in the Hollywood film and music industry. Since graduating from San Francisco State College in 1968 he has worked at the Public Television station KQED in San Francisco and as Displays Coordinator and Designer for the Los Angeles International Film Festival (FILMEX). He began working as a full-time journalist and arts critic in 1982 writing for *Daily Variety*, the Copley Newspapers and News Service, the Southern California Newspaper Group and San Francisco Classical Voice and Creators Syndicate. In 2014, Jim Farber guest curated the exhibition, "Route 66: The Road and the Romance," for the Autry Museum of the American West.

## IMAGE CREDITS

All photographs are from the Stephen White collection except as noted below: Pages 46-47, *At the Round-Up, Fanita Rancho, El Cajon,* and page 140, Untitled (Miners during the Gold Rush), courtesy of the Jim Farber collection.

*A Country Called California: Photographs 1850s to 1960s*

By Stephen White



Design by Amy Inouye, Future Studio

10 9 8 7 6 5 4 3 2 1

ISBN-13 978-1-62640-105-1



Library of Congress Cataloging-in-Publication Data is available

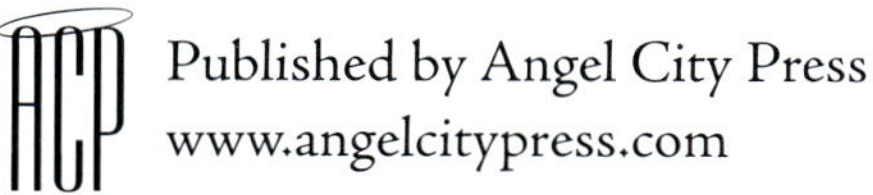

Published by Angel City Press
www.angelcitypress.com

Printed in Canada